CLEMENTINE
CHURCHILL

CLEMENTINE CHURCHILL

CHURCHILL

The Private Life of a Public Figure

JOAN HARDWICK

JOHN MURRAY
Albemarle Street, London

First published in 1997
by John Murray (Publishers) Ltd,
50 Albemarle Street, London W1X 4BD

A catalogue record for this book is available from the British Library

ISBN 0-7195-5552 3

Typeset in 11¼/14pt Ehrhardt by Servis Filmsetting Ltd, Manchester
Printed and bound in Great Britain by The University Press, Cambridge

For Keith with love as always

Contents

Illustrations

The author and publishers would like to thank the following for permission to reproduce illustrations: Plate 1, The Earl of Airlie; 2, 5, 11, *The Sunday Times*/Thomson Trust; 3, © Lloyd's of London; 4, Lord Redesdale; 6, City of Birmingham Museum and Art Gallery; 7 and 8, *Illustrated London News* Picture Library; 9, The Syndics, Fitzwilliam Museum, Cambridge; 10, *Punch*; 12, YMCA; 13, Hugo Vickers; 14, 22 and 24, Hulton Getty Picture Collection Ltd; 15, the author; 16, City of Toronto Archives, Globe and Mail Collection SC266-86725; 17, 18, 19, 20 and 21, The Trustees of the Imperial War Musuem, London; 23, Popperfoto.

Acknowledgements

I HAVE NOT been granted permission to quote any Churchill material either published or unpublished. As a result I have been obliged to paraphrase where I would have preferred to quote directly. Endnotes direct the interested reader to the sources of these paraphrases.

I would like to thank Hugo Vickers for generously allowing me to use a photograph in his possession and Lord Airlie for his kindness in allowing me to reproduce the portrait of Lady Blanche Airlie.

John Chong and Martin Dee Jr of Media Services at the University of British Columbia have been unfailingly helpful and have taken a kindly interest in this book.

The librarians of the City of Lichfield Library have taken great pains to track down some obscure books for me and I thank them. The library of the University of British Columbia, despite unfortunate cutbacks and restraints, has been a wonderful research resource.

I have been most fortunate in having as my copy editor Clare Chambers. Her perceptive criticisms have done much to improve the book and her sense of humour has transformed the often dismaying process of making corrections into a pleasure.

My thanks to Sara Menguc, whose advice and encouragement were invaluable at the outset of this project, and to Caroline Knox, Caroline Westmore and Gail Pirkis of John Murray who have been a delight to work with.

Conversations with some individuals have made vivid for me many details of life during the Second World War. I have in mind especially Mary Hardwick, Rose and Charles Bellhouse, Elsie Alldritt, Catharine and Stephen Idiens, Gertrude Taylor, Marie Wiles and Joyce Holliday.

I want to thank my immediate family. My daughter Miranda Alldritt has always been ready to help me solve technical computer problems. My son Benjamin Alldritt has corrected me on many details of the Second World War and has given me a great deal of help with the preparation of the typescript and index. Keith Alldritt, my husband, has generously taken time to share with me his findings from his work on two books about Winston Churchill and has been, as always, an indispensable source of support, inspiration and encouragement.

Preface

CHARTWELL OPENS TO the public at 11 a.m.; but long before that there are coaches in the bus park and cars are streaming down the tree-lined approach to the house. Entrance tickets are timed and a few minutes after eleven o'clock all tickets for the first two time periods are sold out. Those who have come to Chartwell are of many nationalities and span the generations. But it is not only the house they have come to see, for this is not one of the National Trust's grandest or most curious houses, nor have the spacious grounds and beautiful gardens drawn them all there. Rather it is a seemingly endless curiousity about the life of the man who has by now become a legendary figure.

On the death of Winston Churchill in 1965 Clementine Churchill immediately handed over the house which he had so loved and on which he had spent so much time, energy and money to the National Trust, though under the terms of the agreement by which the Trust acquired the house she was entitled to stay there for the rest of her life. There were several reasons why she was eager for the Trust to have the house, including the worry she had always felt about the cost of its upkeep. But the most important reason was that she wanted to supervise personally the way the house would appear to the public. She saw Chartwell as her opportunity to put the seal on what had been a primary objective of her life for many years: to leave for posterity a particular and flattering image of her husband.

She succeeded admirably in promoting an idea of Churchill that gives pleasure, as the sheer number of admiring visitors to Chartwell attests. But the result is rather strange to those familiar with the lives of its previous owners for the house has become an appropriate image but not in quite the way that Clementine intended.

One of the most remarkable aspects of Chartwell is that there are few overt signs of Clementine's life there. While there are rooms full of displays of Winston's uniforms, his hats, his canes, his letters, his paintings, the gifts he received, Clementine is represented only by her parliamentary robes and the summons from the Queen to take her seat in the House of Lords. She too received honorary doctorates but her academic gowns, unlike Winston's, are not displayed. There are cases of medals and orders awarded to her husband, but the Order of the Red Banner of Labour presented to Clementine by Stalin himself is not visible; neither is the Persian carpet given to her by the Pasha in Marrakesh shown with gifts made to Winston. In a display cabinet in the studio are all the books written by Winston but not the small pamphlet that Clementine published on her return from her visit to Russia in 1945. Among the many photos of Winston Churchill at all stages of his life there are few of Clementine, and in those she appears specifically as Winston's wife. There is only one photo of her standing alone and that is a formal, posed portrait. This absence of visible reminders of Clementine's life perhaps explains why during the time I have been researching this biography I have repeatedly been asked who Clementine Churchill was. Frequently the assumption has been that she was the American, Winston Churchill's mother.

This is not a situation which would have troubled Clementine greatly. She was never a woman who sought the limelight for herself and though she performed admirably in public she was a person who valued privacy and solitude. More importantly, throughout her marriage she saw her role as being that of the supporter and very necessary adviser of someone of greater stature than herself. Indeed the common misconception that she was Winston's mother is not entirely unreasonable, for at times, however reluctantly, this is one of the roles she found herself playing. And like a very proud mother who tries to present her son in the best possible light Clementine has, by influencing the choice of what should be shown to the public at Chartwell, managed to show her husband and their family as totally admirable. In this she was aided by the first administrator appointed by the Trust, for this was Grace Hamblin who had been Clementine's own devoted assistant and who was sympathetic to what she was trying to achieve.

Clementine's first decision was that the house should not be shown as it was in the last days of Winston's life, when there would be signs in the layout of the house of his increasing infirmity, but as it had been in the twenties and thirties, a period which included the time he was Chancellor of the Exchequer and the time when he was a productive writer. Many of the objects, photos and paintings were selected with a view to the light in which they placed Churchill and his family. The photos, for example, suggest a happier and more united family than was, in fact, the case. The same is true of some of the paintings: there is on display a copy of a painting by William Nicholson of husband and wife eating breakfast together as though this was a regular event whereas in fact they led such separate lives that they very rarely shared the first meal of the day. Another painting by Winston himself shows members of the family with guests at dinner. Among the guests is Diana Mitford who later became Lady Mosley. No one would ever suspect that Winston was responsible for her internment in Holloway for some years during the Second World War as a Nazi sympathizer. The prominent display of two crystal bowls with silver decoration showing Volga boatmen given to Winston by Stalin takes no account of the fact that Winston was never afraid of rabidly anti-communist rhetoric in his speeches.

What Chartwell suggests, as a result of the co-operation between Clementine Churchill and the National Trust, is that Churchill was a great man, a fine soldier, a man of decision who could deal successfully with world leaders and influence global politics while retaining the common touch. There are many who would say that this is a fair and accurate picture of Winston Churchill at a certain stage of his life. But after his death as during his life Clementine wanted the personal side of Winston's life to appear equally admirable. And for this some doctoring of available evidence was necessary. What is not shown at Chartwell is as significant as what is. Just as the Graham Sutherland portrait of Winston cannot be shown because Clementine destroyed it, believing that it presented an aspect of her husband which she did not wish the world at large to know about, so too is Chartwell carefully presented to obscure the side of their life together and as a family which was troubled, tempestuous, complicated and far more interesting than the charming portrait suggested by the show house. It could be said that Chartwell mirrors the enigmatic nature of Clementine Churchill's personality. It presents what she wants the public to know. She similarly created a persona which masked the realities of her very private life. In public she was always smiling, gracious, elegant and in control. She always presented herself as

Mrs Churchill fulfilling a public role simply because she was the wife of Winston Churchill. It is a measure of the importance to her that this should be clearly understood that very few people were privileged to call her Clementine and even fewer Clemmie; some of those who had known her for many years and had worked alongside her realized that they would be overstepping the boundaries she had set if they did other than address her formally as Mrs Churchill.

It is the same at Chartwell; Clementine is present exclusively as Winston Churchill's wife. Only in the carefully achieved elegance and comfort of this their home together would anyone suspect how great an influence Clementine had on Winston's life. And there is little here to suggest that beyond the woman who provided him with this background and public support there was a person of strong independent opinions, of painful perfectionism, who frequently found her husband intolerably difficult to live with, who was not a loving mother to all her children and who was capable of doing important things independently in the world outside the home.

So why did Clementine Churchill take such pains to guard from public view the realities of her personality, of her marriage and her family? This is one of the questions that has intrigued me during the course of writing this biography. I have come to the conclusion that she was certainly not motivated by personal vanity. Nor did she believe that a woman is necessarily subordinate to and less than her husband. But just as during the war she visibly worked hard doing public service to help her country so at other times, because she so firmly believed in Winston Churchill and his sense of his destiny to achieve things of world-wide importance, she took seriously her job of supporting him to her utmost to make this possible. Her principles and personality were such that this was rarely easy for her. For by support she meant much more than simply agreeing with her husband and making him physically comfortable. She often believed that Winston's actions and publicly expressed views had made him seem a lesser man than he could be. She was always ready to tell him unpalatable truths and give him advice which went contrary to his own inclinations, in the interests of putting him in a situation in which he could best exercise his substantial talents. As Churchill's wife she was neither passive nor simply decorative but was always well informed and actively interested.

This sense of a great responsibility entrusted to her did not make Clementine's life easy; nor was it always happy. Her relationship with her husband damaged that with three of her children and she carried a guilt about this. At times she felt so physically exhausted by the demands of the life she led that she wondered if she could go on. In the early years of marriage she was emotionally disappointed and subject to outbursts of extreme jealousy. In the middle years she was tempted to look elsewhere for the love she missed in her marriage and even considered divorce. But still she persisted in her self-appointed task. And then in the last years of Winston's life she endured the strain of living with a man who only wanted to die. Even after his death she did not see her role as being at an end but worked hard creating a monument to him at Chartwell and in other ways guarded and protected his image as one of England's greatest men.

It is this complicated, hard-working woman of principle with many secrets to protect rather than the smiling, beautiful Mrs Churchill who interests me and about whom I have written in this biography.

I returned to Chartwell only recently and was struck once more by Clementine's achievement in creating the appearance of openness while contriving to obscure much. And I found in this house which is now owned by the nation a chilling footnote to my experiences in the course of writing Clementine Churchill's biography. There is in Churchill's studio an exhibit of a small selection of letters he received. Prominently displayed with them is a notice from the National Trust indicating that Churchill's papers are to be found in Churchill College, Cambridge, where he wished them to be kept so as always to be available to the public. But this too suggests an openness which is not a reality: the archive is not readily accessible to all scholars and writers who apply to see it. Like others before me I have to say that I have had to rely on sources other than the papers in Churchill College for my biography. The tradition of guarding the family image with the objective of keeping it untarnished apparently continues.

'Do you think that everybody's real life is quite different from what they manage to make it seem? Very likely. No dark secret, but everything different from the façade.'

Nancy Mitford to Evelyn Waugh, 31 January 1951

PROLOGUE

Two Wilful Women

BLANCHE AIRLIE WAS born a Stanley, a family known for its pride and of whom it was said, 'The Stanleys do not marry: they contract alliances'.[1] But the wedding of Blanche Ogilvy, her daughter, to Colonel Henry Hozier solemnized in the chapel of Cortachy Castle on 28 September 1878 broke with the Stanley tradition. It was a marriage in which Blanche Airlie could take no pride: the wedding was less an occasion for celebration than one for simple relief.

Blanche or Blanchy as she was often called to distinguish her from her mother Blanche, Lady Airlie, was intelligent and beautiful. She was also capricious, wilful and unconventional.

These were all characteristics she had inherited from her mother who had also been the cause of much worry to her own parents, Lord and Lady Stanley. They too had been eager to see their daughter safely married. They had contrived many situations to enable her shy suitor, David, Earl of Airlie, to propose to Blanche. They had turned a deaf ear to rumours of his gambling losses and his tendency to drink heavily. But even the prospect of becoming a Countess and presiding over a castle was not, initially, sufficient to overcome Blanche Stanley's reluctance to be married. She was not sure that she loved the man who wanted her for his wife; indeed she was not sure that she wanted to be married at all if that meant leaving Alderley, her many brothers and sisters and the lively company her parents attracted to their home. Her grandmother, Maria Josepha, was inclined to blame that same company for her granddaughter's hesitation. She had even written to her daughter-in-law reproachfully for allowing Blanche to be too much surrounded by clever men, for 'it is setting up for a character which seldom ends well for matrimony'.[2] In her turn Lady Stanley had written to her husband complaining of Blanche, 'She is very capricious and changeable and I shall be very glad when she is married.'[3]

The first year of the marriage of Blanche and David Ogilvy gave every sign of proving Maria Josepha right. The excitement of her wedding and her new responsibilities did not compensate Blanche for her horror at what she found at Cortachy. She was accustomed to a well-run household, where servants knew their place and did their jobs efficiently. She took for granted good food and lively conversation at dinner.

The prevailing notion of what constituted good hospitality at Cortachy came as a very unpleasant surprise to the new Countess. She quickly realized that the men who were invited came solely to get drunk and their wives came only to see that their husbands got home safely when drink inevitably overcame them and they had to be carried out of the dining room and into their carriages. There was not, of course, much in the way of brilliant after-dinner conversation.

Blanche also discovered that the rumours about her husband's gambling were well founded. Although she was still only twenty-one she had a strong will, much stronger than that of her 25-year-old husband, and she took a firm grip on the situation and determined that at all costs she would become mistress in her own castle. She told her husband in no uncertain terms what she thought of his gambling and the way in which he had woefully neglected his estate. She nagged him into taking more interest in politics and becoming more like her own father whom she greatly admired. Lord Airlie was unenthusiastic but to please her and to stop her complaints he agreed to take his place in the House of Lords as a Liberal peer.

The greatest changes she made at Cortachy, however, were in the nature of the entertainment she offered and in the kind of people she now invited to be her guests.

She saw clearly that no improvement of any kind could be made as long as the men were allowed to drink themselves senseless. Her first step, therefore was to ration strictly the amount of wine that could be served with dinner. She sacked the cook and employed one whose food was so good that the shortage of wine was readily tolerated. She invited to Cortachy men she had come to know and respect at Alderley. Instead of the company of gamblers and racing men she now received as her guests men such as John Ruskin, Lord Rosebery and Thomas Carlyle.

She even enticed the fastidious American novelist Henry James to make the long, long journey north and was delighted when he found her home so romantic that he felt he was living in one of Sir Walter Scott's novels.

Even with all the improvements she had made, Cortachy Castle was still remote and in winter few visitors could be expected. Blanche, therefore, persuaded her husband to buy Airlie Lodge on Campden Hill so that she could extend her social life still further. To this London house came Lord Beaconsfield and Robert Browning who read his poetry aloud to select company. Blanche also began to make the acquaintance of some of the many artists who lived in the neighbourhood. G.F. Watts had already painted portraits of the Earl and Countess and their two children. Now he painted a portrait of Blanche which her youngest sister Rosalind described as 'startling at first and exceedingly beautiful'.[4] Through this same sister, whose house close by at Palace Green had been designed by Philip Webb, Blanche now met William Morris and his family, John Everett Millais and Edward Burne-Jones. Rosalind also introduced her to Wilfrid Scawen Blunt and he too became a regular visitor at Airlie Lodge.

Apart from her increasingly active social life Blanche also had a growing family to occupy her. Her first daughter, Blanche, was her pride and joy as she was exceptionally beautiful from birth. But she was soon followed by others and in all the Countess had six children.

By now she had persuaded her husband to take a greater interest in business. He had become a respected breeder of Aberdeen Angus cattle and had begun to take notice of the possibilities for making money in America. Blanche was less pleased with this development as it enabled her husband to escape her watchful eye. The arrival at Cortachy of a series of young American women in whom she felt David took rather too much interest confirmed her doubts about his American business deals.

Over the years by sheer force of will she had made a success of what could have been a disappointing marriage. But this success had not been without cost. During the process she had become hard, severe and autocratic. She was no longer the young woman of whom Jane Welsh Carlyle had written, 'I can give you no idea of her indiscretion, nor the charm of her beauty and childishness that makes me always pardon her.'[5] Instead she was a matron who wanted complete and absolute domination over her family. But as her children grew up so her power over them began to diminish. Her daughter, Blanche, for example, was developing a mind and a will of her own. For she too, just like her mother, had grown up in the company of some of the best minds of the age. Despite her beauty she had not followed the pattern her mother expected, but failed to make a good marriage at the end of her first season. She worried her mother greatly by the way she flirted outrageously with many men but took none seriously. She had suitors, including the much sought-after Arthur Balfour who was to become Prime Minister, but she refused to consider any of them. Her younger sister, Clementine, on the other hand, had married well but had managed to enrage her mother by her choice. She became the wife of Algernon Bertram Mitford as soon as she was twenty-one and did not need parental consent. In theory this match should have pleased Lady Airlie; but she had in fact considered the 33-year-old Bertram Mitford, a cultured man who had only recently left the Foreign Office after many adventures in Russia, China and Japan, as one of her own admirers and had in no way viewed him as a suitor for her second daughter. Although she gave no sign of her anger to the outside world and acted like the perfect hostess to her many guests after the wedding in Cortachy chapel, she expressed her hostility to her daughter by continuing to address her at all times as Lady Clementine Ogilvy.

Even her eldest son was causing her distress by refusing to follow the pattern she had determined for him. He wanted a life in the army and was not interested in becoming master of Cortachy. Her husband was gradually taking her younger son away from her influence with the promise of a good life in America.

Young Blanche was increasingly irked by the restrictions her forceful mother tried to impose on her. She did not want to live a life hemmed in by the social conventions her mother considered important. She saw her younger sister presiding over her own delightful house overlooking the Thames in Chelsea and entertaining men such as James Whistler, Oscar Wilde, Charles Keene, Lord Leighton and Thomas Carlyle. Belatedly she realized that the only way in which she could escape from her family and lead a similar life to that of her sister was to marry.

Colonel Henry Hozier, like Bertram Mitford, was really a friend of the Countess. He had a distinguished career in the army behind him and at the time Blanche began to take an interest in him he had just been appointed Secretary to Lloyd's and was commanding respect for the changes he was making there. Henry Hozier was rather different from many of her mother's other men friends who were for the most part involved in the arts in some way. He was more interested in mathematics and science. Blanche was not at all perturbed by the age difference between herself and Henry Hozier; he was forty years old and she was twenty-six. She was already too worldly to be comfortable with young men of her own age and besides Henry Hozier already had a house in London and a smaller one at Netherton within driving distance of Cortachy. Unlike many young men her family considered eligible, Henry Hozier was passionately interested in his career. Blanche liked the idea that he would not expect his wife to be his constant companion and that as a result she would have the freedom and the leisure to follow her own pursuits.

He was not, however, a man who would ever have been admitted into the company of Blanche Ogilvy's great-grandmother, Maria Josepha Stanley, and even her more easy-going father considered him to be a bounder. He had gained this reputation as a result of his divorce which had attracted a good deal of attention. Divorce was still unusual and still carried a social stigma. One divorce in his background would have been enough to give him a bad reputation but he had compounded his trouble by being cited as the co-respondent in another divorce case and failing to marry the lady concerned once she was free.

Blanche was quite unperturbed by all this: she had her own notions about marriage and they were far from conventional. What she liked about Henry Hozier was his strength of character, his sense of humour and his love of foreign travel. He proposed marriage to her at exactly the right moment in her life. At twenty-six she was eager to leave home and ready to start a family. She was very conscious of the fact that her sister Clementine already had three children. She wanted to become the mistress of her own establishment, to start her own salon and to have the greater freedom she assumed would be hers as a married woman.

When Blanche announced to the Earl and Countess that she planned to marry Henry Hozier they were not at all pleased. There were quarrels and arguments. David Airlie was adamantly opposed to his daughter marrying a man he did not trust. Both Henry and Blanche knew, however, that it would be Lady Airlie who would have the final say and so Henry set out to win over his prospective mother-in-law. What influenced her most decisively was, however, less the charm of her prospective son-in-law than her strong desire to see her unpredictable daughter married before she damaged her reputation irrevocably. Like her own mother before her she looked at her daughter and thought, 'she is very

capricious and changeable and I shall be very glad when she is married.'⁶
Reluctantly she withdrew her opposition to the match.

The newly married couple began their life together in Queen Anne's
Gate and almost immediately both confronted surprises. Blanche discovered several alarming facts about her new husband. First of all he told her
that he had no intention of siring a family. Blanche had hoped for a large
family such as her mother and her grandmother had brought up. Then
she realized that Henry's love of foreign travel excluded her, as he did not
intend to take her with him on the many journeys he had to make on
company business. She discovered that his sense of humour and his
infectious laughter was only one side of him. She had not realized prior
to marriage that he could be just as stern and intolerant as her mother.
Even his passion for mathematics lost its glamour when he applied it to
his regular inspection of household bills.

Blanche had assumed that her husband's reputation as a womanizer
would make him look leniently on any affairs she might choose to have.
She was, therefore, dismayed to find that he had double standards and
that he demanded of his wife not just discretion but absolute fidelity.

Henry, too, found out that he had mistaken the character of the woman
he had married. Because he had seen her in the context of Cortachy
Castle where the Countess ran the household on a tightly controlled
budget he had assumed that Blanche too would have a similar sense of
thrift. But to his dismay his wife proved to be carelessly extravagant and
very fond of new clothes. Although, like her mother, she made sure that
the meals served at her table were good, she took no interest in the cost.
This energetic and purposeful man was irritated to discover that his wife
enjoyed sleeping late and taking life easily. He was offended by Blanche's
flirtatious manner which he had wrongly assumed she would drop once
she was a married woman.

Neither of these two strong personalities was slow to express dissatisfaction. They quarrelled frequently and Blanche, a true Stanley in
her ability to find the weak points in another's armour, more than held
her own. Eventually they achieved a way of living together in reasonable
harmony. Blanche made no scenes about Henry's frequent absences and
he did not enquire too closely into her activities when he was gone.

During the next three years Henry busied himself with the expansion
of a system of telegraph stations along the British coast while Blanche

created a position for herself in English society. It was in London that Blanche really enjoyed herself. She was often in the company of her young Aunt Rosalind. All the artists who had frequented her mother's house on Campden Hill were now entertained by the Hoziers. G.F. Watts who had painted her as a girl at Cortachy now painted her as a young woman. Henry James came to dinner as did Wilfrid Scawen Blunt. Lady Randolph Churchill with whom she had much in common temperamentally became a close friend, and her younger sisters, Leonie Jerome, who later married John Leslie and went to live with him in Castle Leslie in Ireland, and Clara, who married Moreton Frewen, known in the family as Moreton Ruin for his disastrously poor financial judgement, were both full of admiration for the beautiful, witty, daring and unconventional Blanche.

Not everyone, however, looked favourably on Blanche's behaviour at this time. Frederic Harrison, the writer and positivist philosopher, for example, whilst being fond of her was frankly critical of her way of life. He described her in terms very similar to those used earlier by Jane Welsh Carlyle about the young Lady Airlie. He saw Blanche as a spoilt child yielding to her every whim whilst at the same time he was charmed by her ease, her self-possession, alertness and capacity for grace. He believed that no good could come of the frivolous life she led and he disliked the 'deliberate flinging off of delicacy and the fine edge of women's life'.[7]

After three years of marriage Blanche had still not had a child. She looked with envy at her sister Clementine's family. Then, since Henry was still opposed to having children, she took matters into her own hands and in 1882 she was delighted to find herself pregnant at long last.

I

An Unexpected Family

IF HENRY HOZIER was surprised to find himself a father after so successfully avoiding paternity for the first five years of his marriage to Blanche, he did not show it. He accepted the situation with reasonable grace since he knew how unreliable were the available means of contraception.

Lady Airlie and Lady Stanley were rather more suspicious about how Blanche had managed to start a family. She had deeply shocked both of them just before her first confinement. Instead of revelling in the 'sort of delicious mystery'[1] which customarily surrounded an expectant mother, she held forth on the inevitability of infidelity in marriage, saying that all wives liked their husbands 'to take their pleasure even if this did not fit in with their married lives'.[2] The two older ladies tried not to think too much about what this might imply about Blanche's own behaviour. Alarming rumours had reached them about Blanche's recent flirtations, especially with Captain George 'Bay' Middleton.

This tall, attractive man with reddish hair and a dark complexion was a well-known and brilliant horseman. Some years earlier he had reluctantly agreed to lead Elisabeth, Empress of Austria, in the hunting field when she rented Easton Neston near Towcester for the 1876 season. He had fallen in love with her and broken off his engagement to Charlotte Baird, the sister of the Master of the Cottesmore hounds. The relationship with the Empress had lasted for several years but by 1882, the year when he was first seen about with Blanche, the relationship with Elizabeth was at an end and it was assumed by all Blanche's friends, including Jennie Churchill, that the dashing Captain Middleton had become Blanche's latest lover.

Only the excitement of the birth of a beautiful girl whom Blanche named Katharine put these uneasy thoughts about Blanche's reputation and the measures she was prepared to take to become pregnant out of the minds of her mother and grandmother. Even Henry Hozier seemed content to be the father of such an exceptionally beautiful child.

However the birth of Katharine did not put an end to Blanche's affair with 'Bay' Middleton and she quickly became pregnant again. On 1 April 1885 at 75 Grosvenor Street she gave birth to a second daughter whom she named Clementine after her younger sister. Henry Hozier again accepted the situation and his attitude curbed much of the gossip about Blanche. Clementine was christened and one of her godfathers was Jack Leslie who was now married to Leonie Jerome, the sister of Lady Randolph Churchill.

A nursery was established on the top floor of the house and a nanny was employed so that the two baby girls were kept safely out of sight and sound of the adult life in the rest of the house. Blanche continued her social life as though she were still childless and Henry resumed his travels. There was nothing unusual about this situation. In the upper classes in England mothers and fathers rarely had much to do with their children in their infancy. As late as 1911, for example, *Country Life* was praising a new house because 'the whole of the nursery quarters are isolated, as they should be, and served by a separate corridor'[3]; and in 1930, through her heroine Aspasia in her novel *Love's Hour*, Elinor Glyn expressed surprise that in Hungary, unlike in England, even in the most aristocratic of households the nursery always communicated with the rooms of the mother.[4] The nursery staff determined the quality of the children's lives far more than did their parents and in this respect Kitty and Clementine fared if anything rather better than some of their contemporaries.

Blanche's many affairs (Lady Augusta Gregory, W.B. Yeats's Irish patron and at one time the mistress of Wilfrid Scawen Blunt, claimed that Blanche had had at least nine lovers) were not so unusual either. Most Edwardian ladies and their husbands had an unspoken agreement to turn a blind eye on each other's affairs once the continuation of the family name had been assured by the birth of an unquestionably legitimate heir. Everyone agreed, of course, that it was most important to maintain outward decorum and avoid confronting a spouse with overt infidelity. And it was not considered good form to let the lower classes know what their betters were up to. The early novels of Elinor Glyn are full of the intrigues of married ladies which she had observed at first hand and she was less kindly received in society for having exposed these affairs to the general public. The Prince of Wales who had a sequence of well-known sexual relationships with married women set the accepted hypocritical tone for the rest of society when he condemned the publication of Elinor Glyn's *Three Weeks*.

Blanche broke with the conventions of her time by being quite blatant about her affairs and by taking lovers before she had a family. But even so, no one could be quite sure that her husband was not the father of her first two children and for the moment she kept her own counsel. She did, perhaps, reveal something about her own situation when she expressed her support for her Aunt Maisie at the time when that lady found herself unexpectedly and inconveniently pregnant. Maisie was married to Lady Airlie's brother Edward but had fallen in love with George Howard, the husband of her sister-in-law, Rosalind. Venetia Stanley, the child of this affair, born just a year after Clementine, was just one of the many 'rather different-looking children' who appeared at the 'tail end' of a number of Edwardian families.[5]

Blanche was, however, sufficiently conventional to feel that her family was not complete without a son. Henry Hozier was not especially interested in a male heir. He was the youngest of his family and had neither title nor lands to pass on. What he had he had earned for himself. And he already had two more children than he had bargained for and did not want any more.

Despite his attitude Blanche once again became pregnant and in 1888 when Kitty was five and Clementine was three she gave birth to twins, Bill and Nellie. By now Henry Hozier was distinctly suspicious. There was no history of twins in his family nor, as far as he knew, in his wife's immediate family. But he was uncomfortably aware that twins did run in the family of Blanche's brother-in-law, Bertram Mitford, with whom Blanche spent a great deal of time and for whom she seemed to feel more than sisterly affection. For the moment, however, he subdued his doubts and the marriage continued, as it had begun, with quarrels and reconciliations, none of which greatly affected the four children in the nursery.

Shortly after the twins were born Blanche resumed her social life with a visit to her Aunt Rosalind at Castle Howard in North Yorkshire. Rosalind used the visit of her niece to entice her own former admirer, Wilfrid Scawen Blunt, to the Castle. She wrote, 'Blanche Hozier comes about the 15th and when you want frivolity you will find abundance of it in its pleasantest form in her.'[6]

Wilfrid Scawen Blunt already knew Blanche through her mother, and when he had dined with Blanche and Henry shortly after their marriage he had found them a very oddly matched pair. From time to time since then he had called on Blanche in London. At forty-eight years old he was a very attractive man with dark eyes which he used to great effect. His propensity to dress up in an Arab cloak and head-dress made him a romantic figure quite different from the practical Henry Hozier. Although he was married this had never prevented him from being keenly interested in other women. The time spent with Blanche in the romantic setting of Castle Howard led to a new intimacy with her and before long Blunt was one of her lovers. He even took a house near hers in London to promote the affair. But they were not lovers for long: Blunt had a jealous rival. This was not, as might be expected, Henry Hozier, but another lover. Blanche was already involved with Ellis Ashmead-Bartlett, a successful Conservative politician and writer whom Blunt described disparagingly as 'an absurd middle-aged Member of Parliament, married with many children, of no personal attraction but with much underbred pretension'.[7] Blanche might have been ready to give up this man for Blunt who was far more fascinating but Ellis Ashmead-Bartlett was not ready to end the affair. His grievance against Blunt went beyond sexual jealousy. The two men were diametrically opposed on the question of Ireland and Home Rule. Blunt believed passionately that Ireland should have its independence whilst Ashmead-Bartlett believed just as passionately in the Union. He was not about to lose his mistress to such a political rival. He had Blanche's house watched, he threatened blackmail, he threatened to shoot her and finally he promised that if Blanche rejected him then he would instigate a public quarrel with Wilfrid Scawen Blunt. After a particularly alarming incident Blanche was inclined to believe these were not simply empty threats. She had entertained Blunt to dinner one night, but not in an intimate twosome. The highly respectable Henry James, her brother-in-law George Howard and Lady Arabella Romilly were her other guests. Ellis Ashmead-Bartlett who had been watching the house was not reassured by the size of the party and as soon as all the guests had left he burst into the house and forced his way into Blanche's bedroom. Fortunately Henry Hozier was not at home and it was only the maid who heard the ensuing violent scene. Only Blanche's promise to give up Blunt enabled her to persuade her irate lover to depart.

The friendship between Blanche and Blunt flourished despite this disruption and Blunt continued to be a visitor both to the London house and to the house in Forfarshire and to take an interest in Blanche's children. The affair with Ellis Ashmead Bartlett also continued until the day Henry Hozier returned early and unexpectedly from one of his tours of duty and caught his wife and the MP in bed together.

Henry Hozier was not like Lord Londonderry who, when confronted with his wife's infidelity, resolved to avoid the scandal of a divorce: instead he allowed his wife to remain under his roof but never spoke to her again. Henry Hozier was a man of action with a violent temper who had little to lose by going through the divorce courts having already done so more than once. He threw the lovers out of the house and told Blanche that the marriage was over. Blanche had no choice but to accept the situation. She knew very well that she had no grounds for protest and that the courts would definitely side with her husband. The best she could hope for was a reasonable settlement to enable her to bring up her children. Although scandalized by the news of Blanche's infidelities, her relatives stood by her and her brother David, now the Earl of Airlie, did his best to make Henry Hozier treat his wife humanely if not generously. But Henry Hozier was in command of the situation and would offer only a meagre sum for Blanche's support. He argued that he was now confident that he was not the father of the twins and he had no intention of supporting them. If Blanche wanted to contest his decision he was prepared to ruin what little good name she had left by publicly accusing her of numerous acts of adultery and by causing a scandal bigger than they could imagine. He was prepared to accept – indeed to insist – that the twins should live with their mother. But he still believed that the two older girls might be his and, therefore, he intended to keep them in his custody on the grounds that Blanche was clearly an unfit mother. Blanche protested and demanded that all the children should remain with her. She knew, however, that she could not take Henry to court over the custody of her daughters. The law had changed considerably since 1837, largely as a result of the efforts of Caroline Norton, who in that year had written an influential pamphlet entitled *The Separation of Mother and Child by the Law of Custody of Infants Considered*. She had been married to a brutal and violent man whose attacks on her were well witnessed; she was acknowledged by everyone as the innocent party in the break-up of her marriage. Still she had been refused by the courts any access to her three sons.[8] But even with the rather more liberal custody laws the courts would not look kindly on a mother who could not deny adultery.

All this time life in the nursery had continued its calm course with lessons in the morning for the two older girls and walks in the park in the afternoons. The routine was interrupted only for holidays. Sometimes they went to their house Netherton at Alyth in Scotland where they would go for rides in the pony trap or be driven over to their grandmother's rather intimidating home at Cortachy Castle where she still reigned supreme despite there being a new Countess of Airlie since her son David's marriage to Mabell Sudely in 1886. More enjoyable because more relaxed were the times spent at Easthope in Yorkshire with their Great Aunt Maisie whose daughters Sylvia and Venetia Stanley were very close to Kitty and Clementine in age.

While they were in London the Hozier children were only rarely aware of the comings and goings of their mother and father. There were two exceptions; one was the occasion when Blanche took Kitty with her on a visit leaving Clementine at home with the younger children. It was at this time that Clementine began to suspect that her mother favoured her older, prettier and livelier daughter who was closer to her in temperament than the shyer, less confident and easily troubled second daughter. The other, happier occasion was when Blanche took both her daughters to Paris. Of their two parents their mother was undoubtedly the one they were closer to and the one whose company they most enjoyed.

The sudden change in their lives as a result of the separation of their parents was quite shocking to all the children but especially to the two older girls. They were now told that they were going to live with their father who had until then been a very remote figure in their lives. A new governess, Rosa Stevenson, was to take care of them, and one of her first tasks was to buy new dresses for them ready for an excursion with their father. The two little girls aged eight and six were very excited at all the preparations for their holiday in Homburg, the German spa made fashionable by the Prince of Wales, where their father was going to take the waters. They were perhaps relieved rather than dismayed to discover that they were to stay in one hotel with their governess while their father stayed in another. His insistence on the custody of Kitty and Clementine did not mean that Henry Hozier was ready to become a full-time father and risk having his own freedoms restricted. Even during this relaxed holiday period his contact with them was restricted to breakfast time. When they all returned to England he cut himself off still further by sending the girls to live in Berkhamsted with their governess rather than having them in his London house.

Although Rosa Stevenson was called the girls' governess this was a courtesy title only for she does not seem to have attempted to teach Kitty and Clementine even the little that most governesses of the time tried to teach the girls in their charge. After attending a kindergarten for a few weeks the girls ceased to have any education other than picking up something about housekeeping by observing Miss Stevenson as she performed her daily chores.

Henry Hozier must have had some anxieties about the situation in Berkhamsted since he sent his sister Mary to see how his children were and to report back to him. Mary was not impressed by what she saw and on her suggestion the Hozier girls were taken away from Miss Stevenson and sent to school in Edinburgh. For girls of that age and class school of any kind was most unusual. Henry Hozier appears to have chosen Karl Fröbel's school more because it was inexpensive and because it solved the problem of where the girls should live than for its reputation for high educational standards. Karl Fröbel may have shared the name of the man who made such far-reaching improvements in kindergarten education but he did not educate by his methods. The sisters were unhappy and upset by this second inexplicable change in their lives.

As on many occasions in the future Clementine was so dismayed by the situation that she overcame her natural timidity and fear and took action. Clementine, rather than the bolder Kitty, wrote to Henry Hozier to tell him that they were unhappy at school, though it was Kitty who contrived to put the letter in the mail. Their father's reply was brief and to the point. He said he would remove them from the school if they were really unhappy. But before he could do so their position was made worse when the oldest of Karl Fröbel's three daughters who helped him run the school read this letter and realized that the sisters had gone behind her back to complain. Clementine and Kitty were made to feel that they had unworthily betrayed the school.

Perhaps Henry Hozier would have taken the girls away from Edinburgh once he had found an alternative way of dealing with them, but, before he could do so, Blanche discovered their whereabouts and, leaving the twins with her mother at Cortachy, she travelled to Edinburgh. However frivolous Blanche may have been she did genuinely care for her children and she was dismayed and angry to find that they had been sent to school. She regarded her husband's action as a betrayal of the agreement they had reached. After the first meeting which she managed to contrive with her daughters on the street outside the school, she was denied access to them. Henry Hozier had specifically warned the school that his wife might try to abduct the girls and Karl Fröbel and his daughters feared that this was Blanche's present intention. But her charm, her determination and her willingness to adopt unorthodox methods finally enabled her to achieve her objectives. She boarded in a house immediately opposite the school so that her daughters could see her and be reassured that she intended to do something. Then she managed to spend time with them by the simple means of attending their classes in the school. All her life Blanche had the gift of making children and young people like her, and her time in this school was no exception. The children's obvious pleasure in her company made Herr Fröbel's position difficult and he did not, as might have been expected, insist that she leave. But he evidently communicated his uneasiness about her continued presence and the disruptive effect she was having on his pupils to Henry Hozier. Since their father had at that moment no better way of caring for his daughters he allowed them to return to their mother's care. However he made his daughters understand that it was his decision that they should be reunited with their mother by accompanying Blanche when she met the sisters off the Edinburgh train and by going with them to Blanche's furnished lodgings at 97 Cornwall Road in Bayswater where the twins were already living. He clearly did not want them to think that Blanche had made her will prevail over his or that he no longer had any control over their lives. For the moment, however, Kitty and Clementine were content that they had escaped boarding school and were once more part of a family.

2

An Unconventional Childhood

BLANCHE HOZIER NOW set about bringing up her children. As a single parent her position was not enviable. Because she was divorced she could no longer be formally admitted to polite society or be received at court. For herself this mattered little, since she had always preferred the company of artists and men of letters, and they were unlikely to be upset by the failure of her marriage. She could, however, see that in time her daughters would be disadvantaged by her divorce for she would be unable to introduce them into society and help them to find suitable husbands. A greater and more immediate difficulty was her lack of a reliable and sufficient income. Henry Hozier gave her little, and sometimes gave her nothing. She had to rely on her family for financial support. This they provided with a good grace, especially her mother, but none of them were rich, so that, even with their help, Blanche was usually short of money. And Blanche was extravagant in some ways. She liked new clothes and good food and she liked the rooms in which she lived always to be bright and light and pleasant. On occasions she met the expenses of these pleasures by writing pieces for the *Daily Express*. A less reliable source of income was gambling. She moved frequently, always in search of better accommodation at the price she could afford and always keeping one step ahead of her husband just in case he should decide that it was his turn to have custody of Kitty and Clementine.

Because London was always expensive Blanche began to take her family for part of every year to cheaper lodgings in Seaford on the Sussex coast. By doing this she could to some extent claim that, like other children of the aristocracy, her children were getting their share of the outdoor life considered so important at the time. But she took great care that her husband could never accuse her of neglecting her children's education because of the frequent moves. A governess always accompanied them wherever they went. These women were usually French or German since Blanche took seriously her mother's precept that 'There is nothing so inferior as a gentlewoman who has no French.'[1] Whatever disadvantages her girls started out with, an inability to speak French would not be one of them. When the family was in London Kitty and Clementine occasionally attended classes outside home. While Clementine did extra French, Kitty had music lessons. Neither of them was taught much in the way of mathematics for, unlike her sister-in-law Mabell who believed every girl should have the chance to learn mathematics and the sciences, Blanche believed a scientific education was not suitable for a lady. Or perhaps it was that she simply did not want her daughters to have anything in common with her estranged husband. Certainly she was less concerned about keeping them ladylike when she allowed them to have bicycles.

During the months spent at Seaford at 11 Pelham Place the Hozier children were not entirely cut off from their family since Lady Airlie would sometimes visit, staying not with the family but in the Seaford Hotel. The girls had to be on their best behaviour during these visits. Another visitor who was much easier to be with was Mrs Mary Paget, a friend of Lady Airlie, who had a house at West Wantley in Sussex. It was apparent to her that Kitty was Blanche's favourite and that Clementine suffered from a lack of affection. Blanche was never very happpy about Mary Paget's singling out of Clementine for invitations to stay at her house. She understood the implied criticism and Clementine's evident delight in such opportunities to spend time away from her family reinforced her resentment.

A month of every year was spent in Scotland with Lady Airlie. In Blanche's view Scotland offered her children the opportunity for greater freedom than they could ever have in furnished rooms. In the wild and empty countryside they could walk and fish and breathe good fresh air. Although she was always glad to see these grandchildren to whose support she contributed as much as she could afford, Lady Airlie also felt it necessary to see that they maintained certain standards of behaviour. She was not pleased to learn that the girls had been given bicycles, and Clementine and Kitty had to be careful that she never caught them riding back from fishing expeditions. She did not approve of croquet, a game about which Clementine was already passionate, so that this became another activity that they had to do secretly. She took an interest in the progress of their education and although she was pleased with Clementine's aptitude for French she was critical of her handwriting.

In Scotland Kitty and Clementine could not fail to see how very different their lives were from those of their cousins. Kitty Ogilvy was just two years younger than Clementine but, although her father was in the army and moved frequently, her future and her education were carefully planned, whereas the Hozier girls had no idea of what the future held for them. It was generally accepted that Kitty's younger brother David, who would become the Earl of Airlie, would be educated at a public school. Whether the money could be found for Bill Hozier to have such an education was extremely doubtful. When they visited their Stanley cousins at Easthope they again could see how differently and with how much more security Sylvia and Venetia were being brought up.

Kitty Hozier who was generally more carefree than her younger sister does not seem to have been worried by the uncertainty of their future and by the generally unstructured life they led. She was very pretty and at fifteen already had admirers and had little doubt that she would marry young. Clementine, always in her shadow, and aware that she was considered to be far less pretty and not such good company, did not have such confidence and this explains why when she began confirmation classes she became for a period intensely religious. The church offered her certainties and a structure that her normal life lacked. She was confirmed in the church at Kirriemuir towards the end of 1898 when she was thirteen years old.

Between 1894 and 1899 Clementine saw very little of her father. The pleasant times in Homburg were largely forgotten and the image of Henry Hozier she now carried in her mind was of a rather frightening and threatening figure who had the power to send her away from her mother to live with uncongenial strangers. Blanche did nothing to dispel this antagonism towards her husband with whom she was constantly embattled about the inadequacy of the allowance he made her. By 1899 she was desperately short of money and was in fact in debt. She felt that Bill should be going to school like other boys of his age and class but unless her family paid his fees this would not be possible. Lady Airlie was fully aware of her daughter's plight and she also blamed Henry Hozier for his meanness. When Blanche became ill and could not even supplement her income with occasional journalism, Lady Airlie approached her former son-in-law and insisted that he took greater financial responsibility for his children. Henry Hozier's response was that if Blanche would return the two older girls to his care then he would certainly make sure that they lacked for nothing. But Blanche had no intention of giving up the girls, especially Kitty whose lively company she increasingly enjoyed. She was afraid that Henry would get his way by abducting his daughters, and to make this difficult for him she decided, without informing him of her intentions, to move out of easy reach. The family found the money to put Bill into Summerfields Preparatory School whilst she hastily packed up and then accompanied by three daughters and two dogs made for Newhaven and from there in July sailed to Dieppe.

By 1899 there was a regular ferry service between Newhaven and Dieppe on boats which were English-owned but manned by French sailors. As the ferry sailed into the harbour the girls were excited to see the whole town spread before them in a panorama. Behind Dieppe they saw a bay formed by striking white cliffs broken by smaller bays at Puys and Pourville. The ferry docked in the heart of the town and the Hoziers disembarked at the Gare Maritime. Immediately the girls felt abroad. The French language they heard all about them, the brighter colours and something in the quality of the light all contributed to make them feel more than just a few hours away from England.

Blanche had decided not to stay in Dieppe itself. Perhaps she feared that Henry Hozier could find her there too easily. Instead she piled daughters, luggage and dogs into a cab and headed for one of the small fishing villages they had seen from the sea, Puys, and once there she took rooms with Madame Balle at La Ferme des Colombiers. Here the family remained for the rest of the summer.

By the autumn Blanche had made up her mind to stay in France for a while. For many reasons Dieppe suited her very well. But she had to consider the education of her daughters and as there was no school in Puys she decided to move into the centre of Dieppe itself where there were three schools to choose from. She took a small furnished house at 49 rue du Faubourg de la Barre. The door opened straight onto the street and from the downstairs windows all the comings and goings from the town's meeting place at the nearby eighteenth-century Café des Tribunaux in the Place du Puits Salé could be observed.

Blanche found she had less choice in deciding on a school than she had expected. Money determined where the girls should go. Of the three schools Miss Cunnick's was considered to be the most elegant, but Miss

Shackleton's had the higher academic standards. The third school run by nuns, the Pensionnat des Soeurs de la Providence, was the one Blanche could afford and so Kitty and Clementine now aged sixteen and fourteen found themselves the only Protestants in a school run by Catholics for Catholics. They felt almost as out of place here as they had done in the Edinburgh School. But at least they were close to home and were not boarders. For the time being they put up with the webbing belts they wore to show what year they were in and the ugly black aprons. They disliked intensely the lack of hygiene in the school and having to wash their spoons and forks after lunch in the same greasy water as everyone else used. They were always afraid of catching the lice which they knew were a problem in the school. And although they liked the calm Mother Superior they were uneasy at the inevitable emphasis on the Catholic religion.

Blanche herself was well pleased with her new home. She liked the low rent she had to pay and the supply of maids ready to work for a pittance. She enjoyed the quality and cheapness of butter and eggs and milk and the variety of fresh and inexpensive produce she could haggle for in the Place Nationale. She quickly gained a reputation as a woman who struck a hard bargain and when she sent Clementine to do the shopping she expected her to do the same. Unlike the French women in the town she never felt it was a servant's job to do the shopping.

The people of Dieppe found the Hoziers inexplicable oddities. They could not understand why a titled lady should dress as eccentrically as Lady Blanche did with her hair in a long plait down her back and why she would dress her girls in cheap cotton gingham. They were puzzled that she always did her own shopping and often her own cooking and that she sent her daughters to the convent to be educated. Although this handsome and striking woman carried herself with dignity and pride and expected to be treated with respect, she participated in the everyday life of the town in a way no other aristocratic visitors from England had done previously. Lord Salisbury, for example, had built himself a large villa on the edge of the town. He had spent his summers at Chalet Cecil every year until in 1895 he had sold the property. But neither he nor his family had ever mingled with the ordinary people of Dieppe. Even the scandalous Duchess of Caracciolo, reputed to have borne a daughter to her regular visitor the Prince of Wales, kept herself to herself in the Villa Olga.

Lady Blanche did not seek out the company of the established and respectable British colony. Rather she kept company with the town's artists and writers of whom there were many. French painters had discovered Dieppe and the quality of its light in the 1870s. In the 1890s English writers and painters had been attracted there because the town was so close to England and yet offered a completely different life-style. Oscar Wilde, who was a friend of Blanche, had sought refuge there after his release from jail in 1898. Aubrey Beardsley had helped plan the Savoy review with Arthur Symons in the Café des Tribunaux and had returned in 1897 just before his death. The novelists George Moore and George du Maurier were regular visitors.

The Blanche family was one of those which had been longest resident in Dieppe and the painter Jacques-Émile Blanche was intimate with the British colony in the town and with both French and English artists. His close friend was Walter Sickert who had spent much of his boyhood in Dieppe and who had returned there to live in the 1880s. He was known as '*un vrai Dieppois*' because he not only spoke French fluently but he was also able to talk in the local patois. Blanche Hozier already knew Jacques-Émile Blanche through her contacts with many artists in London and before long he introduced her to Walter Sickert. The friendship between Lady Blanche and Walter Sickert quickly became a close one. The tall handsome man who had once been an actor was energetic and high spirited. He was quite comfortable with Blanche's odd marital situation since he also had many adulterous relationships behind him and he too had parted from his spouse, though in his case the parting was very amicable. He was at the time Blanche came to know him living with Augustine Villain, ostensibly as her lodger, though it was remarked that her son Maurice had colouring remarkably similar to that of Walter Sickert with his thick honey-coloured hair. He too cared little for conventional dress and could easily have been mistaken for one of the fishermen among whom he lived. He was a frequent visitor to the house on the rue du Faubourg de la Barre and since he always got on well with young people and children his friendship included Blanche's three daughters. In this small house there was no way in which the children could be segregated from the life of the adults as would have been the case if Blanche had lived the way her peers did. Walter Sickert teased and flirted with Kitty but took Clementine more seriously. They met frequently in the streets of the town when Clementine was shopping for her mother and he was painting. Clementine was not too impressed by his painting but he was an early admirer of her unusual looks which were just now beginning to blossom. He invited her to have tea with him at Madame Villain's at Neuville where the fishermen lived. Unfortunately when Clementine arrived at the house Sickert was out shopping and she had to deal with his intimidating, tall, beautiful, red-haired landlady who allowed her to wait in Sickert's bedroom. Clementine had never before seen such squalor as the painter lived in and after waiting some time in vain for her host to arrive she decided to do him a good turn by cleaning up for him. Sickert was not well pleased when he returned with their tea to find that Clementine's cleaning had included throwing out the bones of a herring which he had been about to use as the centre-piece of a still life. His dismay was short lived, however, and his normal jolly manner quickly made Clementine feel at home in these unusual surroundings.

Blanche's friendships with painters helped to develop in Clementine a lasting interest in the arts. Had she been brought up conventionally in England she would not at her age have come into contact with men such as Sickert and certainly would not have been allowed to have unchaperoned meetings with a painter of questionable morals.

But another of her mother's activities which also had a lasting influence on Clementine was far less positive. One of the greatest attractions in Dieppe as far as Blanche was concerned was the casino. There had been a casino in Dieppe since 1822 and the building where Blanche now gambled was the third one to occupy the spot. Built in the Moorish style with horizontally striped red and buff bricks, domes of green copper, minarets, and surrounded by flower beds, the casino was one of the most striking features of the town. Lady Blanche Hozier whom Jacques-Émile Blanche described as 'an impenitent gambler' spent a great deal of her time and money within its walls. How she financed her habit at this time is something of a mystery; in later days she unashamedly borrowed from any family member or friend who stayed with her in Dieppe. Clementine who was already embarrassed by her mother's eccentric dress and way of life was now distressed that while her mother found the money to visit the casino she also needed credit in the local shops because she lacked cash. She was ashamed of her mother's obsession and of their lack of money and throughout the rest of her life she tried to dissuade, not always successfully, those whom she cared for from gambling.

In October the Boer War began and the events taking place so far away soon had repercussions on the lives of the English living in Dieppe. The French, like the Irish, were entirely on the side of the Boers and against British Imperialism. In the shops the usual postcards for tourists with views of Dieppe were replaced with brightly coloured cartoons mocking and denigrating the British. Crowds demonstrated on the streets against the British and on one such occasion Nellie was knocked to the ground. At school the Hozier girls were the only ones who did not support the Boers and they felt isolated and offended to such an extent that when their fellow pupils cheered at the announcement that Ladysmith had not been relieved they staged their own protest by walking out of the school. Many of the British colony decided to leave France, if only temporarily, but Blanche, who was not unaccustomed to disapproval and cared nothing for it, had no intention of being driven away from the place where she was otherwise content.

Word reached Henry Hozier of the life-style of his wife and daughters. Blanche had earlier been made angry by Henry's choice of school and she had attacked him for breaking their agreement. He now turned the tables on her by objecting strongly when he learned that the girls were being educated in a convent school and were living in an atmosphere which was hostile to the English. He approached Lady Airlie and told her of his intention to intervene and possibly to reassert his right to custody. Lady Airlie tried to warn Blanche of his intentions but she could not stop Henry Hozier from discovering his wife's whereabouts since *The Citizen*, a London weekly, published detailed accounts of visitors to Dieppe and their activities. The presence of the forceful Lady Blanche could hardly go unremarked.

In December 1899 Henry Hozier took the steamer from Newhaven to Dieppe making no secret of his resolve to return with his two oldest daughters. He established himself in style at the Hotel Royal and then set out on a cold night for the address where he understood Blanche to be. When he reached the house on the rue du Faubourg de la Barre the windows were all lit up. He peered in and saw that he had the right address for there were his wife, Kitty and Clementine and a large handsome man whom he did not recognize. He rang the doorbell and waited but no one answered. Instead all the lights in the house went out. So he posted under the door the invitations he had brought with him before peering once more through the window where the room now appeared to be occupied only by the tall man.

Inside the house Blanche insisted that the girls remain crouched below the window until the visitor's footsteps could be heard echoing away in the distance. When Blanche opened the envelope left by her husband she found an invitation each for Kitty and Clementine to have a meal with their father. Kitty was invited to dinner the following evening and Clementine for lunch the day after. Much to their surprise Blanche said that they must see their father but that the maid must take them and fetch them back from the hotel. The following evening Kitty arrived home safely in high spirits full of talk of what she had eaten and all the things her father had promised to give her if she went to him for a visit.

Clementine was, nevertheless, extremely nervous the next day when it was her turn to go to the Hotel Royal. Her father was more accustomed to dealing with men than young girls and he had never lost his military manner. Clementine was a little afraid of him and did not fully trust him after his failure to rescue her from the Edinburgh school. She was alarmed when at the end of the meal and after many searching questions her father announced that she would be living with him or Aunt Mary in the future. The very idea of Aunt Mary was enough to make Clementine eager to return to her mother. She was greatly relieved when the maid arrived promptly to take her home and terrified when her father dismissed the young woman with a bribe. She firmly believed that unless she managed to get out of the hotel her father would make her go back to England with him. The moment he turned his back she ran from the room. Outside she found the maid waiting uncertainly and the two of them ran off in the direction of home. Henry pursued them briefly before returning to the hotel.

Although she was not to know it then, this was Henry Hozier's last serious attempt to regain custody of the girls he believed to be his daughters. Only two months later there was a tragedy in the family which changed everything.

3

A Little Knowledge

JUST TWO MONTHS after the disturbance of Henry Hozier's visit when it was clear that there would be no repercussions, and when Clementine was beginning to feel confident that she would not have to live with her father and Kitty to feel disappointed that there would be no pony for her, Kitty fell ill. The far from clean conditions at the convent may well have been responsible for the typhoid fever which Kitty now contracted. Blanche became distraught as she realized increasingly that Kitty's recovery was extremely doubtful. But unlike other women of her class she pulled herself together and determined to nurse her daughter herself. Walter Sickert helped his friend in every way he could undertaking the heavy task of carrying cold water upstairs by the bucketful to try to reduce Kitty's fever. When Blanche decided that she could not look after her younger daughters and care for Kitty at the same time and that they must be sent back to England until Kitty was well, Walter Sickert made all the arrangements and even saw the girls safely onto the ferry. Clementine and Nellie were allowed to see their sister very briefly before they left only on condition that they did not alert her to the fact that they were leaving. Blanche was concerned not to let Kitty know just how ill she was.

Clementine and Nellie, worried and frightened about their older sister, made the long journey alone from Dieppe to Scotland at a time when it was unheard of for young girls to travel by rail unaccompanied. They were met in St Andrews by their aunt Griselda. Normally they would have gone to stay with Lady Airlie but she was preparing to leave for Dieppe to help their mother. For almost two weeks Clementine and

Nellie had no word about their sister. Then came a telegram which suggested that all was well, for in it their mother said that she was taking Kitty to Batsford, the home of their Aunt Clementine and Uncle Bertram, and that they should join her there. They thought that Kitty must be very much better if she could travel across the channel and the two girls looked forward to a happy family reunion. But the hope inspired by this telegram did not last long. Another telegram had been sent earlier to Cortachy which told of Kitty's death and Blanche had assumed that the news would have been broken to Clementine and Nellie before her telegram summoning them to Batsford for Kitty's funeral arrived. The sisters were all the more devastated by the news after their brief period of renewed hope.

Why did Blanche in her distress turn to Bertram and Clementine Mitford rather than her family at Cortachy and why did she choose to have her daughter buried at Batsford rather than in Scotland or in France? Does her decision suggest that those who believed that Bertram Mitford was Kitty's real father might have been right? When Blanche had told Wilfrid Scawen Blunt that Captain 'Bay' Middleton was the father of her first two daughters she may have been attempting to establish a credible rumour that would screen her relationship with her brother-in-law, since this almost incestuous relationship would have been even less acceptable to society than an affair with the Captain and might even have harmed her sister Clementine's position. A portrait of Bertram Mitford as a young man which shows a striking resemblance not only to Clementine but also to her son Randolph lends some credence to this theory. Whoever had fathered the two girls, one thing only is certain and that is that Blanche wanted it clearly understood that it was not Henry Hozier.

With Kitty gone the relationship between Clementine and Nellie changed. Now Clementine was the older sister and she began to adopt a protective attitude towards Nellie which lasted for the rest of their lives. Clementine did not, however, replace Kitty in Blanche's affections. Clementine was, if anything, even more serious, reserved and anxious after the death of her sister and these were character traits to which Blanche was temperamentally unable to respond favourably. The distance between mother and older daughter increased rather than diminished. The preference Blanche had once shown for Kitty she now began to show for Nellie.

For the time being Blanche felt a revulsion towards Dieppe where her favourite daughter had died and she did not wish to return there. Perhaps she also felt some guilt for having sent her daughters to the convent where Kitty might have contracted her fatal illness. Uncharacteristically she now made the decision to settle down quietly in England while her children finished their education.

There was a certain irony in that the place Blanche Hozier now chose to live was the very same place where Clementine and Kitty had briefly attended kindergarten while in the custody of their father. A very English town dating back to Saxon times, Berkhamsted in Hertfordshire had several features to recommend it to Blanche. It was far enough from London to be inexpensive yet within easy reach of the capital by the good train service. She was able to rent an eighteenth-century house on the High Street which, like the house in Dieppe, enabled her to be at the centre of the town's activities. Also on the High Street was Berkhamsted School for Girls to which she intended to send her two daughters. Bill had by now finished his time at his preparatory school and in other circumstances would have gone with his peers to a public school. But such an education was entirely beyond Blanche's means especially now that she had the extra expenses of living in England. So, although she believed in educating boys well, the best she could do for Bill was to send him to Berkhamsted Grammar School. She knew that she would be wasting her time appealing to Henry Hozier to pay for Bill's education since he continued to assert that the twins were not his children and that he had no responsibility for them. He made one last attempt to claim Clementine however. He insisted that she be brought to his house in North Audley Street, London, for a visit. Clementine was even more afraid of her father's intentions than in Dieppe. Blanche escorted her right to her former husband's door and tried to reassure her daughter that she would be there to take her home. Unfortunately Henry Hozier spotted his wife outside his house and took the opportunity to berate her there and then on the street. Blanche gave as good as she got while Clementine stood there in agonized embarrassment listening to this public row. After such a disruption there was no chance at all for the meeting between Henry Hozier and Clementine to be anything but awkward and unsatisfactory. Neither of them knew then that this was to be the last time they would see each other.

Once again her own unusual circumstances obliged Blanche to put her children into a situation unlike that of their cousins and unlike that of other daughters of the aristocracy, none of whom attended school with children outside their own class. But this did not worry Clementine and Nellie at all. Although at times in Dieppe Clementine had been uneasy about her family's life-style, in Berkhamsted she was much happier. After all the changes and upsets of the last few years she was delighted to settle into a more or less regular routine. Although her education to date had been patchy and she was humiliatingly behind in subjects such as mathematics and science, her talent for French gave her a status in her new school. She found she enjoyed working hard and the structure that attendance at school imposed on her life suited her well.

Blanche, however, was not entirely pleased by the way Clementine took so readily to school life just as she had once done to religion. She was more in sympathy with Nellie's happy-go-lucky attitude towards school than Clementine's serious intensity. When Clementine tried to do her homework Blanche could always think of something else that her daughter should be doing. If the homework happened to be mathematics or science then Clementine had to hide herself away or pretend to be doing some other subject. It was Blanche's view that girls were not expected to know, they were expected to amuse. She regarded Clementine's seriousness as a distinct social disadvantage.

But Blanche was pleased with Clementine's prowess with the French language as she regarded this as a far more useful accomplishment than all the rest of her schooling put together. When Clementine won the silver medal for French from the Société des Professeurs Français en Angleterre Blanche marked the occasion by arranging for Clementine to be accompanied by her French teacher of earlier days, Mademoiselle Henri, on a trip to Paris. She considered this excursion in much the same way as other mothers thought of finishing school: it would enable Clementine to pick up some Parisian culture and make her better able to converse at society dinner parties.

Blanche was still in contact with Walter Sickert who had by now moved to Paris. She told him of Clementine's success and that she would be in Paris. Walter Sickert was interested to see whether Clementine had fulfilled the promise he had detected in her, so he arrived one day at the small hotel where she was staying with Mademoiselle Henri and, although he was the most unlikely of chaperones, he managed to charm Clementine's companion and instructress into allowing him to take her pupil out for the day. The Paris Sickert introduced Clementine to was not the Paris known to tourists or the one shown to her by Mademoiselle Henri. Sickert lived in a comparatively poor neighbourhood in which he was as established and as well known as in Dieppe. He had his regular places for eating and Clementine was intrigued that in the small cafés he patronized money did not exchange hands; instead the bill was chalked up to be settled at a later point. Sickert dutifully took Clementine to look at paintings in the Luxembourg Gallery but what interested the seventeen-year-old girl far more was being given a sense of bohemian Paris when she was taken to meet Camille Pissarro and his friends in what seemed to her to be a typical painter's garret. Sickert also took her to the home of Jacques-Émile Blanche just outside Paris. Clementine had known this painter earlier in Dieppe. His home was elegant and well appointed, quite unlike the place where Pissarro lived. Dinner there was not at all like the meals Sickert had provided throughout the day. Jacques-Émile Blanche was far more middle class than bohemian in his views as well as in his life-style and he was slightly scandalized that even the unconventional Lady Blanche had gone so far as to allow her young and unmarried daughter to spend a day alone and unchaperoned in the company of a man like Walter Sickert. No French mother would have allowed her daughter's marriageability to be threatened by such behaviour.

When she returned to Berkhamsted Clementine began to think seriously of what the future held for her. The headmistress at the High School, Miss Beatrice Harris, was all for Clementine setting her sights on a university education and a career which would give her financial independence. She assumed, correctly, that the only alternative for a girl in Clementine's position was to enter the marriage market within the next couple of years and hope to secure a husband who would support her. As an independent woman herself with strong views about women and education she found this prospect for her pupil degrading. Clementine was strongly attracted to the idea that she could create for herself a life very different from that of her mother. But Blanche's opposition to the idea of a university education for her daughter was immediate and emphatic. Her view was the same as that of Moreton Frewen who responded to his daughter Clare's determination to find work with the words, 'I should advise you, my dear, to find a husband; it is more permanent.'[1]

Clementine had every reason to be both surprised and dismayed by her mother's response for there was a strong tradition of support for the full education of women in Blanche's own family. Blanche's grandmother, Henrietta Maria Stanley, as a widow had dedicated herself to improving the education of women. She had not only helped found schools for girls which concentrated on academic subjects rather than feminine accomplishments but she had also been a strong supporter of university education for women and had helped to found Girton College. Blanche's aunt, the youngest sister of her mother, who had married into the Russell family, was a feminist who advocated the same possibilities for education for women as for men. The present Countess of Airlie, Blanche's sister-in-law, had as early as the beginning of the 1890s written a little book entitled *The Real Rights of Women* which she had made sure was widely circulated in high schools for girls. In this book she had forthrightly declared that girls should be taught to think that 'work is as necessary for a woman as a man'. She was entirely against the notion that marriage and household duties should be enough for a woman. She believed that all women should be educated to accept that 'they have work to do outside as well as inside their own homes'.[2]

However unconventional she was in other respects Blanche Hozier was just like most other women of her generation and class in her attitude towards her daughter's future. She regarded the prospect of Clementine's going to university as little better than her going into a convent. She firmly believed that such a step would ruin Clementine's chances of marriage. And what did life hold for a spinster, however well educated? In Blanche's view all a girl really needed at Clementine's age was the ability to be charming and to make conversation at dinner. Time enough to educate herself when she had found a husband.

By now Blanche was quite hopeful that Clementine might make a good marriage. As she had grown older so had her looks improved. She was at seventeen quite beautiful with thick ash blonde hair and unusual striking hazel-green eyes. Sir Alan Lascelles describing her at this time said that when she entered a room her appearance was 'quite electrifying' and that she was 'the loveliest creature you ever saw'.[3] Blanche was convinced that if only Clementine could meet the right people she would quickly find a husband. The problem was that Blanche herself was not able to introduce her daughter to the right people. Her position as a divorced woman was one problem, another and even greater difficulty was the lack of money. She determined, therefore, to approach Lady St Helier and ask for her help.

Lady St Helier was the former Mary Mackenzie. She had been married and widowed twice. Her first marriage was to Colonel John Stanley, Blanche's uncle, and it was this relationship by marriage that gave Blanche some claim on the older woman's assistance. After the death of John Stanley his widow had married Sir Francis Jeune who was, ironically enough given Blanche's situation, a judge who presided over divorce cases. With her husband's elevation to the peerage Lady Jeune had become Lady St Helier. She was a woman with plenty of money and a very broad social acquaintance, so that all sorts of people could be met at her house at 52 Portland Place. She liked famous people and was pleased to entertain frequently the well-known novelist Elinor Glyn despite her scandalous reputation. The introduction of such a young and inexperienced girl as Clementine into society was a new venture for her but she agreed to do her best by her great-niece.

Blanche wasted no time. She was so keen to launch her daughter that she did not even wait until Clementine had finished school. So during the London season of 1903 Clementine had what must have been the very odd experience of both continuing her education at the High School and being introduced into London society. Despite her double existence she managed to pass her exams in French, German and, to Blanche's disgust, Biology. But Blanche's tactic of letting Clementine have a taste of London life succeeded in making Clementine accept that more education would not necessarily make her more acceptable for the kind of life she had to look to in the future.

What convinced Clementine to fall in with Blanche's wishes was something quite other than the latter's arguments. For Clementine, who had always regarded herself as second best to her older sister, now found that she was in demand. Within a very short time she was being spoken of as 'the beautiful Miss Hozier' and she had plenty of invitations. What was even more gratifying to a young woman with little experience and no financial prospects was that she had no shortage of potential suitors. Lady St Helier was very pleased with her protégée especially when she saw that one eligible man in particular had fallen in love with her great-niece and was very likely to propose to her.

Sidney Cornwallis Peel was the third son of the 1st Viscount Peel. He was fifteen years older than Clementine so that when he first met her in 1903 he was thirty-three to her eighteen. He had been educated at Eton and New College, Oxford, and was a Fellow of Trinity College, Oxford. He was also pursuing a career as a barrister after having reached the rank of Colonel during the Boer War in South Africa. It is not at all surprising that Clementine was flattered and delighted by his unexpected attentions. What inexperienced eighteen-year-old with low self-esteem could resist a man who wooed her by sending her violets every day and by being available to escort her whenever he was needed?

At the end of the summer term Clementine left school with fewer protests than might have been expected. Blanche had no hesitation in terminating Nellie's education at Berkhamsted too, before she also developed unsuitable ideas. Since Bill had decided to become a naval cadet there was, in Blanche's view, no good reason for remaining in Berkhamsted. And so the house was packed up and Blanche took her two daughters back to France. Not to Dieppe which still held painful memories, but to Paris. Here she took a short lease on a house in the rue Oudinot in an inexpensive area on the fringes of Montparnasse. As in Dieppe she was once more living among artists and writers. From this house Clementine continued her French studies by attending classes at the Sorbonne. There was no question of her being accompanied on her journeys around the city by a chaperone: she went to and from her lectures alone. She loved being in Paris and she did not mind unduly Blanche's alternations between economizing one moment and splashing out on an expensive meal the next. And to prove that he was pursuing her in earnest her admirer, Sidney Peel, spent every possible weekend in Paris as long as the Hozier family was resident there. Both Blanche and Lady St Helier expected that at any moment the couple would announce their engagement.

If Sidney Peel had had his way then this certainly would have happened. But the most he could persuade Clementine to agree to was a secret engagement. Inexperienced and unsure, she was not ready to make a firm commitment and to set in motion all the preparations for a wedding. What held Clementine back? She could not have had a more ardent and caring suitor. She might have thought his age a disadvantage but at least she could be confident that he knew his own mind and was ready to settle down. For Clementine most certainly did not want a marriage like that of her mother and father. She wanted marriage for life and with Sidney Peel she was likely to have this. But there was, perhaps, a little too much of her mother in her for her to settle so young for such a steady and predictable life with an admirable but rather unexciting husband. She had, after all, been in society for only a few months and seemed likely to attract more suitors. It was neither sensible nor necessary to accept the first man who proposed when she was not sure of her own feelings.

It was customary for young girls of good family to complete their education by a spell in Germany. Most were sent to establishments in Dresden where they learnt a little music, saw some paintings and improved their German accent. But these finishing schools were clearly too expensive for Blanche Hozier. Instead she arranged for Clementine to spend the spring of 1904 with a German family who lived just outside Berlin and who would give her daughter a taste of fashionable life there. Clementine found that she did not miss Sidney Peel at all during her time in Germany and her uncertainty about marriage increased.

By the summer of 1904 when Clementine returned to London to the house at 20 Upper Phillimore Place in Kensington which Blanche had by now rented, her education was as complete as possible in the circumstances. In the view of all those who took a kindly interest in her all that remained to be done was to settle her with a husband. Given her mother's precarious financial situation a good marriage was regarded as unusually urgent. Lady St Helier encouraged Clementine to accept Sidney Peel. She thought that he was an excellent catch for her impoverished great-niece and that she was unlikely to have a better offer. But still Clementine held back; she explained that she was not in love even though she was very fond of her suitor. Lady St Helier's response was that being 'in love' was perhaps a luxury that Clementine could not afford and that a marriage based on affection and respect was more likely to prove happy in the long run than one based on notions of romantic love. She pointed out that at least Clementine had been given plenty of opportunity to get to know her suitor whilst many a young girl in her position married despite hardly knowing her future husband. She painted an enticing picture of how much marriage would change Clementine's status. She would no longer have to live at home and she would have both more freedom and more security. Despite such rational arguments, Clementine stubbornly refused to commit herself. And so she continued the social rounds considered appropriate for a well-born young woman of the time. The important distinction between Clementine and her peer group was that she had no money. Clementine's style was considerably cramped by the limitations of her wardrobe. Edwardian ladies regularly travelled to long weekends in country houses, with trunks full of dresses, hats and shoes. Several changes of clothes a day were needed in order to be appropriately dressed for the predictable programme of events. And, of course, a maid was necessary to keep all those clothes in order. Clementine had neither fine clothes nor a maid. She could do nothing about the maid but she could do something about her wardrobe. To earn the money she needed she put her excellent French to good use and gave French lessons. Then she made the money she earned go as far as possible by learning how to sew from her cousin who had a dressmaking business. Her Aunt Mabell, Countess of Airlie, recorded how Clementine had appeared at Cortachy Castle one evening dressed for a formal dinner in a white satin dress she had made for herself and how very beautiful she had looked in the simple style she had of necessity chosen. It was fortunate for Clementine that simple white dresses were considered the only suitable apparel for a young unmarried girl at that time.

For the next few years she lived a strange divided life. Her home, which was now 51 Abingdon Villas, was always pleasant since Blanche had a gift for bringing out the best in her surroundings. But the house was modest and a far cry from the large and elegant country houses standing in their own grounds where Clementine would spend the weekends. The food at home was generally good, if not elaborate, because Blanche employed a French cook, but it was not on the lavish scale with meals of many courses such as she encountered in the homes of her weekend hosts and hostesses. At the weekends she was 'the beautiful Miss Hozier' with young men at her feet. At home she was Miss Hozier the French teacher and the daughter of the vigorous Blanche who would tolerate no airs and graces. The girls she met in the country were for the most part in surroundings which were familiar to them and they would be returning home to similar establishments where they would spend their days in idleness and writing letters and diaries. Amongst those she regularly encountered were her cousins Venetia and Sylvia Stanley, Cynthia Charteris and Violet Asquith, all of whom had homes where they could reciprocate the hospitality they received. Only Horatia Seymour whom she met at this time had anything like similar circumstances and it was with her that she developed the closest friendship of her young womanhood based on their difference from the company they found themselves in.

In 1904 Clementine was invited to a ball at Crewe House, a lovely Georgian house on Curzon Street, the home of Lord and Lady Crewe. As usual she was not short of admirers and she was aware that she was the focus of attention of many young men. She was usually quite unselfconscious about the way her beauty affected people. But on this occasion she was disconcerted by the persistent stare of one young man. He was of medium height, five feet six and a half inches tall, and not especially distinguished looking with his sandy hair already beginning to recede. Only his obvious confidence and the singlemindedness of his attention made him seem different from the other young men in the room. She knew who he was even though he clearly did not know her. His recent defection from the Conservative party to the Liberals had made him the centre of a storm and he was at that moment very unpopular in many circles but known to everyone. She recognized also the woman who was with him for she too had caused something of a scandal when she had married George Cornwallis-West, a contemporary of her own son. Clementine also knew that Jennie Jerome, as she had been before she had married Lord Randolph Churchill, was an old friend of her mother, though the two women had not met since Blanche's divorce. Jennie was the sister-in-law of Jack Leslie, Clementine's godfather, and it was this relationship she now used as the excuse for introducing her son Winston to Clementine Hozier. Winston was taken with Clementine's appearance but Clementine responded in the way most people did to the forceful young man. It was Lady Pamela Lytton who said, 'The first time you meet Winston you see all his faults.'[4] Clementine's first impression was of a stuck-up and rather objectionable young man. As soon as she politely could she broke off the stilted conversation that was all they could manage and left him to dance with someone else. Although Winston had sought the introduction and had seemed bowled over by Clementine, he made no attempt to develop the acquaintance. He quickly turned his thoughts to politics and his career. Women did not play a major role in his life at this time; men were more important to him because they were 'the ones who made the world go round'.[5] It was almost four years before they were to meet again.

Clementine could not forget Winston altogether because he was so often in the news. But she did not follow his career with particular interest and she certainly did not see in him a prospective husband. By contrast with his awkward social behaviour and abrasive manner the pleasant courtesies of Sidney Peel and her other admirers had a new attraction.

Although Blanche Hozier had no desire to push her daughter into an unhappy marriage she did become increasingly concerned as time went by and Clementine continued to refuse to marry not only Sidney Peel but every other young man who approached her. For it was absolutely essential that Clementine should marry someone. Life as a spinster in Edwardian England was a desperate fate to contemplate and in any case Blanche was keen for someone else to shoulder the financial burden of her daughter. There was a great deal of tension in the household as

Blanche saw her daughter go to one social occasion after another without the result she longed for. She began to be annoyed when Clementine attended balls apparently unconcerned that the reason she had initially been encouraged to do so was to find a husband. On one occasion her annoyance was such that she boxed her daughter's ears. Clementine had a temper to match her mother's and she immediately left the house rather than tolerate such an indignity as physical punishment at her age. It took the intervention of her sympathizer of earlier days, Mary Paget, to reconcile mother and daughter.

The pressure was beginning to tell, however. In 1906 Sylvia Stanley, the cousin Clementine most admired and respected, became engaged to Anthony Henley. The match was considered a good one since Anthony Henley was not only a director of a company of shipowners and coal exporters and the heir presumptive to the 5th Baron Henley, he also had a well established career in the army. However, what impressed Clementine far more than the bridegroom's eligibility was Sylvia's obvious love for him. She would let nothing, not even the pain of a broken arm, delay her marriage. Because Clementine had been asked to be her cousin's bridesmaid she saw a great deal of her immediately before the wedding took place. So she was in a position to contrast Sylvia's certainty about her feelings for her fiancé with her own recurring doubts about whether she really loved Sidney Peel. She decided that her uncertainty was not a good basis for a marriage and once again, this time irrevocably, she broke off her unofficial engagement to her long-suffering suitor.

Nevertheless she was now more open to the idea of marriage and settling down than she had been before her cousin's wedding. In July of that year she was invited to a party at Castle Ashby in Northamptonshire to celebrate the coming of age of William Compton, the heir to the Marquess of Northampton. It was an even more glamorous and splendid occasion than the many parties Clementine had already attended. Guests were taken from London in a special train and were met at the station by several brakes. There were chaperones who were supposed to see that the young people did not pair off but walked the grounds in threes. But the chaperones never had a chance. For three days fifty young people, most of them under twenty-five, were constantly in each other's company. The weather was warm, there was plenty of champagne and dancing until the early hours of the morning. The young women slept in the castle but the young men were housed in tents hung with tapestries and equipped with electric lights. Gradually a general air of eroticism stole over the company and many a new romance sprang into being. Clementine was as affected as all the other young women; she seems to have been intoxicated with the idea of love. She spent a good deal of time in the company of Lionel Earle whom she had met, as she had met Winston Churchill, at the home of Lord and Lady Crewe. Like Sidney Peel, Lionel Earle was much older than Clementine. When she met him again this summer he was forty years old and a successful civil servant. To the unworldly and inexperienced Clementine he seemed dazzlingly a man of the world. He had been educated at universities in Germany and France as well as at Oxford and he had lived and worked in Paris for two years. She was flattered by his attention, by his appreciation of her ability to speak fluent French and her knowledge of Paris. In the highly charged atmosphere of Castle Ashby Lionel Earle seemed a delightful and congenial companion, and when he proposed to her she accepted. She returned to London engaged and for a few days basked in the approval of her grandmother and Lady St Helier. To her surprise her mother seemed less enthusiastic than she had expected but Lady Blanche nevertheless made a formal announcement of the engagement and began preparations for a wedding.

Her contemporaries were aghast at what she had done. Not one of her friends approved of the match of the beautiful young girl and the man they regarded as pedantic and boring. Away from Castle Ashby and the special atmosphere of the party Clementine herself began to reconsider her rash acceptance of a proposal from a man she barely knew. Some time spent in his company while holidaying in Holland brought home to her the fact that she cared for him even less than for the unfortunate Sidney Peel. She was horrified when congratulations and, worse still, wedding presents began to arrive and she seemed trapped. If she had been doubtful about marrying Sidney Peel she was certain that she could not go through with marriage to Lionel Earle. She now realized that her fiancé was pompous and set in his ways and that she had nothing in common with him beyond a shared interest in France. She now found his attentions irksome rather than flattering and she discovered that he was not at all physically attractive to her. But arrangements for her marriage were so far advanced that she was afraid to confess her doubts to her mother. In the event Blanche, who had never warmed to Lionel Earle, was kind and understanding. Not so her grandmother who regarded Clementine's decision to break the engagement as disgraceful. But break it she did and it would be a long time before she was once again admitted into Lady Airlie's favour.

4

Love at Last

No one was more shocked at the mess she had made of this affair than Clementine herself. She became quite ill with the shame and worry. But the next season came around and with low spirits Clementine once more attended balls and dinner parties and the occasional country house weekend. She continued to attract admirers but her recent experience made her careful about encouraging more proposals of marriage.

She was depressed because her younger, lively sister Nellie was ill with tuberculosis and had left England for a clinic in Nordrach. Not only did she miss her high spirits she was also afraid of losing her just as she had lost Kitty. The death of Henry Hozier in February did nothing to raise her morale. She did not know that there was any question about her parentage and she had a sense of having failed as a daughter; now she would never have the chance to put that right. But in the spring of 1908 her life unexpectedly took a new direction.

Both Clementine and Winston were fond of telling their family and friends with some awe of how close they had come to missing that occasion which changed both their lives. Lady St Helier who did much to put potential suitors Clementine's way had no such motive in mind on the day when she invited her protégée to make up the numbers at a dinner party held for Sir Frederick Lugard, the explorer of West Africa, and his wife, Lady Lugard, in late March. She had invited Winston Churchill because his knowledge of Africa and his career as a journalist were both likely to make him congenial company for a couple who were deeply interested in colonial affairs. Lady St Helier arranged the seating at table with Winston Churchill placed next to Lady Lugard. Because one of her guests had cancelled she put Clementine on the other side of Churchill.

Clementine was not really keen on attending this particular party. She would be one of the youngest present and she had nothing in common with any of the other guests. Only because she felt under a great obligation to Lady St Helier for all her kindnesses did she dutifully appear at the appointed time.

Winston too had benefited from Lady St Helier's intervention in his career in former days but he was even less inclined for a party than Clementine. He was late for the dinner and the company was already seated at table when he arrived. He was amazed and delighted to find that he was to sit next to the beautiful girl who had attracted his attention several years ago but whom he had not encountered since. Normally he would have focused all his attention on Lady Lugard because there was always a chance that she might prove politically useful to him at some time in the future. But at this dinner party he forgot political expediency and turned the full force of his charm on Clementine. He was at his sparkling best and Clementine was delighted with and amused by their exchanges. She was impressed by how much he had done and how much he knew and by the number of books he had already published. She had to confess that she had not read his most recent publication, a biography of his father Lord Randolph Churchill. He promised to send her a copy. After dinner when the ladies left for the drawing room and the men as usual settled down for port, cigars and political discussion Winston, most uncharacteristically, was restless and showed an unusual eagerness to rejoin the ladies, even though his close friend and political sparring partner Frederick Smith was one of the men present. His behaviour did not escape notice and there was a great deal of amused comment.

Clementine reported to her mother that she had enjoyed meeting the son of Blanche's old friend Jennie. She waited expectantly for the promised copy of the biography of Lord Randolph Churchill. This never arrived; instead mother and daughter were surprised when a few days later they received an invitation to visit Jennie and her husband George Cornwallis-West at their home, Salisbury Hall, near St Albans, on 11 April. When they arrived at the seventeenth-century manor house with its moat, its Elizabethan hall with stone plaques, its grand carved wooden staircase, wood-panelled rooms and magnificent fireplaces they found that Winston was already there to greet them. Because the two older ladies had much news to catch up on after so many years, Winston and Clementine found plenty of opportunity to get to know each other better. By the end of the weekend Jennie, Blanche and Clementine herself were aware that Winston was falling in love. As she wrote in her 'thank you' letter to Jennie, Clementine was already deeply impressed by Winston.

Blanche had known Lord Randolph Churchill, Winston's father, through Bertram Mitford and she had known Jennie since before Winston was born. She was more than ready to tell Clementine all she knew about Winston's background and early life.

The beautiful and dynamic Jennie Jerome had burst onto the London social scene in 1873. She was different from some of the other American 'dollar princesses' sent to England to marry into the aristocracy, providing a much-needed infusion of cash in return for a title. Jennie had been for the most part educated in Paris rather than America and she was not a great heiress like Consuelo Vanderbilt who married Winston's cousin. Her father Leonard Jerome was an inveterate gambler; sometimes he was a millionaire, sometimes he was close to bankruptcy. He also had an estranged wife and not one but three beautiful daughters to provide for.

During Cowes week in 1873 Jennie Jerome and Lord Randolph Churchill, the 24-year-old younger son of the Duke of Marlborough, met and fell in love. Both families opposed their urgent desire to marry. The Marlboroughs wanted a better-connected, wealthier and preferably English woman for a daughter-in-law. Lionel Jerome, who believed his family to be every bit as good as the Marlboroughs, resented their attitude towards his daughter and himself. He had no desire to be connected to such snobs and to pay heavily for the privilege. But eventually the young couple managed to prevail against their parents' hostility and they were married in Paris in April 1874. Seven months later their first son was born so unexpectedly that not even a layette had been prepared for him.

Winston Leonard Spencer Churchill was born at Blenheim but most of his early childhood was spent in Dublin. For, like Blanche Hozier, the Churchills found themselves ostracized by polite society. Divorce was again the issue but this time at one remove. Lord Randolph had unwisely attempted to blackmail the Prince of Wales in order to prevent his brother, the Marquis of Blandford, being named as co-respondent in a divorce case and had not unnaturally incurred royal displeasure. The Duke of Marlborough had, therefore, accepted the post of Viceroy of

Ireland and had appointed Randolph his secretary in order to remove him from England until such time as the Prince of Wales saw fit to forgive him.

On his return to England, largely because of the Prince's fondness for Jennie, Lord Randolph and his wife were once again received in society. Lord Randolph's ability as an orator was responsible for his spectacular career within the Conservative Party so that by 1886 he was Chancellor of the Exchequer and seemed a likely candidate to be the next Prime Minister. But an ill-judged resignation after being Chancellor for only six months put an end to that prospect. When Winston entered Harrow in 1888 his father was no longer even a member of the Cabinet.

Winston's relationship with his father was as troubled as Clementine's was with hers. The increasing effect of syphilis on Lord Randolph's nervous system together with his disappointment at the failure of his career made him intensely critical of his elder son. With little or no consultation with Winston, Lord Randolph determined that the only career his son could aspire to was the army. For some time it seemed as if even this was beyond Winston's grasp when he failed the examination for Sandhurst and had to be sent to a crammer in order to pass for the more expensive cavalry.

On 24 January 1895 Lord Randolph died leaving little but debts. In February, with some anxiety about how he would pay his way, Winston had joined the 4th Hussars as a second lieutenant.

The years before Winston met Clementine had been rich in experience. He had served in India during which time he had read widely and formed many of the opinions which shaped his subsequent career. He had reported on the war in Cuba and the expedition of the Malakand Field Force. He had been taken prisoner and escaped during the course of the Boer War. But in 1900 he had turned his attention to politics.

Clementine herself knew the rest of his story as a public person. But she was eager to know the man himself. For a short time, however, Winston and Clementine had to be content with getting to know each other better through an exchange of letters. Nellie was due to leave the clinic where she had been for a year and Blanche had arranged to take both her daughters to stay with her mother in Florence. Not that things would necessarily have been different if Clementine had been in England during the next few weeks, since Winston was more often in his constituency than in London and his time was taken up with his election campaign. For, shortly after the occasion at Salisbury Hall, he had been appointed President of the Board of Trade and, as was customary, he had to stand for re-election for his seat in North West Manchester.

The newspapers had extended coverage of the by-election and Clementine read the reports with an avidity she had never before shown for politics. Winston himself reported on his progress to his new correspondent revealing to her just how important a part of his life politics was. He also told her about her mother's cousin Dorothy Howard who had thrown herself into the task of drumming up votes for him. Clearly the daughter of Rosalind, Countess of Carlisle, had inherited not only her mother's good looks but also her strong political commitment to the Liberal party. Fortunately for Clementine, Dorothy Howard was also passionate about women's suffrage and eager to promote teetotalism. Neither of these was a cause dear to Winston's heart and so the Countess's hope for a match between her daughter and Winston Churchill was never likely to be fulfilled.

Clementine now had the opportunity of seeing what strong responses the man who was showing such an interest in her could arouse in others. She must have pondered this when his defeat in the election was announced and *The Daily Telegraph* reported, 'Churchill out . . . We have all been yearning for this to happen, with a yearning beyond utterance . . . Winston Churchill is out, Out, OUT.'[1] She saw and admired the way he recovered from his defeat and quickly managed to get himself elected in Dundee the following month.

In his letters at this time Winston was also allowing Clementine to see a side of himself that few people saw. This ambitious, aggressive and sometimes ruthless politician confessed to her that, despite all the bustle and activity of his life, he was essentially lonely. He appealed to her to write to him and to be kind to him. Clementine cannot have failed to appreciate the significance of his willingness to show her his vulnerable side.

In April, the engagement of Jack Churchill and Lady Gwendeline Bertie was announced. Clementine had met Lady Gwendeline, who was an exact contemporary, at parties over the last few summers and she rather liked the dreamy and attractive young woman. She also knew that Lady Gwendeline's parents had been hoping that she would make a good match as the family had no money. Gwendeline's marriage to Jack Churchill who had neither money nor title could only be for love and Clementine knew Winston approved of this.

When Clementine, Blanche and Nellie returned to London Winston had begun work at the Board of Trade. But he contrived to be present at occasions to which Clementine was invited. Such public meetings were less intimate than their exchange of letters and Clementine felt less confident about both her own feelings and those of Winston. She now knew a little more about his past relationships with women. It was common knowledge that he had been very much in love with Pamela Plowden, the beautiful blonde-haired, blue-eyed daughter of the Resident of Hyderabad, Trevor Chichele-Plowden. This young woman, whose father had tended to spoil her since she had lost her mother at an early age, had lived for long periods of time in the London home of Lady Granby (later the Duchess of Rutland) and it was there that Winston had wooed her. What had caused the relationship to end was Pamela's feeling that Winston's career would always take first place, a feeling that his reluctance to marry until he was well and truly established seemed to confirm. She had married Lord Lytton but continued to be close to Winston. Quite recently there had been rumours of his engagement to two other women, Muriel Wilson, a shipping heiress, and Helen Botha, the pretty nineteen-year-old daughter of the Prime Minister of the Transvaal, whom he had escorted around London during the Colonial Conference. There were whispers about an affair with the American actress Ethel Barrymore, whom he had taken with him on a visit to Blenheim.

Clementine took herself off to stay with her Great Aunt Maisie, the mother of Sylvia and Venetia, to think things over away from the charisma of Winston's presence. At the end of the summer she was to go to Cowes Week but then, as in April, she and Blanche were invited to Salisbury Hall. Blanche regarded this invitation as a further step towards a proposal of marriage. During the weeks of summer Clementine and Winston once again advanced their relationship through letters and it was Clementine's impetuous expression of her relief in a telegram after hearing that Winston had escaped harm in a fire at the house of his cousin Freddie Guest that gave him a clearer idea of how she felt about him. Her reserve and shyness when he was in her company had caused him some doubts. Indeed he had wondered whether it would be fair to ask a young woman like her to marry a man like himself. He had confided his fears to Frederick Smith saying, 'Is it fair to ask this lovely creature to marry so ambitious a man as myself?'[2] His brother Jack's letter the previous November had reminded him that his relationship with Pamela Plowden whom he had loved had failed because he had devoted most of his energies to his career and future.[3] His mother had reassured him with her perception that underneath Clementine's loveliness and shyness were qualities of strength and integrity which would make her a good wife for Winston. After witnessing the miserable break-up of the marriage of his cousin Sunny, Duke of Marlborough, and the beautiful American Consuelo Vanderbilt, Winston was determined to make a marriage that would last and one in which he was not dependent on his bride's money. The wedding of Jack and Gwendeline, an obvious love match, determined him to follow suit quickly. He wrote to Clementine to modify their previous arrangement to meet at Salisbury Hall asking her to come straight from Cowes to meet him at Blenheim Palace as the guest of Sunny.

After all the talk of weddings in Winston's letter Clementine had little doubt about what his suggestion implied. At this crucial moment she hesitated. She knew instinctively that by agreeing she was taking an almost irrevocable step, and she was suddenly assailed by doubts. Blenheim Palace intimidated her and she knew she would be ill prepared for a large social gathering since after her time in Cowes all her clothes would need attention. She was accustomed to travelling without a chaperone but she was fearful of turning up at Blenheim without a maid.

Winston, however, had made up his mind and his letter in response to her hesitation left her little choice but to agree, whilst at the same time making his intention very clear. He told her that if she had serious doubts about the visit he would send a telegram to Sunny changing the arrangements. But he pointed out that Sunny would have already invited another couple, Frederick Smith and his wife Margaret 'to balance us'. In an attempt to reassure her he told her that there would not be a big party present. Clementine agreed to go to Blenheim.

The long journey from Cowes to Oxford with no company but her own gave Clementine plenty of time to question the wisdom of accepting Winston's invitation. All through that sunny day of 10 August she thought not only about the man she was going to meet but she also worried about the clothes she had with her and feared that her shabbiness would let him down in the company of his friends. His last letter to her in which he hoped that she would fascinate Sunny with her strange mysterious eyes was very flattering but made her fear that his cousin would have expectations of her which she would not fulfil.

At long last the train reached Oxford and there, on time for once, was Winston waiting to meet her and drive her to Woodstock and Blenheim

Palace. His warm welcome was flattering though little conversation was possible on that drive which was marked more by Winston's enthusiasm for than skill in driving a car. They arrived in front of the magnificent facade of the palace built by Winston's ancestors and there were greeted by their host the Duke of Marlborough, Winston's mother, Jennie, as well as Frederick Smith and his wife, Margaret, and Eddie Marsh, Winston's Private Secretary who accompanied him almost everywhere. Clementine had the uncomfortable feeling that everyone knew why she had been invited.

Her discomfort was in no way lessened when the party climbed the shallow flight of stairs and entered the immense hall with its domed ceiling. The small group of guests already seemed dwarfed and lost in that space meant to impress rather than to please. When she was shown to her bedroom she found herself in a smallish, high-ceilinged room. There was a fire in the grate despite the heat outside and in front of it was a round bath-tub, hot and cold water jugs, towels and sponges.

Unlike most young women who visited Blenheim Clementine had no maid to unpack for her and see that her clothes were pressed and laid out ready for the evening and then to fill the tub ready for her evening bath. There was no way she could attend to the latter task herself. She was quite dismayed until Jennie, who had quickly assessed the situation and who remembered vividly her own dismal first experiences of Blenheim and its ways, sent her maid to help Clementine and to ensure that her dresses were ready not only for that evening but also for the next couple of days.

Dinner that night was in the huge but dark dining room. Clementine was shy and like her melancholy host contributed little to the conversation. But Winston had so much to say himself that he hardly appeared to notice her silence. And before the company dispersed after dinner Winston pointedly arranged to meet Clementine early the next day when he would walk with her in the grounds and show her the rose gardens.

As usual Clementine was up early but found when she appeared downstairs that the other guests were still in bed. Only Sunny appeared to keep her company and the two of them had a slightly awkward breakfast together. Every moment both guest and host expected the appearance of Winston. The situation grew uncomfortable and eventually Sunny sent a message to his cousin's room to remind him of his appointment. In the meantime to prevent Clementine feeling abandoned he took her for a ride round his extensive property.

It was not until after lunch when the fine weather showed signs of breaking that Winston and Clementine set off for the promised walk. When the rain forced them to take shelter Winston at last made his proposal in the romantic setting of a small Greek temple by the lake. Clementine accepted. As they set off back to the palace Clementine asked Winston to keep their engagement a secret until she had told her mother about it. Winston agreed but his delight and excitement were such that he could not help pouring out the news to Sunny, the first person they met on their return. Not that secrecy was ever a real possibility; the happiness and radiance of the newly engaged couple would have given them away without any words being spoken. Nevertheless Clementine insisted that she must return to London the next day and give the news to her mother.

Winston could hardly bear to let his bride-to-be out of his sight. He even managed to get up early to walk with her in the rose garden and he decided to drive her to the station himself. He should have returned to Blenheim to work on government papers but his excitement was for once greater than his interest in his work and he made a last-minute decision to travel to London with his fiancée. Clementine was both delighted and alarmed. She was eager to go to Abingdon Villas alone as she was by no means sure that her mother who frequently did not dress until late in the day would be presentable and she wanted her to make a good impression. Blanche, however, was ready for her daughter and her news and she received Winston gracefully when he called to ask formally for her daughter's hand in marriage. Blanche was delighted to welcome him as her son-in-law and so Winston was now free to give Clementine the ruby and diamond ring which his father had always intended him to use as an engagement ring. Then in high excitement the trio travelled back to Blenheim and a celebration before making the long planned visit to Salisbury Hall and a family party which included the newly married Jack and Gwendeline. Blanche lost no time in relaying the good news to her family that at last Clementine had made up her mind and was to be married.

5

Marriage

ON 15 AUGUST 1908 the engagement of Winston Spencer Churchill and Clementine Hozier was officially announced from Salisbury Hall. It was not quite six months since their courtship had begun and their wedding was to be in under a month.

Not everyone was delighted with the news. Sidney Peel who had always hoped that Clementine would reconsider her broken engagement to him was bitterly disappointed when he learnt that she was to marry Winston Churchill within the month. It would be some years before he married also.

Violet Asquith had been very close to Winston and she had perhaps hoped that she would be the one he chose for a wife. At dinner parties in her father's house he had paid her a lot of attention and had even learnt poems by heart to entertain her. She took herself off to the country to hide her disappointment and to compose herself.

Winston's cousin Clare Frewen who felt she had a special relationship with him was also sad that he was not marrying Violet. She considered Violet, with her knowledge of politics and her sharp mind, a most suitable match for her brilliant cousin. Clare was less sure about the reserved Clementine and feared that she would no longer be so close to her cousin once he was married.

The Countess of Carlisle, too, was disappointed; she had rather hoped for Winston for her own son-in-law. Nancy Astor who had chosen her second husband with an eye to his wealth was surprised by Winston's choice of a bride. She commented, 'The girl Winston Churchill is to marry is *lovely* but v. stupid. As poor as a rat – but nice. Everyone said he would only marry for ambition – this proves them wrong.'[1] Lord Hugh Cecil, who was to be Winston's best man, warned Winston about taking his marriage vows lightly. Perhaps he wondered whether Winston with his quicksilver nature and tendency to be careless of the feelings of others was suited to marriage at all. The King himself expressed irritation about the way in which Winston was using his impending marriage to draw attention to himself.

Clementine, too, may have had her doubts as the wedding presents poured in, including one from the King, and she now realized just how public a figure was her husband-to-be. She had, after all, spent little time with this man to whom she was about to dedicate her life. Much of their courtship had been conducted by letter and, even now that they were engaged, letters continued to be their most important form of communication. During the last few months she had, however, been given a chance to learn a great deal about Winston's character and behaviour. She had seen the worst side of him on their very first meeting. Since then she had experienced his lack of punctuality even on the most important of occasions. He had, after all, been known to keep the King waiting for his dinner; he had been late for the very dinner at which their relationship had begun, as well as failing to get up in time to propose to her. Although Clementine hated lateness she regarded her fiancé's failing with amusement at this stage; she hoped that in time she would cure him.

His dedication to politics and his career was unmistakable and he had gone so far as to suggest a wedding date which would fit in neatly with parliamentary sessions. Clementine did not mind this; she was full of admiration for his accomplishments and glad to think that she was marrying a man who was powerful enough to effect change in the country. Her own interests were so undeveloped at this time that she was ready to make his passions hers.

His impetuosity had shown itself in his decision to drop everything and accompany her to London to ask Blanche's permission to marry her and in his headlong haste to settle upon a date once she had accepted him. This too she could accept, for in the present situation such urgency was headily romantic.

She had met some of his few close friends and was not too sure that she found them congenial. Already she was puzzled by Winston's ability to be on extremely friendly terms with men and women whose political views were at odds with his own. Frederick Smith was a good example. He had been present at two of the most important occasions in their relationship: at the dinner party at Lady St Helier's and at Blenheim when Winston had proposed. Frederick and his wife had known of Clementine's engagement before her own mother. But far from being a Liberal he was an ardent Conservative and held the seat for Walton. He was undoubtedly good looking with his black hair, dark eyes and pale skin. But his flippancy and cynicism made Clementine uneasy.

Then there was Mrs Cornwallis-West, Winston's mother. Clementine was uncomfortably aware of how very much like her own mother Jennie was. Dramatically good looking, she was unconventional, she dressed flamboyantly and extravagantly, she loved to be the centre of attention, and there were as many rumours about her amours as about those of Blanche. But there was no mistaking Winston's devotion to her and Jennie's influence on him. Both Blanche and Clementine's grandmother Lady Airlie were inclined to take the optimistic view of Winston's relationship with Jennie saying that a devoted son usually made a good husband.

On the positive side Clementine could see that she really could fill a gap in Winston's life. She saw that he was not truly intimate with anyone now that his mother had taken a young man for her husband and his brother Jack had married, breaking up the establishment they had maintained together for some years; his loneliness echoed her own. His letters which expressed his overwhelming love for her thrilled her and she, too, in letters at least, found herself pouring out her love for him in a way which in person she would have found hard to do.

The letters she wrote to her family at this time reveal her excitement and love. Her Aunt Mabell declared that she had always believed that Clementine would make a romantic marriage and Clementine agreed with this view of her engagement. Even her mother's old admirer and advocate of passion, Wilfrid Blunt, approved of her marrying Winston. Blanche insisted that she visit her uncle Bertram and aunt Clementine to give them the news. Perhaps Blanche felt that Bertram had a special right to give his blessing to this match. Henry Hozier was no longer alive to give his view of the marriage, but from people who had known him as Clementine's father, Henry Labouchere and the Earl of Dundonald, for example, there came good wishes.

Four weeks was not very long to plan a wedding which, given the bridegroom's background and public position, was likely to be a major social event. St Margaret's, Westminster, was booked and eight hundred guests were invited. Clearly the rather small terrace house in Abingdon

Villas was entirely unsuitable for the occasion so Lady St Helier, who felt to a great extent responsible for the marriage, offered to hold the reception in her eminently suitable premises in Portland Place. It is not recorded who paid for the far from quiet wedding which was certainly beyond Blanche's means.

At two o'clock on 12 September Clementine, dressed in white satin with a tulle veil and a headdress of orange blossom, arrived at St Margaret's with her brother, Bill, in his naval uniform. There was a great crowd to see the nervous young woman step out of the carriage on the arm of her handsome young brother. Her bridesmaids were already waiting for her; there was Nellie, her sister and Bill's twin, Madeline Whyte and Venetia Stanley, her cousins, Clare Frewen, Winston's cousin, and Clementine's own closest friend who had been through several seasons with her, Horatia Seymour.

The church was so full that Wilfrid Scawen Blunt arriving a little late had difficulty in finding a seat until Blanche, strikingly dressed in purple silk, came to his rescue. She directed him, from her front seat alongside Bertram Mitford, Lord Redesdale, to sit in the family pew between her sister Maude Whyte and Hugo Wemyss. The latter, Blunt noted, was also a former lover of the incorrigible Blanche. Sitting together on the groom's side was the formidable trio of sisters, the former Jerome girls, Clara, Leonie and Jennie. The latter, looking a trifle stout, was handsomely dressed in dark mushroom with a hat trimmed with dahlias.

The church was a mass of white flowers, chrysanthemums and lilies and spiraea offset by the green of palms. Clementine carrying white roses and a white prayer book given her by her godfather, Jack Leslie, made her way to Winston who was looking unusually anxious and far less confident than usual. As the service proceeded Winston made his vows loudly and with conviction but the assembled guests could hardly hear Clementine's responses.

Then it was back to Portland Place and the reception. Clementine changed into her going-away outfit of a grey suit, with a black satin sash matching her large black hat adorned with an ostrich feather. Outside the house were the Cockneys known as Pearlies dressed in their unmistakable costumes covered all over with mother-of-pearl buttons ready to cheer on his wedding day the man who had fought for their rights as street traders. Even then the newly married couple were only without company for the time it took to travel by train to Woodstock, where they were met by more cheering crowds and the ringing of church bells. Their destination was

Blenheim Palace, in which vast establishment they finally found themselves alone.

Many people, including Clementine herself, regarded Jennie
Cornwallis-West as a frivolous and irresponsible woman. Certainly there
was this side to her. But she also had some delicacy of perception especially when it came to young people. The younger members of her
extended family were frequently touched by her thoughtfulness towards
them. On Clementine's first visit to Blenheim Jennie had unobtrusively
helped her to feel more comfortable in her unfamiliar surroundings.
Without Clementine's ever knowing, Jennie had similarly attempted to
protect Clementine from a different kind of awkwardness on her honeymoon visit. It seemed to Jennie that Clementine, unlike herself and
Blanche Hozier, did not have an overtly sensual nature. She saw her as
physically fastidious, even prudish, and she realized that the wedding
night might be difficult for her. And so she warned Winston, whom she
knew had no physical modesty or reticence, to treat his new wife carefully
and with consideration. If the honeymoon couple's first night was a
success, and there is reason to suppose it was, then Jennie's thoughtfulness for her daughter-in-law should have some credit. The next day, 13
September, Winston wrote to his mother reassuring her that all was well,
that Clementine was happy and that there had been no need for anxiety.
Had Clementine known of her mother-in-law's concern would she have
been a little less censorious in her attitude towards the older woman or
would she have resented Jennie's interference in such an intimate matter?

Once Clementine and Winston had recovered from the wedding and
all the emotions and hasty preparations that had preceded it, they set off
on their travels to Italy and Austria. Already on their honeymoon
Clementine and Winston began to make discoveries about each other.
Clementine must have been slightly dismayed to find that Winston had
brought some work with him. He had written a series of articles about
East Africa for the *Strand Magazine* and he was keen to make this work
pay twice by extending the essays and publishing them as a book. She
must have been even more anxious when she learnt how important to
their future finances was the advance on the book. She had expected to
spend the time in romantic Venice wandering through the churches and
galleries with her husband. To her consternation she found that,
although Winston was prepared to go to some galleries with her, he was

not really interested in looking at paintings. In Austria they stayed with Baron de Forest, an old friend of Winston and the stepfather of George Cornwallis-West, Jennie's young husband. They might just as well have been at a country house in England as in Austria, for there were the same shooting parties and large formal dinners. Winston revelled in such entertainment and the extensive company; Clementine did not enjoy it at all and she longed to be back in London and alone with her husband.

Despite these differences between them husband and wife were well pleased with each other and confirmed in the choices they had made. In London they began married life in the house in Bolton Street which Winston had shared with his brother Jack before he married Gwendeline. It was not their intention to stay there long but, nevertheless, Jennie had tried to make the place less of a bachelor establishment by having the bedroom decorated. Clementine hid her dismay at the discrepancy between her mother-in-law's taste for the fussily feminine and her own desire for simplicity.

They had barely had time to settle in before they journeyed north to Scotland with two objectives. Clementine had seen Blenheim Palace, the ancestral home of her husband's family. Now it was her turn to show him Cortachy Castle, the home of the Airlies, and to show herself to her grandmother as a married woman. She was fully aware that Lady Airlie expected her to show respect for her husband and to bow to his opinions. Lady Airlie aproved of Winston's prominent position in the Liberal party: it was after all what she had hoped for from her own husband. Clementine did not find any difficulty in pleasing the old lady on this occasion.

After a short visit Winston took his bride to Dundee, his constituency. He placed as much importance on Clementine making a good impression on his constituents as on his family for he wanted his wife to be a positive addition to his life as a politician. On this occasion Clementine was able to give her whole-hearted support to everything her husband said in the speeches he made to large crowds. His emphasis in Dundee was on his party's achievement in making government-financed pensions available to those over seventy and on its commitment to intervene in issues of unemployment and to attack poverty with vigorous measures. These were issues for which, with her Stanley background, she felt great sympathy. She was proud of the warmth with which her husband was received, and he was pleased with the admiration expressed for his beautiful and elegant wife. He was not aware that her decorative appearance was looked upon somewhat cynically by those members of the crowd who were desperately poor and living in conditions of utter misery. In their turn the people of Dundee were not to know that Clementine knew first hand something of what it meant to be poor and that her sympathy for their plight was genuine and not merely political rhetoric.

By November Winston and Clementine were back in London and both were satisfied that their marriage had got off to an excellent start. Only one thing was lacking to complete their contentment and they did not have to wait long for that. Early in 1909 Clementine was able to confirm that she was pregnant with their first child.

6

Adjustments

IN A SOCIAL group where marriages were rarely based simply on mutual love the Churchills appeared to be a romantic exception. There were many contemporary observers of the newly married couple who noted enviously the loving way in which Clementine would hold Winston's hand in public whilst he would gaze at his beautiful bride with delighted admiration and pleasure. Clementine in particular was anxious that they should be seen this way. But there was another side to this seemingly idyllic life of married bliss.

There were many good reasons why these two people, and especially Clementine, would find that marriage meant adjustments and changes not fully anticipated. Before their marriage neither Winston nor Clementine had experienced a really intimate relationship with anyone else. Clementine had always felt that her mother cared more for Kitty than for her and then, when Kitty died, it had been Nellie who had replaced Kitty in her mother's affections rather than Clementine. Almost in self-defence she had developed a veneer of reserve and had not allowed anyone to become close to her. It was no accident that she was generally known before her marriage as the 'beautiful Miss Hozier'. There were very few people who knew much about Clementine beyond the fact of her undoubted beauty. In her life there had been no one like Winston's motherly and physically affectionate nurse, Mrs Everest.

Mrs Everest had taken a very close interest in Winston as a child, while his mother had largely ignored him until he had reached a more interesting age at which time his father, who was increasingly ill and irritable, had begun to criticize him relentlessly.

Perhaps it was because Winston had not enjoyed a warm relationship with a woman since he had left Mrs Everest and the nursery that he chose to express his new, and to him delightful, intimacy with Clementine by regressing to the language of that time. Clementine became his golden cat whilst he was her amber pug. It was a playfulness new to Clementine which delighted her but with which she was more comfortable in letters than in conversation.

Just as when they were engaged, Clementine soon found that letters had to play a major role in her marriage, for the times when she was alone with Winston were few and far between. This was not at all what she had expected: she had hoped that as a married woman her life would be completely different from the life she had so far led. She had thought that she could escape that round of socializing required of those of her contemporaries in search of a husband, and she had looked forward to being free of the demands of the season and what Cynthia Asquith described as 'that awful *bustling* idleness'.[1] She had anticipated with pleasure evenings of quiet intimacy with her loving husband.

In fact she had simply changed one kind of life in society for another as she quickly discovered. By the time he married Clementine Winston had established a social routine for himself as President of the Board of Trade and as a Cabinet Minister. His assumption was that the only changes marriage would bring to his way of life were that his beautiful wife would now sometimes accompany him when he went out, that she would provide a stable background in which he could do his work, and that she would be a pleasing hostess who would help him reciprocate hospitality.

He did not feel it necessary to discuss these assumptions with his wife; nor did he question whether the friends of his bachelorhood would fit into his new life. Clementine found that she was now expected to take her place in a group which consisted almost exclusively of Winston's family and friends, and people whom he thought might help him politically. He accepted her family as his own but he took little interest in her friends.

During the first months of their marriage the Churchills rarely dined alone. During the week when parliament was in session they were either being entertained by the Asquiths, the F. E. Smiths, the Lloyd Georges, or other political friends and acquaintances, or they were themselves holding dinner parties for the same group. Winston regarded these occasions as a necessary part of his political life and essential to forwarding his ambitions and prospects. It was at these dinners that gossip about the government was exchanged and unofficial alliances established. Winston believed that if he was not in constant close contact with his colleagues he would be at a political disadvantage. Although she wanted to be a good wife and help her husband advance his career in any way she could, Clementine would have preferred to live less in such company. For it was not only the men who talked politics on these occasions; their wives in their own way were just as involved. Aubrey Herbert, the brother-in-law of Cynthia Asquith described the kind of conversation that Clementine would have encountered regularly, particularly at the Asquiths. 'They chatter, the women do, about things of great importance, as if they were talking of daisies. They are intelligent, inconsequent, informed and partisan, and one is liable to be either a spy in their camp, or untrue to one's party.'[2] In the first months of her marriage, with no first-hand experience of politics, Clementine felt very much an outsider in this company. It was the same after the meal was finished, for it was a rare evening when dinner was not followed by a game of bridge. Although Clementine did not mind playing cards as such, her aversion to gambling extended to playing bridge for money and in this she found herself alone. Most of Winston's social group accepted that gambling added a necessary spice to the game and the evening.

But more than the conversation and the bridge Clementine disliked the way that the men would insist on staying late, drinking heavily and growing ever more riotous and noisy. She was often reminded of the stories told of her grandmother's early married life and how she used strong measures to change the nature of evening parties at Cortachy Castle. But Clementine's husband was very different from Blanche's. Winston thoroughly enjoyed this aspect of these social occasions and had no intention of changing his ways. His delight in being a man among men was a side of him that was new to Clementine, one that she had not been aware of when he was courting her with flattering gallantry and when he was focusing the full intensity of his attention upon her in his determination not only to make her his wife but to do so quickly.

The expense of these frequent dinner parties was a great worry to Clementine. Her instinct to spend as little money on them as possible was not acceptable to her husband. Winston felt he had an image to promote and he expected her to keep up to the high standards set by his friends who were considerably wealthier than they were. He wanted the best food and the best brandy and as much of everything as his guests desired to be served in his house regardless of cost. He might challenge his colleagues about extravagant government spending but he never looked closely at the demands he put upon the household budget.

Forced to accept that expensive dinner parties and late drinking were to be an inevitable feature of her married life, Clementine, who had received as a wedding present a helpful book on how to manage a household on twelve shillings a week, tried to compensate by economizing in other ways. On the rare occasions they did eat alone she had cheaper food and drink served. She kept meticulous account books and looked for any way, however small, in which she could reduce their expenses. Winston did not like this kind of frugality but in the early days of marriage, believing that in time Clementine would change her ways, he made little protest. Only when Clementine tried to make him economize on the matter of his underwear did he take a firm stance.

Clementine was horrified to discover that Winston treated himself to pale pink silk vests from the Army & Navy Store at the cost of £85 a year. When she challenged him with this extravagance he explained that he had very sensitive skin and that the silk vests were essential for his comfort. Whatever arguments she used Clementine could not make Winston change this habit. She was shocked not only by the expense but also by this revelation of her husband's almost feminine cosseting of himself and of his sensuous pleasure in having silk next to his skin. His attitude was alien and puzzling to her and her puritan self was greatly offended. She had not fully realized before she married him just how much Winston enjoyed luxury and how little attraction it had for her.

It was this love of luxury which he could not easily afford for himself, Clementine believed, that led Winston to keep company with men of whom she disapproved. His eagerness to accept invitations to certain country houses for long weekends was similarly motivated. She could understand why he enjoyed spending time at Blenheim Palace. He had after all been born there and his relationship with his cousin was based on genuine mutual affection despite their political differences. She was less easy about visits to the homes of Bendor, Duke of Westminster.[3] She did not dislike the Duke himself, a strikingly tall, handsome man, with blond hair, blue eyes and a charming manner, who had been Winston's friend since their time together in the Boer War. She admired his concern for his tenants and his interest in housing schemes for the poor. She was less kindly disposed towards his beautiful and self-assured wife Constance, prejudiced by the fact that Constance was a close friend and the sister-in-law of Winston's mother of whom Clementine was increasingly critical.

But the true source of her uneasiness was the knowledge that Bendor was the richest man in England, able to afford to gratify his every whim. She was overwhelmed by his home at Eaton Hall where every bathroom had a fireplace and a staff of three hundred was employed. Her fear was that Winston would try to keep up with his friend's lavish life-style which was far beyond their means.

There was, however, another man, whose extravagance in every aspect of his life was not balanced by the kind of responsibility the Duke of Westminster showed, and it was this man whom she greatly feared would corrupt her husband. Unfortunately Ivor Guest was not only Winston's cousin, the son of his favourite aunt Cornelia and Lord Wimborne, he was also a Liberal and, just like his brother Freddie, had been a close friend since childhood. Through the circle of women Clementine had known before she was married she had heard much of Ivor's drunkenness, his wild escapades and his relentless pursuit of women, often much younger than himself, whom he wooed with expensive gifts. An evening spent in Ivor's company during which he had lost at bridge and expressed his frustration and anger by throwing his cards at Clementine only confirmed her distrust and dislike of him. Left to herself she would never have set foot in Canford Manor, the Wimbornes' home, ever again. But Winston was determined not to break with his cousins even on Clementine's account. If Clementine would not accept invitations from his aunt he would visit the Wimbornes alone.

Clementine continued to be afraid that Ivor would tempt Winston to follow his example and look for excitement in affairs. For from the outset of the marriage Clementine was fiercely jealous of Winston and could not bear him to show attention to any woman other than herself. There were many angry scenes when she accused him of still being in love with Pamela Lytton, of flirting with Violet Asquith or Venetia Stanley. She was even at times jealous of her sister-in-law Gwendeline – 'Goonie' – and her own sister Nellie. Both Violet Asquith and Goonie had been close to Winston long before she knew him: Violet had been in love with him and there had been a time when it seemed Goonie might easily have chosen Winston rather than his brother. Winston had not stopped liking these women simply because he had married and he saw no reason to change his manner towards them. But Clementine did not like him to confide in Violet, as he often did, and she was suspicious of his ease with Goonie. She was jealous when he flirted with the beautiful, vivacious Nellie who had far more of her mother in her than did Clementine; she could not accept that everyone flirted with Nellie as a matter of course without necessarily intending anything by it.

Clementine's jealousy was the result of her own lack of confidence rather than Winston's behaviour. Part of the trouble arose from Winston's frequent absences from home. But, if she had been rational about the matter, she would have seen for herself that Winston was a workaholic with no time for love affairs: politics was his real passion. Her insecurity was such that she was anxious to make everyone see that Winston was truly hers. This explains why, although she was generally undemonstrative and reserved, she showed Winston public affection, and why she confided in Violet Asquith about her husband's silk under-wear, thus asserting her superior intimacy with Winston. She had not been married long when, in the presence of George Riddell, she said to Winston, 'I've got you. The real question is how to keep you now that I've made my capture.'[4] The joking tone did not disguise Clementine's very real fear.

Clementine's pregnancy, though a source of delight to husband and wife, also put further strain on their relationship. Clementine was often unwell and her doctor recommended plenty of rest. So at this early stage in their marriage Winston, who continued to socialize as usual and who was greatly absorbed in his work, frequently had to leave Clementine at home alone. His loving letters were not an adequate compensation for his absence and all her jealous feeling increased as she felt herself becoming less attractive as her pregnancy advanced. She began to resent the unborn child who was keeping her away from her husband and she was often overcome by fits of anger so intense that she herself was worried by them.

They had never intended to live for long in the house on Bolton Street. It was not a place where Winston could entertain adequately now that he was a married man and there was certainly no room there for a baby, and the nursery and nurserymaid which they both considered essential. When the lease on the house expired and, much to Clementine's chagrin, they were obliged to accept the loan of Freddie Guest's house in Carlton Square, the need for a new home became urgent.

The house they settled on at 33 Eccleston Square had one drawback as far as Clementine was concerned: the Smiths lived at number 77. She feared that Winston would inevitably spend even more time with his friend, Frederick. Already many well-wishers in the Liberal party had advised her that Winston could only harm his prospects by being seen to be so intimate with such an arch-Conservative.

However, the house was suitable in every other way. It was located in a pleasant, quiet square with mature trees and a large central garden for the use of residents, and it was conveniently close to Westminster and the Houses of Parliament. The five-storey, Georgian-style, Victorian terrace house was much the largest that Clementine could remember living in and she would require more staff than she was accustomed to. All her life she had moved from one house to another with her restless mother. This was not the way of life she would have chosen for herself and she now had high hopes that things would change and that she and Winston would settle for some considerable time in Eccleston Square since they had signed an eighteen-year lease.

So, despite her anxiety about the expense of living in such a large house, Clementine threw herself into preparing their new home with enthusiasm. She salvaged what she could of carpets and curtains from Bolton Street and used them in the servants' rooms. In the rest of the house she was free to do as she wished, limited only by money since Winston was content to give her a free hand. He was not himself very interested in furnishings, as long as his study replicated the one he had already enjoyed in two other houses, but he was careful to praise the way Clementine was transforming the place. Clementine herself was pleased as she discovered that she had just as much of a talent for creating a beautiful home as had her mother.

All the work on the house, however, was contrary to her doctor's instruction to rest as much as possible. Winston became worried that she was doing too much and would harm herself or the baby. Unfortunately he chose to mention his misgivings whilst Blanche was visiting them and he even appealed to his mother-in-law to use her influence to make Clementine take things more easily. He was not aware what a big mistake he was making in so doing. For as soon as her mother had left Clementine flew into a rage with her startled husband. She was bitterly angry with him for aligning himself with her mother in criticizing her behaviour. She was also resentful that the unborn child was once more coming between her and something she wanted to do.

They had not yet been married a year but already Clementine and Winston were discovering just how little each had known of the other's true personality during their courtship. Winston had married a beautiful woman whom he assumed to be gentle and calm, whose nature would balance his own more volatile and pugnacious character. He had expected and hoped that marriage would bring a new serenity and order into his life and that his wife would provide a stable background against which his political career would advance more readily. He had imagined that because she had little experience of the life of a politician his young wife would be ready to be guided both by him and by his worldly mother.

He now discovered that Clementine's calm was precarious, that she was capable of violent anger and jealousy. She had undoubtedly improved the quality of his life in terms of running his house and making sure he kept a good table but she had made emotional demands upon him for which he had not been prepared. His hope that the two women he loved, his mother and his wife, would be good friends had not been fulfilled. The young woman who had been only too glad of Jennie's assistance on her first visit to Blenheim now made clear that she had distinct reservations about her mother-in-law. She disapproved of her extravagance, her love of gambling, her frivolity, her marriage to such a young man. Most of all she was jealous of the way Jennie could influence Winston. She did not dare criticize Jennie openly but she avoided her company when possible and rarely took her advice.

Clementine had come to realize that Winston did not really take women as seriously as she had imagined. He protested that he loved her deeply and in her more optimistic moments she believed this, but she could see that he thought that in the larger scheme of things, outside the home, it was men who mattered. It was men who had power and made things happen while it was the place of women to please and inspire them. It was no accident that he chose to communicate with her, his wife, in baby language. His continued need of male companionship and his absorption in work to the detriment of home life underlined his attitude. Clementine was not sure that she was prepared to accept this view of her role in her husband's life. But for the moment she was hampered by her pregnancy.

Clementine began to look forward to the time after her child was born when she would be able to take a larger and more central role in Winston's life. Winston similarly looked forward to the birth of the child hoping that some of Clementine's emotional instability would disappear once she was no longer pregnant and that she would be less upset by his absences once she had a baby on which to focus her attention while he was away. It was with these unspoken and dangerously different views of their future together that the couple made the move into their new home in Eccleston Square.

7

Maternity

THE ECCLESTON SQUARE house was much bigger than Winston's establishment in Bolton Street. And with the greater amount of space some of the intimacy enforced upon Winston and Clementine by the small house disappeared never to return. They were now able to have separate bedrooms just like most of the other married couples they knew. Clementine, however, felt a need to justify this new arrangement. In the first months of married life she had discovered that one of the many differences between herself and her husband was that while she liked to rise early, and would continue to do so all her life, Winston liked to stay in bed and even to do some of his morning's work there. Clementine disliked staying up late at night, especially when she was pregnant and easily tired. By contrast Winston considered the hours after dinner as some of the best of the day and he would rarely go to bed before the early hours of the morning. Whilst Clementine would entertain friends such as Horatia Seymour and her cousins Sylvia and Venetia in the drawing room during the day Winston would entertain his men friends until late at night in the overtly masculine atmosphere of his study and library. And so a pattern was established in which their two lives overlapped increasingly little on a day-to-day basis. They breakfasted separately; Winston often had lunch out with colleagues and, as her pregnancy developed, Clementine frequently excused herself from dinner invitations because she was too tired whilst Winston readily accepted them. Clementine knew that it was by no means unusual for married couples to spend the greater part of their time apart but she had hoped for something different from her marriage.

The one compensation for Clementine in these lonely days was her growing friendship with her sister-in-law Goonie. Pregnancy made an obvious and immediate bond between the two young women and the time they spent together at Blenheim in April without their husbands made them closer. When Clementine voiced her uneasiness about her mother-in-law she found that Goonie shared her disapproval of the way Jennie could still influence her sons and make claims upon them; she, too, disliked the way Jennie treated them as amusing girls and not as married women. But in every other way their friendship was an unlikely one and had they not married the Churchill brothers they would probably have remained only distant acquaintances. They had after all moved for some time in the same social circles without ever becoming particularly friendly. Their looks were very different and expressive of the difference in their personalities: Clementine was tall and stately with an almost classical beauty. Goonie was slender and vivacious with a prettiness that had much to do with her animation and attentiveness and which the camera could never capture. Cecil Beaton described her as 'that divine, mysterious, sphinx-like creature'.[1] She was dark while Clementine was fair, she had a ready wit and a lively sense of humour which contrasted sharply with Clementine's solemn earnestness and lack of frivolity. Both women considered themselves uneducated and both regretted that they had received so few educational opportunities. But this did not make Goonie shy as it did Clementine. Goonie never was at a loss in company; she enjoyed social occasions and, unlike her sister-in-law who tended to keep acquaintances at a distance, she made friends easily and inspired a great affection in all who knew her. It was her habit to address people as 'darling', an informality which Clementine would not dream of. As the daughter of Lord Abingdon, Goonie had a clear sense of her place in society whilst as a result of her upbringing and her mother's social disgrace Clementine still felt herself to be an outsider.

There had been a time when Goonie had hankered after marriage to Winston rather than to his quieter, though more handsome brother. Seeing what Clementine's life as Winston's wife was like she now began to think that she had made a better choice. Of course she saw that Winston was more flamboyant, more powerful, more exciting to be with. But she also saw that Pamela Lytton had been right, when she had decided against marrying Winston, about that driving ambition which kept him away from home a great deal and meant that his wife and any future family would have to be fitted into his busy life rather than having a place at the centre.

Already, despite the new house and despite Clementine's pregnancy, husband and wife were more often apart than together. For example, as Winston arrived at Blenheim for three weeks under canvas with the Queen's Own Oxfordshire Hussars, Clementine departed for a visit with her cousin Dorothy Allhusen, at her house, Stoke Poges Court, in Buckinghamshire. She had been invited to stay at Blenheim along with some of the other wives whose husbands were taking part in the military exercises. But the company did not attract her; nor did the parties, the dancing, the drinking, the card-playing and gambling into the early hours of the morning. What seemed a three-week treat to her husband repelled her more than usual in the late stages of her pregnancy. Far more appealing to her was a time spent in the civilized company of one of the Stanley family, for Dorothy was the daughter of the first marriage of Lady St Helier to Clementine's great uncle, John Stanley. She was warmly hospitable and the calm and familial atmosphere in her house suited Clementine well.

It was while she was in Buckinghamshire that she received the news of the birth of a son to Goonie and Jack whom they had named John Spencer-Churchill. She was encouraged to know that Goonie had been very little inconvenienced by her confinement. The previous evening Goonie had dined out and gone home to bed. She had woken at two in the morning with labour pains and had by four o'clock been delivered of her son. Clementine who was a little frightened of what lay ahead of her hoped that she would have a similar experience.

When she returned to London in June her husband was no more company that he had been earlier. If he had any apprehensions about what changes in his life paternity would bring, he showed no signs of them for he was thoroughly immersed in his work at the Board of Trade preparing the Trade Boards Bill and working for a minimum wage and the establishment of Labour Exchanges throughout the country. Clementine saw with some dismay that even at this important moment in their lives and in their relationship work mattered more to Winston than anything else. His Private Secretary Edward Marsh saw more of him than did his wife.

On 11 July the baby which had been referred to throughout the pregnancy as Puppy-kitten, to allow for it being either a girl or a boy, was born. The birth was not especially difficult but left Clementine exhausted and depressed. Was she disappointed that their first child was a daughter and not the son she knew would have delighted Winston with his notions of dynasty? Winston expressed himself as thoroughly pleased with the small red-haired girl and immediately claimed that she looked like him but Clementine quickly handed the baby over to a nanny and did not even consider breast-feeding her daughter. In her biography of Winston Churchill Violet Asquith voices the sentiments of her class when she says, 'A Nannie must enter her kingdom when the baby is a month old, not a day sooner or later.'[2] Clementine showed even less maternal feeling than was common among her contemporaries. After two weeks she set off for Southwater near Brighton where her mother and sister were staying in a small house called Carpenters lent to them by Wilfrid Scawen Blunt. Her tiny daughter was left in the care of a nursery-maid and Winston, whose contact with the baby was limited to bath-time.

After ten days Clementine was in London again for a brief visit only to find Winston heavily involved in trying to negotiate a settlement which would avert a threatened coal strike. Taking Diana and the nurse with her this time she returned to Southwater and from there in September she took refuge not at her own home but in the pleasant and orderly establishment of another Stanley, her Great Aunt Maisie, Lady Sheffield, at Alderley in Cheshire. Aunt Maisie was a staunch Liberal and a great believer in Asquith as Prime Minister. When Asquith spoke in Birmingham she took Clementine along with her to the meeting and Clementine was able to report to her husband how kindly she had been received as the wife of Winston Churchill. Another cause for pride at this time was the enthusiastic reception of baby Diana. Clementine was gratified, but her comments on the baby are curiously impersonal and it is clear from her remarks that she had far less to do with her daughter than did the nanny. It is the nanny who is blissfully content because of the compliments on her charge she was receiving below stairs.[3]

The first anniversary of their wedding found Clementine and Winston apart as they had been for most of the preceding months. While Clementine was in Cheshire, Winston had gone to Germany along with Edward Marsh and his cousin Freddie Guest. Ostensibly he was on government business observing German military manoeuvres and inspecting the German version of Labour Exchanges in Frankfurt. But he was also on a jaunt in his cousin's car and clearly enjoying the companionship of his male friends. His absence at this particular moment was certainly insensitive and Clementine must have wondered whether it was absolutely necessary. Winston had earlier told her how his best man

Hugh Cecil had warned him that keeping his marriage vows meant more than simply abstaining from adultery: he must be prepared to take seriously the notions of loving and cherishing. At that particular moment Clementine did not feel very cherished.

To compensate his wife of one year for not being with her on this sentimental occasion Winston sent to her a letter intended to be a tender summary of their time together. Surprisingly this letter is always read by Winston's biographers as a wonderful love letter. But it is not the spontaneous effusion they describe. It is a carefully worded document but it inadvertently gives away a great deal about the relationship between the recently married couple.

Churchill begins his anniversary letter by recalling that it is just a year since the September morning when Clementine, whom he describes as his beautiful white cat, came to him as his wife. He expresses his hope that a year later she does not regret her decision. He tells her that the occasion of their wedding is brought vividly to his mind by the sound of the ringing of those same bells he had heard on that day. Has the year fulfilled her expectations, he wonders. He claims that for him that year of marriage has made him desire an even greater intimacy with his wife.[4] It is not so much the content of the letter which is worth commenting on as the language in which it is written. The opening and the conclusion of the letter are written in the nursery language they were accustomed to use for intimate exchanges. This intimacy is somewhat diminished, however, by being expressed in the third person: Winston does not address his wife directly as 'you' but as 'she'. And the conclusion of the letter suggests that Winston regards his wife less as a lover than as a protective female presence. His expression of his desire to curl up in her arms where he feels safe and needs no protective disguise might as easily have been written to his nurse Mrs Everest as to his wife. The central section of the letter is written in the rhetorical style of a man in the habit of making speeches. It is written with an eye to future readers with such fine-sounding phrases as 'the chimes which saluted our wedding' and 'the clear bright light of happiness'. But it also suggests that Winston is aware that the marriage has not lived up to Clementine's expectations. He expresses the hope that she feels no regrets about her decision to marry him but the words 'however vague or secret' give away his doubts. Similarly in the next sentence the conditional clause, 'if it has not brought you all the glowing and perfect joy which fancy paints', balances the notion of 'clear bright light of happiness' and concedes that

Clementine may have found the relationship less than she had hoped for, while suggesting by the use of the words 'fancy' and 'paints' that her expectations had been unrealistic.

Clementine's letter written on the same day is more honest and more clearly ambivalent. She writes in terms conventionally suitable for a wife writing to her husband after the first year of marriage saying that the year she had been with him has been the happiest in her experience. Given the more or less unhappy nature of Clementine's life to this point this is not saying a great deal but the second half of the sentence modifies what has gone before in a very strange way as she says that even if it had not been a happy year, it had been worthwhile.[5]

In the first week in October the couple were together again, not as a family in Eccleston Square but at a house party given by Wilfrid Blunt at Newbuildings. Clementine had regained her figure and she was able to dazzle her husband and the assembled company in a tight-fitting gold dress of crimped silk that resembled fish scales. She was once again the beautiful wife of whom Winston could be proud and she enjoyed the role.

But then, despite Winston's expression of his desire to curl up in Clementine's arms the couple continued to lead separate lives. Winston had hoped that Clementine would go with him when he visited his constituency in Dundee; instead she retreated to Crowborough in Sussex where she continued her protracted convalescence. But he was sure that the growing division between the Lords and the Commons on the issue of Lloyd George's People's Budget would force a General Election and if that were to happen he would certainly need her support in his election campaign. So for the moment he encouraged Clementine to rest, albeit in words more appropriate for a public address than a private letter, telling her to dedicate herself to accumulating health accepting that in some circumstances dullness is beneficial.[6]

When Clementine returned to London she found Winston at the centre of a crisis which inevitably affected her too. As soon as she was married she discovered how closely political events could affect her personal life. As the 'beautiful Miss Hozier' many houses had been open to her which were firmly closed against Mrs Winston Churchill. Conservative hostesses such as Lady Londonderry could not forgive Winston Churchill for what they considered a betrayal of the party, and their disapproval extended to Clementine. Lloyd George, who had been a witness at Clementine's wedding, had been the man next to whom

Winston had sat when he crossed the floor of the House and it was Winston's vehement support for Lloyd George's budget which had once again made him the focus of much Conservative hatred.

Clementine quickly discovered that her husband was spending as much if not more time with Lloyd George than with her, and most evenings he was out promoting Lloyd George's budget. The relationship was a puzzle to Clementine and she was more than a little surprised to see how much the Welshman could influence her normally independent and stubborn husband. The two men were as different as could be in appearance, temperament and background. Lloyd George was much older than Winston and he had been a Liberal throughout his political career. He had been passionately opposed to the Boer War in which Winston had taken an enthusiastic part. Unlike his younger colleague Lloyd George was emphatically not an imperialist. He not only did not have Winston's aristocratic connections, he actually despised that class and all it stood for. Winston had been educated at a public school and he had been to Sandhurst, while Lloyd George's formal education had ended at twelve. The Welshman neither drank nor ate to excess and was not the avid diner-out that Winston was. He neither belonged to nor approved of the gentlemen's clubs which were so important to Winston. While Winston's attire was often careless – he had even been criticized for his appearance on his wedding day – Lloyd George was most concerned about how he looked and he was always immaculately turned out.

But for all these differences the two men were jokingly referred to as 'The Heavenly Twins', a nickname which was hardly flattering since it was taken from a novel in which the twins so named are 'gifted, irresponsible and inseparable children'.[7] Clementine had seen for herself Winston's devotion to his colleague, for if anyone dared to criticize David Lloyd George in his presence Winston would leap to his defence. Clementine wondered whether Lloyd George was as faithful to Winston.

There was a great deal in that controversial budget that Clementine sympathized with and part of her was delighted to see her husband so whole-heartedly committed to dealing with the problems of the old and the poor and the unemployed. But like everyone else she was aware that for Winston to advocate such policies was to go against the best interests of many of his friends and relatives. She was not sure how her husband could reconcile his delight in the life-style of the rich and the aristocratic with the radical political measures he was now supporting. Was it Lloyd George's personality as much as his politics which had such an influence over her husband? She could see how easy it would be to succumb to the charm of this man who had a way of looking at you when you spoke to him that suggested he was giving you his whole and undivided attention and that what you were saying was of tremendous importance to him. People had suggested that his eyes had a hypnotic power. Even Clementine who was not disposed to gossip was aware that Lloyd George had the reputation of being an accomplished and compulsive seducer of women. Being quiet and observant and immune to the sexual flattery implied in Lloyd George's manner with women, Clementine had also noticed that he treated everyone this way, men and women alike, and she wondered just how sincere he was and how far he could be trusted. For the moment she reserved judgement and said nothing of her doubts to her husband who would anyway have been disinclined to listen to her.

The Finance Bill was passed by the Commons despite Lloyd George's lengthy and uncharacteristically uninspiring account of it. But, as anticipated, the Lords refused to go along with a budget which threatened their wealth and status. Parliament was dissolved and a fierce election campaign began in which, for the first time, Clementine played her part as the Liberal candidate's wife.

8

Women's Rights

A BURNING ISSUE of the day on which Lloyd George had little influence over Winston was the very one which concerned Clementine closely and the one which caused perhaps more angry exchanges between husband and wife than any other at this time.

Woman suffrage was not a question which Clementine and Winston had discussed during their courtship and engagement. In a letter to Clementine about her cousin Dorothy Howard, Winston had given some hint as to where he stood on the matter when he joked about Dorothy's passion for temperance and votes for women, two issues which he assumed were irrevocably linked. But, as Clementine later told Lord Birkenhead (the son of F. E. Smith), she was at the time dazzled by Winston and she did not think clearly about the implications of this casual remark. She could not possibly have known that some years earlier, while he was in India and considering his position on many political issues, he had made up his mind that it was 'contrary to natural law' to give women a say in governing a country and that women best served their country by marrying and giving birth to children. In his view husbands and fathers adequately represented their womenfolk in political matters and he resolved there and then that he would always resist what he saw as a ridiculous movement.[1] Until he married Clementine, Winston had pursued this unswerving course. One great fear that motivated him and many other men was that there were more women than men in England. If they had the vote they would also hold the balance of power. This would not suit Winston at all since he not only enjoyed power for himself he also believed that men in general were better fit to wield it.

There was little in his background to make him question his beliefs. His father had been against votes for women and his mother had been at the forefront of those Conservative upper-class ladies who had signed an anti-suffrage petition. Most of the men he knew shared his views, some of them, such as his cousins the Guests, Sunny Marlborough, F. E. Smith and Prime Minister Asquith, most vociferously. Sir Edward Grey and Lloyd George were unusual in his aquaintance in being in favour of votes for women. Clementine recognized that to make her husband change his mind would be a difficult task.

But if Winston Churchill's standpoint on the issue of votes for women is quite explicable, Clementine's is less so. Why was she so passionate about woman suffrage that she was prepared to take a stance against her husband and risk a breach between them so early in her marriage? Lady Blanche had not wittingly brought up her daughter to be a suffragist. She, like so many other women who were actually better placed to demand change, especially political hostesses such as Lady Londonderry, believed in influence behind the scenes as being more effective than the vote. If Clementine was sufficiently disapproving of her mother to be deterred from adopting her views unquestioningly she was close to another older woman whose views she generally respected. Her favourite great aunt, Maisie, Lady Sheffield, was a devoted admirer of Asquith and she accepted whole-heartedly the Prime Minister's forth-right anti-suffrage position. Why did Clementine not accept her great aunt Maisie's judgement in this particular matter?

Then there was the example of her distant cousin by marriage, Gertrude Bell, a courageous traveller and archaeologist who had carved out for herself a career any man would be proud of and who had never allowed the fact of her being a woman to restrict her. Yet far from feeling that she was as much entitled to the vote as a man, when she was in England Gertrude took the trouble to campaign against woman suffrage. There were other women who had worked as hard as men for social reform but who did not support this particular change. Beatrice Webb, for example, who had educated Winston about many aspects of society, had supported Mrs Humphry Ward's campaign against votes for women and had only very recently announced that she had changed her mind and was now a suffragist. Few of the young women in Clementine's immediate social circle shared her convictions. Venetia Stanley, Gwendeline Churchill, Sylvia Henley and, at this time, Violet Asquith, were not interested in acquiring the vote. Without sharing Margot

Asquith's passion for the notion, they tended to agree with her that women exercised power best through influence and gained 'importance by position and ability, not votes'.[2] These women from cocooned and privileged backgrounds could not understand that this 'influence' that they valued so highly was possible for only a very small number of women in England. The June meeting of the Council of Women's National Anti-Suffrage League, chaired by Lady Jersey, demonstrated this fact vividly since it comprised mostly middle-class and upper-class women.

Clementine, however, knew from her own experiences just how vulnerable women were in the larger world of which her friends had little or no real understanding. Clementine knew what it was like to be really short of money and to have no power to change the situation. Her limited experience of being a seamstress and a teacher had given her a glimpse of the way many women had to live and had shown her how utterly helpless such women were to change their circumstances by any other means than marriage.

Because Blanche had often spoken rather disparagingly about her aunt, Rosalind Howard, Countess of Carlisle, Clementine had taken an interest in her and she knew how devotedly she had worked with the Women's Liberal Federation to change that organization's objective from the simple one of the 'protection of women and children' to the more forceful and forward looking goal of promoting 'just legislation for women including local and Parliamentary franchise for all women on the same terms as men, and the removal of their legal disabilities'.[3] All through her childhood Clementine had lived with the fear that her father might take her away from her mother and her mother's position in law had made her painfully aware of women's 'legal disabilities'. And since marrying Winston and seeing at close hand the behaviour and attitudes of such members of the governing body as F. E. Smith, who was in the process of drinking himself to death, any faith she might have had in the natural superiority of men to rule the country had been completely undermined.

In her arguments with her husband about this issue, so calculated to raise tempers and cause divisions in families and between friends throughout the country, Clementine did not have an easy time in defending her position. The classic argument against allowing women the vote was the accepted view of the time that women were more emotional than men who were generally more rational. Winston could easily demonstrate the truth of this generalization by pointing to Clementine's own uncontrollable outbursts of temper and what he considered to be her irrational fits of jealousy. Then there was the familiar argument that nature had not intended women, who were inevitably physically weakened by child-bearing and the demands of raising a family, to take on the hurly-burly of a politician's life or to fight in the army. Since they were not physically able to either govern or defend their country, the argument ran, what need or right had they to the vote. Again Winston could point to Clementine's own experience as an example of this objection to woman suffrage. After all Clementine had been physically and mentally undermined by childbirth and had taken months to convalesce after the birth of Diana.

There was another argument Winston could and did use against Clementine. He appealed to her as a good Liberal to understand that giving votes to women was simply giving votes to the Conservative party. If he had voted for a bill such as that put forward by W. H. Dickinson which would enfranchise unmarried women householders then, he argued, he would simply have been increasing the vote of the propertied class which was generally Conservative.

When Clementine answered that she wanted the vote for all women not just those with money Winston countered with the argument that women were more influenced by the Church than men and the Church was Conservative.

There were other points which Clementine found difficult to refute: for she could not deny that woman suffrage had not been part of the Liberal party's platform at the election and that, therefore, it had no mandate to legislate for it. She had to acknowledge that the party had its hands full enacting that legislation it had been elected for and which the House of Lords was hampering at every step.

But the most potent argument that Winston used was the one which gave Clementine herself and others like her cause for discomfort, and that was the behaviour of the militant suffragettes some of whom were already in jail for assault. She could not condone their violence and she feared that it damaged the cause. She did point out, however, that a male government was in its turn using unacceptably violent methods when it authorized the force-feeding of jailed suffragettes who were on hunger strike on the grounds that they did not have the status of political prisoners. Whatever Winston said Clementine would not accept that it was right to deny women the vote. Winston now found himself in the altogether unfamiliar position of being resisted not only by a woman but the one closest to him.

That sharp words were exchanged and that Clementine held her own in the argument is evidenced by the letter Winston wrote to her in October 1909 from his constituency in Dundee. Because the suffragettes believed him to be one of the members of the Cabinet resolutely opposed to woman suffrage his meetings were frequently disrupted by them. On this occasion he had, by his own admission, spoken harshly to the women who had tried to shout him down. Knowing that the meeting would be reported in the press and that much would be made of his outburst against the suffragettes, Winston wrote to his wife expressing the hope that she would not be angry when she read an account of what he had said. In his letter he acknowledges that their opinions on this difficult subject are very different. But he goes on to say that he hopes his harsh response to the suffragettes will not make Clementine angry. He promises that he will never try to change her principles and that he hopes she will treat him similarly. He reports having told the women that, though he is sorry for them, he cannot help them while they persist in violence.[4]

Just as in the letter written to Clementine on their first wedding anniversary, there is a formality of tone that suggests a distance between man and wife. And that distance was not lessened by a jealous outburst from Clementine at the beginning of November. The details of the cause of her anger are lost but it is not difficult to conjecture what had led up to her distress. Aware that the suffrage question divided them Clementine was especially vulnerable when she saw Winston being supported in his views by other women in their social circle. Her cousin, dark-haired, vivacious and flirtatious Venetia Stanley, already a close friend of Prime Minister Asquith, was a particular threat as was Asquith's daughter Violet. Clementine resented Winston's tendency to discuss important issues with Violet, especially as she could see that Winston respected Violet's political judgement more than her own at times.

The formality of the letter Winston wrote early in November belies the sentiments it expresses. He writes of her unfounded suspicions which take no account of his feelings of love and loyalty. And any fears she might have had that he put her personal feelings second to his political concerns and that he viewed women as essentially inferior creatures can only have been confirmed by the concluding lines of this letter meant to reassure her but which belittle the importance of her personal concerns in the context of larger issues.[5]

It was one thing, however, for Clementine to take a stand on behalf of the suffragists from the safety of her own home and to take exception to Winston's public declaration of his refusal to be 'hen-pecked' on the issue of woman suffrage, and quite another to go out on the hustings with him and confront the actualities of the suffragettes' violent behaviour herself.

Just a few days after the disagreement described above Clementine set off with Winston to address the Liberals in Bristol. They travelled by train and were greeted on the station platform by Liberal party officials. Suddenly, from the welcoming crowd erupted a young woman brandishing a horse whip. She made straight for Winston, raised her whip and was about to slash him across the face. Instinctively Winston reached out to grab her wrists. She pushed forward so that Winston stepped backward. Clementine saw with horror that her husband was about to be pushed under the wheels of the departing train. All the anger between them was forgotten instantly as she scrambled forward and grabbed at her husband's coat to pull him back from the edge of the platform. Meanwhile others responded by tackling the suffragette and removing her from the scene.

Clementine's convictions were to be further tried at public meetings for, on Winston's birthday on 30 November, the Lords voted against Lloyd George's budget. Immediately parliament was dissolved, an election was called and campaigning began. The issue which dominated all Liberal party election meetings was 'Peers versus the People'. Woman suffrage once again was not included in the Liberal manifesto. But the suffragettes refused to be ignored in this way as the Churchills discovered when in early December they made a tour of Lancashire and Cheshire. In this part of the country the women in the labour force were especially well organized. At every political assembly women were out in force demanding to be heard. Was it the presence of Clementine that inspired Winston in Manchester to invite a well-known agitator, Mary Gawthorpe, to be admitted to his meeting escorted by police and to give her the floor to ask him three questions? His tactic paid off as even other suffragettes considered that Mary Gawthorpe had made a poor showing.[6] On other occasions the attacks went beyond words: in Bolton one woman hurled at Winston's car a piece of iron wrapped in the message, 'Votes for Women'.

On 9 December the Women's Liberal Federation held a great rally in the Albert Hall. There had been a good deal of concern among politicians that this organization, frustrated by the lack of any mention of women's suffrage in the election promises, would fail to support candidates with their valuable voluntary work behind the scenes. So Lloyd George himself, in an attempt to harness this invaluable source of energy and political force on behalf of the Liberal party, addressed the rally. To give credence to his stance as one who would support women when the time was right he invited to sit on the platform with him his own wife Margaret, the wife of the Home Secretary, Mrs Herbert Gladstone, and Clementine Churchill. Clementine knew, as did Lloyd George, that a vast majority of those present were suffragists. From her vantage point on the platform she looked on with interest as Lloyd George tried to win the women's support without actually giving them what they wanted. He declared his personal belief in votes for women and he rather glibly asserted that the majority of the Liberal Cabinet shared his view. But he excused his party's not making this part of their electoral programme on the grounds that in both parties there were hostile minorities 'of influential responsible men whom no party would risk a quarrel with'. He told the women in the Albert Hall that to insist on making woman suffrage part of the legislative programme would be to risk splitting the party, to risk losing the election and thus the opportunity to bring about other most necessary changes. He declared the time was not yet ripe to take up the issue of votes for women since 'We have a few accounts to settle before then.'[7] The most convincing argument he brought forward was that immediately the franchise was extended a new register of voters would have to be compiled. Parliament would have to be dissolved for this to happen so that the Liberals, having only recently won the election, would immediately have to face the electorate all over again. In his view this was not a good policy.

Clementine, like many other women, accepted this point of view. But his reasoning was not acceptable to many of those present who believed that, like other male politicians, Lloyd George put too much emphasis on whether giving women the vote would strengthen or weaken his party rather than on the justice or injustice of the present situation. As long as politicians were influenced by this point of view, woman suffrage might always be regarded as less important than other political considerations. These women were determined to make their views heard: Lloyd George was equally determined that his speech should be heard to its conclusion. Two hours after the meeting began he was still doggedly attempting to make himself heard against the clamour. From time to time the organist drowned out both speaker and protesters with his rendering of 'Oh dear, what can the matter be?'

The Christmas holiday put a temporary stop to electioneering but the issues were still very much on the contestants' minds. Clementine and Winston along with baby Diana had been invited by Sunny as head of the family to a large family gathering at Blenheim Palace. The festivities barely masked the underlying tensions in the disparate group that assembled at Woodstock. Clementine felt herself especially isolated in that context. For not only was she a Liberal supporting policies which Sunny, her host, saw as a great threat both personally and financially, she was the only person present who whole-heartedly supported 'votes for women'. Naturally forthright she had difficulty in keeping her views to herself and refraining from becoming involved in arguments. She was slightly dismayed and even a little disapproving to see that Winston had no difficulty in simultaneously accepting the hospitality of the Duke of Marlborough while supporting Lloyd George who had very recently stated in parliament, 'A fully equipped duke costs as much to keep up as two Dreadnoughts and dukes are just as great a terror and they last longer.'[8] Indeed Winston's own words in Bristol after his encounter with the young suffragette, when he had described the House of Lords as a group of men who felt the government was of less importance than their positions and money,[9] would have seemed grounds for keeping a distance between himself and his titled cousin rather than spending Christmas in his palace. Clementine was not yet accustomed to that trait in Winston described so well by Violet Bonham Carter: 'His blood relations were accepted without question and *en bloc*.'[10] Even had Clementine shared this disposition, Sunny Marlborough was not her blood relative. Clementine was far less able to compartmentalize her feelings and so she was far from comfortable spending Christmas in a Tory stronghold.

She was undermined also by other worries. As long as Winston was in the Cabinet he had a salary (even though he had gallantly and perhaps unwisely accepted a lower salary than those who had the status of Secretary of State), and the upkeep of Eccleston Square and the kind of life they led there were sustainable. But what would happen to them, she wondered, if the Liberals should lose the election and Winston should become simply an MP and as such be without a salary?

9

Conflicting Loyalties

As soon as Christmas was over Winston left Blenheim to return to the election campaign. Clementine had to acknowledge that if her husband did find himself out of office it would not be for want of vigour in fighting for his seat. She herself felt uncomfortable that after accepting Sunny's hospitality Winston set out as determined as ever to battle against the Lords. His language now was more extreme than previously as he described their Lordships in terms of greedy pigs.[1] A cartoon of the time by Max Beerbohm echoes Clementine's uncertainty about the consistency of her husband's political stance and his personal life-style. The cartoon which is entitled 'The Budget' shows Winston remonstrating with the Duke of Marlborough in front of Blenheim Palace saying, 'Come, come! As I said in one of my speeches, "there is nothing in the Budget to make it harder for a poor hard-working man to keep a decent home in comfort".'[2]

The campaign over, Clementine waited anxiously for the result which would determine their financial position for the next few years. She feared that Winston's stance on votes for women had not done him any good in his own constituency of Dundee. There woman suffrage had such strong support that when protesting suffragettes had been jailed and threatened with force-feeding, two thousand men had staged their own protest against the imprisonment of the women. The prisoners had been released before they had served their full sentences and Dundee prison officials were noticeably reluctant to force-feed any suffragettes on hunger strike. The full significance of this was to strike Clementine some weeks later.

On 26 January 1910 the anxiously awaited election results were announced. Just days before, the Conservatives had been hopeful that they would gain a majority but in fact the Liberals held on to power though with a greatly reduced portion of the vote. Since Winston held his seat and also secured a place in the Cabinet which carried twice the salary he had been earning before the election, Clementine's immediate money worries were over. The post to which Asquith had appointed her husband was that of Home Secretary. Now, at the age of only thirty-five, he had a major position in the Cabinet. Clementine's delight at her husband's success was tinged with anxiety, for one of the major problems that would now become his responsibility was the treatment of suffragettes in the prisons. Clementine foresaw that Winston's position would be made especially difficult because during the last weeks of January a relative of close friends had served a prison sentence for her part in a suffrage demonstration.

The matter of force-feeding had troubled Clementine, as it did many other non-militant suffragists, for some time. She was newly aware of its full horrors since the release of Lady Constance Lytton from Walton jail in Liverpool on 23 January 1910. Constance Lytton was the sister-in-law of Winston's early love, Pamela Lytton, the former Pamela Plowden, and she was the sister of Neville Lytton, a good friend of Clementine's sister, Nellie. Lady Constance's story of her treatment at the hands of prison officials could not easily be dismissed. She had disguised herself as Jane Warton to ensure that she was treated as just another prisoner and not accorded special privileges. She had got herself arrested for throwing a stone at Lloyd George's car and had then gone on hunger strike to protest at the treatment of suffragette prisoners and the government's failure to grant women the same civil rights as men. Even before Constance's address to a meeting at the Queen's Hall on 31 January some of the details of the horrors of force-feeding which had come close to killing her had reached Clementine. She had heard that any woman who refused to eat would be held down by the wardresses while the doctor, sitting on her knees to prevent her kicking, forced a steel or wooden gag between her teeth to hold her mouth unnaturally wide. This was a painful and sickening process in itself, but then a tube about four feet in length would be forced down her throat causing extreme irritation. Down the tube food would be poured quickly, often causing a terrible choking sensation followed by vomiting even before the tube was removed. After the tube had been extracted the prisoner, shocked and weak, had to clear up her vomit.

She was disgusted to realize that Herbert Gladstone's assurances about this treatment had been deliberately misleading. Other suffragettes who had served time in prison made public the disgraceful conditions in some jails. All of this together with widespread labour unrest and unemployment promised to ensure that the new Home Secretary would have a busy and extremely difficult year ahead of him.

Clementine herself would inevitably be affected by her husband's changed role in the government. As wife of the Secretary of the Board of Trade she had felt comparatively free to speak out about her position as far as votes for women were concerned. But as wife of the Home Secretary she found herself in a most delicate position. Her loyalty to Winston and her ambition for him to succeed in his Cabinet position were such that she could not now say or do anything which might in the slightest way undermine his position. It was fortunate for her peace of mind that other events made it easier for her to remain silent. A new all-party committee known as the Conciliation Committee had been formed with a view to trying to solve the matter of woman suffrage and Clementine was hopeful that at last a peaceful solution might be found. A further bonus for the new Home Secretary and his wife was that as long as the committee was meeting, other women who wanted the vote clung to the hope that their wishes would be met and for a while there were fewer violent demonstrations. Suffragists and suffragettes alike had confidence in at least two members of the committee, Mr Brailsford, the husband of a well-known suffragette who had been imprisoned more than once, and the chairman, Lord Lytton, the brother of Lady Constance.

In the meantime Clementine did all she could to exert her influence on Winston in private. When she and her husband visited Wilfrid Blunt at Newbuildings in March she found a strong ally in the poet. Blunt, who had himself spent time in prison, was always agitating for improved conditions for prisoners. Winston was ready to listen to his suggestions on this matter and to act on them. But Blunt had a particular interest in the imprisoned suffragettes and especially in the way in which they were being force-fed. Constance Lytton was his daughter's sister-in-law and he had taken her account of events in Walton jail seriously. At this point, however, Winston would make no promises to end force-feeding though he agreed to investigate. When in April Lord Lytton invited Winston to his home, Knebworth, to look into his sister's case which the former Home Secretary, Herbert Gladstone, had refused to do, Clementine urged her husband to seize the opportunity to find out more for himself, and this he did. For reasons of political expediency he could not pursue the matter in the way the Lyttons wished but at least as a result of Clementine's influence he allowed himself to be further educated.

In another serious case of mistreatment of a suffragette prisoner which Constance Lytton brought to his notice his wife's influence is surely visible. The case was that of Mrs Meredith Macdonald who had slipped and fallen while taking exercise in Holloway Prison. Though it was apparent to everyone that she had sustained a serious injury and although she was in great pain, she had received no treatment and indeed had been asked to do things which made her condition worse. Her request for an X-ray was refused, as was her petition to Herbert Gladstone that she might see her own doctor. When she was finally released from prison it was into a hospital where it was confirmed that her leg was broken and had been from the time of the fall. Because she had not received any treatment her leg had shortened and she was left with a limp for life. When Winston became Home Secretary he was asked to review the case with the result that he awarded Mrs Macdonald compensation of £500.

When Mr Brailsford wrote asking for his views on the Conciliation Bill and his support during its passage through the Commons, Winston was prepared to say in writing that he was in principle in favour of no longer discriminating against women on the grounds of sex.[3]

Despite these hopeful signs Winston still held that the violent behaviour of the suffragettes was wrong, unnecessary and deserving of punishment. He would not or could not hear the argument that Clementine urged, that the violent treatment of the women both by the police at demonstrations and in the force-feeding in prison was in excess of any violence on the part of the protesters.

Although outwardly the couple continued to lead their lives in a pattern already well established, spending holidays together at Blenheim followed by periods which Clementine spent away from London usually at either Alderley or Penrhos, Holyhead, with her Stanley relatives, and although outwardly Winston was his usual ebullient, even aggressive self, a change had taken place in their marriage. Despite the money and the prestige of the Home Office Winston was not really happy in his new work. He was especially perturbed by the need to consider the appeals made by those sentenced to death. The kind of careful and considered judgements he felt he must try to make were alien to his nature.

Clementine now realized that her husband's energy and restlessness were a way of warding off and combatting a tendency towards deep depression. As Home Secretary his energies were not fully employed and at times he succumbed to those fits of depression which he fittingly described as 'Black Dog'. Clementine was deeply shocked to discover how little true self-esteem her seemingly over-confident husband possessed and how little comfort he took from her praise of everything he had already achieved in his life. He later described this time as being one in which all the colour faded from life. Paradoxically this bleak time in Winston's life brought out the best in Clementine. When she had married Winston she had set her heart upon being a good wife. But for most of their time together she had felt herself to be little more than a decorative figure in the background of his very busy life. Winston had not appeared to notice her growing dissatisfaction with this limited role except on those occasions when her outbursts of temper shocked him into paying attention to her needs. Now, for the first time in their marriage, Clementine felt that Winston really did need her, not just physically, but also emotionally. For it was only to his wife that he could expose his vulnerabilities and uncertainties without fear that she would care for or respect him any the less. Both realized fully at this time that their very different personalities could be complementary, and a period of stress which might have undermined the marriage did not; on the contrary it strengthened it.

The death of Edward VII in May plunged Winston, the ardent royalist, into further depression. The uncertainty as to how long Asquith's government could stay in power once again made Clementine fearful about their financial prospects. But neither these worries nor the massive Conciliation Bill demonstration in which suffragists and suffragettes alike, led by Lord Lytton marched from the Embankment to the Albert Hall, nor the subsequent two-day debate in the Commons were much of a threat to their new-found harmony.

In August they took a holiday together cruising on the yacht of Baron de Forest who had been their host for a part of their honeymoon. After a brief separation while Winston participated as usual in army manoeuvres on Salisbury Plain, husband and wife set off together to Wales to the home of Lloyd George on the outskirts of Criccieth.

Margaret and David Lloyd George had begun married life in Criccieth and had maintained a home there even when Lloyd George's appointment to a Cabinet position had required him to spend more and more time in London. Margaret Lloyd George had never liked being a minister's wife in London. She knew none of the other wives and was not comfortable with them or the way they lived. After the death of their seventeen-year-old daughter Mair Eluned in 1907 in London, Margaret Lloyd George, grief-stricken, had retreated to Wales. Her husband had bought an acre of land on a hillside above Criccieth and there built for his wife and family a spacious house with views of the sea from the front and the mountains from the back. The house was called Brynawelon – Hill of Breezes.

Margaret Lloyd George and Clementine Churchill were very different women. Clementine admired but had no wish to emulate the older woman's intense involvement with the lives of her children. She did not entirely approve of the way Margaret distanced herself from politics and was prepared to let her husband spend a good deal of the year living alone or with his youngest daughter at 11 Downing Street.

At Criccieth Clementine gained a new perspective on her husband's friend. Here at home he was not treated as the Chancellor of the Exchequer: his wife seemed to regard him less as an important political figure than as a 'much beloved and very foolish child whom it is her business, in so far as she can, to look after'.[4] Was there a lesson here for herself, Clementine wondered.

After the luxuries of the baron's yacht and the grandeur of Blenheim, Clementine enjoyed the familial hospitality of the house in Criccieth with picnics by the river or on the seashore and games of golf, which she had recently begun to play. She found common ground with her hostess in their mutual love of gardening.

Unlike Margaret, however, Clementine was very interested in the political discussions – some would say conspiracies – between Winston and his host. During this visit Lloyd George told Winston that, as he saw it, there were two possible courses open to the Liberal government at that moment, when issues such as Home Rule and the powers of the Lords were taking up time that should have been spent on social legislation. He suggested that the government could try to form a coalition government and thus harness Tory support to deal with outstanding issues, while recognizing that this would inevitably mean a watering down of Liberal reform policies. The second possibility was to steamroller ahead and hope to carry through their policies for imposing land taxes and introducing radical social changes.

Just how far apart politically Winston and Clementine still were shows in their different responses. Clementine, 'a better natural Liberal' as Violet Bonham Carter described her,[5] was firmly for a vigorous programme of reform. Whilst Winston, the former Tory, was just as convinced that the idea of a coalition was the better option.

The events of the next few months had great potential for bringing into the open such differences between Clementine and Winston. As the all-party Constitution Committee, which had been formed to discuss the role of the House of Lords, failed to reach any kind of agreement, Asquith felt he had no choice but to dissolve parliament on 18 November and hold yet another election.

Immediately the suffragettes took to the streets and assembled in a mass protest meeting in Parliament Square. There followed six hours of violent disruption in which police and protesters clashed. The police, believing they had popular and certainly government support, treated the women with great brutality before making 120 arrests. As Home Secretary Winston Churchill was held responsible by the women who had taken part in the protest for the events of Black Friday as the day was quickly named. Clementine, appalled by the stories of women being thumped in the chest, seized by their breasts, pushed against brick walls and verbally as well as physically abused, nevertheless knew that the police had not acted in accordance with her husband's orders. She may have had some influence on Winston's decision to counteract police action by ordering the release of all the women because 'no public advantage' would be gained by prosecution.

Clementine's scepticism about Herbert Asquith's honesty was only increased by his response to Black Friday. He made a public statement promising that on the following Tuesday he would make an announcement about woman suffrage in the Commons. When he failed to do so a group of militant suffragettes led by Mrs Emmeline Pankhurst tried to have a meeting with him at 10 Downing Street. When he refused to see them and thus, they believed, violated their civil rights, they broke into the house and so began the 'Battle of Downing Street' which ended with the arrest of all the women while Asquith made an undignified escape from his own home under police guard. Once again the Home Secretary took the blame for police action, though in this case he had in no way helped his own image by urging the police to arrest Mrs Pethick-Lawrence, a friend of Lady Constance Lytton, as a ring leader.

Although Clementine sympathized with the frustrations which had led to the new outburst of violence she stood by her husband loyally. For not only did he have the suffragettes to contend with he was also attempting to prevent violence erupting in the coal strikes in Wales. The Rhondda valley miners had gone on strike for better pay and conditions. The pits had closed and the men picketing had come into conflict with the police. The Chief Constable had asked for troops to be sent but Winston had felt this was excessive. He ordered the troops to be held back and had extra police sent from London instead in an attempt to avoid provoking the miners excessively. Clementine saw her husband doing his best to control violence, and to a certain extent succeeding, but being reviled from all sides. The Labour press accused him of pitting the army against unarmed strikers while the Tory press accused him of failing to act with sufficient firmness by holding back the troops. His obvious need for Clementine's unconditional love was greater than ever before in his increasingly lonely and isolated position.

By now there was also a new element in Clementine's relationship with Winston which was likely to bring them closer. She was pregnant for the second time and she was sure that this child was going to be a boy. Instead of giving the unborn child a nickname that would do for either a boy or a girl as she had done in her first pregnancy with the name Puppy-kitten, from the outset she called her second child by the uncompromisingly robust and masculine name of Chumbolly. During her first pregnancy Winston had urged her to rest as much as possible. But there was no such cosseting this time. More than ever with the prospect of another child both Clementine and Winston saw the vital importance of making sure that the Liberals won the election and that Winston secured a paying ministerial position. When Winston began his election campaign Clementine was with him adding her beauty and charm to his pugnacious energy. She witnessed more of the suffragettes' violent hostility to her husband when a young man named Hugh Franklin not only disrupted a meeting in Bradford but then, on the train back to London later that day, attacked Winston with that weapon so favoured by the suffragettes, the horsewhip. He followed this with a verbal attack in a vitriolic article in the magazine *Votes for Women*.

Clementine, however, had her reward for her patient, behind-the-scenes pressure on her husband when in his own constituency of Dundee in early December he stated publicly, if guardedly, that 'in principle' he favoured women being enfranchised.

A cold kept Clementine in London towards the end of this campaign. When Winston visited her Great Aunt Maisie at Alderley to relax after the rigours of the campaign she was not able to be with him, but the letters exchanged at this time are different from those of the previous year. There is a real intimacy and affection expressed and their regret at being apart seems genuine and not merely formal. Often careless and thoughtless for others, at this time Winston delighted his wife by unexpectedly sending her flowers and fruit as a love token.

Nevertheless, when the Liberals were re-elected and the family finances secured once more, life continued much as before. Winston was deeply involved in the affairs of the Home Office and this brought him little popularity. Clementine suffered when this was demonstrated openly as cinema audiences booed the footage of the Sidney Street incident in which he had taken part. Police had surrounded a house at 100 Sidney Street in the East End of London. They were convinced that in the house was an anarchist gang, including a man known as Peter the Painter, wanted by the police. Hearing of what was happening Winston had hurried to the scene where he found two hundred police, some of whom were armed. He had taken command and ordered more police so that the building could be taken. Then the house caught fire and Winston refused to let any firemen risk their lives for men he regarded as criminals. The house burnt to the ground and only two charred bodies were found inside, neither of whom was Peter the Painter. Winston was accused of interfering in the work of both the police and the fire brigade, motivated simply by an irresponsible love of adventure and danger for its own sake. Clementine herself was not pleased that her husband should have taken what seemed unnecessary risks at such a time.

As in all the years of their marriage so far the couple spent a great deal of time apart. After their usual Easter visit to Blenheim Clementine spent the last weeks of her pregnancy with the Sheffields at Penrhos. Husband and wife continued to disagree about the reliability of Herbert Asquith, Clementine maintaining her critical stance to the man who was now being nicknamed 'Old Squiffy' whilst Winston, despite having to stand in for his leader on the nights when Asquith was too drunk to answer questions, retained a loyal respect for and belief in the Prime Minister.

Early in May Clementine returned to Eccleston Square ready for the birth of the baby which was expected mid-month. But Chumbolly did not arrive on time and Clementine had two more weeks to wait. It was now that her husband established yet another all-male group, the Other Club, where members of all political parties could meet for discussions. His new closeness to his wife did not mean that he was ready for quiet domesticity. Male companionship in a setting other than his home was still extremely important to him.

On 28 May 1911 Clementine gave birth to a large and lusty baby; it was a boy as she had predicted. She was delighted to have produced the Churchill heir and given to Winston the satisfaction that his own family dynasty had been begun.

10

Seduced by the Enchantress

CHUMBOLLY CAME INTO the world to a very different reception from the one that had greeted Diana. The baby boy was not abandoned to the care of a nursemaid as soon as possible; instead his mother was with him constantly since she had decided to breast-feed him. Winston's delight at the birth of a son did not prevent him from going to Blenheim as usual for his annual two weeks' training with the Reserves. But the letters Clementine wrote to him now show none of her earlier reticence. Her happiness is evident and she clearly takes pleasure in being physically close to her son. Randolph's arrival unquestionably thrust her small daughter further into the background.

The coronation of King George was an event which Clementine had anticipated with interest but it seemed as if the late arrival of her son and his regular demands on her would make it impossible for her to take a part in the ceremonies. Her devotion to the baby was such that she did not resent this sacrifice as she might have done after the birth of Diana. In the event she got the best of two worlds. Hearing of her situation the King made special arrangements so that she could be taken by carriage to the Abbey at the latest possible moment and so would not have to spend long hours waiting like the rest of the congregation. She was given a place in the King's own box. At the last coronation that very box had been dubbed the 'loose box' when occupied by three of King Edward's mistresses. As soon as the time arrived for Chumbolly's next feed Clementine was whisked discreetly away, back to Eccleston Square.

Once the coronation was over Clementine went to the calm and healthy atmosphere of Seaford taking with her the two babies and their nurse. Seaford was generally agreed to be a good place to recover from the ravages of a winter in London and many of her acquaintances were there. Blanche was also making one of her regular visits and so Clementine had plenty of company. The only slightly jarring note was the absence of Winston. He wrote her loving and amusing letters describing his drive through London as part of a royal procession to celebrate the coronation in the company of a duchess and a countess who detested him. He forwarded Lloyd George's complimentary remarks made about Clementine when the two men had dined together.

When there was nothing left to keep him in London, instead of joining his wife and children in Seaford, he accepted an invitation to stay with Maxine Elliott at her home Hartsbourne Manor in Hertfordshire. Maxine Elliott was an old friend of Jennie. An American by birth and an actress by profession she too had been for a time one of King Edward's mistresses. She was now jolly and fat but her home still boasted the 'King's Suite'. It was emphatically not a house where a nursing mother and her two children could readily be accommodated. Its charm for Winston, as Clementine very well knew, was that he could live there with all those luxuries he so much enjoyed and that he would be the centre of attention and not have to compete with the babies.

For her part Clementine was glad enough to be away from London in the summer that was one of the hottest on record. It was bliss to be able to swim in the sea and to know that having regained her figure quickly her appearance in her swimsuit attracted general admiration. She felt pleasantly distanced from what seemed to be a prevalent feeling of unrest in the country which the hot weather exacerbated.

During the course of this summer Clementine realized fully that however much Winston wanted a family and whatever importance he put on having an heir, family matters must always be in the background and that her role as mother must come second to her role as his wife. This was made quite clear to her soon after the birth of Randolph when Winston wrote from Blenheim to arrange for a dinner party at Eccleston Square in June for the King of Portugal. He expressed his hope that Clementine would receive the King even if it meant her lying on the sofa in the library to do so. She knew that if she wanted to make her marriage a success then she must always put Winston first. In the months prior to Randolph's birth, as Clementine had responded to Winston's need of her in his state of depression, she had realized that in many ways he was demanding from her the mothering and reassurance that Mrs Everest had provided in his childhood. Even though they now had two small children of their own, Winston still wanted that kind of attention from Clementine. A letter she received from him in August prior to a weekend visit he made to her at the seaside is almost comic evidence of this: the Home Secretary writes from London asking his wife to explore and to find a good sandy beach with a stream where he can spend his time happily making an elaborate sand fortress. Fully understanding her husband's needs and, at this stage in their marriage, willing to supply them, Clementine made sure that by the time she left Seaford and entered society again Randolph was fully weaned. From the intimacy of the summer when his mother was available at all times Randolph was suddenly thrust, along with his two-year-old sister, into the care of a nursemaid, and his mother became a distant figure in his life.

The first use Clementine made of her freedom from the demands of the nursery was to go to Bavaria with Goonie to spend a quiet time in the cool of the mountains at Garmisch. Then she planned to join Winston at the Villa Cassel as guests of Sir Ernest Cassel. The villa was luxurious and since there would be good food and congenial company Clementine had looked forward to holidaying there with her husband. She felt no qualms about accepting hospitality from Sir Ernest who had been Winston's financial adviser for many years. She knew that since the death of his daughter he welcomed the company of young people and especially those such as Winston who had known her well and had visited her while she lay dying. However, Clementine's hopes were dashed. Winston was far too busy dealing with the problems of industrial unrest at home. There were dock strikes in Birkenhead and Liverpool accompanied by riots which the Home Secretary felt obliged to quell with troops. Then, when the railway workers came out in sympathy there were fears of a general strike. Instead of enjoying something approximating a second honeymoon Clementine returned to London and from there travelled to Scotland to pay a duty visit to her grandmother at Airlie Castle whilst Winston went to Balmoral at the invitation of the King.

Although she had now been married for three years and had two children, Clementine was still a little afraid of, and indeed in awe of, her grandmother. Her Aunt Clementine was also there along with her husband Bertram. Aunt Clementine reported on the progress of her beautiful granddaughter Diana born in June to her son David and his wife Sydney. Bertram wanted to know all about Clementine's son. Lady Airlie, however, was more interested in giving her granddaughter some instruction in how she as a gentlewoman should behave. Appalled by Clementine's handwriting she reduced her granddaughter to the status of a schoolgirl insisting that she should spend time each day of her stay copying the handwriting of Lord Melbourne and Lord Palmerston with the objective of improving her own.

As always Clementine found the atmosphere in her grandmother's home oppressive and she longed for the arrival of Winston to provide some relief. She was most anxious, however, that Winston who was driving his new red Napier of which he had just taken delivery would not get carried away with the pleasure of driving and cause trouble by arriving late.

From Airlie Castle the couple, alone for the first time in months, drove to the coast of East Lothian where they were to be the guests of the Prime Minister and his wife. Archerfield, a lovely Adam house at the end of a long drive of lime trees, had been lent to the Asquiths by Margot's brother, Frank Tennant. It was as impressive inside as out with a fine library and a large salon beautifully decorated with motifs taken from the ruins at Pompei. It was not only the classical ambience which made the house especially pleasing to Herbert Asquith but also the delight of private golf links stretching right down to the sea.

Clementine's pleasure in escaping Airlie Castle to the much more relaxed and casual house was lessened by her anxiety about two things. First of all Violet Asquith was of the party and, much as she liked the Prime Minister's daughter personally, she did not like Winston's habit of taking long walks alone with her. Secondly she knew that Winston hoped that during the course of the visit he could persuade Asquith to make him First Lord of the Admiralty. Because it was a position that Winston had long coveted, Clementine hoped that he would get his wish. She was aware of how frustrated he had felt being at the Home Office rather than the Admiralty when, in July 1911, the Germans had sent a gunboat to threaten the Moroccan port of Agadir, which the French claimed as being under their sphere of influence. It had seemed at the time that Britain might have to back up the French with a display of British naval power. Despite these considerations, a part of Clementine feared the changes that an appointment to the Admiralty would bring into their lives.

Asquith was excruciatingly slow about deciding whom he would appoint to the Admiralty. When he did at last offer the position to Winston, just as on the day of his engagement Winston blurted out the news to the first person he met. This was not Clementine but Violet Asquith. Her account of this occasion in her book about Winston leads the reader to the conclusion that Clementine's jealousy was not misplaced. Violet writes as though Clementine had not been present at all on that important day in Winston's life and that she, Violet, had been the sole recipient of the confidential information about his new position. Clearly Violet would have preferred Clementine to have been absent.

When she did receive the news Clementine was full of praise for her husband's achievement and outwardly she shared his pleasure. Inwardly she had grave doubts and worries. She wondered how it could be that the man who had fought so vigorously to reduce the Naval Estimates, or the Admiralty's claim for the amount of money it required from the government's operating budget, in the previous year could now become the man who would throw himself into the fight to secure for the navy all that he could. She did not share Winston's almost childish enthusiasm for moving into the grand establishment of Admiralty House. Whilst her husband revelled in the thought of the lavish entertainments he could preside over there, Clementine worried about all the extra expense that would result from living in such magnificence. She did not want to move out of the Eccleston Square house which she had decorated and furnished to her own taste into premises which she would have to furnish from a Ministry of Works catalogue.

Her concern was not confined to money matters. While Winston had been at the Home Office they had grown closer. He had discussed his problems with her and she believed that she had been helpful. She feared that such closeness would disappear when he took over his new office and that the very nature of the work would take him increasingly away from her and the family and into a world populated almost exclusively by men.

In an attempt to resist these changes Clementine put up obstacles in the way of the immediate move into Admiralty House that Winston favoured. She said that it was no place for children to live, that she did not like the ugly furniture, that they could not afford the necessary extra staff to run such a large house and that they could not let the Eccleston Square house stand empty.

Arrangements had been made for Randolph's christening to take place on 26 October. Winston readily accepted that this occasion would delay their move. His appointment as First Lord was announced just two days before Randolph was christened in the crypt of the House of Commons. The very location suggested Winston's hopes that his son would follow in his footsteps and become a political figure. The choice of godparents was Winston's also. Clementine was by no means pleased that F. E. Smith should be one of these but she had to accept that as Winston had stood godfather for the Smiths' first son it was only courteous to return the compliment. Winston went further: Smith's son had been named Frederick Winston and now his son was named Randolph Frederick. Lady Ridley, the daughter of Winston's favourite aunt Cornelia, Lady Wimborne, was godmother. The only godparent of whom Clementine fully approved was Sir Edward Grey, the Liberal Foreign Secretary, a quiet man who still mourned the death of his wife. Clementine had an affection for him which he reciprocated. A bond between them was his belief in women's suffrage.

Although Clementine successfully delayed the move into Admiralty House, she was not able to circumvent the other changes she feared. Winston flung himself into his new job with enthusiasm and alacrity and was away from home more than ever before. He loved his office in the Admiralty with its huge chart of the North Sea, and the study-library which Clementine had created for him at Eccleston Square was now neglected. But what literally carried Winston away from her was the yacht *Enchantress* which was traditionally at the disposal of the First Lord and which became for Winston a second home or even, as some said, his first home. Winston himself described his love affair with his new work: 'From dawn to midnight day after day one's whole mind was absorbed by the fascination and novelty of the problems which came crowding forward. And all the time there was the sense of the power to act, to form, to organize.'[1] There was little room left for Clementine in this new and busy life. She felt excluded and resentful, and on more than one occasion she threw a temper tantrum before Winston left on the *Enchantress* to inspect yet another ship, yet another dockyard. Then when her husband had left she would regret her bad temper and would have to write a letter of apology.

Before long, however, she discovered that she still had an important role to play even in this male–dominated society. Winston was still a poor judge of character and he was still insensitive to the kind of responses his actions were likely to provoke. When he set about making dramatic reforms in the navy and making changes of personnel even at the highest ranks Clementine saw, as he did not, that he was everywhere making unnecessary enemies. She alerted him to this and pointed out some long-term consequences which he might avoid if only he would treat people more kindly, give them salves for their pride, inform those entitled to know what he was about and what he intended doing, instead of assuming that he was free to make all decisions unilaterally.

Clementine's advice was usually good and frequently Winston listened to her. But just as he had refused to accept her judgement of F. E. Smith and Ivor Guest so too he turned a deaf ear when she expressed her misgivings about the former First Sea Lord, seventy-year-old Lord Fisher, now living in retirement in Lucerne, whom Winston proposed to bring back to the Admiralty as his adviser.

Lord Fisher had been very friendly with Winston at one time but the friendship had suffered when in the early days of the Liberal government Winston had joined Lloyd George in attacking the Naval Estimates. Fisher was a forceful but strange man. Although he had been born to English parents in Ceylon and had lived in England from the age of six he had a distinctly asiatic appearance. His hair was cut unusually short and brushed forward over his brow. His thickly hooded eyes gave him a sinister look which was underlined by his hard mouth turned down at the corners. He had been married since he was twenty-five and had sired four children but still he preferred the company of men. He loved to waltz, and when no suitably pretty woman was available to partner him he was just as happy to dance with one of his naval officers. He had in common with Winston an amazing energy, a love of power, a zeal for reform and a manic desire to prevent the German navy from becoming more powerful than the British.

Clementine feared that Winston was over-impressed by Fisher and might become his cat's-paw. She was afraid of Fisher's uncertain temper and his openly expressed conviction that 'the secret of efficiency is favouritism'. What is more she knew that he was violently opposed to women having the vote or having any influence whatsoever on public life. His own wife had always been content to remain a subordinate, background figure. In Clementine's view Fisher could only reinforce the worst side of Winston.

The question of the vote for women was at this time very much to the forefront of Clementine's mind. How could it fail to be when after two readings of the Conciliation Bill in the Commons, when hopes were raised that some positive action on the issue might be forthcoming, Prime Minister Asquith had effectively undermined the whole process by announcing on 7 November that in the next session he would introduce a bill to give suffrage to all adult males with British citizenship. To this, he calmly added, there could be an amendment to give votes to some women.

Even the most law-abiding, moderate suffragists such as Millicent Fawcett were appalled by Asquith's interference. She wrote, 'If it had been Mr Asquith's object to enrage every woman suffragist to the point of frenzy, he could not have acted with greater perspicacity.'[2] Mrs Bernard Shaw, normally a calm woman and one who had taken no part in the suffragettes' violent demonstrations, said that the Prime Minister's speech had filled her with 'an angry impulse of blind rage'.[3]

In the privacy of Eccleston Square Clementine echoed these sentiments. Winston was alarmed by her reaction and that of other seemingly moderate women. Clementine was almost certainly unaware that her husband had written to various members of the government expressing his fears. To the Master of Elibank, Liberal MP Alexander Murray, he wrote on 16 December, 'What a ridiculous tragedy it would be if this strong government and Party . . . has to go down on Petticoat politics.' Winston's idea was to hold two referendums, 'first to the women to know if they want it [the vote], and then to the men to know if they will give it'.[4] While Winston had been Home Secretary Clementine had believed that her views on suffrage had gained some influence, however slight, over her husband. This November of 1911 she realized that she and Winston were as far apart on this issue as they had ever been. If Clementine felt that her loyalty as a wife prevented her from speaking out publicly and vigorously, other women were not so constrained, as she would soon discover.

11

Fears and Anxieties

AT THE END of 1911 Clementine discovered that she was pregnant again and so was able to further delay the move to Admiralty House. Christmas was as usual spent at Blenheim but this time when Winston set off for Ireland to make preliminary arrangements for an official visit in February, Clementine remained as Sunny's guest. For some time he had been extolling to her the pleasures of hunting. Now, despite her pregnancy and cautionary letters from Winston, Clementine decided that the time had come for her to ride with the hounds. She found the experience just as thrilling as Sunny had promised. Like him she lost her habitual reserve and her inhibitions in the excitement of the chase. Her enjoyment in this new activity was such that during the early weeks of January she rode out with him as often as possible.

The letters which came from Winston were disquieting and brought her down to earth. In Belfast he had met with strong opposition to his official visit from the Unionists led by Edward Carson. The Ulster Hall which he had planned to use for a public meeting was being held by armed Ulstermen who refused to leave. There were open threats of violence against him in the press and Edward Carson was taunting him with his defection from his father Lord Randolph's Unionist position of 'Ulster will fight and Ulster will be right.'

Neither verbal nor physical violence could persuade Winston to cancel his meeting but he did have second thoughts about Clementine accompanying him to Ireland as they had originally planned. The fact that his wife was pregnant made him doubly anxious. But Clementine, who could have used her condition as a graceful way of excusing herself from the engagement, would not hear of a change of plans. She thoroughly approved of Winston's support for Irish Home Rule especially as he had only six years earlier been as strong a Unionist as his father; she wanted to be visible as his supporter now that his views coincided with her own. Because they were so much at odds on the issue of women's suffrage she was particularly keen to support him on a matter on which they could agree. She also hoped that her presence might give pause to those intent on violence.

The weather was cold and wet as, on 7 February 1912, accompanied by Winston's cousin Freddie Guest, Winston and Clementine travelled by train to Stranraer from where they would take the overnight ferry to Belfast. Any fears Clementine had about what faced them were in no way diminished by the knowledge that cousin Freddie was carrying a loaded revolver. What she had not anticipated was that even before they left England they would be the focus of intense hostility and violent abuse.

Still enraged by Asquith's November speech militant suffragettes were determined to make life difficult for every member of his government. They believed, rightly, that Winston Churchill represented opposition to their cause. It was public knowledge that Winston was going to Belfast and so a crowd of shouting, protesting women had gathered on the docks to confront him. In the eyes of the crowd Clementine was as much at fault as her husband. They saw her as a member of a leisured class of women who, protected by social position and money, did not fully understand just how unfair present legislation was to most women. Clementine received her fair share of abuse; how could those women have known that in her heart she agreed with them but felt unable to voice her beliefs?

The protests did not cease when the ferry pulled out into the Irish Sea. A number of militants were on board and all night as the ferry ploughed through stormy seas Clementine and Winston in their cabins were kept awake by the protesting women beating on their windows, stamping loudly overhead on the deck and shouting loudly 'Votes for Women'.

Tired and tense they arrived in Belfast to be greeted by more unpleasantness. The car which was to take them from the docks to the Grand Central Hotel was without windows. The police explained that they were afraid that the dockers would smash them and that flying glass would injure the car's passengers. Clementine, Winston and Freddie climbed into the car and the driver attempted to pull away from the docks. But the dockers had other ideas and began to manhandle the car in an attempt to overturn it. Clementine watched with helpless horror. She had never known before what it was to be hated by an enraged crowd. The police tried to beat back the protesters' hands with canes, and in the temporary confusion the driver was able to get away. In the hotel matters were not much better. They were greeted by fist-shaking and had to be hustled quickly to a specially prepared room. But the crowds gathered round the hotel waving flags, brandishing sticks and shouting abuse. When Winston unwisely drew back the curtain a little to see what was happening, the shouting increased and he had the experience of seeing an effigy of himself burnt before his eyes. He suggested that Clementine might like to stay in the hotel when he went to address the meeting. But, having come so far, Clementine did not intend to leave her husband's side. Shortly after noon police arrived to take them to the car which they then escorted first through surging hostile Unionist crowds and then through cheering Catholic ones out to the football ground at Celtic Park where a huge marquee, specially shipped from England, had been erected for the meeting.

Clementine accompanied her husband onto a makeshift and rickety platform and looked down on the seething mass of people talking loudly and gesticulating wildly. She did not find it easy to distinguish supporters from opponents. Tempers were not improved when the canvas roof of the tent, no longer able to support the weight of all the rain which had accumulated, suddenly released a great torrent of water which drenched a large part of the audience.

Eventually Winston was able to make himself heard and his final remarks in which he turned his father's words to suit his own ends delighted all of his supporters and provoked the rest of the audience to fury.

He claimed that the Tories were trying to regain office by using Ireland as a cat's-paw but that he believed that Irish nationalism was unquenchable. He then went on to say:

> It is in a different sense that I adopt and repeat Lord Randolph's words 'Ulster will fight and Ulster will be right.' Let Ulster fight for the dignity and honour of Ireland; let her fight for the reconciliation of races and for forgiveness of ancient wrongs; let her fight for the unity and consolidation of the British Empire; let her fight for the spreading of charity, tolerance and enlightenment among men. Then indeed Ulster will fight and Ulster will be right.[1]

At last the seemingly endless day was over and they were back on the ferry and then on the train to London.

Once safely home Clementine began to feel unwell. At first she thought she was simply experiencing a reaction to the extreme tension of the Belfast adventure. Then she began to have pains that she recognized as being labour pains as her body spontaneously aborted the child she was carrying. The miscarriage left her weak, distressed and vulnerable. Winston worried about her but could not or would not stay with her; as soon as he was sure that she was in no physical danger he sent her off to Brighton to convalesce while he set off once again on the *Enchantress*.

The medical attention that Clementine received at the time of the miscarriage was inadequate. Along with the normal depression the loss of a child brings with it Clementine also suffered great physical discomfort. She was, therefore, very sensitive at this time to the pains specific to women and more than a little cynical about the ability of men and especially male doctors either to sympathize or to do anything to help. This was her state of mind when she opened *The Times* of 28 March to read a letter three columns in length from a fanatical opponent of woman suffrage, the bacteriologist Sir Almroth Wright. Writing as an 'expert' he attacked the wisdom of allowing women to participate in politics since their very physiology made them unsuitable. He described the militant suffragettes as immoral women and blamed their behaviour on the fact that they were sexually embittered.

While Winston had been Home Secretary Clementine had kept silent but now that her husband was at the Admiralty she felt free to respond to this virulent letter in which the writer went so far as to claim that 'there is mixed up with the women's movement much mental disorder'.[2] On 30 March a letter signed 'C.S.C. (One of the Doomed)' appeared in *The Times*. Adopting the method of Swift's 'A Modest Proposal' Clementine pursued Sir Almroth Wright's argument to its logical conclusion asking, 'how much happier and better would the world be if only it could be purged of women' and a race of males could be maintained 'by purely scientific means'. She expressed the hope that Sir Almroth Wright himself would 'crown his many achievements by delivering mankind from the parasitic, demented, and immoral species which had infested the world for so long'.[3] Even anti-suffrage Asquith had to confess to an admiration for Clementine's trenchant letter.

Buoyed up by her success and taking a quiet pleasure in having done something for women Clementine felt well enough to contemplate going to Paris for a short holiday. She arranged to stay with friends at first and then to move with Winston into Ernest Cassel's apartment for a week.

Her new-found composure was ruffled by a letter from Winston in which he jokingly told her that her brother Bill had visited him and reported losing £100 gambling. He had asked Winston not to tell Clementine. She was worried to know that Bill, who more often lost than won, had not given up gambling, even though she had begged him to do so. She did not like the fact that Winston, on his part, took the matter so light-heartedly.

Then she fell ill again and was dismayed when a French gynaecologist she consulted expressed disapproval of the way her condition had been treated in England. His advice was that she should rest completely for a month. Clementine found her continuing ill health not only irksome but also lonely. Winston sent frequent loving letters and telegrams and was always anxious for news of her but he was rarely with her. His absorption in his work was only one reason for his absence. Clementine knew that sickness in others made Winston uncomfortable and even depressed and that he would go to some trouble to avoid being in the company of someone who was ill.

So when Winston broached the idea of a cruise on the *Enchantress* in May Clementine did her best to simulate good health in the hopes that sea air, leisure and a change of scene would make her pretence become a reality. She was also attracted by this novel and glamorous way of repaying hospitality which involved her in little work or expense.

The party which set off from London on 22 May comprised not just Winston, Clementine and Goonie but also Prince Louis of Battenberg, the Prime Minister and his daughter, Violet. They were given a lively send-off by friends and family on the first stage of their journey to Dover. A smooth crossing in bright weather was followed by the train journey to Paris where the party stopped off to refresh themselves with hot baths at the Ritz and a splendid meal at Voisins. Then they were back on the train for Genoa where the *Enchantress* was waiting to take them on the first part of their cruise to the island of Elba which Winston, as an admirer of Napoleon, was keen to see.

As the 3,800 ton ship, with a crew of more than eighty, an excellent chef and supplies of good food and drink, set off the cruise promised to be idyllic. The weather was marvellous, their ports of call interesting. After Elba they sailed to Naples and explored Pompei. They visited Paestum where they picnicked by temples of golden stone standing by the sea surrounded by masses of colourful wild flowers – poppies, marigolds, love-in-a-mist and cornflowers. In Syracuse they swam in the clear waters of the harbour. They visited the ruins of a Greek fortress where they were assailed by the perfume of rosemary and wild lavender and they saw the old Greek theatre by the romantic light of the setting sun. Then it was Malta where there were dinner parties and dancing and a visit to the house of Sir Ian Hamilton, the soldier whom Winston had greatly admired since the time of the Boer War, at San Antonio where the garden was full of bougainvillaeas and flowering pomegranate. They witnessed a battle practice and a review of the troops before sailing for Bizerta which Goonie, who had expected the coast of Africa to be more exotic, described as 'not unlike the environs of Bournemouth'.4

Clementine desperately wanted to enjoy this luxurious holiday as much as the rest of the party seemed to be doing. But she did not. She felt weak and debilitated and her lack of energy troubled her all the more as she saw Violet in sparkling form monopolizing Winston. The nightly bridge games which the men insisted upon troubled her as she saw Winston gambling recklessly. And then were was Lord Fisher whom Winston had lured on board the *Enchantress* at Naples. She disliked him from the start and was dismayed by her husband's evident infatuation with the man and his eagerness to please him. Fisher was equally unimpressed by Winston's wife describing her as a beautiful but stupid woman.

By the time the *Enchantress* reached Bizerta Clementine felt too ill to join the party's excursion to Tunis and she kept to her cabin for most of the remaining days of the voyage which ended in early June at Gibraltar.

During the next months Clementine saw a sequence of doctors but her condition remained unchanged. Winston continued to press for the move to Admiralty House but even he could see that Clementine was in no fit state to organize such a major upheaval.

Although she had only just returned from the cruise on the *Enchantress*, Clementine began to think about possibilities for a family summer holiday. Like every other woman of her class at that time she took for granted the need to be out of London for the summer months. Unlike most of her contemporaries she had no country house of her own nor did she have parents who could receive her and her family. Blanche herself was dependent on the generosity of her brother-in-law, Bertram, for the loan of a small cottage on his estate when she rented out her home, the Villa St Antoine at 16 rue des Fontaines in Dieppe, for the summer months. Jennie had Salisbury Hall but Clementine did not see that as a holiday home. Fortunately Nancy, Lady Astor, had heard about Clementine's ongoing illness and she offered to let her use 'Rest Harrow', overlooking Sandwich Bay in Kent. Clementine was delighted to take up residence in the 'cottage by the sea' which Nancy had had built for herself. Since the 'cottage' had fifteen bedrooms there was plenty of room for Clementine and her children along with Goonie and hers as well as the nannies and other staff.

Clementine had hoped that this holiday would enable her to return to London refreshed and ready for the new parliamentary session. But she continued to feel ill. A letter she sent to Winston at this time is a cry for help expressed in the nautical terms she felt sure would claim his attention. She describes herself as a 'poor wrecked ship' and she asks Winston to put the same thought and energy into solving her problem as he does into reforming the navy. Help came from an unlikely source. Ernest Cassel who had learnt why Clementine had returned early from Paris happened to have a niece who had similarly suffered from the after-effects of a miscarriage but who had been restored to health after a curettage operation. Clementine, who was by now willing to try anything, in July put herself in the care of the gynaecologist recommended by Cassel and by the end of the year she was feeling well. But so shaken was she by her experience that she was anxious to avoid another pregnancy in the near future.

Her fear of pregnancy created a tension between husband and wife and this was exacerbated by what Clementine saw as Winston's excessive concern for his mother. For while Clementine had been economizing ready for the move from Eccleston Square, Jennie had been organizing a lavish pageant. She had been confident that it would make money but instead found that it had left her in debt. To add to her misery she could no longer pretend not to be aware that her young husband was less interested in her than in Mrs Patrick Campbell. At the end of the year he asked for a divorce. Jennie turned to Winston for comfort and Clementine was not pleased with the demands her mother-in-law made on Winston's rare leisure moments. Harsh words were exchanged.

In September, however, tranquillity was restored when Winston's inspection of the docks and the ships on the Tyne was also made the occasion for a holiday. Blanche and Nellie were invited this time. When Winston went to Balmoral in his official capacity as a Minister, Clementine and Nellie were also invited to dinner. Blanche, as a divorced woman, could not be received.

In 1912 Nellie was twenty-four and very handsome. Like her mother before her she attracted men like bees to a honey-pot. Prime Minister

Asquith himself found her very appealing and his nicknames for her were 'The Bud' and 'Mlle Beaux Yeux'. Clementine was more concerned about Nellie's future than her mother appeared to be. It was Clementine who worried that Nellie flirted with everyone but took no man seriously and it seemed to her likely that Nellie was on her way to making as unsatisfactory a match as their mother had done. She found her sister something of a puzzle; was Nellie's air of light-hearted innocence which so drew men to her something of a pose? That she had grounds for doubt is supported by a comment in Nellie's novel *Misdeal* written years later in 1932 under the pseudonym of Anna Gerstein which evidently relates to Nellie's own life. The central character, Nancy, shares many of her author's characteristics. At one point in the novel she turns down a potential lover confessing that she has a lover already. The rejected man retorts, 'You've got such an innocent face, such an innocent expression, and your voice and the things you say, and your eyes, why, you might be the Mother Superior of a convent. You're the most complete and awful little humbug I've ever met.'[5] There were rumours about Nellie's behaviour which troubled Clementine. Her sister was, she considered, too much in the company of the Coterie, the children of the Souls – that tightly knit group of friends led by Lord Curzon who prided themselves on their superior wit and intelligence. The Coterie was an equally exclusive group, but they were intent on behaving with a frivolity that shocked their parents. With some dismay Clementine had heard that, along with Venetia Stanley, Nellie had been responsible for putting opium into Raymond Asquith's pipe for a joke. When she discussed her fears with Winston he merely laughed and said Nellie was well able to take care of herself. Clementine's suspicions about Nellie's sincerity and sense of responsibility were far outweighed by her own sense of family loyalty, and as the young woman always entertained Winston she continued to spend much of her time with the Churchills.

There was now no good reason for further delaying the move into Admiralty House and for Winston it had become a matter of urgency. Clementine suspected that he was in part motivated by the fact that the F. E. Smiths were leaving Eccleston Square and going to a larger, more prestigious house in Grosvenor Gardens. Moving to the Admiralty was a way of keeping up with them. As a concession to Clementine's fear of the expense of running a larger establishment Winston agreed that one floor should be sealed off. Sir Edward Grey was interested in taking over the lease of the Eccleston Square house and Clementine had to admit that they could not find a more suitable tenant. She began the laborious task of packing up and selecting furniture from the Ministry of Works catalogue complaining bitterly about the ugliness of what was available. And all the while there was a new, nagging worry at the back of her mind, for it was in March 1913 that Winston decided that he should learn to fly. Clementine accepted that he needed to find out how planes could be used to augment the power of the navy, but she did not believe that to do so it was essential for him to fly himself. Only too aware of her husband's frightening lack of co-ordination when driving a car she was thoroughly alarmed by this new venture. She feared that Winston was testing and proving his personal physical courage rather than undertaking something which would genuinely help the navy. She protested, but to no avail.

For the weekend of the move to Admiralty House Jennie had offered to have the children with her at Salisbury Hall and since Winston was away on the *Enchantress* Clementine was free to accept an invitation to stay with the Asquiths at their country retreat, the Wharf, at Sutton Courtney near Abingdon in the Thames valley.

Such occasions were something of an ordeal for Clementine. Margot Asquith, small and thin with a hawk-like nose, shrewd eyes and a deep, vehement voice could be difficult company. She prided herself on her outrageous honesty and guests at the Wharf were often surprised by short critical notes from her when they got up in the morning. Although Asquith was quite different from his wife, Clementine was never quite easy with him either. She felt slow-witted and ill-educated in his company and she envied the ease with which both her sister and her sister-in-law dealt with him.

Although Clementine would have dearly loved a country retreat of her own, she did not particularly envy the Asquiths theirs. It was a strong red-brick house with leaded windows, which had been made by knocking together a public house and a cottage. The result was a series of small, inconvenient rooms. Margot did not herself sleep in the house but in a converted barn and guests were accommodated in the Mill House across the street from the Wharf. The only charm of the house was its proximity to the river and the ever-present noise of the nearby weir. Close by were the indispensable golf links, and during Clementine's visit golf was the party's occupation during the day and bridge at night.

It was not the kind of weekend that Clementine particularly enjoyed, but she accepted invitations from the Asquiths for the sake of Winston's career. For the same reason she found it hard to refuse an outright request from Margot for an invitation for herself, husband and step-daughter for a cruise on the *Enchantress* in May.

There was just time to take the children to their new home in the Admiralty and for Winston to sample the joys of his imposing bed decorated with gilded dolphins before they set off once more. This time the children were left in the care of a nanny; Winston had invited Jennie to accompany them, hoping that the cruise would take her mind off her impending divorce. He had warned his mother that she must try to avoid quarrelling with Margot, but the party had no sooner started on its way than the two women began an exchange of sarcasms creating an explosive atmosphere. This time they joined the *Enchantress* in Venice. Clementine would have loved to spend some time in the galleries and churches but Winston longed to be away. They set sail for Greece where they visited Athens and saw the Acropolis by moonlight before going on to Malta. The ostensible reason for this voyage was to enable Winston to examine the preparedness of the navy there. As on their previous visit there were naval exercises and receptions. And then it was back to England and a new way of life in Admiralty House.

There was no summer holiday by the seaside this year. For once Clementine remained in London. As she had remarked on leaving Eccleston Square, a chapter in her life had ended and she was now more than ever conscious of her position as the wife of an important member of the government. Winston might claim that they had few friends[6] but still there were plenty of people who, for whatever reason, wanted Clementine to grace a social occasion or dinner party, and she in her turn, as she had anticipated, was obliged to do much more entertaining. Her daily consultations with the cook were now longer and more intense as she strove to make Winston proud of her capacities as a hostess.

In July Clementine had an unusual outing with Margot Asquith when they went to hear a court case which involved Lady Sackville. The family of Sir John Murray Scott was contesting a will by which Sir John had left to her, his close friend, £150,000 and the very valuable contents of his house in rue Lafitte. The family argued that Lady Sackville had used undue influence on a dying man to secure his fortune for herself and they retained F. E. Smith to prove this and invalidate the will. The case had attracted a great deal of publicity so Clementine agreed to go with Margot on the day that F. E. Smith was to cross-examine Lady Sackville. F. E. Smith was accustomed to crushing his opponents in the Commons and he was confident that he could easily outwit a mere society lady. But to Clementine's utter delight Lady Sackville's responses to cross-questioning were witty and ingenious and she quickly had the sympathy of the whole court. Clementine, who hated Smith's attitude towards women, was not at all unhappy to see him lose this case because a woman had outwitted him. A far less entertaining court case was Jennie's divorce. By the end of July her marriage was over and she now dropped the name Cornwallis-West and reverted to Lady Randolph Churchill. She moved into a house at 24 Brook Street which she declared, to Clementine's consternation, would make it easier for her to be in close contact with her sons and their wives.

The absence of a summer holiday this year did not unduly trouble Clementine since there had already been so many journeys and so much upheaval with the move from Eccleston Square. The ones who suffered were the children. In previous years they had enjoyed at least two months of being close to their mother. This year they saw very little of her indeed and most of their time was spent in the nursery with nurserymaids. Although this was not an unusual situation, it was made worse for Randolph and Diana by the fact that the maids rarely stayed long and cared nothing for them as individuals. Before long Randolph had discovered that the way to make his mother pay attention was to be naughty. The more troublesome his behaviour the more the nurserymaids were driven to appeal to Clementine to intervene. The more unmanageable Randolph became, the more quickly the maids gave notice. There was no stability in the nursery whatsoever. Unconsciously Randolph must have hoped that the supply of maids would run out and his mother would have to be more present and available.

The problem was made worse by the fact that both children were handsome, Randolph especially so, and Winston liked to show them off and to hear them praised. And already he favoured his son over his daughter. Clementine was irritated by both children and at a loss as to how to control them. So Randolph and Diana had a see-saw existence of being ignored for long periods of time and then being made the centre of attention and admiration.

Troublesome children did not prevent Clementine from joining Winston for a further voyage on the *Enchantress*; Nellie and Goonie were invited too on this excursion first to Criccieth to visit the Lloyd Georges and then to Scotland where Winston left to pay his respects at Balmoral. The ladies spent a day at the races in Ayr where they unexpectedly met up with Nellie's twin, Bill. He was accompanied by a very pretty girl and Nellie immediately speculated about whether he intended to marry her; but Clementine had little doubt that the relationship would be short-lived, and she was right. Then the *Enchantress* took them all to the Isle of Arran where Liberal party meetings were interspersed with social gatherings. The end of the holiday was marked by an evening's entertainment on board the *Enchantress*. Winston and Nellie went on to stay with David and Ethel Beatty at the Invercauld Estate which the Beattys rented yearly for the grouse shooting. Winston had made Admiral David Beatty his Naval Secretary when he had moved to the Admiralty. Although Clementine liked the Admiral she was less fond of his wife. Ethel Field, the rich American heiress of the Marshall Field Company, had been married once before to Arthur Tree who had divorced her for desertion. It was not the fact of her being a divorcée which troubled Clementine, but that Ethel was spoilt, gambled heavily and often fell into childish tantrums. She was already showing signs of the mental disturbance which would claim her entirely in just a few years and she was not easy company. So Goonie and Clementine excused themselves from the visit to Invercauld on the pretext that they must attend to their homes and children before reassembling at Blenheim as Sunny's guests.

The awkwardness between Winston and his cousin had become less apparent since Winston had moved to the Admiralty and was less directly involved with the proposed land reforms which would affect the Duke of Marlborough. But it was unfortunate that during Clementine's stay Lloyd George made an important speech on Land Reform at Swindon. It was less than tactful of Clementine and Nellie to spend the morning following the speech reading aloud an account of it and praising its trenchancy. In response Sunny calculatedly put Clementine on the defensive by mocking the drunkenness of the Liberal Prime Minister Asquith and even went so far as to allude to Asquith's affair with Clementine and Nellie's cousin, Venetia Stanley. The latter was a matter on which Clementine was particularly sensitive since she herself disapproved of the Prime Minister's evident infatuation with an unmarried girl so very much younger than himself. The atmosphere at Blenheim was already strained when a telegram from Lloyd George himself arrived. Without thinking, Clementine went to the nearest writing desk to draft a reply. Sunny objected to Blenheim Palace notepaper being used to communicate with the man he saw as an enemy, and said so. At his words Clementine left the room, marched upstairs and ordered her maid to pack immediately. Goonie, who took her politics more lightly, urged her to calm down and to stay but Clementine would not be deterred. Sunny's apology for upsetting her and his request that she remain in his home were ignored also. Clementine swept out of the palace and returned to London. She quickly discovered that she had offended not only Sunny but also Winston. He regarded his family relationship to Sunny as being above politics and he was not pleased that Clementine had failed to observe his unspoken code.

In December, however, Clementine found herself in an unlikely alliance with both Sunny and F. E. Smith. Winston's flying instructor, Captain Gilbert Wildman Lushington was killed when his plane crashed. Horrified, Clementine realized just how risky were Winston's attempts to learn to fly. Her appeal to Winston to give up this new and dangerous pastime were supported by vehement requests along the same lines by the two men of whom he was most fond. It was the wrong moment to urge this on him: to stop flying because of the death of his instructor would have seemed like an act of cowardice to Winston and so, despite Clementine's distress, he continued.

Early in 1914 Clementine became pregnant for the fourth time and now she was anxious not only about Winston but also about her unborn child. She dreaded a repeat of the miserable experience of her last pregnancy and was, therefore, more inclined on this occasion to listen to her doctor and to take good care of herself. Always alarmed by speeding cars she now developed a fear of any but the most cautious driving and thus earned the contempt of Asquith. Clementine was staying at the Wharf on a weekend in March when terrible weather had made golf impossible. Asquith wrote to Venetia Stanley that the weekend's entertainment had consisted of trundling about 'at snail's pace (in deference to Clemmie's fears) in a shut up motor'.[7] In April, when she was invited to Spain as the guest of Ernest Cassel, along with his old friend Mrs Keppel and her daughter, Violet, she excused herself from accompanying the rest of the party to a bullfight for fear that it would be harmful to her condition. When, after the fight, she saw the white faces of her companions she knew she had been right.

She was in Paris, still Cassel's guest, when she received a series of letters from Winston expressing his concern about how much money they were spending and how necessary it was for them to economize in the future. Clementine knew that matters must be serious indeed for Winston to talk of economy: that was usually her role. She had anticipated and feared exactly this situation when she had first heard of the move to Admiralty House. She could have turned round and said 'I told you so'. But she did no such thing. Resisting the temptation to accept the offer of a valuable ring from one of Winston's associates she made her own attempt to raise money and alleviate their situation without telling anyone. She sold a valuable necklace which Winston had given her when they married to help pay their debts. With an additional, unborn Churchill to think about she could not bear the idea that they were in debt.

This puritanical side of her was reinforced by a visit, on her way back to England, to Dieppe to see her mother. Clementine was very uneasy at the way her mother continued to borrow money to enable her to gamble. When Winston wrote to tell her that Nellie had been a great success and had looked beautiful in a new dress at a ball given by Lord Curzon, Clementine wondered anxiously where Nellie had found the money for spectacular new clothes.

She had intended to return to London at the end of April but because she felt unwell delayed her journey. Then Winston wrote to say that the children were clamouring to join her in Dieppe. Whether they really were or whether he simple wanted them away from the Admiralty, they were soon in Dieppe staying with their grandmother while Clementine and Nellie shared Blanche's other property, a converted coach house, Petit St Antoine. The old routines of her girlhood were resumed as Clementine made daily trips to the market to bargain for vegetables and fruit. Just how distant she had become from her own children is shown in a letter written to Winston at this time in which she comments that she has had time to be with them and get to know them and that they seem to have some affection for her.[8]

In early June Winston made arrangements for the *Enchantress* to dock in Dieppe so that he could visit his family. He simply laughed at Clementine's disapproval of Blanche and her carelessness about money and to prove his point joined his mother-in-law at the Casino. These two saw eye-to-eye on many things. Unconventional and eccentric herself, Blanche did not at all worry that Winston drew unfavourable attention to himself by sitting 'outside the Hoziers' cabin on the promenade reading the daily papers with his bathing costume rolled down to expose an unusual amount of flesh roasted to an unlovely scarlet'. Simona Pakenham, a young girl who spent all her school holidays in Dieppe at that time and who knew Blanche Hozier well, recalls how 'ladies felt unable to walk on that part of the beach when he was there'.[9] In his turn Winston turned a blind eye to the way Blanche repeatedly broke quarantine laws by smuggling her scotch terrier into England under her voluminous clothes.

It was on this visit that Clementine at last convinced her husband that his flying really did disturb and upset her and she extracted from him a reluctant promise to stay away from planes at least until her child was safely delivered.

After almost three months' absence Clementine at last returned to London to join Goonie and her children at Overstrand in Norfolk where they planned to spend the summer by the sea at Pear Tree Cottage and Beehive Cottage. Somewhat misnamed, these houses, each with six bedrooms and a billiard room, had originally been rows of fishermen's cottages and had been converted into more substantial accommodation by the architect Edwin Lutyens, the brother-in-law of Constance Lytton. In this attractive setting everything seemed set for peace and quiet in the last stages of Clementine's pregnancy.

12

'This is your war station'

CLEMENTINE HAD KNOWN that Winston had viewed Germany as a potential enemy for some time and she knew that this had spurred him on to fight for increased spending on the navy earlier in the year. She herself had not felt that war with Germany was imminent and she was inclined to think that Winston's desire to see the navy in action had something to do with his attitude. Like most other people in England she had been more afraid that there would be civil war in and about Ireland as Unionists armed themselves in the north and National Volunteers did likewise in the south of Ireland. The break-down of the Buckingham Palace Conference intended to decide whether Fermanagh and Tyrone should be included with other Northern counties excluded from Home Rule reinforced this fear.

The assassination of Archduke Franz Ferdinand at Sarajevo had made little impression on her as on most people. There were many English in France in July 1914 who had no idea that war was possible. Elinor Glyn, for example, only realized that something was afoot when the Austrian Ambassador to France left a house party near Paris abruptly and without explanation and she found herself unable to change money to pay for her journey home. At another house party in Berwick-on-Tweed where the novelist Mary Borden was the hostess, Ford Madox Hueffer was alone of their number in anticipating that a war was imminent.[1] As late as August it was not certain that there was sufficient reason for cancelling the annual Cowes Regatta which the Kaiser usually attended.

So Clementine was far from unusual in taking her summer holiday with every hope of undisturbed tranquillity. Winston was due to visit his family at Overstrand on 24 July. Clementine's first real inkling that the situation was graver than she had previously understood came when her husband telephoned to cancel his visit because he felt he must be in London. Even then she was not unduly worried because Winston had so often in the past cancelled holiday arrangements for more important government business. When he did appear on the Saturday she was satisfied that there was no real danger. Like others now looking for signs she felt sure that Winston would not have left the Admiralty if there was the smallest chance that he would be needed there. On Sunday night Winston telephoned London to find out if there had been any further developments. He then decided that the situation was sufficiently critical for him to cut short his time with his family and return to London immediately.

Clementine's position was now difficult. On the one hand she desperately wanted to be with her husband if there really was a crisis; on the other hand if she were to leave the coast abruptly taking her family with her this would be read by everyone as a clear signal that a dangerous situation was developing and might result in a general panic. Clementine's sense of duty won out and she stayed where she was. When war was declared at 11 p.m. on 4 August there was a mass exodus from the coast, much to the dismay of those who earned their living from holidaymakers. Mrs Churchill's continued presence at Overstrand was pointed to by the local authorities attempting to reassure everyone that there was not the slightest danger in remaining at the seaside.

Winston himself was by no means so confident that his family was in a safe place and he urged Clementine to make sure that the car was in good repair in case she should need to leave Overstrand in a hurry, though it is difficult to see how all the members of both households could have fitted into one family car.

Blanche Hozier was still in Dieppe when war was declared. Quite unperturbed by the unfamiliar presence of uniformed French soldiers in the casino she continued to play *chemin de fer* nightly until the French authorities decided as a wartime measure to close the casino. It is rumoured that Blanche's addiction to gambling was greater than her fear of war and that she was the very last person to leave the place which was almost a second home to her.

Clementine's letters to her mother urging her to leave France had been ignored. When the ferry between Dieppe and England was suspended on 3 August Clementine grew seriously worried about what to do. As soon as a limited service was resumed Clementine sent Nellie to remove Blanche, by force if necessary, from Dieppe. She had offered to have her mother to stay with her at Pear Tree Cottage and, although she was not looking forward to the problems of entertaining her mother in that quiet place where there was no casino to satisfy Blanche's obsession, she hoped that Nellie's presence would be helpful. Nellie, however, had other ideas which did not include looking after her mother. Wild and irresponsible, Nellie had suddenly become aware of a world beyond her own tight social circle. Like so many other young women at this time she seized upon the opportunity presented by the war to do something more exacting than the usual social round. Learning that Lady Astor was setting up a convalescent home for the war wounded at Cliveden, Nellie abandoned her mother once they had reached London and left her to continue her journey alone while she travelled to Buckinghamshire. But the work at Cliveden quickly looked less exciting than the possibility of joining a nursing unit which was about to set out for Brussels and real action.

Clementine was angry with her sister for so readily turning her back on family responsibilities and setting off for the war as if to an unusual party. As her pregnancy came to term she was nervous and upset and haunted by nightmares that the baby would not be born normal. Now she had the additional burden of her mother, who was herself unwell after her hasty retreat from Dieppe and who was bored by family life at Overstrand. Then the news that the Germans had reached Brussels threw Blanche and Clementine into a fever of anxiety about Nellie. Their fears proved justified for, although Nellie and the unit had escaped Brussels in time, they had become mixed up in the retreat of the British Army from Mons where it had suffered a heavy defeat.

In September Clementine and her family returned to the Admiralty for the last month of Clementine's pregnancy. She was happy to be back with her husband, though she saw little of him since he was constantly on the move, visiting Dunkirk and British headquarters in France. Letters now began to arrive from Nellie with details of her capture by the Germans and her temporary imprisonment in a station waiting-room along with other members of the nursing unit. She described how she had written a patriotic and provocative jingle on the walls of the waiting-room. The Germans had not been provoked but had decided to make use of this supply of nursing help to deal with the many British wounded. Whilst admiring Nellie's spirit, Clementine fretted about her foolhardiness and feared that her attitude would bring more trouble on the unit.

Both she and her mother waited anxiously also for news of Nellie's twin brother Bill who was taking a more orthodox part in the war serving on a torpedo destroyer.

As September drew to a close these anxieties were further compounded by Winston's restlessness. The years he had spent building up the navy and making it a force capable of defending the country had been satisfying because full of positive action. But now the navy's role was essentially a waiting, defensive one and this did not suit Winston's temperament at all. His dissatisfaction was increased by the frequent questions in the press as to what exactly the navy was doing.

Clementine knew all this but even so she was not prepared in the last week of her pregnancy for Winston's precipitate departure to the heart of the action. A telegram from Belgium announcing that the King and army were about to leave Antwerp for Ghent and that Antwerp was likely to fall quickly to the Germans had determined the Cabinet to try to bolster up the Belgians by promising British reinforcements quickly. In the meantime someone with authority was needed in Antwerp to emphasize the need for resistance and the continuing presence of the King. Without hesitation Winston volunteered to go to Belgium immediately.

Clementine was devastated: she had hoped that for once her husband would be with her at the birth of their child. She was not sure that he was really needed in Antwerp or that he was the right man for the job. She could not help feeling that it was not only Winston's keen desire for action that motivated him but also a fear of being with her when she went into labour. Seemingly indifferent to her distress and her fears for his safety Winston left London on 3 October for beleaguered Antwerp. As Violet Bonham Carter commented, 'He could not turn his back on action',[2] not even for Clementine.

Throughout the time when Clementine had been in Overstrand and Winston had been in London she had insisted on knowing exactly what was going on. She has been criticized for her desire to know the precise details of Winston's thinking and planning at this time when he carried great responsibilities, and she has been described as being 'more than usually unimaginative and selfish'.[3] This is to misunderstand the nature of the relationship between husband and wife and to undervalue Clementine's accurate perception of her husband. In a letter written in November 1913 Winston had himself acknowledged that Clementine knew and understood him and that with her intuition she had 'measured the good and bad in his nature'.[4] She knew that Winston was accustomed to being politically and socially isolated. She knew that he was not fully sensitive to the new spirit abroad in the country after the declaration of war. A general feeling of euphoria had led to a greater sense of unity and a desire to co-operate. This could be seen in the way the leader of the Irish Nationalists, John Redmond, had declared his support for England during the war. Irishmen from the south were volunteering for the army; the Unionist Sir Edward Carson had agreed to postpone the Amendment Bill in the interests of unity; suffragettes had ceased hostilities against the government in order not to weaken the country internally during wartime; Conservatives had pledged their support for the war declared by the Liberals.

Clementine was aware that Winston had not adapted to these changes and that he was still in a confrontational mood and was likely to act in ways which would cause dissension and opposition rather than co-operation. As long as she knew what he was about she could advise and persuade and, she hoped, prevent him from taking damaging action. She already knew from his letters that Winston was no longer satisfied with being First Lord of the Admiralty; that he was impatient with the way others were managing the war; that he yearned for overall control and the leadership that was to come his way in the next war. Clementine knew instinctively in 1914 that it would be a mistake for him to make these feelings apparent. She urged her husband to be content with the very real power and position he had and to be careful not to alienate others by appearing to doubt their competence.

At the moment Winston appeared to be working amicably with Lord Kitchener who had once been his opponent and whom he had criticized freely as a young man. That they were able to co-operate now was in part the result of Clementine's friendliness to Kitchener and her hospitality to him at the Admiralty. But Clementine could see this delicate relationship being shattered if Winston continued to go to France to monitor the activities of the army there without consulting Kitchener. Her advice to Winston to tread more warily proved sound. Similarly she could see that Winston's desire to replace Admiral Callaghan, whom he considered past his best, with Admiral Jellicoe was not in itself a bad idea, but that his insensitive handling of the situation could cause resentment and lack of unity among naval hierarchy.

Her desire for information was not mere meddling curiosity but an attempt to understand the situation and so be able to give advice which was helpful to the country and to the progress of the war. This becomes especially clear when we see what happened when Clementine was for once without any influence over Winston's behaviour.

Once in Antwerp Winston was in his element. He was greeted as a saviour, his orders were obeyed and he could see that the Belgians were suddenly reinvigorated by his presence. Now he realized fully how much more to his taste was being in the thick of battle than sitting at a desk in the Admiralty. On an impulse, which Clementine surely would have curbed had she been in close contact with him, Winston sent a telegram to the Prime Minister offering his resignation from the Admiralty so that he could take command of the relieving and defensive forces assigned to Antwerp. His confidence in himself was such that he saw nothing wrong with the notion that he who had been a lieutenant in the Hussars was asking to be put in charge of Major Generals, Brigadiers and Colonels. It was exactly that complete lack of awareness of how his actions and words affected those around him that Clementine tried always to balance. When she heard of this telegram she was appalled and not even a kind and congratulatory letter on her hero husband from Sir Edward Grey disguised from her the fact that Winston's rash impulse had not only made him enemies it had also diminished his authority at the Admiralty in the eyes of his government colleagues. For Asquith, with some malice, had read the telegram aloud to the Cabinet as a whole. Even Winston's close friend and admirer, Violet Asquith, had to concede that he had behaved like 'a romantic child'.[5]

On 6 October as her labour pains began Clementine was relieved to know that her husband was on his way back to England. However, their child, a pretty, red-haired girl, was born in the early hours of 7 October many hours before Winston reached home. He returned full of the excitement of directing troops and decided that his daughter should be called Sarah after the wife of that most successful fighting man, the first Duke of Marlborough.

Now that she was divorced Jennie was more a part of the Churchills' life than she had previously been. She regularly walked across Hyde Park to see Winston at the Admiralty but Clementine rarely visited her and Goonie, now living on Cromwell Road, did not visit her at all now that Jack had gone to France with the Oxfordshires. Edwin Lutyens who dined with Jennie in the early months of the war wrote to his wife Emily telling her of Jennie's complaints about the lack of attention from her family and especially her daughters-in-law. She had told Lutyens that 'In her old age she is forsaken and has no friends – no strong arm to lean on.'[6]

This must have been one of Jennie's more melancholy evenings because what she said was not particularly true. As both Clementine and Goonie observed, there were plenty of men both young and old willing to escort their still beautiful mother-in-law to social occasions.

Jennie's nephew, Norman Leslie, was one of the earliest casualties of the war. Rather than stay at home grieving, his mother, Jennie's sister Leonie, had volunteered for the less than glamorous job of washing up at a canteen for servicemen at Victoria Station. Before long Jennie, too, decided to make a contribution to the war effort. Initially she chose the more congenial occupation of touring the troop camps and hospitals along with her friend Lady Warrender bringing some lightness and glamour into the men's lives by playing the piano and singing. For the moment Clementine was too frail to think of war work but she would anyway have been deterred by Winston's attitude towards those close to him undertaking any occupations which might diminish their attentions to him. When Violet Asquith told him that she was planning to train as a nurse he wrote reprovingly to her saying that she must stay at home by her father's side because, 'We who are directing these immense and complicated operations . . . need every comfort, care and cosseting . . . *We* are your duty. This is your war station.'[7]

When the war had begun in August there had been optimistic predictions that it would be over by Christmas. But as Clementine and Goonie set off to Kent to enable Clementine to recover from the birth of her daughter there was no sign that another two months would bring victory to England. They had been invited to stay at Belcaire later renamed Port Lympne, the constituency home of the fabulously rich MP for Hythe, Sir Philip Sassoon. When an unrepentant Nellie arrived back in England after being thrown out of Belgium for refusing to nurse German soldiers, her stories brought into the tranquillity of Kent some of the horrors already being experienced by British soldiers. Goonie more than ever felt grateful that Winston had used his influence to get Jack removed from the trenches and into a safer staff position.

It was while Clementine was safely out of the way in the country that Winston made another reckless move. This time it was not only Clementine who protested but also the King. Ugly feeling had been growing against Germans in England as the list of the dead and wounded grew at an alarming rate. A victim of this hostility was Prince Louis of Battenberg whose parents had been German. Public opinion was such that he felt unable to continue as First Sea Lord and offered his resignation. Winston was in no doubt about who to appoint as his successor: he wanted Lord Fisher. The King did not; he argued, on the grounds of Fisher's age, the fact that the navy did not trust him or have any confidence in him. Clementine argued that he was malevolent and a megalomaniac. But Fisher had an attraction for Winston similar to that of F. E. Smith and he was deaf to Clementine's advice. The new First Sea Lord was appointed and began to work in close harmony with the First Lord. Clementine knew that when she returned to the Admiralty Fisher would be very much in evidence. But the Admiralty was her 'war station' and return she did.

Clementine and her contemporaries were now beginning to take the war seriously as they lost friends and relatives. Clement and David Mitford, sons of Bertram and Clementine were both at the front. Clement was in active service while David who had been seriously injured in the Boer War was a Transport Officer. Early in 1915 Clement was killed in action; the cousin who so closely resembled Clementine in both appearance and temperament was now Lord Redesdale's heir.

The earlier euphoria which had swept England was gone and London itself was transformed. At night the streets were almost completely dark as a result of the tops of the street lamps being painted black and the black curtains and shades at every window. Everywhere there were young men in uniform, some heavily bandaged, many limping, all overseen by the accusing eye and pointing finger of Kitchener in his recruiting posters. Many of the young women now wore nurses' uniforms and there was a palpable tension in the air. Violet and Margot Asquith accompanied by Cynthia and her husband went to France to review the work of the Red Cross. Jennie moved on from being an entertainer to organizing buffets at railway stations, chairing a hospital committee and even acting as Matron for the Lancaster Gate Hospital. Venetia Stanley, despite opposition from every quarter, began her training as a nurse. Nancy Astor was running the Canadian Red Cross hospital at Cliveden. Clementine's cousin Gertrude Bell was working in the Paris office of the Red Cross tracing the missing and the wounded. Cynthia Asquith was talking of doing factory work. Ethel Beatty, the wife of Admiral Beatty, was converting her yacht *Sheelah* to be used as a hospital ship. All over the country mansions and large houses were being prepared for use as hospitals and convalescent homes.

But as long as Winston was at the Admiralty Clementine's war work was of a very different nature. She now had a Scots nanny, Isabelle, whom she could trust and who seemed to have the children well in hand so that they occupied little of Clementine's time. It was her responsibility to be the gracious hostess at dinner parties at which she was often the only woman present and at which the business of war was discussed. She had to accompany Winston to naval occasions such as the inspection of the *Hood* in February. The sumptuous luncheon enjoyed by all present including Goonie, Violet and Edward Marsh already seemed faintly scandalous in view of what was happening in France. Clementine, however, was not merely a decorative addition to the party. When it was discovered by chance at the last moment that the *Hood* was about to sail with totally inadequate medical supplies it was Clementine who worked quickly and with ingenuity to remedy the defect, gaining praise even from Asquith.

On the whole, however, Clementine's life during the first months of 1915 was far less affected by the war than were the lives of many women. She continued to visit the Asquiths at the Wharf and Walmer Castle. She watched anxiously as her sister Nellie flirted with any man in sight, but her own standards remained as inflexible as ever. She would not, for example, accept a couturier dress from Alice Keppel for fear of becoming in some way obliged to the older woman, and she recoiled in horror when this former mistress of King Edward suggested that Clementine could promote Winston's career by taking a rich lover and even offered to suggest some likely candidates. On 1 April her birthday party was held as usual despite the war. At this time she could not have echoed the words of her mother-in-law who in an interview for *Harper's Bazaar* of January 1915 had pointed out that the war had changed the lives of women and taught them about work. So far Clementine continued with the routines which Jennie declared, but for the war, would still be women's common lot: 'We might have been pottering out our little humdrum lives, eating our chickens and going through our daily routine in comfort and smug complacency.'[8] Already, however, in April events were building up which would dramatically change the lives of many people, including Clementine.

13

Disgrace

SINCE THE BEGINNING of the year Clementine had listened to conversations in which Winston explored ideas for bringing the war to a speedier conclusion than could be envisaged if the trench war in France were to continue. Right at the outset of the war he had seen the possibilities of sending naval vessels through the narrows of the Dardanelles to Constantinople to secure passage for Russian ships blocked in the Black Sea. This plan had come to nothing but in February his impatience with the passive role of the navy in the war made him think once more of the Dardanelles.

Admiral Carden, who was on the spot in the Eastern Mediterranean, proposed a course of action whose potential pleased Winston immensely. He discussed the details with Clementine and then with the War Council. Everyone responded enthusiastically, so eager were they to find a way out of the slaughter going on in France. As the plan evolved the talk in the Admiralty and at 10 Downing Street was all of the Dardanelles and Constantinople. There was suddenly an air of optimism and the feeling that *the* plan for achieving victory had been found. Over her own dinner table Clementine heard Asquith and Lloyd George comment favourably on Winston's lucidity in explaining Carden's strategies which had achieved unanimous support in the War Council. A British Landing in Turkey would make possible an attack on the Austrian and German Empires from the east. It would also assist the Russians and above all compel Germany to divert troops from the Western Front. After Sir John French's admission that success on the Western Front was no more than barely possible the War Council was doubly eager to make a success of the

Dardanelles expedition. Even Clementine's dislike of Fisher was tempered during the early days of January by Winston's account of the older man's co-operation and his willingness to countersign all the commands being telegraphed to Admiral Carden.

But her suspicions were newly alerted when a puzzled Winston told her on 25 January 1915 that Fisher had produced a written renunciation of the whole Dardanelles plan which he wanted to distribute to all the members of the War Council. It now emerged that Fisher had not agreed with the actions that Winston was taking; that at the same time as he was signing orders he was writing to Admiral Jellicoe at Scapa Flow saying that he entirely disapproved of the Dardanelles plan because it would dangerously deplete the Home Fleet. Winston, with Jellicoe's backing, produced the documentation to prove that this fear was unfounded, and was therefore stunned to find Fisher's resignation on his desk. Asquith intervened, the resignation was withdrawn, but Fisher's behaviour at the War Council left no one in any doubt that he was unhappy about the Dardanelles plan. Even so the War Council reiterated its confidence in the strategy. Clementine was fearful about what Fisher would do next. She knew that such lack of confidence could damage the daring plan to seize Constantinople. At this very moment she noticed that suddenly the Dardanelles plan was being described as Winston's plan and she sensed danger.

Despite the way Fisher blew hot and cold, planning continued and on 19 February the attack on the fortifications guarding the entrance to the Strait was carried out successfully. But then after this promising start there were delays caused by bad weather and by the perceived difficulty in clearing mines in the Strait. At the Admiralty everyone waited in tense expectation for the next attack. When the telegram came to say that Carden expected to take Constantinople in two weeks there was great excitement. Clementine noted with cynicism Fisher's complete identification with the plan he had so nearly wrecked.

One of the advantages of living in the Admiralty which Clementine now appreciated was being at the nerve-centre of the war. With 10 Downing Street just a few steps away and the Admiralty's close contact with the Fleet there was little going on that Clementine did not know about. Sometimes Winston's excitement at news received was such that he would rush to tell his wife, as on the occasion when he thought that Greece had been persuaded to help in taking the Gallipoli peninsula. And then there were the days when the news was bad or frustrating, as when Admiral Carden had a break-down and had to be replaced the day before a planned attack. There was also the ongoing problem with Fisher. Whenever he feared that the Dardanelles plan was not going smoothly he offered his resignation. Clementine understood all too clearly that this man so beloved by the general public as a sort of reincarnation of Nelson was intent on being associated only with victory. She would have liked his resignation to have been accepted but understood that this would undermine public confidence in the management of the war. She hated to see Winston coaxing and persuading this man she so destested. But as the wife of the First Lord she had to keep her personal views to herself and be content with prompting Winston behind the scenes just as she had done when she advised him in the early days of the war to be careful not to offend Kitchener. He had taken her advice then on that particular matter but he had not realized, as Clementine had, just how necessary it was to avoid damaging Kitchener's dignity in any matter whatsoever. So that, although he had consulted with Kitchener about his visits to Sir John French in France, he had not thought of informing him about the nature of their discussions. Now, as Clementine had foreseen, Kitchener was offended and vital co-operation between navy and army broke down. During the impasse the Dardanelles operation was at a standstill. The original plan had presumed prompt and sustained action and the delays while hurt pride was soothed doomed the whole venture. By the time Kitchener had decided that he would make troops available under the command of Ian Hamilton it was too late. Winston, however, had high hopes of Hamilton whom he greatly admired. He did not pay attention to Clementine's comments about Hamilton's own large ego and unsuitability for a job that depended on a delicate balance of power between the Admiralty and the War Office, not even when Hamilton's parting words indicated that he would communicate only with Kitchener and not with Winston at the Admiralty.

By the middle of April when the campaign should have been long over the navy idled, waiting for Hamilton to act. Letters from Clementine's brother Bill caused further anxiety by describing how enforced idleness was eroding naval morale.

Only dimly aware of how completely her own fate was bound with that of the Dardanelles campaign, Clementine presided over the social life of the Admiralty in much the same way as usual. She was not so preoccupied with the war that she did not take a great interest in Nellie's latest conquest, the handsome Scots soldier Sir Archibald Sinclair. She approved of him and hoped that Nellie was about to settle down. She was aware of the continuing gossip about her cousin Venetia and the Prime Minister. Goonie had confided in her that she was sure that Venetia was Asquith's mistress. At the same time Clementine knew that Edwin Montagu, the ugly but charming and gentle Private Secretary of the Prime Minister, was in love with Venetia and wooing her persistently. Clementine found it hard to understand her cousin's behaviour, so alien was it to her own standards of conduct. At the same time she admired Venetia's perseverance in training as a nurse, despite all opposition, and her determination to go to France to join a nursing unit in May.

By the end of April the Dardanelles operation was no longer spoken of at Admiralty House with hope and enthusiasm. Clementine saw Winston's anxiety as the original plan which had been for the navy to achieve the capture of Constantinople changed to one in which the movements of the Fleet were entirely subordinated to those of the army seeking to establish a bridgehead at Gallipoli. Her husband was no longer in charge of the attack. Now that Ian Hamilton and Lord Kitchener had taken over entire responsibility for action she feared what the effect would be on Winston and the campaign. Every fear was confirmed when letters came from Jack describing what was happening at Gallipoli. Under the command of Hamilton and Kitchener the daring, swift naval attack had been transformed to a more terrible extension of exactly the kind of infantry warfare going on in France which it had been Winston's hope to bring to an end.

Clementine felt Winston's pain at the horror of this lost opportunity. She was angered by all the attacks on Winston in the press knowing as she did where responsibility truly lay. When Winston went to Paris to conclude delicate negotiations with Italy she wanted to defend him against those who criticized him for being away from England enjoying yet more jaunts. But to speak out would be to betray trust. All that she could think to do was to try to reduce some of the tension in the Admiralty itself by some judicious hospitality. She knew Winston's increasing difficulty in working with Admiral Lord Fisher. But, rather than admit that he had misjudged Fisher as a man, Winston had shown unusual patience in attempting to instil new faith in the Dardanelles expedition in the Admiral. Putting aside her dislike Clementine decided to reinforce her husband's efforts by showing good will and inviting Fisher to lunch. The occasion concluded amicably and as she said goodbye to the Admiral Clementine felt she had performed a useful service. But to her consternation, some time later in the afternoon, she found that the Admiral had not left but was wandering up and down the corridors in a seemingly nervous state. When Clementine appeared he spoke to her strangely. He told her that she was foolish and misguided not to understand what everyone else knew; that Winston's trips to Paris were not really for the purpose of negotiation but to visit his mistress there. Totally taken aback and very angry Clementine shouted at the Admiral telling him he was a silly old man and ordered him to leave immediately. When she reported these events to Winston she told him that she was sure that Fisher was no longer a stable person, that he was absolutely untrustworthy and that, for whatever reason, he clearly bore great ill will towards Winston himself. But even now she could not persuade Winston that Fisher presented a real threat. She could only hope that events themselves and the support of the Prime Minister would vindicate and protect her husband. What she did not know was that a member of her own family was taking steps which would make Asquith useless as an ally for some time to come.

Rumours about Venetia Stanley's intimacy with the Prime Minister had been well founded, though it was not until many years later that the incredible way in which Asquith had divulged every State secret in his possession to the young woman with whom he was infatuated became known. Until 14 May, when Venetia announced to her elderly admirer that she intended to marry Edwin Montagu, she knew at least as much and sometimes more about the country's business than any member of the War Council or the Cabinet. The Prime Minister was devastated by Venetia's defection and, as he saw it, betrayal. Overwhelmed by misery his grasp on escalating events slackened. He was in no mood to defend anyone, least of all Winston for whom, he had recently learned with some chagrin, Venetia had a soft spot, and certainly not Clementine, whom he suspected, incorrectly, of encouraging Venetia to marry rather than continue her affair with him. For some months he had been denigrating Clementine to Venetia calling in question her intelligence saying she was 'by no means a deep well', describing her as 'a thundering bore' and comparing her unfavourably with Goonie and Nellie both of whom had less rigid moral codes. He had even mocked her response to Mrs Keppel in the matter of the dress calling her very 'particular' in a way which did not suggest approval.[1]

Clementine was dismayed but not surprised when on 15 May Fisher again tendered his resignation. She was not even surprised to learn that this man whom she had never trusted was spreading word abroad of his resignation and that he was demanding absolute power over all the navy and its disposition as the condition of his return to office. But she was in no way prepared for the course events now took.

Winston had explained to her that now Fisher's resignation was common knowledge he would be obliged to defend the Dardanelles policy in the Commons. On the morning of 17 May Winston, as so often before, walked the short distance to Downing Street to show Asquith the speech he had prepared. There he learnt to his amazement that Asquith, who had earlier refused to entertain his suggestion of a coalition, had now responded positively to a Conservative request to form a National Government. The carefully prepared speech would not be suitable in the circumstances since in the new government Winston would no longer be First Lord of the Admiralty.

Clementine knew as soon as Winston returned to the Admiralty that something dreadful had happened. Although he had looked tired and strained when he left, he had looked like a man ready and eager for battle. He had so much wanted to put the true facts about the Dardanelles before the Commons and to be judged on them, not on the wild rumours which were flying about. He returned to the Admiralty looking like a man who had been dealt a mortal blow. Her own disbelief and anger at the apparent treachery of those they had trusted was as great as his despair. But she did not agree with Winston's decision to appeal to the Conservatives to look at his record in the hope that they would see that he must be left in position at the Admiralty. She did not share Winston's belief that the facts would vindicate him, knowing all too well how thoroughly the Tories hated him and how sweet they would find their revenge for his defection by keeping him out of the office in which he had taken such pride and pleasure. Even Sunny, remembering his quarrel with Clementine about Lloyd George, could not resist pointing out what a false friend the Welshman had proved to be: he had made absolutely no effort to support Winston's appeal for an opportunity to put the facts before the Commons.

After his initial depression Winston, with Clementine's support, determined not to give in without a fight. Still unwilling to see the full extent of Fisher's determination to have him dismissed from office, Winston tried to negotiate with him. Clementine went straight to the top and wrote a most forthright letter to the Prime Minister himself. Her defence of her husband was admirable and her perception of Asquith's motives accurate. But politically she was unwise to confront Asquith with his real weakness and to pronounce that she believed he had acted from reasons of expediency using the politician's well worn battle cry 'to restore public confidence'. Nor was her final rhetorical flourish likely to endear either herself or her husband to a man who was fighting to retain office himself. She suggested that it was not in England but in Germany that public opinion would be boosted by the dismissal of her husband.[2] She was right, of course, but this counted for little in the face of the formation of a new government, and all the wheeling and dealing that implied. Asquith in his position of weakness had to dismiss her comments as those of a maniac.

By 22 May there was no hope left, no possibility of finding a way of keeping Winston at the Admiralty. Asquith's words were brutally frank as he announced that the decision that Winston must leave the Admiralty was irrevocable.[3]

There were friends who remained loyal, even within Asquith's own family. His daughter-in-law Cynthia called on Clementine to try to comfort her and to sympathize. Edwin Montagu who found her in tears did his best and also wrote to her. Jennie was, of course, full of sympathy and as full of indignation on Winston's behalf as was Clementine herself.

It was not just the feeling of being betrayed and humiliated that Clementine found hard to accept. There were also immediate practical problems to solve. The elegant establishment in which they were living was no longer theirs by right. They could not simply return to Eccleston Square as this was still leased to Sir Edward Grey and in any event they could not now afford to live there. Asquith, apprised by his daughter Violet of the very real problems of rehousing a family of five at short notice, offered to let the Churchills stay at the Admiralty until they had made suitable alternative arrangements. But Clementine was in no mood to accept any favours from Asquith. Her pride was against doing so but she was also scornful that the Prime Minister did not realize the impossibility of running such an establishment on only half the salary that Winston had been paid as First Lord. She was in a fever of impatience to leave the premises she had not wanted to occupy in the first place. So desperate was she to move that she was willing to accept the temporary use of Wimborne House, Ivor Guest's luxurious and elegant establishment in Arlington Street.

Fortunately the Churchills had already negotiated to rent Hoe Farm in Sussex as a country retreat so that at least they could leave London for the weekends and lick their wounds in the quiet of the country. But it was unthinkable that they should leave London altogether at that moment. Winston was still negotiating for a Cabinet position. He still had hopes of playing a part in running the war. An agonized Clementine faced the reality of his situation. The papers were full of approval for his dismissal from the Admiralty. Even in his own constituency of Dundee the press was out for his blood. The rights and wrongs, the inspiration and the mismanagement of the Dardanelles and the Gallipoli campaign are still disputed today. Clementine was no military strategist and probably could not have argued her husband's case from that point of view, but she did have complete faith in his abilities in that direction. She was angered by what she saw as the gross disloyalty of both Asquith and Lloyd George whom Winston had considered his closest friends and political allies. She believed, probably correctly, that they were almost relieved to have found so suitable a scapegoat to divert attention from the mismanagement of the war and the seriousness of Britain's position. But she saw that public opinion was now so strongly against her husband that no government could easily contain him. At this moment she realized with full force the importance of a politician's public image. It was a lesson that she did not forget and which determined many of her actions in the future.

Eventually Winston was offered the sinecure position of Chancellor of the Duchy of Lancaster. He was humiliated to accept such an appointment but saw it as the only way of retaining a seat on the War Council. Clementine found some compensation in the salary; it was less than half what Winston had been earning but at least they would not be penniless. However, their reduced circumstances meant that they would have to live very differently. There could be no more exotic cruises at government expense; no more repaying of hospitality in the same way and there could be no grand establishment.

But the problem which confronted Clementine most vividly and most urgently was how to deal with Winston. The events of that week in May had utterly transformed him. Where he had been youthful, buoyant, energetic and optimistic, full of new plans and ideas, always cramming more into a day than was humanly possible, he now seemed to have aged suddenly and he carried himself like a man defeated. During the first weekend at Hoe Farm he had shown a flash of anger about Asquith, venting his rage to the most inappropriate person, Venetia Stanley, who was visiting with her fiancé, Edwin Montagu. But for the most part he was too depressed to show any fight at all.

When Clementine saw him stop short in his tracks with a blank unseeing gaze in his eyes she knew he was going over in his mind the sequence of events which had led to his downfall. Clementine felt how it pained him that he had been given no opportunity to explain himself either to his peers in the Commons or to the public at large. She knew that he was, therefore, apt to justify himself when any opportunity presented itself, even to those likely to be sympathetic to him. E. Ashmead-Bartlett, who had been the cause of Blanche's divorce, found himself a less than willing audience at a luncheon party given by Jennie. He described Winston at this time: 'He looks years older, his face is pale, he seems very depressed and he feels his retirement from the Admiralty.' In Bartlett's view Winston's downfall had come about because 'his nature rebelled at the prospect of sitting in an armchair directing naval strategy when others were actually fighting'.[4]

Clementine had to face a personal ordeal herself in June. She was not fond of speaking in public at the best of times. But earlier in the year she had been invited as a former pupil, now married to the First Lord of the Admiralty, to open a new wing at her old school in Berkhamsted. To go to such a public occasion when the papers were full of abuse of her husband was almost more than Clementine could bear. But if she went back on her word she feared she would confirm the view that she had something to be ashamed of. She determined to go through with the arrangement. She dressed with care and captured everyone with her elegant appearance. Her words were carefully chosen and expressed not only her sympathy with all the women in England suffering painfully the loss of husbands, fathers, brothers and sons, but also indicated how she had chosen to deal with her own misery. She spoke of 'stoic fortitude' in the face of 'agonizing sorrows'.

If Winston had found even the Admiralty an insufficient outlet for his energy he now had far less to occupy him in his new position. Denied the pressure of office and constant hard work he was overwhelmed by a depression far worse than that which had threatened him during his years at the Home Office. Clementine was frightened by her inability to reach him and to comfort him. She feared he might die simply because he had lost the will to live. No one, it seemed, could do or say anything to rouse him more than temporarily. She invited people to the Hoe Farm whom she thought he might like to see. Eddie Marsh came, bringing literary and social gossip, but Winston did not appear interested. Jennie came to do her best but Winston was merely polite. Even Nellie who usually made him laugh had no success.

Now Clementine was grateful for the presence of the children. For she discovered that in their company Winston could for short spells cast off his despair. They were of another world, they knew nothing of his failure, to them he was still exciting and powerful. And so instead of sending telegrams of national importance to the Fleet, Winston played rowdy games such as 'gorilla' with his children and nephews. Instead of supervising the laying down of ships he joined the children in making elaborate structures from Meccano.

Clementine found these the hardest days of her life so far. How could it be that she, his wife, could do so little for her husband at the worst time of his life? She found her position almost unbearable; to be the witness of such depths of despair and disillusionment and to feel the hopelessness of all her attempts to alleviate her husband's distress. It was, she found, almost more difficult to live with a man in a chronic state of depression than to suffer it herself.

It was Jennie who, almost by chance, set in motion the process which was to draw Winston to some extent out of his isolation and preoccupation with failure. Casting about for something which might interest him she had reminded him of how he had sometimes accompanied her when she had drawing lessons and she had recalled his own pleasure in painting when he had been at school. At the time her words appeared to have made little impression on Winston. Goonie had taken the process a step further. Like all well brought-up young ladies of the time she had learnt to draw and to paint watercolours. At Hoe Farm she often sat out in the garden and painted. She was surprised to find Winston taking an interest and she encouraged him to use the children's watercolours. Winston was diverted. But, as he explained to Clementine, watercolours were a lady's pastime. Real men used oils. Clementine seized on this, the first positive signs of interest in anything outside himself that her husband had shown for weeks. She rushed off and returned excitedly and hopefully with oil paints and brushes and all the paraphernalia necessary to get Winston started. Family rumour has it that she forgot vital turpentine, though it seems unlikely that Clementine, who had observed painters like Sickert at work at close quarters in Dieppe and later in Paris, would have been unaware that every oil painter needs turpentine. And she did contact Hazel Lavery, the wife of John Lavery, and a professional artist in her own right, who knew exactly what a beginner in oils would need. Clementine invited the beautiful Hazel, whom she had known as a neighbour in London, to visit Hoe Farm. It was an inspired move and one which Clementine never regretted. At last Winston had an occupation which absorbed and excited him and which lifted some of the burden of his constant brooding from those who loved him, especially Clementine.

Clementine's speech at Berkhamsted had referred to people putting aside their private griefs in order to concentrate their energies on winning the war. Her words had been sincere and she felt an almost desperate need to do something positive to prevent herself from being sucked into the vortex of Winston's depression. She felt that she could better help him if she herself had an outside occupation. She considered the possibilities open to her. Nursing was out of the question: the time she would have to spend training and the possibility of being sent abroad presented practical problems. She felt that her future was too uncertain for her to make any kind of long-term commitment and she knew that Winston would be opposed to her doing so. She could, like Cynthia Asquith work part-time in a factory making parts for respirators. She could learn to fold bandages for the Red Cross. Or she could join the likes of Leonie Leslie and Elinor Glyn and wash up in a forces canteen. She rejected all these but not because she was afraid of the work. What was uppermost in her mind at this time was that it was important for her to hold her head high and to act with a dignity which would enhance Winston's reputation. The notion that Winston had an important image to protect was beginning to motivate her actions and behaviour.

When the invitation came for Clementine to join the Young Men's Christian Association's newly formed Munition Workers' Auxiliary Committee she recognized that this was the opportunity for which she had been looking.

As the war had progressed many factories had been converted from other uses to supply the increasing need for ammunition and more and more people, especially women, were being employed. Some factory managers and owners had set up their own canteens. But these were usually inadequate in every way. In other factories the workers simply ate food they had brought from home amidst the dust and fumes of their workplace.

Lloyd George, who was now in charge of the production of munitions, recognized that productivity was better where the workforce was healthy. The idea of special canteens operated independently of factory owners was seen as a measure likely to bring about this improvement. Clementine's initial task was to set about creating new canteens at factories in north and north-east London. To achieve this she first had to interview factory managers and owners and persuade them that it was in their best financial interests to set aside a suitable space in which food could be served. All her powers of charm were brought to play in this the most difficult stage of the operation, for factory owners were inclined to see such measures as unnecessary pampering of the workers. Then the staff to run the canteens had to be found. There was very little money available, so for the most part Clementine had to appeal for voluntary workers. Recruiting was not so difficult; there were plenty of middle-class and upper-class women who had little to do, especially when their men were at war, and who welcomed the diversion and the notion that they were helping the war effort. But many of these women had never worked in a sustained way before and they did not fully appreciate the need for regular commitment over a long period of time. Some found the work less congenial and amusing than they had anticipated. Others would take time off at a moment's notice if a particularly attractive social function came their way. Clementine found it difficult keeping her volunteers up to the mark.

She had no formal training for the work she had undertaken but her recent experience running Admiralty House now proved useful and the capacity for resourcefulness and ingenuity she had already shown in the matter of the *Hood*'s medical supplies now came into full play. The relief she found in activity made her doubly sympathetic to Winston's frustration and dissatisfaction in being merely on the fringes of all that was important to him.

But there were more blows coming the way of the Churchills before that dreadful summer came to an end. Clementine shared Winston's astonishment and rage when Lord Fisher, the man who had abandoned his post and whom Asquith was reported as having said should be shot for treason, was now appointed chairman of the Admiralty's Committee on Invention and Research. The pain of this blow was only slightly alleviated the next week when briefly husband and wife had reason to hope that something might be salvaged from Winston's political career and his involvement with the Dardanelles. Asquith authorized Winston to go to the Dardanelles and Gallipoli to see for himself what was happening there. Clementine knew that Winston's mission was very dangerous because he would be under fire constantly. She was afraid that he would not come back alive, especially when she learnt that he had taken out a new insurance policy and arranged for a letter to be delivered to her in the event of his death. Nevertheless she made none of the objections she had made when Winston insisted on flying or going to Antwerp. She knew now as she had never known so completely before that such activity was vital to her husband's well-being and sense of himself. As he packed and prepared to leave that weekend she saw a return of some of his old spirit and vitality.

And so when, at the very last moment, his old Tory enemies vetoed his departure they both felt the blow with double force.

By now the housing problem had been solved, at least temporarily. Goonie and her children would share Hoe Farm at weekends while Clementine's family would share Goonie's house on Cromwell Road the rest of the time. The house was undeniably crowded with three adults, five children and servants. But all the costs were shared and only one staff needed to be maintained. Both women were grateful for this financial relief. Winston was to some extent sustained by his painting at the weekends and by being part of the Dardanelles Committee and having the opportunity to put forward schemes and to know at first hand how the war was progressing. It was not an ideal life, but it was by no means as bad as what others were facing. This came home to Clementine very vividly in September when unexpectedly Winston's cousin Clare appeared at Cromwell Road. She held her small daughter by the hand and carried in her arms her baby son. She was dressed entirely in black. Since Winston was not at home as she had hoped she poured out her sad tale to Clementine. Her beloved Wilfrid had been killed at the Front and she was now penniless. Knowing how Clare had suffered recently from the death of her one-year-old second daughter Clementine felt keenly for her grief at this terrible blow. And, on top of everything else, to have no money. In comparison her own lot was tolerable, Clementine reflected.

But it ceased to be so in November. The first significant sign that Winston's chances of improving his position in the government were negligible was Asquith's speech to the Commons on the matter of the Dardanelles on 2 November 1915. Clementine had hoped against hope that the speech would contain some word that would vindicate Winston. But it did not and Clementine recalled that other November speech which by its omissions had betrayed the cause of women's suffrage. Her anger against the Prime Minister was refuelled. Then on 6 November the Dardanelles Committee was renamed the War Cabinet. Winston was not offered a place in it. Now there was no escaping the fact that Winston had been firmly removed from the centre of activity. Despite the financial hardship which would result, Clementine accepted that her husband really could not stay in the Cabinet but must resign. At the very least this would give him the opportunity of making a speech in the Commons which would explain the Dardanelles campaign from his perspective.

Clementine was not the only person to be impressed by the speech he subsequently made. Violet Asquith described it as 'flawless'. And there was another small point of hope: not all the press was as confidently hostile to Winston as it had been in May. The editorial in the *Manchester Guardian* asserted of Winston, 'he has the best strategic sense in the Government'.[5]

Clementine had long sensed what Winston's next move would be. And she knew she had to accept it whatever it cost her in worry, distress, loneliness and hardship. The only way that her husband could be at peace with himself after the senseless loss of life at Gallipoli was to risk his own life and join those fighting at the Front. Clementine hoped that he might be given a command but Asquith and Kitchener were in no mood to offer him anything, despite his experience and knowledge. And so it was as a Lieutenant Major in the Oxfordshire Hussars that her husband prepared to go to France.

14

A Soldier's Wife

THERE WAS JUST one week between Winston's resignation and his departure for France. In that time all his kit had to be assembled and packed and there was a farewell luncheon to arrange. During that week there was chaos in the Cromwell Road house. Emotions ran very high: Jennie wept, fearful of what might happen now that she had two sons in France. Violet Asquith was in and out making suggestions and offering gifts. Eddie Marsh, whose own career was so closely bound with Winston's, feared for himself as well as for his friend. The children, picking up on the emotionally charged atmosphere, were naughtier than usual. There was a steady stream of callers wishing to say goodbye to Winston. But through it all Clementine gave the impression of calm. Everyone who called at the house remarked upon her serenity with surprise. It was not just the 'stoic fortitude' of which she had spoken at Berkhamsted that sustained her, but also relief at her husband's decision. It was true that he would be in danger, more danger than absolutely necessary, she suspected. However, during the time since he had left the Admiralty he had been in danger of a different kind. She had feared for his sanity and she had feared that his grief might kill him. The days of enforced inactivity had placed a heavy burden on her and on their relationship. She had been distressed to see him grasp at remote hints and chances that the government needed him after all, only to have his hopes dashed time after time. Seeing Fisher restored to favour, despite all he had done, had been the most insufferable insult as far as Clementine was concerned. Now, to see Winston busy, making plans and arrangements and above all having a sense of a future, which he had sadly lacked of late, gave Clementine herself renewed hope.

She accepted that the only way for her husband to cauterize his feelings of shame was for him to participate in the dangers and horrors to which the policies of the government of which he had been a part had condemned so many other men. Seen in this context Clementine's calm is less surprising.

The farewell luncheon was one that she could have done without. She knew it was a necessary act of bravado on Winston's part to leave with his head held high. For that reason Margot and Violet Asquith had to be invited as well as Nellie and Edward Marsh. Inevitably Winston and Margot crossed swords but, despite Nellie's attempts to lighten the atmosphere, the luncheon resembled nothing more closely than a wake.

On 18 November Clementine saw Winston off on his way to France. He again left a letter for her to be opened in the event of his death. He did not, however, leave her with the impression of a man facing death; rather, she felt his sense of purpose and destiny which had deserted him during the months of grief.

Clementine returned to Cromwell Road; the house seemed larger and emptier with Winston and all his kit gone. Now the two women had to reassess their situation and make decisions about their immediate future. The most pressing problem was money. Both Jack and Winston were now earning less and, although there was a saving in combining household expenses, everyone still had to be fed and clothed. Jennie had turned her hand to journalism of late and she offered to make a financial contribution to the joint household. Goonie and Clementine alike treasured their independence but had to accept this offer of help. They even agreed with Jennie that it made no sense for her to spend money on separate accommodation and that as soon as she could rent out her house she too would move into Cromwell Road. It did not take both Goonie and Clementine to run the house, especially when Jennie was willing and eager to spend more time with her grandchildren. Goonie had little inclination to work outside the home and it was, anyway, her house. So it was agreed that Goonie would keep house, Jennie would write and work on her committees, while Clementine continued with her canteen work.

When Clementine and Winston had decided to economize in order to manage on his officer's pay, the first sacrifice had been the car. Now with several canteens established Clementine had to visit them all using public transport. Just as when she was a girl she found herself leading a life far closer to that of most ordinary people than she had become accustomed to since she had married Winston. She realized again how tiring it was to travel by train and tram and how much energy was wasted standing about waiting. But if her days were long, she was aware that the working hours of the women in the munition factories were worse. The factories were working at full stretch and that meant everyone working on shifts. Each shift was twelve hours long and those twelve hours were spent doing tedious, repetitive but dangerous work handling toxic materials. The women and girls who worked in the munition factories were readily identifiable, for the 'munitionettes', as the newspapers patronizingly called them, all had yellow-tinged skin from their contact with chemicals.

Clementine's objective was to make sure that these women and the men they worked with could spend at least a portion of their working day in more civilized surroundings with adequate toilet facilities, seats during meals and cheap but nutritious food. It was an uphill struggle at times. One of the biggest problems she encountered in the early days was one which existed on the factory floor itself. The men in the factories were resentful and suspicious of the influx of female labour. They feared for their own jobs and for those of men returning from the war. At first they grumbled about mixed sittings for meals, then they objected to seeing women smoking in public. But Clementine was on the side of the women and she usually managed to smooth the ruffled pride of the men. In some of the canteens there were protests about the cost of the meals provided; but as the war dragged on and good food became scarcer workers began to express appreciation that they were guaranteed at least one good meal a day without having to queue for the ingredients.

Clementine was seeing first-hand how most people's lives were being affected by wartime conditions. But still she was more privileged than most. She certainly returned home at night tired and sometimes frustrated. She did, however, return to a comfortable, well-run house in which her children had been adequately cared for. She did not have to start queuing and cooking and cleaning as did so many women after their shift at the factory. She was, like all soldier's wives, worried about her husband, and Winston's letters to her left her in no doubt about the vile conditions in the trenches and the dangers he was exposed to. However, unlike many women receiving letters from the Front, she found that those from Winston gave her a sense of renewal. In the first week he was clearly glad to be where he was, active and in the company of men. The reports she received from those who had actually seen him suggested that, contrary to her fears, army life was suiting him and he looked a younger and healthier man than the one who had left London. To her surprise, the long days of hard work were not proving detrimental to her health either. She was a perfect example of the phenomenon observed by the Health of Munitions Workers Committee, that women's health actually improved during the war 'thanks to more interesting work'.[1] As Jennie prepared her book *Women's War Work*, Clementine was surely one of the women she had in mind when she asserted, 'We shall be able to clear our minds of the empty cant that may survive about women's physical limitations. No one was ever much concerned with these limitations in the case of charwomen or sick nurses.'[2]

Nevertheless war work had not entirely replaced Winston as Clementine's central focus. From France he sent long lists of items he needed or wanted. Clementine searched assiduously for such things as trench wading boots and a sheepskin sleeping bag, although this kind of equipment was becoming increasingly difficult to obtain in London. She sent food parcels and even bottles of old brandy and peach brandy he asked for. How many other soldiers in France at this time felt able to write home for such luxuries? Every letter brought more requests and each request took time and trouble to meet. Clementine never complained: she was only too aware of the discomfort of life at the Front and willingly did all she could to improve Winston's situation. She was very much like Mrs Everest in the old days when she had sent food parcels with treats to Winston at school.

When Winston had first left for France one comfort that Clementine had drawn from his departure was that he would be far removed from the London political scene and what she saw as its infighting, treachery and disloyalty. She herself had been glad to withdraw as far as possible from the social-political scene in which she had once been a central figure. She missed knowing exactly what was going on but she did not miss the company of those in government. She found it especially difficult to put her relationship with the Asquiths on a new footing, and in this Goonie's immediate presence was very helpful to her. The Asquith women tried to behave as if nothing had changed. Margot and her daughter Elizabeth took tea at Cromwell Road. Clementine and Goonie were invited for lunch at 10 Downing Street, though Asquith himself was not present. Violet even chose Randolph to be her page when she married the Prime Minister's Private Secretary, Maurice Bonham Carter, on 30 November in St Margaret's Westminster. Clementine had reservations about such a glamorous affair in wartime. She suspected Asquith, whom she described to Winston as being 'sleek and complacent', of using the occasion to bolster his own popularity. Nevertheless, she delighted in the way Randolph charmed all the wedding guests, especially the ladies, and she wrote of it to Winston, knowing how he revelled in his son's success. She described to him how beautiful Randolph had looked in his Russian velvet suit trimmed with fur.

Violet's wedding was not the only one that concerned Clementine as this troubled year drew to a close. For almost a month Nellie had blown hot and cold about marrying Bertram Romilly, as planned, on 4 December. She had met him during the summer when he had returned from his regiment, the Scots Guards, with a head wound and had soon after become engaged to him. Blanche had no objections to the match, especially since Bertram's mother, Lady Arabella, was an old friend. Clementine, on the other hand, worried that Nellie had fallen for Bertram's good looks and charm. She feared that the head wound Bertram had suffered would make him something of an invalid for the rest of his life and that he would not be able to keep up with the hectic social life Nellie enjoyed. She was not sure that the pity Nellie clearly felt for her fiancé was an adequate basis for marriage. Nellie was first convinced by Clementine's arguments but then rejected them completely and resented the fact that her sister had expressed any reservations. Goonie, who agreed in principle with Clementine, advised her to let Nellie have her own way with a good grace.

In Nellie's autobiographical novel the central character, Nancy, had, like Nellie, 'found herself swept away in the passionate zest of serving her country'.[3] She nurses a young man who has been wounded and he proposes to her repeatedly. Just as Nellie had havered so does Nancy 'but a voice seemed to whisper to her, "No, no. Escape while there is yet time."'[4] Nancy marries Gerald but after some years her verdict on the relationship is 'that they were like two animals penned in a small cage, who might, if life had turned out better, have been roaming the wilds'.[5] So, as Nellie's novel suggests, Clementine's apprehensions were by no means misplaced.

On 4 December Nellie was married from the Cromwell Road house with Diana and Randolph and Goonie's son, Johnny, as attendants. Just as she had done for Clementine in 1908, Lady St Helier gave the wedding reception in her house in Portland Place. The three children looked angelic but Clementine knew that their appearance was deceptive. In that household of five children with no adult male present Randolph was already the ringleader and his behaviour was increasingly troublesome.

None of her worry on this score was expressed in her letters to Winston. On the contrary she went out of her way to recount anything that Randolph said or did which suggested his precosity. The only concern she did express was about Sarah who was worryingly frail and whose painful bouts of neuralgia greatly distressed her. Letters between husband and wife were exchanged almost daily and Clementine found this close contact a great comfort. Yet there were matters which could not be dealt with adequately either through letters or the occasional exchange over the phone from the Admiralty where Clementine had to shout into the mouthpiece, uncomfortably aware of being overheard. Winston who had accepted his rank of Major without complaint on his first arrival in France was now impatient to be promoted to a rank where he had some real power. As he told Clementine, he was confident that he could achieve far more than those in power who were, he considered, bungling the war. A visit to general headquarters in late November increased his restlessness but he was prepared to accept the advice of Lord Cavan to proceed carefully, to give his enemies nothing to exploit and to be satisfied with the command of a battalion before aspiring to a brigade. This was advice with which Clementine, far more sensitive to the current political atmosphere in London, agreed whole-heartedly and she expressed her views to Winston in a letter written on Nellie's wedding day. But by the time her letter reached him, Winston, encouraged by Sir John French, had his sights once again set on a brigade. So certain was he of receiving command of the 56th Brigade that he asked Clementine to secretly order him the appropriate uniform. When Clementine reported to him that she had heard via Goonie that Kitchener was impressed by his paper on trench warfare, he began to regard his promotion as secure.

But Clementine still had doubts. Conversations she had with Lord Esher and Eddie Marsh convinced her that the Tories at home would protest Winston's promotion vigorously and would be likely to sway the ever-wavering Asquith to their point of view. She continued to urge Winston to move carefully. Clementine's perceptions and her judgements of how key figures were likely to act in this matter were accurate. Winston was angered by her insistence and wrote in no uncertain terms to tell her so. Clementine was upset by two letters attacking her and the first note of reproach enters the correspondence at this time. But both she and Winston, mindful of how the future might view the sender of the two bitter and angry letters, were in agreement that they should be burnt.

Clementine was, of course, vindicated, but this was cold comfort to her. Sir John French did recommend Winston for a brigade, Asquith did agree with apparent pleasure, then only hours later, learning that the Tories would attack this appointment, withdrew his approval.

At least, Clementine hoped, the episode would have disabused Winston of any hopes he might have had of Asquith's friendship. She was not all dismayed by Winston's directive that she should refuse to discuss his affairs with the Prime Minister and should in every way hold herself aloof from him; it was exactly what she wanted to do. She was, however, sad that Winston's reputation had taken a further knock. Had she been able to talk to him and influence him by her presence, she was confident that things would have turned out differently.

Winston had been gone only a month when he and Clementine began to talk of his getting leave. It was Clementine's suggestion that she should meet him in Paris for a few days which they could spend alone. In the event he was back in London on Christmas Eve but his leave was only three days long. Clementine had so looked forward to this reunion that it could not fail to disappoint. She had anticipated spending time alone with her husband but she managed to have him to herself for brief snatched intervals only. At home everyone wanted to be with him, especially the children to whom he seemed like a hero in his uniform. Winston himself wanted to see people to keep his finger on the political pulse. He even had an interview with Asquith. By the Monday of his departure Clementine was exhausted and frustrated. Even their last moments together were spoilt by a frantic dash to catch the train.

Clementine's poise and security had been shattered by that whirlwind weekend. But she had to pull herself together to do as Winston had requested and attempt to keep all political avenues open by having lunch with Lloyd George. Her personal choice would have been to have nothing further to do with him: she trusted him not at all, describing him as being descended from Judas Iscariot.[6] Once in his company, even though she was aware that his eyes never met hers, his habitual charm towards women made the occasion easier than she had feared. Most importantly the conversation enabled her to supply Winston with information about what was going on in the Cabinet.

With this meeting behind her Clementine thankfully left London for Alderley, the countryside and a household which ran smoothly and was undisturbed by political upheaval and intensity of emotion. Three of her cousins were there and Venetia joined them later. They were all very conscious of their menfolk in France: only Venetia's husband had a London job. Being at Alderley gave Clementine an opportunity to assess and plan for the future. She agreed with Winston that their fortunes could hardly suffer again such a rapid decline as they had done since the last New Year. Winston's appointment as Lieutenant Colonel with the 6th Royal Scots Fusiliers gave her some hope that their fortunes might actually be on the mend.

In company where Asquith was regarded with respect and affection (Venetia had recently been the object of his devotion and now Sylvia was his intimate confidante) Clementine saw that it would be a tactical error to risk alienating the Prime Minister. She could be most helpful to Winston by cultivating the friendship of the Asquiths rather than allowing them to see herself and Winston as problems. Winston had reservations about her judgement but as soon as she arrived back in London Clementine began her campaign to re-establish good relations with the Prime Minister and his family by taking tea with Margot. This was quickly followed by a lunch at Downing Street at which Asquith himself was present. Asquith had no high regard for Clementine's intellect or abilities though he admired her beauty. He was completely unaware of the skilful way in which Clementine created a situation in which he suddenly felt more warmly affectionate to her than he had done for some time. He had no idea that she was playing a role and pretending to be the kind of woman he liked when she turned the conversation to feminine topics such as he enjoyed. She made no mention of politics and when Asquith tentatively asked her about Winston she painted for him a picture of her husband happy in his new command and delighting in taking a physically active part in the war. Her tone was calculated and based on an acute and accurate perception of the kind of man Asquith was. She described him to Winston as 'a sensualist' who, if she had spoken her heart and presented her husband in the 'tragic and sinister light' in which she saw him, would have failed to enjoy his meal and would, therefore, have been reluctant to invite her again. Clementine's strategy worked. More invitations were given and accepted and Clementine was even invited to Walmer Castle to play golf with Asquith.

The only pleasure she derived from these occasions was the knowledge that they gave her the opportunity of observing Asquith and assessing his strengths and weaknesses, thus enabling her to give Winston informed advice. She was, for example, far more aware than was Winston of the strength of the Prime Minister's position and his means of sustaining it. Her description in a letter written on 11 January is as vivid as it is accurate. She identifies Asquith's strategy against his enemies as one that does not rely on considered and swiftly delivered attacks but on behaving like a rubber ball, absorbing all attacks until the enemy gives up hope of making any impression.[7] This is a far more telling description than the commonly used one of Asquith as 'The Block'. Her account of the measures she would need to take before shaking Lloyd George's hand gives a new meaning to his nickname, 'Welsh Wizard'. She says she would need every kind of charm and to cross herself.[8]

In the early weeks of 1916, with her husband away in France, Clementine was discovering new powers in herself. Not only could she manipulate and charm people, she could also grasp a situation and explain it clearly and logically with well-chosen and telling details. Her letters to her husband at this time show this ability very clearly. They are different from the letters of their early marriage and they reflect a difference in Clementine herself. The rather shy, earnest, unsophisticated and somewhat prudish young woman had gone completely. She was to say later in the year in a different context that no character went unsearched by war.[9] In the search her character had not been found wanting. Somewhat reluctantly, even Winston accepted that Clementine had often perceived situations with a greater wisdom than his own and that her advice had been worth following.

Gone now were the days when Clementine would receive her cook in her bedroom and leisurely plan the day's menus. Now she was up early every day writing letters to Winston before breakfasting downstairs, occasionally with the children. She was usually at one of her canteens by nine o'clock and often worked until about 7.30 p.m. She was especially busy at this time organizing a new canteen at Hackney Marshes to feed over a thousand. She was very keen to have all in order by opening day since Lloyd George himself was to officiate. There were rumours that the men at the factory would strike as a protest against Lloyd George because they resented the way he had encouraged the use of female labour. In the event the opening was a great success and Clementine was touched by the way the men singled her out for their expressions of appreciation.

She was very interested in the way women had adapted to work normally considered suitable only for men. She saw for herself that one reason why the men felt threatened was the speed with which women learnt new tasks. She was impressed by how much these women could

earn, whilst being conscious of the fact that there was even in these circumstances no thought of equal pay for equal work. When she visited the
Woolwich Arsenal with Lady Henry Grosvenor, she noted the high
spirits of the young girls and, remembering the suffragettes, she perceived that it was the kind of strong-minded purposeful women who had
fought for women's rights and had been identified as unnatural who were
now indispensable in positions of responsibility as forewomen in heavy
industry. When she visited the Office of Munitions where women and
girls were employed in jobs traditionally regarded as women's work, she
found the workers less admirable. While the women at Woolwich read
advanced books, the clerks in the Office of Munitions seemed more concerned with their appearance than anything else.

After a hard day's work in what Clementine was increasingly beginning to see as 'the real world' she found it an effort to change her clothes
and do a second job by entertaining or being entertained by those who
could be useful to Winston's rehabilitation as a prominent figure in the
government. She found it difficult on these evenings to relate to the
women she met who did not, like herself, have a husband in danger, and
she found the men in government unbearably smug and complacent. It
was at one of these social occasions that she met a 'South African poten-
tate', Sir Abe Bailey. Little did she know at the time that he would one
day become the father-in-law of little Diana who with her new shorter
hair cut at this time looked like Peter Pan. At another dinner party Arthur
Balfour warned her to watch out for Jacky Fisher.[10]

So it was with a sinking heart that Clementine received Winston's
request that she make contact with 'The Fiend', as he had come to
describe Fisher. She knew Winston had never ceased to fret about the
Dardanelles. When the possibility of the publication of the papers relating to the expedition was rumoured, she had urged him not to write to
Asquith, not to take any step at all without consulting her. She had done
all that she could to further his future, consorting with Curzon, with
Lloyd George, McKenna, Balfour and Asquith himself. But she
absolutely refused to approach Fisher. She could hardly believe that,
after all that had happened, her husband would make this request of her.
It was an instance of Winston's complete insensitivity to the feelings of
others.

Afraid that Winston was preparing to make new and strange alliances,
Clementine was glad that he was due for a week's leave. Her hope was that
faced with the reality of the political situation in England he would be

more inclined to accept the validity of her perceptions and to take her advice.

Winston's plans for his leave left her in no doubt that he was not intending to spend his time in the bosom of his family. It was true that he wanted time slots allocated to dinner with Jennie and dinner with her but he wanted at least one night out with the men and he wanted political friends and associates invited for lunch every day. One of those he insisted must be invited was Lord Fisher. Despite her misgivings, Clementine dutifully set about making complicated plans for the first week in March. To prepare the ground with Asquith she arranged a dinner party designed to give him maximum satisfaction. She contrived delicious food, invited handsome women, and the numbers present allowed for the two tables of bridge in which he delighted.

When Winston arrived in Dover Clementine made sure of spending some time alone with him by meeting him there and they spent the first night of their reunion together at the Lord Warden Hotel. As far as Clementine was concerned this was the high point of her husband's leave. Once they were back in London very little went as she had hoped or planned. The lunch with Lord Fisher was a disaster. Clementine could see before her very eyes Winston becoming fascinated all over again by the Admiral, being drawn into accepting an unreal assessment of the situation and talked into actions designed primarily to benefit Fisher. She is reported to have become so angry that she violated all her own notions of hospitality and, making no attempt to hide her hostility, said to Fisher, 'Keep your hands off my husband. You have all but ruined him once. Leave him alone now.'[11]

It was as if Winston were mesmerized by the old man and could not hear his wife's pleas to have nothing to do with this person whom Clementine some days later described as a powerful and dangerous machine.[12] At the dinner party Clementine had arranged for the Asquiths her careful preparations to make Asquith look favourably on her husband were undermined when Winston revealed to Asquith something of what he intended to say when he spoke in the House in the debate on Naval Estimates. Clementine had always been opposed to his making that particular speech at that particular moment. Nevertheless, along with Eddie Marsh, Violet and others she sat in the Visitors' Gallery to hear her husband speak. His speech was an out and out attack on his successor Balfour and his work at the Admiralty; it was forceful and well documented. The House listened respectfully. Clementine was proud of his performance and she began to think that she had been wrong to advise him against speaking. But in the closing words of his speech came the shattering blow. Seemingly oblivious of all that he had said publicly in the recent past, Winston now called for the reinstatement of Fisher as First Sea Lord. Clementine was shocked and angry. There was laughter in the House as the absurdity of Winston's demand struck MPs and she could see clearly that all the good he had achieved in his speech had been completely undermined by his call for Fisher. She could hardly bear to look at her companions. Eddie Marsh was in tears; Violet was white with distress and Margot was glaring at Winston as though she would have liked to hit him. Clementine never saw Margot's letter to Balfour in which she described Winston as 'a hound of the lowest sense of political honour' and 'a fool of the lowest judgment and contemptible'[13] but her demeanour said it all.

So absorbed had Winston been in hearing only those he wanted to hear that he was completely taken aback when he left the House by Clementine's distress at what he had done. She knew, as he had apparently not anticipated, that all Balfour had to do in response to Winston's speech was to quote back at him his public criticisms of Fisher. Winston had himself effectively provided Balfour with the means of rebutting the substance of his speech. For he could claim that no man could take seriously the criticisms of someone who could say such contradictory things and show such uncertain judgement.

The atmosphere at Cromwell Road can be deduced from the conversation a pale and strained-looking Winston had with Violet Bonham Carter. His very first words to her were, 'I suppose you are against me like the rest of them.'[14]

Clementine's hopes that Winston would see for himself that he was better off at the Front than in parliament were dashed when he announced his intention of resigning from the army. He went so far as to send his resignation to Kitchener. Then he was persuaded by Asquith to retract. Even on the train to Dover Clementine and Winston tossed the argument backwards and forwards. When Winston had left, Clementine spent a miserable night alone at the Lord Warden Hotel looking back over the last few eventful and bitterly disappointing days. She found herself in a most painful situation. She knew that Winston's return to political life at that very moment when his reputation was once again in shreds and when no one in the Cabinet could or would offer him support would be a great mistake with far-reaching consequences. On the other hand it was almost intolerable as his loving wife to argue the alternative that he should remain at his post when at any moment a bullet could take him from her.

In deep depression she forwarded a letter to Asquith from Winston in which he asked to be released from his commission. When she finally reached Cromwell Road she discovered that Winston had sent a telegram to the Prime Minister cancelling the contents of the letter she had forwarded.

Clementine's mind was in a whirl. She simply did not know how to assess this latest move by her husband. As at Christmas, Winston's leave had left her emotionally and physically drained and consumed with anxiety. She quickly became incapacitated with bronchitis and was confined to the house, unable to carry out her visits to her canteens, an activity which might have taken her mind off her troubles. She was in no fit state to receive visitors when Winston sent word that his second-in-command, Archie Sinclair, would be arriving to spend his leave at Cromwell Road. Archie brought with him a letter from Winston which added to her unhappiness for its tone and attitude seemed to distance her and to discount her opinions. In rather bald terms he asked her not to use arguments or take up attitudes which conflicted with his intentions and to refrain from discouraging those who wanted him to return to England. Clementine's distress was only slightly alleviated when she discovered that Archie Sinclair agreed with her assessment of the situation and not Winston's.

Once Archie had left Clementine accepted an invitation from Sir Ernest Cassel to recuperate at his house in Branksome Dene near Bournemouth in the company of Mrs Keppel. For once living in luxury was what Clementine wanted and needed. Her letters to Winston continued to urge him not to return precipitately, even though she knew that he did not want to hear this advice from her. She used every argument she could think of. Her letters are thorough, dealing with all the points pertinent to the issue in a logical and shrewd way. But they are not coldly logical, on the contrary they are passionate with her desire to convince her husband. When his letters begin to convince her of his intentions she tries to make him see that he cannot return and behave as he had done on his last leave. She advises him to forget the past and the desire to recriminate and to focus calmly on the future.

The exchange of letters following Winston's leave is markedly different from earlier ones. The focus is entirely on Winston and his future.

Clementine's situation, the children, the titbits of gossip she had been accustomed to relating are all absent.

In a letter written on 25 March there is a clear suggestion that, despite her great love for him, Clementine is less than satisfied with the marriage. As she contemplates their immediate future she wonders if the relationship can stand the strain of Winston's manic determination to regain a place at the centre of political affairs. There is something of a warning in her words when she tells him that they are still young but that as time passes so does the ardour of love. She does not want mere friendship so soon.[15] From this and other letters it would appear that Clementine wanted a more physically passionate relationship than Winston needed. There is no equivalent in his letters to her forthright admission that she had desired him even at the station.[16] Winston's love letters either express a desire to be held in her arms or they are couched in terms of romance and courtly love. In a letter written just before Clementine's thirty-first birthday on 1 April 1916 he confesses to being consumed by egoism. But he makes no pretence that this will change. The best he can offer is his desire to meet her in another world where he can be to her as a knight in a courtly romance.[17] In the meantime his demands on Clementine to do things which went against her better judgement continued. There were more letters to forward: Clementine reluctantly complied with his wishes with one exception. She asked him to reconsider his letter to Lord Northcliffe, which Winston had asked her to read before sending it on. At the time of Winston's return to France the newspapers controlled by Lord Northcliffe had given him a very bad press. But Winston had then heard indirectly that Northcliffe's papers might be interested in running a series of articles by him on the needs of the army. The idea appealed to him and so he had written a letter directly to Northcliffe asking for the articles to be commissioned. The tone of this letter offended Clementine. She objected to her husband writing in such a conciliatory tone to the man who had used the press to abuse him. Her reason is interesting especially in the light of future actions. Just as Winston had wanted his bullying letters burnt because he did not want this aspect of him known in the future, so now Clementine uses the argument that, if sent, the contentious letter would become part of his biography.[18] This was a point which had some influence on Winston's thinking: the letter was not sent.

Clementine made one last attempt to dissuade her husband from leaving the army. Just as she had earlier catered to Asquith in order to influence him so now she tried to reach her husband by appealing to the romantic side of him, the side of him responsible for his novel *Savrola*. She asks him to imagine the figure he could cut in the future as the man 'who prepared & mobilised the Fleet who really won the war for England in the trenches as a simple Colonel. It would be a great romance.' It was her last throw of the dice and it failed.

When Winston had a few days' leave in April before his battalion went to the Front, Clementine was forced to accept that Winston would take the first viable opportunity to leave the army. She suffered agonies of uncertainty as heavy casualities and losses in Winston's battalion were reported. Because of these depletions two battalions were to be merged. Winston was again without a command and he seized on this as the best possible reason and best possible time to leave the army.

Clementine was profoundly relieved to have him home safe and sound. He had survived attack by the Germans. Now she wondered how he would fare against his own government.

15

False Friends

CLEMENTINE WAS, OF course, right about Winston's position. But she found no pleasure in having prophesied correctly that the newspapers would criticize her husband for leaving the army, that he would find himself politically isolated, that he would be frustrated by his powerlessness, that he would miss the respect and admiration of his men, and that he would soon come to regret his decision.

Winston's return had relieved Clementine of a great burden of worry about his safety but had imposed a different kind of weight upon her. There were some practical matters to solve first, including the pressing need for money. Without a Cabinet position Winston received no money as an MP and now he had forfeited his army pay also. Winston did what he had always done when he was in need of money and turned to journalism. He could earn £250 for each article the *Sunday Pictorial* printed and with two pieces could equal his army pay. But to Clementine this seemed a doubtful and precarious way of earning a living.

Her own life had become very full in the months that her husband was away. Now, while she continued to fulfil all her outside obligations, she also had to encourage and support Winston who had too little to do. He was a more silent and brooding figure than she had known before. His very appearance reflected the trauma of the last months. She was horrified by the careworn expression on his face, and his eyes which had a haunted, withdrawn look. He no longer held his head high and jutted out his chin pugnaciously but seemed always to be looking down or away. His shoulders drooped and his hands when not occupied were held tensely and tightly closed. In the past, weekends at country houses had been his delight. Her role had been to look beautiful and his had been to talk and talk. Now he was silent in company as at home. In June they were offered the loan of a small house in the park surrounding Herstmonceux, a fifteenth-century brick castle complete with towers, medieval hall, galleries with Grinling Gibbons carvings, a drawbridge and a grassy moat. Their host was Claude Lowther. One evening they were invited to dinner in the castle where Jennie and the Bonham Carters were guests. But even Jennie with her lively account of her horror and terror at being confronted by Lowther's huge mascot ram wandering at will through the castle failed to rouse her son from his despondency. Clementine knew how low an ebb he had reached when he returned the next day from a conversation with Violet convinced that she had ceased to have respect for him.

During the week while Clementine visited her canteens, Winston went to the Commons. He would return home increasingly depressed by his failure to get anyone to listen to his ideas for changing the direction of the war. His famous ability to command the attention of the Houses had, it seemed, failed him. Clementine saw the ironic parallel between her inability to make Winston see the rightness of her judgements and his to convince parliament. But this was not the moment to say such things. For the first time perhaps, she appreciated F. E. Smith's friendship towards Winston. He made a point of keeping Winston informed of Cabinet policies and divisions of opinions. He even went so far as to have Winston's analysis of the way war strategy could be improved printed and distributed to the House.

One friendship, however, to which Clementine was still violently opposed was that with Fisher. She deplored the fact that Winston was still in touch with him and had even sent him a birthday card. She was confident that much of Winston's present unhappiness was the result of just this sort of bad judgement. On the other hand she still believed that his policy for the Dardanelles would have worked if he had not been let down in so many ways. She was convinced that his position as scapegoat could only be changed by a public disclosure of all the documents related to the by now infamous campaign.

When, under great pressure, on 1 June 1916 Asquith agreed that the Dardanelles papers should be made available to parliament Clementine allowed herself a glimmer of hope. The news seemed too good to be true and she did not trust Asquith to keep his word. There had been his promise to the suffragettes, his change of heart over Winston's promotion. She could understand Winston grasping at this new possibility as his means of regaining his position in the government but she cautioned him against too much hope. Then, just a few days after Asquith's announcement, came the news that the *Hampshire* on which Kitchener was travelling to Russia had struck a mine and sunk with total loss of life. In Winston's view and that of others such as Ian Hamilton, Kitchener had a lot to answer for. Would there be a sentimental aversion to making accusations against a man no longer able to defend himself? A month later Clementine's instinctive distrust of Asquith was shown to be justified when the Prime Minister once again changed his mind. But this time Winston's was not the only voice raised in complaint. There were others in the House who had begun to feel that the government was covering something up. Lloyd George devised a compromise: a Royal Commission sitting in secret should carry out the investigation into the Dardanelles campaign.

This was by no means the full public hearing that Winston and Clementine had hoped for but it was better than nothing and both hoped that at last Winston could clear his name and that the nightmare of the last year would be dispelled in some measure. There was hope too in the signs that Asquith was on his way out. Even public sympathy for the loss of his son Raymond at the Somme in September was not enough to enable him to regain the support he had once enjoyed. F. E. Smith, a Conservative, stood by him, but not Lloyd George the Liberal. Clementine warned Winston that Lloyd George was out for himself and would do whatever was necessary to become Prime Minister. In her view the Welshman could not afford to champion Winston's interests at that moment. Her views, however forcibly expressed, did not damp down her husband's growing optimism. Violet Bonham Carter pinpointed the problem when she described Winston: 'Poor darling W. – there is a naive and utterly disarming truthfulness about him. He is quite impervious to the climatic conditions of other people.'[1]

In December Lloyd George tricked Asquith into a position where he was forced to resign. Asquith had been persuaded to set up a small War Cabinet with Lloyd George as the leader, but when the Prime Minister had decided that he must chair the committee Lloyd George had resigned from the Cabinet taking with him other key members of the government. Since he could no longer hold together the Cabinet Asquith had resigned. When Bonar Law had failed to form a government the King had appealed to Lloyd George. Suddenly Lloyd George was Prime

Minister and about to select his Cabinet. As Liberal after Liberal resigned in support of Asquith, Clementine saw clearly that there was no chance of Winston being included in the new Cabinet. There were simply too many Tories who would resolutely refuse to serve with him and these were men Lloyd George would not wish to alienate at the outset of his premiership.

For all her pessimism Clementine herself was surprised and even hopeful when F. E. Smith invited Winston to dinner at his house along with Max Aitken and Lloyd George. To Winston this seemed a clear sign that he was to be offered a Cabinet position. He even made up his mind that a return to the Admiralty was a possibility. Clementine saw him leave for dinner in better spirits than for a long time. She did not expect to see him again that evening for such male gatherings were likely to last until the early morning.

She was, therefore, dismayed when just a couple of hours later Winston returned home in a rage. During the course of the evening he had suddenly realized that he was not after all to be included in the new government. Not only was he angry, he was humiliated at the position he had found himself in. He had to face the fact that perhaps Lloyd George was the Judas figure Clementine had claimed him to be.

The Churchills had a long-standing invitation to spend Christmas 1916 at Blenheim as guests of Sunny. What should have been a pleasant escape from London, politics and the cramped quarters at Cromwell Road was less of a success than everyone had hoped. At a time when F. E. Smith had seemed to be a strong supporter of Winston, Sunny had invited him and his family for Christmas also. But there was now an uneasy tension between the friends. F. E. Smith had become a supporter of Asquith at the very time when Winston was losing all faith in him. But whereas Winston, who had supported Lloyd George, was excluded from the Cabinet, Smith, who had opposed him, was in. Clementine and Winston felt a certain bitterness at this apparent unfairness. Then there was the problem of the children. Clementine had hoped that the space at Blenheim and the extensive grounds would be good for them. She had been able to explain away a good deal of Randolph's wild behaviour on the grounds that he felt cooped up. But it quickly became apparent to her that more space simply gave Randolph greater scope for naughtiness. She was also aware of the difference between the well-disciplined Smith children and her son. Randolph seemed to revel in defying any kind of authority and he was completely indifferent to any punishment. What worried her did not, however, concern Winston. He continued to see his son as precocious and spirited and none the worse for these qualities.

After Christmas the family at last returned to the house in Eccleston Square. When Sir Edward Grey had resigned he had left London for Scotland. But the house no longer meant quite the same to Clementine. So much had happened since she had first moved in, full of hope, seeing the house as a symbol of her new status and security. In London in 1917 no one felt secure with nightly Zeppelin raids when children and adults alike had to be bundled down into the cellars. Everyone was tired from lack of sleep and strain. The shortage of food was beginning to be felt now. As Cynthia Asquith confided to her diary: 'At last we are beginning to feel the pinch of the war in material things . . . It has been an exclusively emotional experience for most of us, but these last days each hostess's brow has been furrowed by mentally weighing meat, bread and sugar.'² New clothes were almost unobtainable and bomb damage made every journey hazardous. Fuel was in short supply and in the extreme cold of January and February Clementine found it impossible to heat her large house adequately. When Goonie had paid a visit to Blenheim she had been shocked that not only was a six-course meal served, there were fires even in bedrooms not in use. Whereas in London everyone felt the need to wear outdoor clothes inside.

Clementine felt that the advantages of all the extra space and privacy of Eccleston Square were almost outweighed by the sudden, frightening increase in expenses. She consoled herself with the knowledge that she had weathered all the upheavals of the time since leaving the Admiralty far better than Margot Asquith who was responding to her exodus from Downing Street with floods of tears and many bitter words. But Clementine had few hopes of the New Year. The end of the war seemed as far away as ever, as did Winston's return to a political career. She believed that she was about to face another year of hardship, anxiety and isolation.

The future looked a little brighter when in January the Dardanelles Commission issued an interim report and it seemed as if Winston's name might be cleared. At last both Asquith's and Kitchener's parts in the disaster were now acknowledged.

Since the early days of their marriage Winston and Clementine had hankered after a place in the country. Most of their friends had such a retreat but so far the Churchills had been content with renting or borrowing a summer place. So why did Clementine now set her heart on buying a place of their own? They had less rather than more money than previously and their future was very uncertain. In part Clementine was attracted by long-nourished romantic ideas of having a place where they could grow their own food and use horses instead of cars. In war-battered London the idea of the 'countryside' and peace and quiet had become even more attractive.

Romance apart, the ever-practical Clementine had other good reasons for pushing the idea of a country property at that particular moment. Unsure of how Winston's career would develop she was determined that he would have a place where he could paint. The solace this brought him also brought relief to her. As the bombing of London grew more frequent and more and more nights were spent in cellars, she wanted to get the children away from the city to a place where they could lead more normal lives. She was oppressed by the knowledge that when the lease of their house expired, as it soon would, the family would have no permanent home. A house in the country would provide this.

After some searching the Churchills found Lullenden Farm in a lovely wooded valley near East Grinstead. The house itself was attractive, being built of local grey stone, and there was a large barn which could be converted into extra living space. With the farm came a light carriage and pony. Remembering her desire right at the beginning of the war for such a mode of transport rather than a car, Clementine was charmed by this detail. The romance of Lullenden certainly attracted both Clementine and Winston. In March Winston sold some railroad stock and bought the farm.

Before they could move in there was a great deal to do including laying water pipes to the main supply. To make room for the Churchill children of both families the barn needed extensive work. There were few men available to do such jobs and everything took time. In spite of the increasing number of problems the farm presented Clementine was cheered by the thought that soon the family would have a new and permanent home and a sense of a future. The promise of the publication of the Dardanelles Report seemed to confirm this.

In the event the publication of the report solved nothing. Asquith had severely limited the Commission's access to the relevant documentation. It had not, for example, been able to see the War Council's minutes for the meeting at which Winston had stated that he would not be held responsible for the failure of the expedition if the appropriate troops were not made available immediately.

Winston had been confident that he would be exonerated and that immediately everything would come right; that the press would cease hounding him and that he would be invited to take his rightful place in the government. Clementine knew that it would not be so simple. She was aware by now that the Dardanelles had only provided a focus, an excuse for feelings that existed anyway. Those who disliked Winston's arrogance, his ambition, his driving and sometimes misdirected energy would not see him any differently after the Commission's report. And indeed the Conservatives in the coalition government continued to refuse to serve alongside Winston Churchill. In private Winston sulked and was bad tempered. But in the House he had a new confidence. When Lloyd George talked of trying to get him the Duchy of Lancaster he refused the offer as an insult. But then in July he was made Secretary of State for Munitions. It was not exactly the job he would have chosen. But as Clementine, who had her own experience with munition workers to draw on, pointed out it was of vital importance to have a strong and able person in that position if Britain was to have a chance of winning the war.

Before Winston could take up his new job he had to go through the usual process of standing in a by-election in his Dundee constituency. Deeply anxious that there should be no hitch that would prevent her husband rejoining the Cabinet, Clementine joined in the election campaign with a will. She was no longer the shy young woman who had simply accompanied Winston on visits to the constituency. She was a mature woman of thirty-two. She was, if anything, more beautiful than she had been when she married. During the time Winston had been in the army she had learnt how to use her good looks and charm to win people to her side. In 1917, however, good looks and charm were not enough. At electioneering meetings there was a new mood of dissatisfaction. Everyone was weary, everyone had been touched by loss and hardship, and someone had to be held responsible. The Dardanelles Commission might have cleared Winston's name but among ordinary people such as those in his constituency this news had made little impression. There were large numbers in the crowds gathered to hear him speak who still held him entirely responsible for the terrible loss of life. So it was not so much her beauty which stood Clementine in good stead now but the experience she had in her work in the munitions canteens. She was used to dealing with working men and women; she knew more about what their lives were like and she was prepared to listen even to hostile hecklers. Her presence in Dundee did Winston incalculable good. He was re-elected and once more the Churchills had an income.

Winston's appointment transformed Clementine's life. She no longer had to bear the burden of her husband's depression and anger and disappointment. He no longer needed her to bolster him up and give him confidence and hope for the future. He was immediately involved in his own work and was now frequently away from home. Once again he became a regular flyer but now he was content to be a passenger. Clementine saw the risks and worry involved as a small price to pay for the revitalization of her husband.

Now Clementine redoubed her efforts to make Lullenden habitable so that Winston would have a quiet place to return to after his many flights to and from France. But the romance and glamour of Lullenden faded somewhat as she realized that the farm presented problems they had not anticipated. It was not only the house that needed work but also the surrounding land. In other times the overgrown and untended state of the place might have been seen as a pleasing wilderness area. But in 1917 when food was in short supply it was literally criminal to let such good arable land remain untended. She now realized that there was no equipment to cut the hedges, to clear the overgrown ditches and the fields full of brambles and thorn bushes. To take even the modest step of planting a field with potatoes some help was essential. The only able-bodied men in the area were German prisoners-of-war.

As a desperate measure the Churchills resolved to employ three. It meant finding space for them to sleep on the farm as there was no way of transporting them daily to and from the camp. For four months Clementine with her school-girl German supervised the prisoners trenching and draining a field ready for the potato planting. From the outset their neighbours protested. They felt unsafe with Germans at liberty so close by. The men themselves were sullen and reluctant to work hard. Clementine began to feel that the money spent on their wages was not justified by the amount of work they did. At the end of four months the experiment was declared a failure and the prisoners were sent back to the camp.

Clementine now contented herself with creating a garden around the farmhouse while the hay rotted in the fields. Eventually Winston bought some bullocks and found an old gardener and a man too crippled to be fit for war work and two small boys to help on the farm.

There was no invitation to Blenheim that Christmas. Sunny's patience with his cousin had at last come to an end and the two men had quar-relled. Clementine's efforts to effect a reconciliation had failed. She sus-pected that Gladys Deacon, who had an increasing influence over Sunny, had played a part. The future Duchess of Marlborough did not like Winston, nor was she pleased by the continuing friendship between the Churchills and Sunny's ex-wife, Consuelo. So Christmas 1917 was spent at Lullenden along with Jack and Goonie and their children. The barn was by now the children's principal home and Randolph and Johnny attended the local village school. Through Randolph's contact with chil-dren at the school, Clementine learned that even here in the countryside Winston was disliked and blamed for the Dardanelles. There were by now other reasons for doubts about whether Lullenden had been such a good idea after all.

In March 1918 Winston received an official letter of complaint about the state of the land around the farm and the fact that arable land was being left uncultivated. In excuse Winston listed the problems they faced, ones which had escaped their attention in their first flush of enthu-siasm, but which without extra capital they could not overcome.

Equally problematical were the children. The separate living quarters devised for them was an outward sign of the separation of their lives from those of the adults. Clementine and Goonie were frequently absent – Clementine working and Goonie socializing with one of the several men who professed to be in love with her. The grandmothers were only occa-sional visitors since Jennie preferred London and Blanche spent her time in cottages lent to her by the Blunts and by the Redesdales. Jack was away in France and made only rare visits while Winston managed to get there for occasional weekends only. Randolph was growing wilder and more of a bully while Diana was becoming more withdrawn. Sarah was too young to be really troublesome, but her life was endangered by Randolph's experiment of putting her along with Goonie's son, Peregrine, into a small cart which he then pushed down a steep hill. The cart was destroyed but the babies escaped with bruises only. Even Winston, who generally laughed at Randolph's exploits, felt that his son had gone too far when he tipped the contents of a chamber pot from an upstairs window onto the white head of the unsuspecting Prime Minister Lloyd George, sitting on a bench below.

Apparently it escaped the attention of the adults that the children were drinking water which was potentially dangerous and no one was aware that Sarah was regularly drinking unpasteurized milk which was causing

her to develop tubercular glands. Her generally sickly condition despite
the country air was put down to trouble with her tonsils and adenoids.
Winston arranged for a visit from a surgeon and there on the kitchen
table the troublesome organs were removed.

Why did Clementine become pregnant again in early 1918? She found
the three children she already had a trouble rather than a joy and she was
guiltily aware that she experienced little in the way of maternal feelings.
Perhaps Winston wanted another son to ensure his name was carried on.
So many families had lost sons in the war that he might well have felt that
his one son was not enough. Throughout her pregnancy Clementine
referred to her unborn child as though it were a boy. It was even called
Chumbolly as Randolph had been. It could be that Clementine was
affected by the heavy propaganda of the time encouraging women to have
babies as a necessary patriotic gesture. She enjoyed her pregnancy this
time, experiencing better health largely because she remained active.
There was also a hopeful feeling in the air that perhaps the horrendous
war was grinding to a halt.

The prospect of victory allowed many resentments and dissatisfac-
tions that had been repressed for patriotic reasons to come to the surface.
Just at the moment when the last great effort was needed, there was
trouble in the munitions industry with strikes which were potentially so
disabling that Winston had to stop them by threatening conscription of
those who had been exempted on the grounds that they were doing war
work. Clementine was quietly triumphant when Winston received a telegram from the Manchester Women Munitions Workers condemning the
men on strike and pledging themselves to work without cease until the
war was ended. Manchester had, after all, been a stronghold of the
suffragettes. Coming as it did so soon after the granting of the vote to
women over thirty in January 1918, the telegram demonstrated that all
those who, like Clementine, had held that women were just as responsible
as men had been right. Winston was silenced.

A surprise of another kind was the request to Winston in May from
Montagu Porch for permission to marry Jennie. At this time Winston
was forty-four and his mother's suitor was forty-one. Tall and handsome
with fine moustaches and a head of prematurely white hair, Porch nevertheless seemed an unlikely husband for the flamboyant Jennie. His family
was not of the aristocracy but had made its money from Australian sheep.
When Jennie had first met him her future husband had held the far from
prestigious position of Third Resident in Nigeria. Since then he had

served as a Lieutenant in the Nigerian Regiment of the Cameroons and it was while he was on leave from his regiment that he had proposed to Jennie on the way to pay a visit to Jennie's sister, Leonie, at Castle Leslie. Porch was mild-mannered and steady, but he evidently loved Jennie. In June the wedding took place at the Harrow Road Registry Office with Winston as a witness. The bride wore a grey coat and skirt and a light green toque with a soft veil and gave every appearance of being happy.

In September Clementine and Winston had themselves been married for ten years. It was an occasion like so many in the past that Clementine celebrated alone. Winston's loving letters to his wife declare that the years of marriage have been the happiest of his life. Apart from the fact that they both knew that some of those ten years included ones in which he had never been more unhappy, the letters suggest that Winston is not entirely sure how his wife feels looking back over the time she has been married to him. He wonders if they have been less or more happy than other couples and he acknowledges that in the relationship she has been the giver and he the taker. His letter of 12 September suggests that he feels a trifle uncertain about whether he has been the husband she had hoped for. But rather than promising to change he implies that the empty place in her life where she had wanted him to be will be filled by new interests and new possibilities. He concludes his letter by saying that he will always be at her side in 'true and tender friendship'. Had he already forgotten Clementine's assertion that 'friendship' was not enough. We do not know how Clementine reacted to these letters: to Winston's chagrin she did not write in reply.

16

Life and Death

AUTUMN 1918 BROUGHT ever-increasing hope that the end of the war was close. Clementine was among those who saw that with the end would come new problems. She would have agreed entirely with Cynthia Asquith's sudden recognition of what the prospect of peace meant.

> I am beginning to rub my eyes at the prospect of peace. I think it will require more courage than anything that has gone before. It isn't until one leaves off spinning round that one realises how giddy one is. One will have to teach one's wincing eyes to look at long vistas again instead of short ones and one will at last fully recognise that the dead are not only dead for the duration of the war.[1]

When Clementine looked at the 'long vistas' she wondered what would happen to that group of war workers she knew best, those who worked in the munition factories. In particular she was concerned about all those women who had discovered that they were capable of earning their own living. She knew that already, as munitions work became less of a priority, it was the women who were losing their jobs. She was also aware from her regular contact with the workers that they had expectations of a better England after the war. What they had been prepared to accept in the way of poor housing and living conditions because of the war would no longer be acceptable in peacetime. She wrote a letter to Winston at this time in which she expresses a wish to see all the munition workers employed building garden cities to replace the slums. It is a Utopian vision of which William Morris would have approved. Clementine knew realistically that, although such changes were necessary, they would come slowly, if at all. But she also knew that if changes were not made there would be trouble. The Bolshevik revolution in Russia was a potent example.

Her own immediate problem as her pregnancy came to term was housing. Her efforts to find a house that was both suitable and affordable had come to nothing. In the end the family moved into a house in Tenterden Street which Winston had persuaded his Aunt Cornelia to lend them. It was not an entirely satisfactory arrangement as Clementine did not like to have to accept favours or charity but at this time she had no alternative.

For a brief moment in November both long-term and short-term worries were forgotten in the collective relief and then jubilation that swept through England as the Armistice was announced. Clementine joined Winston at the Munitions Office in the Hotel Metropole in Northumberland Avenue to share the moment with him when Big Ben struck eleven and at long last England was at peace. They went by car through the dense crowds to 10 Downing Street and Lloyd George. Then while London became one enormous, loud party Clementine, only days from giving birth, went back to Tenterden Street to celebrate more quietly. Four days later on 15 November her fourth child and third daughter was born: she had the same red hair as her sisters. As a compliment to the new wife of their friend Archie Sinclair, she was named Marigold.

At Christmas of 1918 there seemed much to celebrate. The Churchills were now reconciled with Sunny and they were invited to a big family party at Blenheim which turned into a more public occasion for the twenty-first birthday of the Duke's oldest son, Lord Blandford, a tall, ungainly and apparently not very bright young man. The party was on a grand scale with a huge bonfire on which a whole ox was roasted. Clementine did not greatly enjoy this vast gathering of the Churchill clan and she was dismayed by the implications of the burning on the bonfire of an effigy of the recently defeated Kaiser.

Elections had been held at the end of the war. As usual Clementine waited anxiously to know if Winston would be in the Cabinet of the newly elected coalition government in which the Conservatives were now the dominant partners. The Churchills needed the money more than ever now that they had a fourth child and no settled home of their own in London. She was not, however, pleased when Winston took on not just one but two Cabinet positions. He became Secretary of State for War and for the Air Ministry. She could read for herself in the daily Press that this double appointment was unpopular. She feared, rightly, that Winston would have even less time for his family and she saw this desire for excessive power as what had led to his downfall over the Dardanelles campaign. She attempted, unsuccessfully, to persuade him to accept one office only by appealing to his sense of humour and the ridiculous: 'you want to be a statesman not a juggler'.[2]

Winston had at first grumbled at being given the War Ministry at the very moment when hostilities had ceased. There was, of course, plenty to occupy him with the Peace negotiations in Paris and he was rarely at home. Moreover, to Clementine's consternation, he soon began to behave in a manner which suggested that he was looking for a war to be Minister over. His virulent hostility to the Bolsheviks was apparent even before the end of the war but throughout 1919 he became progressively more obsessed with them and his language became less and less temperate. Mary Borden, the American novelist, recorded in her diary of 24 January 1919 that Winston had told Lloyd George that 'one might as well legalise sodomy as recognise the Bolsheviks'.[3] By February he was advocating a military committee to see how Russia could be invaded if necessary. This was all very worrying for Clementine who like most people was utterly sick of war, and who was experiencing no luck in finding a family house.

In March her problems were compounded when her reliable Scots nanny, Isabelle, succumbed to the influenza which was claiming thousands of lives from a European population already weakened by prolonged war. Isabelle's temperature soared and she became delirious. Horrified, Clementine discovered that the young woman had taken the five-month-old Marigold into her own bed for safe-keeping. She rescued Marigold but Isabelle was beyond saving and died.

Even Lullenden was not proving the haven Clementine had hoped for. With demobilization she had been able to hire a bailiff to run the farm. But his energy and his radical plans alarmed her. Everything he suggested involved spending money they did not have. Winston rarely had time any more to take much interest and she now admitted to herself that Lullenden had, after all, been a mistake. It was a burden to her rather than a pleasure and it was tying up money that they really needed for a house in London. She began to consider selling the place.

In August she spent a brief period with her husband when he inspected the British Army on the Rhine at Cologne. Here she saw for herself the devastating effects of the war on Germany and Germans and she was reminded again of the burning of the Kaiser's effigy when she saw the haughty, bullying attitude of some of the army officers' wives to the civilian population. There had been a plan for Clementine to travel to Scotland to stay with the Sutherlands at Dunrobin Castle and to join Winston at Lochmore as guests of the Duke of Westminster. But in the event Winston went alone while Clementine spent a few days with Lord and Lady Londonderry. The two of them were once again apart for their wedding anniversary: on this occasion there was no real reason to keep them apart. Winston, keeping up their custom, wrote to mark the occasion thanking Clementine for all she had given him, but in his letter there is a formality of tone reminiscent of the earlier letters. Clementine did not even remember the date until too late. Her letter too lacks warmth, and the sentence commenting on the swift passage of Time[4] brings to mind her earlier letter warning of the danger of love becoming simply friendship. This year of the marriage had been a difficult year and they were still without a home in London. Winston was put in the position of having to beg a room in Ernest Cassel's imposing mansion, Brook House, when he and Clementine met again in London at the end of September before staying at Freddie Guest's house, Templeton. When Sir Ian Hamilton expressed an interest in buying Lullenden Clementine was eager to accept his offer and to put the proceeds into a London house. Winston, however, was still attracted to the idea of owning a country property and asked the estate agents Knight Frank and Rutley to look out for a fruit farm in Kent for him.

In the meantime Templeton had its attractions. There was a swimming pool and an indoor tennis court where Clementine could play to her heart's content. But it was a strain living in other people's houses, always in the public eye. Winston did not mind as he was frequently away and then, when he was at Templeton, he had plenty of the kind of male company he so enjoyed. Then there was the question of the children. It was too much to expect the Guests to house them also, especially given Randolph's exuberance and naughtiness. So Diana and Randolph along with their cousin Johnny were sent to a small boarding school at St Margaret's Bay in Kent. Clementine and Winston frequently disagreed about Randolph but now they were at one in deciding that the time had come for him to go to a preparatory school. Nurserymaids and governesses alike could not control him. Since the arrival of Marigold, to whom everyone was instantly attracted, he no longer paid much attention to Clementine when she reprimanded him. The only person to whom he showed any respect was his father who was rarely at home. Clementine tried to suppress her awareness that already people regarded her son either as an amusing and precocious smaller version of Winston or as a monster. She concentrated on assembling his uniform for the school they had chosen, Sandroyd near Cobham in Surrey. During the Spring holiday in March Clementine enjoyed one of those brief spells of being close to her son. When he was dressed in his new uniform she saw him for the small boy he really was, whilst on his part Randolph was very pleased to have such an array of new and grown-up clothes. He showed nothing but pleasure in the idea of going to school. It was the last time for many years that Clementine and Randolph were pleased with each other.

The temporariness of everything in her life from late 1919 to the summer of 1920 did not suit Clementine at all. Through all the strains of the war she had maintained her composure largely because she had been concentrating on work she knew to be valuable. Now she had little to do. The older children were at school, nurserymaids looked after Sarah and Marigold. She had no house to maintain, no cook to instruct. Winston had much less need of her than formerly. At weekends he was very happy to spend his time with Freddie Guest, painting. His cousin, Clare Sheridan, visited often as she had been commissioned by Freddie to make a portrait bust of Winston. Clementine now became aware that F. E. Smith was having an affair with Clare; she disapproved but Winston did not mind.

More serious friction between husband and wife was caused by politics. There was a difference in their attitudes to what was going on in Ireland. Clementine read with horror of the activities of the Black and Tans sent to Ireland by her husband and of their brutal reprisals, repressions and indiscriminate destruction. When in August it seemed that England might suddenly go to war with the Soviets she was dismayed to think that Winston's anti-Bolshevik obsession, with which she did not agree, might have been in part responsible.

Throughout the early part of the year she felt drained and depressed. Goonie, who had been her confidante during the war years, was now preoccupied with her own affairs. She too had spent a year wandering around as a guest in a series of houses belonging to friends and relatives since she had found it necessary to rent out the Cromwell Road house to provide her with an income. But Goonie had not much minded the situation. Once back in London she had become the centre of a group of admirers. Both Augustine Birrell and the Honourable Harold Baker were rumoured to be in love with her. And then she had become pregnant and to her utter joy had in this year given birth to the daughter she had longed for and whom she named Ann Clarissa Nicolette.

Fortunately Jennie now spotted a house which she thought might be suitable for Clementine and Winston. In Sussex Square, just north of the Bayswater Road and close to Hyde Park was a cream stucco, mid-Victorian family house with plenty of spacious rooms. It was not dissimilar to the Eccleston Square house. Like Jennie, Clementine saw its potential though she also saw what a lot of work would be needed before it would be ready for the family to move in. At the back of the house was a mews property which was also for sale and which would make an admirable studio for Winston. The search for a new home was at last over and Clementine felt that she could begin to live her life again.

There was an added and unforeseen bonus to being in this part of London. Not far away, down Holland Park Road, was Notting Hill High School for Girls. Everything she had heard about this school determined Clementine to send her daughters there. Even from its earliest days this school had offered just the kind of education her Aunt Mabell, Countess of Airlie, had argued for in the pamphlets she had written as a young married woman. The curriculum emphasized academic excellence rather than genteel accomplishments. In many ways it reminded Clementine of the school she had attended so happily in Berkhamsted. Among its former pupils were Georgiana Burne-Jones, Jennie and May Morris, Violet Hunt and, very briefly, Lilu Yeats. The girls were enrolled in the school, Randolph began as a pupil at Sandroyd and Clementine left with Winston for a short holiday in Italy.

When they returned to London, although a great deal still remained to be done on the Sussex Square house, it was work that could be done gradually as money became available. In the meantime the family could move in. Clementine hoped that was just the beginning of a more settled period in their lives.

Throughout the preceding months Clementine had heard much about two Russians named Krassin and Kamenev employed at the Russian Soviet Office. Winston was convinced that they were involved in propaganda work and that he had evidence to support his claims. He wanted them expelled from London. Lloyd George hesitated about such a drastic measure at a delicate moment in relations between the two countries.

In this context neither Winston nor Clementine could hardly believe the news that greeted them on their return to London. Not only had Clare Sheridan been making busts of Krassin and Kamenev, she had actually left her forthcoming exhibition in the lurch and set off with Kamenev for Moscow. Winston was beside himself with anger at what he saw as a betrayal by his own cousin. And the atmosphere at Sussex Square grew worse when the further news came that Clare had sculpted the men Winston most detested, Lenin and Trotsky, and that the latter had actually fallen in love with her and offered to take her with him to the Front in the civil war between the Reds and the Whites.

To compound Winston's anger, when Clare did arrive back in England her exploits were reported in every paper; on the street were placards for *The Times* announcing in large purple letters the serialization of 'Mrs Sheridan's Diary'. Labour leaders and known communists flocked to Clare's studio to hear about her adventures. Clementine was heartily thankful that Clare was Winston's cousin and not hers.

She found Winston very difficult to live with these days. Not only did he feel that Clare had made him a laughing stock, he also felt that he had failed at the War Office. He wanted another Cabinet position which would give scope to his talents. At the end of this difficult and tense year Clementine felt exhausted and on edge. She hoped that 1921 would be better. But the year opened with the first of those deaths which were to shake the whole family. In January Clementine's grandmother, Blanche, Dowager Countess of Airlie, died in her ninetieth year. She had remained a force to be reckoned with until the end. Clementine had not been close to her and she grieved more for this marker of the passing of time than for the actual person. Neither this death nor the poor health of Diana and Sarah, however, seemed reason enough to change her plans for a holiday in Nice where she and Winston were to stay with Ernest Cassel and his granddaughter Edwina. While she and Winston travelled to France and the sunshine the girls were sent to Broadstairs with a maid where, it was hoped, they would grow stronger in the sea air.

When Winston returned to London Clementine was easily persuaded to stay in the south for her health. Away from the family and from Winston she quickly began to recover. It was as though Winston's anger and frustration had been sapping her own energy and only when she was apart from him was there a chance for her to recover her own vitality. She swam, she played tennis and she visited friends.

Later in January came the second death of the year. This time it was one of Winston's relatives, Herbert Vane-Tempest, who was killed in a train crash. As the result of this entirely unforeseen eventuality, Winston suddenly inherited an estate in Ireland which brought in £4,000 a year. Overnight their income had been doubled. One of Clementine's major concerns had been the cost of doing all the work on 2 Sussex Square. Now this was one less problem to face. She had also been worried about how little money her mother had; with this extra income she could afford to give her more. Nellie too was struggling now that she had two sons, Giles born in 1916 and Esmond in 1918. Winston felt able to give her some money to help her to start a hat shop.

Still in France in February Clementine moved into the Hotel Bristol in Beaulieu. Already the prospect of more money made her feel able to indulge in the luxury of a hotel. Here she met Ashmead-Bartlett. She disliked him intensely for criticizing Winston's part in the Dardanelles but she appears not to have known what a dramatic part he had earlier played in the break-up of her family when she was a child.

Now that she was at a distance from her husband Clementine put into practice a technique she had come to adopt with him. She knew that if she confronted him directly with a disagreeable difference of opinion he would be likely to shout her down. But there was always a chance that he would take notice of something committed to paper. Therefore on 18 February she expressed her opinion about the state of affairs in Ireland, pleading with him to bring some moderation to the Irish situation. She asked him to try to put himself in the position of the Irish and to understand that brutality and reprisals were more likely to stiffen their attitude against the English than to browbeat them into submission. She went so far as to say that she was disappointed in his attitude towards the Irish which she described as 'rough, iron-fisted, "Hunnish"'.[5] When at about this time Winston became Colonial Secretary rather than Secretary of State for War she hoped that this would give him a different perspective on the Irish.

The news sent by Winston of the girls in Broadstairs and 'combative' Randolph at Sandroyd was good. More disquieting was the fact that little Marigold was once again ill with the cough and cold that rarely left her. However, Clementine did not find the baby's illness sufficient reason for turning down Winston's suggestion that she should join him on board the *Sphinx* and travel with him to Egypt in the company of the famous T. E. Lawrence and their friend Archibald Sinclair. In Egypt Clementine found that her husband was as unpopular as in England. Crowds gathered on their arrival with the intention of stoning them. They were rushed by armoured car to the safe luxury of the Semiramis Hotel. Here Clementine met up with her cousin, Gertrude Bell, who was to take part in the Cairo Conference. She was still an impressive-looking woman with white hair and a pink complexion. Her intelligence was as formidable as ever. Throughout the last twelve months she had been sending back to England invaluable weekly reports on the Civil Administration of Mesopotamia. Despite her official involvement in the conference as the Oriental Secretary to Sir Percy Cox she found time to talk to Clementine and to exchange family news and to accompany her and Winston along with T. E. Lawrence on a camel ride to see the Pyramids and the Sphinx. The party also went to see the Nile dam which their friend Sir Ernest Cassel had helped to build by organizing the financing.

It was an interesting and exciting time for Clementine, and at a farewell ball given by Lord Allenby, she had been a great success and danced until midnight. But she was not altogether sorry to set off home. She had been greatly alarmed by Winston's refusal to admit there was any danger in his setting up his easel in the open wherever he saw a view he wanted to paint, despite the hostility of onlookers.

At the end of March Clementine was back at Sussex Square. The children who had been staying with Jennie and who had not seen their mother for three months were there for her homecoming. On 14 April, however, she left them again and with Nellie set off for France in response to the devastating news that their brother Bill had committed suicide in a hotel room in Paris. They could not understand why he had done so. At thirty-four he seemed established in business. Gambling debts which might have worried him had earlier been settled for him by Winston and at the time of his suicide he had money in his bank account.

In Dieppe they found their normally high-spirited mother in a state of collapse; she looked old and shrunken. She had been staying in rented rooms whilst the Mitfords had been renting from her her own home when the telegram had come. It now fell to Clementine to organize her brother's funeral and to deal with the delicate matter of his burial as a suicide. She was desperately eager for Winston to attend the funeral to lend it an air of respectability and this he did.

Clementine was still grieving for her brother when Jennie suddenly became ill. She had been staying with Lady Horner at Mells when she had fallen downstairs wearing new high-heeled shoes. She appeared to have fractured her left leg above her ankle. She had been brought back from Mells in an ambulance to her own home to recover. But after two weeks it was clear that something was wrong. Gangrene had set in and the only thing that could be done was to amputate the affected leg.

Clementine knew what this would mean to the woman who had prided herself on her pretty feet, who had loved to dance and be with young people. All her grievances against Jennie and her scorn of her frivolity were now overcome by her admiration of Jennie's courage in facing this terrible ordeal. She spent time with her every day and she was as delighted as Winston when after the operation Jennie seemed to be making a good recovery. So she was all the more shocked when Winston was summoned one morning before he got out of bed to go to his mother who was dying. A main artery in the thigh of the amputated leg had burst, and Jennie was in a coma from which she never recovered.

Condolences arrived in great numbers and Winston answered them bravely, saying that Jennie had been spared the pain of growing old. But to Clementine he poured out his grief and she knew that for him a stage of his life was now over. His mother had been one of his greatest supporters. Now there was only Clementine.

Winston organized the funeral and made sure that Jennie would be remembered as a Churchill. A special Victorian coach was attached to the Oxford train and the mourners were taken from Oxford by car to the little church at Bladon where Jennie was buried alongside her first husband, Randolph. July was spent in the miserable business of selling off Jennie's possessions to pay her debts.

Clementine hoped to forget all the miseries of the year in a tennis tournament at Eaton Hall, the Duke of Westminster's Cheshire home. Marigold was again unwell but Clementine hoped that the sea air at Broadstairs would benefit her as it had her sisters earlier in the year. So the four children were sent off with their friend, the nurserymaid Rose, to stay at their usual boarding house, Overblow.

Clementine received letters from the children which gave her some uneasiness while she was at Eaton Hall since they all mentioned Marigold's illness. But as there was no word from Rose she put her doubts aside and flung herself into her favourite game. She was not prepared when the telegram came summoning her to Broadstairs and her sick child. The landlady who had taken alarm at Marigold's condition had insisted that Rose send for Clementine. When Clementine arrived on 14 August septicaemia had developed and Marigold was very ill indeed. She sent Randolph, Diana and Sarah off with her own maid to the Duke of Westminster's estate in Scotland where they were due anyway in a few days' time. Winston was still in London and unable to get away, but Clementine let him know the seriousness of Marigold's condition and then devoted herself night and day to her frail daughter. On 22 August Marigold seemed a little better, but when Winston arrived he decided that a specialist should be brought from London. On the night of 22 August Winston and Clementine did not leave the side of their sick child. At one moment Marigold awoke and asked Clementine to sing to her the song which she had learnt to sing for herself. So in that sick-room Clementine haltingly began to sing the jolly little song 'I'm for ever blowing bubbles'. After the first few lines Marigold said she was sleepy and would like to hear the song the next day. But there was no next day for Marigold. On 23 August Marigold died aged just two years and nine months. Clementine, who had kept calm until that moment now lost control completely. The sound of her howls of pain when she realized that Marigold was dead haunted Winston for the rest of his life so that years later he was able to describe the scene vividly to his youngest daughter, Mary.

Clementine hardly knew how to deal with her anguish and self-reproach. Why, she asked herself, had she not sent someone more experienced with the children? Why had she not responded to the children's letters? How could she have enjoyed herself at the tennis tournament while her child was dying? Now she grieved for how little she had seen of this delightful child during her short life.

Marigold was buried in Kensal Green Cemetery and then the bereaved parents had to face their other children and tell them that Marigold was no more. They spent two weeks at Lochmore where their host Bendor was able to understand their grief. He had lost his beloved son and heir, Edward, when the boy was just four years old.

In September Clementine tried to establish normality in their lives. While Winston left for Dunrobin Castle to stay with the Duke and Duchess of Sutherland, she returned to London with the children and prepared them for school. The shock of Marigold's death made her pay more attention to her three other children and she took them on picnics and outings and even showed them Marigold's grave.

Then came the news that Ernest Cassel who had been such a good and kind friend to the whole Churchill family had died. Clementine wondered what else could happen in this year in which they had already seen five deaths.

There was more to come. After a quiet Christmas at Sussex Square

Winston set off on Boxing Day with Lloyd George to Cannes. Immediately influenza struck the household again. Maids and children alike fell victims, and, instead of joining Winston in France as soon as the children were safely back at school, Clementine had to stay in London to nurse them. As soon as they were better Clementine collapsed from physical and emotional exhaustion. While she lay prostrate in bed, Winston in Monte Carlo entertained Blanche, now sufficiently recovered to have become established as a character at the Sporting Club. He gave dinner parties for their friends. In a state of deep depression Clementine wrote the bitterest letter to Winston she had ever written. He was only too ready to obey her subsequent telegram to burn this letter which put him in a very bad light. But he did take advantage of Clementine's feeling in the wrong to confess that he had been losing money gambling.

Before long Clementine was able to travel to Cannes and there she was reconciled with Winston. She soon began to hope that she was pregnant and that the loss of Marigold might be made less painful by the arrival of a new baby.

17

A Country Estate

ONCE WINSTON HAD returned to London, Clementine, left behind in Cannes, began to recover quickly. Despite Winston's anxiety that she might suffer another miscarriage, she took the opportunity to play plenty of tennis. By now she was a very good player and with her partner won the doubles section in the Cannes Tournament. While she was away work on the house proceeded so well that by the time of her return to London Winston was ready to resume his search for a country property. In March they went to see a place in Kent called Chartwell situated near the attractive village of Westerham with its red-brick houses, some of them tile-hung and all with red roofs. Their responses to the house itself were quite different. Winston fell in love with the magnificent views over the Kentish Weald and he saw great potential in the house and its grounds.

Clementine saw a basically charming red-brick house of the time of Henry VII made ugly by numerous nineteenth-century additions and made dark by overgrown ivy and a great clump of rhododendrons. She saw how neglected both the house and the grounds were. She remembered how they had fallen in love with Lullenden and how they had both greatly underestimated the time, cost and sheer hard work needed to make it habitable and then to run it. She did not want to repeat that experience and told Winston so forcefully. Reluctantly he accepted her verdict, or at least he appeared to do so, and other matters drove the house from her mind.

In April 1922 Winston was hurt quite badly when he fell getting off his pony after a game of polo at Eaton Hall. He even talked of giving up the sport altogether. Then in May there was the question of the portrait of Diana and Sarah which they had commissioned from the artist Charles Sims. A great deal is revealed about Clementine and Winston's attitude towards their daughters in the correspondence about this portrait. For as it progressed Clementine began to take a dislike to it. She had envisioned a painting in which the girls were not the central feature but merely charming adjuncts to a garden scene. The painter, however, had become more interested in Sarah and Diana and had made them the focus of the painting. What really troubled Clementine was the way he had seen them and presented them. She recognized that the portraits were a good likeness but she had wanted them portrayed at their best. Such a portrait, after all, should be a message to the future that the Churchill girls had been both beautiful and happy. Instead of which the portrait, as it stood, would give a very different impression. Diana appeared to be priggish and without animation or appeal. Sarah on the other hand looked rather insolent.[1] Clementine did not care to acknowledge that the portrait did reveal a truth about the girls at this time.

In December 1921 Winston had been involved in negotiations with the republican Irish which had led to the signing of the December Treaty. By this, Ireland would be divided, with the Unionist provinces in the north remaining under British rule while the south would be self-governing on terms similar to other countries, such as Canada, which had been British colonies. The Black and Tans, whom Clementine had so detested, would no longer cause terror in Ireland and there could be peace at last. But the Treaty was not well received by everyone in Ireland; civil war broke out which had repercussions in England. For, shockingly, on 21 June 1922, Field Marshal Sir Henry Wilson, one of Winston's Cabinet colleagues, was murdered right outside his own home by IRA gunmen. This was bad enough in itself, but then Winston learned that he could well be the focus of the next attack since his name was on the IRA hit list for the part he had played in negotiating the December Treaty.

The effect on the Churchill family was immediate. Plain-clothes police arrived at Sussex Square and searched the house thoroughly for bombs. Winston was given strict instructions about not exposing himself to unnecessary risks and advised to have a bodyguard with him at all times. He took the threat to his life seriously and Clementine was frightened when he determined to sleep in the attic in a specially reinforced chair with his revolver to hand.

This new anxiety did not prevent Clementine from taking a holiday in

Devon in July with Goonie while Winston visited his rich friends and organized a dinner party for the Prince of Wales. Clementine had planned to spend a few days in London before going to Scotland. Sarah, however, put a stop to both the dinner party and her mother's return home by catching measles. Clementine was obliged to take a room at the Ritz rather than take any chances at this late stage in her pregnancy.

Winston was as usual busy, so busy in fact that he had not time to see her on the day of her return. She looked forward to having him to herself in August when the whole family moved to a big house she had rented in Frinton. But Winston could not resist other more glamorous invitations for the month. While Clementine entertained the children he was entertained by Max Aitken at Deauville and the Duke of Westminster at Mimizan. So his visit to Frinton was short, but for the children it was the most important part of the holiday for he threw himself wholeheartedly into organizing the building of the biggest sand fort they had ever seen. Clementine looked at her delighted, absorbed children and wondered why she was not able to engage them in quite that way. She had tried that very holiday to instil in Randolph and Diana her own passion for tennis. She had even entered them in the local tennis tournament. But neither of them had shown much promise or interest and although, as the handsome Churchill children, they were much photographed for the newspapers, she had felt let down when all they could win was the booby prize which she herself had the embarrassing job of presenting to them.

When Clementine returned to London for the birth of her child the other children remained at Frinton. During these last weeks Winston was at home very little and he was staying at Lympne with Philip Sassoon just days before the baby was due. On 15 September Clementine gave birth to another daughter, Mary, and on that same day Winston had his own 'adventure'. Despite all Clementine's objections to and fears about Chartwell, he had made up his mind to have it and on 15 September had made an offer of £5,000 which was accepted. Clementine knew nothing of this and even now Winston did not tell her. Instead he collected the children and took them to see the house, pretending that he was still considering buying it. As he had hoped and expected, Randolph, Diana and Sarah were delighted with the large, wild grounds of the house and they saw none of the disadvantages. They urged him to buy what seemed to them a wonderful place. Even though the news of this purchase had not yet been broken to Clementine Winston let his children into the secret, so when he finally confessed to her what he had done, he had the children's

1. Clementine's grandmother,
Blanche Countess of Airlie,
in her youth, painted by
G.F. Watts. She was a woman
who wanted complete
domination over her family
and Clementine was rather
afraid of her

2. Lady Blanche Hozier,
Clementine's mother,
whose disregard for
convention and obsession
with gambling frequently
embarrassed her daughter

3. Colonel Henry Hozier, Clementine's father, a highly respected Secretary to Lloyd's and a gifted mathematician. Clementine saw him only once after 1899

4. Bertram Mitford, later Lord Redesdale, Blanche Hozier's brother-in-law, to whom Clementine bore a remarkable resemblance

5. Clementine (*left*) and
her older sister Kitty before
their parents divorced.
Kitty was Blanche's
favourite until she died
in 1900 aged seventeen

6. The rue Pequet close
to the Hoziers' home in
Dieppe. Clementine
watched Walter Sickert's
progress with this painting
as she ran errands for
her mother

7. Clementine's engagement photograph in September 1908. She was already of great public interest as the fiancée of Winston Churchill

FIEL·PERO·DESDICHADO

MISS HORATIA SEYMOUR

MISS MADELEINE WHYTE

THE HON. VENETIA STANLEY

MISS CLARE FREWEN

MISS NELLIE HOZIER

8. Clementine and her bridesmaids: Madeleine Whyte, a cousin on the Ogilvy side; Horatia Seymour, her closest friend; Venetia Stanley, a cousin on the Stanley side; Clare Frewen, Winston's cousin on the Jerome side; and Nellie Hozier, Clementine's younger sister

9. Clementine and Winston gaze proudly at Diana, their first child born in 1909 at Eccleston Square. Within days, however, Clementine left London, putting her newly born daughter in the sole charge of a nanny

10. As this cartoon shows, Clementine was not alone in believing that not all Winston's cruises on the *Enchantress* were strictly necessary

11. The Enfield Munition Works in 1915.
Winston addresses the workers while Clementine listens

12. Clementine with Violet Bonham Carter and David Lloyd George at the opening of the Ponders End Canteen in February 1916. Clementine had feared that the resentment of the male workers against Lloyd George might wreck the occasion

13. Clementine at the Grand National accompanied by Winston's cousin Sunny, Duke of Marlborough, in an uncharacteristically cheerful mood

14. A rare photograph of Clementine alone with her son Randolph.
She strongly disapproved of his wild behaviour which is here temporarily
masked by his conventional Eton attire

15. Chartwell from the back. Clementine took pleasure in the beautiful gardens she had created but the house itself never ceased to be a burden to her

16. Clementine, Winston and Mary arrive for the Quebec Conference in 1943

17. Clementine with Eleanor Roosevelt in Quebec City in 1944 making a radio broadcast. Clementine shows little of the nervousness she felt on this occasion

18. Clementine at the opening of a YWCA hostel in Brussels in 1945

19. Workers' playtime at a London canteen. Despite her fur coat Clementine finds no difficulty in mixing readily

20. Clementine in Russia in 1945 wearing the Red Cross uniform of the Vice-President of the County of London Branch. She placed such great importance on this visit to Russia that she was willing to sacrifice her part in the Victory celebrations in England to be there

21. Clementine on her way to vote in 1945. She kept her own counsel about which party she voted for

22. Leaving 10 Downing Street for the coronation of Elizabeth II.
The gorgeous robes mask the fact that Clementine has her arm in a sling

23. Clementine and Winston celebrate their golden wedding anniversary. Randolph and his daughter Arabella had flown out to Lord Beaverbrook's villa especially to present the book of Golden Roses from the family

24. In the last year of her life, 1977, Clementine attends the christening of her namesake, her great-granddaughter Clementine Hambro

enthusiasm on his side. Clementine was angry and fearful about what the house would do to their lives. It was too late for her to do anything as the contract had already been signed, but she would always remember that Chartwell had been bought against her wishes and without her knowledge.

Winston was in a way lucky that shortly after his announcement he fell seriously ill and Clementine's anger turned to concern. On 18 October, just a day after a General Election was declared, Winston was operated on for appendicitis. Clementine was in a difficult position. She was still nursing Mary and in normal circumstances would not have taken part in the campaign. In this situation, however, she felt she had no choice; she was sure that Winston would not be re-elected if neither he nor she appeared in Dundee in person. So taking Mary along with her she set off for Scotland to do the best she could. This campaign was unlike any other in which she had taken part. In the aftermath of war the people of Dundee were more than ever aware of their poverty and the discrepancy between their lives and those of the rich people of the south. As a result the new Labour party's platform which seemed to take account of their needs and problems had been very well received in this constituency. In this atmosphere Clementine found that all those aspects of herself that she had previously been able to use to good advantage now told against her. Her voice with its pleasant accent was mocked as alien; her elegance which had once been admired was now resented as representing a richer life-style than was possible for the women of the constituency. On one occasion when she was unwise enough to wear a string of pearls to a meeting where many of those present had barely enough to eat, she was spat on. Hecklers interrupted her at large meetings so that she could not be heard. At one venue Winston's opponents had filled the hall with sneezing powder and Clementine could not say a word. She tried dealing with small groups, listening attentively to complaints and wishes. She learnt a great deal, but she convinced very few people that her husband was the right MP for them. She passed on what she had learnt to Winston and urged him to fight his campaign on positive lines by telling his constituents that he was dedicated to solving the labour problem rather than by denigrating the socialists. She gave him good advice but when Winston did manage to put in an appearance looking weak and ill he did not profit from it. Throughout the weeks of the campaigning Clementine tried to be cheerful and hopeful. In her heart she knew the likely outcome. It was no real surprise to her when Winston lost his seat.

Clementine was not altogether sorry for this chance for a respite from politics. More clearly than Winston she saw that political changes were taking place and that he would be better off on the sidelines until things settled down. She was herself very tired after a depressing campaign so soon after Mary's birth and Winston was by no means fully recovered from his operation. She was happy to let their London house and rent the Villa Rêve d'Or near Cannes. When the children finished school for the holidays the whole family joined her in France. When they returned to England and school there was no lack of company because before leaving London Winston had booked in a series of visitors. The days were passed in tennis and swimming and, less pleasing to Clementine, gambling in the casino.

For the first time in their married life Winston was not an MP. If Clementine had hoped that now their marriage could develop the intimacy and focus she had always found lacking in the relationship, then she was disappointed. When Winston had been out of office in those difficult days after the Dardanelles he had turned to her and relied heavily on her. Now, however, he had interests almost as demanding as those of his political life and he frequently left Cannes for London to attend to these. He was working hard on his as yet untitled book about the First World War and just as hard negotiating favourable publication and serialization terms. Clementine appreciated that this was necessary if they were to maintain their standard of living. What she resented was that the time left over from business was spent on Chartwell. It seemed to her that Chartwell was as great a rival for Winston's time and loving care as any mistress could have been. The house absorbed her husband more than even the *Enchantress* had done.

He had employed the architect recommended by Lloyd George, Philip Tilden. Now began the process, which Clementine had foreseen and feared, of discovering just how much needed to be done to their bargain house to make it habitable. Ironically, at this very time Winston was successfully suing for libel newspapers which had published an article about Clementine claiming that both Lord Randolph and Winston Churchill made life 'hell' for their wives.

Since Chartwell could not be ready to live in during the summer of 1923 Winston rented a house near by at Hosey Rigge. When the children's school holidays began they joined him there along with Mary and her nanny. The children adored working in the garden, building dams, riding the polo ponies, and being able to be wild and get dirty with impunity. Clementine felt excluded from these happy family activities but she had little desire to take part in them herself. She spent those summer days staying with Goonie at Pear Tree Cottage and then she did her bit politically for Winston by staying with Oliver Locker Lampson, a Tory MP keen to see Winston back in parliament and willing to do all he could to that end.

So Clementine was not there on that day in August when Brendan Bracken who worked on Locker Lampson's journal, *Empire Review*, turned up at Chartwell in search of Winston. It was the weekend that Winston had begun work in a lime tree making a tree house for the older children. Before the day was out Bracken had endeared himself to the whole family including Mary's nanny. By the time Clementine put in an appearance at Hosey Rigge he was an accepted member of the family party. People tended either to like or dislike Brendan Bracken. Clementine disliked him on sight. She did not understand how this, to her, unattractive, uncouth 22-year-old with an Australian accent, large spectacles and a mop of unruly curly red hair, had come to be so intimate with her husband when she had not even known of his existence until she found him at Hosey Rigge. She was cold and reserved in her manner to him, addressing him formally as Mr Bracken; but he appeared not to notice.

Shortly after Clementine arrived at Hosey Rigge, Winston set off to join Bendor on his yacht *Flying Cloud*. His ecstatic descriptions of life on the yacht made Clementine nervous that he might be thinking of a yacht as his next purchase. Then while Clementine worked and planned at Chartwell, Winston hunted at Mimizan and gambled at Biarritz.

Living at close quarters to Chartwell Clementine became ever more convinced that the place was beyond their means. After a year it had already absorbed a considerable amount of money and she could see no end to it. She had wanted a country place in which to relax and here she was saddled with a house which needed endless work. She hacked away at the detested rhododendrons behind the house and ordered drastic tree-cutting. Her physical violence in these activities expressed her pent-up anger and disgust at the house and her situation. In her letters to Winston she complained bitterly about the expense of his dream home and suggested that it was not too late to sell the house and look for somewhere more modest. But Winston was not to be moved. In his imagination Chartwell was already the family seat to be handed on to Randolph. To Clementine's horror he was even prepared to sell the house in Sussex Square if need be rather than sacrifice his country house.

When an election was called in November 1923 Winston was back ready to fight once more for a seat in parliament. Clementine saw the way he was tending politically when he decided not to stand as a Liberal against a Conservative in Manchester, where he had a good chance of winning, but to take on the far harder task of fighting a Labour candidate in the Labour stronghold of West Leicester.

The campaign was the worst Clementine had experienced to date, worse even than Dundee. Everywhere the Churchills appeared they were booed and mocked. The meetings they tried to speak at were rowdy and sometimes violent; their car window was smashed by a hostile opponent. There were two other factors which distressed Clementine. Firstly the Labour candidate was Mr Pethick-Lawrence, the husband of the suffragette for whom she had some respect. Secondly her husband was relying heavily in this campaign on the organizational skills of Brendan Bracken. But, even with the vigorous support of the young man and the declared support of some Conservatives, there was never a chance that Winston would win the seat. In fact he was soundly beaten by Mr Pethwick-Lawrence. Not for the first time Clementine had the frustration of seeing that the rejection of her advice had brought about a bad result. The only good thing to come out of this campaign, as far as Clementine could see, was her husband's realization that he and Lloyd George were no longer political allies. Lloyd George together with Asquith had declined to support the Conservatives against the Labour party thus giving Ramsay MacDonald the opportunity to form the first Labour government.

Back in London Clementine discovered that she was not the only person to wonder at Winston's close relationship with Brendan Bracken. Horrified, she discovered that rumours were circulating that Bracken was Winston's illegitimate son and that neither man was refuting the rumour. When she confronted Winston with this he gave a teasing reply, saying that he would have to check the dates. She never could be sure; her children grew up half-believing that Bracken was their brother. And even if she had known that Bracken was no relation to Winston she was deeply hurt by society's conviction that he was. Her dislike of Bracken intensified and her relationship with Winston, already severely strained over Chartwell, worsened. In February 1924 they both set off for France, but once there they intended to go their separate ways. Winston joined the Duke of Westminster at Mimizan while Clementine accepted an invitation from the former Duchess of Marlborough, now Madame

Balsan, to stay with her at Villa Lou Sueil looking over Eze-sur-Mer near Monte Carlo.

Clementine lingered in the warm south when Winston returned to Chartwell from where he issued detailed reports of the progress being made there. His letters seem to be an attempt to convince Clementine that he was doing the right things and to break down her resistance to and dislike of Chartwell. But not only did Clementine feel distanced from him and his building activities she seems to have felt remote also from her children. Mary had measles and then influenza; Clementine expressed distress but made no suggestion that she might return to be with her child of just over a year. She sympathizes with her young son in his cold school[2] but obviously feels no urge to improve his situation. Her keenest interest is in Winston's political career as she observes him moving ever closer to the Conservatives. She is concerned that he is too eager to rejoin the party which he had only recently left when they first met. Although she had not felt it necessary to return to London for her children's benefit, she did return to help with Winston's campaign for the Westminster seat. She was offended by the very visible presence of Brendan Bracken. As an Independent, Winston had no party organization to back him but Bracken's energy was a good substitute. Clementine was not too sure that she approved of his enlisting the help of the Drury Lane chorus girls to address and fill envelopes and she was extremely annoyed when without her permission he paraded Diana and Sarah round the constituency bearing the placard 'Vote for My Daddy'. Winston did not win this by-election but he did well enough to make many Conservative MPs urge him to rejoin the party.

As soon as the election was over Winston turned his attention to the exciting prospect of moving into Chartwell. All the many previous moves of their married life had been planned and organized by Clementine. But she had no intention of participating in all the hard work for a move to a house she had not chosen and did not want to live in. She decided to visit Blanche in Dieppe and she left Winston and the children to start to make Chartwell their home at Easter.

Instead of the hurly-burly of the move Clementine had a quiet time in France feeling almost drunk on the sea air. Her mother, now seventy-two, was visibly an old woman but she lived her life in much the same manner as she had always done. She still insisted on letting out the larger of her two houses and living in the much smaller one. If she could make a good let for the small house as well, she was quite prepared to move out of there and to take a room in a hotel by the casino. For she was as addicted as she had ever been to gambling and she drank more than Clementine felt was good for her. Since she did not go to the casino, Clementine spent her days idling and reading and considering the future. She had been thirty-nine that April, and in September Winston would be fifty. Whilst she was still beautiful and slim and had retained a good carriage Winston was fatter than he had been, he was almost completely bald, and his face was becoming lined. His great asset was the conviction and mobility of his face. She believed that his political career was on the upswing, his books were doing well and now he had his passion for Chartwell which she could see would provide him with an occupation for many years to come. With Chartwell he had drawn the children much closer to him than they had ever been to her.

So what did life promise for her? What was to be her role in the future? Clearly she was not central to her children's lives; she had deliberately exercised a choice not to be. As she observed her sister's obsessive mothering of her two boys Giles and Esmond and Goonie's possessiveness of Clarissa she was not altogether sorry about her decision. It had always been her intention to make Winston the centre of her life and she had hoped for the same from him. But was that any longer possible or likely? It seemed to her that Brendan Bracken was offering political support such that Winston's need for her was diminished. Winston's greed for affection and admiration was now being satisfied by his children's adoration of him rather than by her. He was even managing to establish a home at Chartwell without her help. At this moment she felt very much alone; her life seemed to be without much purpose and lacking a centre and her marriage had failed to live up to her expectations. What should she do next?

18

11 Downing Street

WINSTON'S ACCEPTANCE OF an invitation to speak to the Liverpool Working Men's Conservative Association was a clear signal. Now Clementine knew that it was only a question of time before Winston stood once again as a member of the Conservative party. She was resigned to this necessity but not happy about it. Winston was approached by several constituencies but after two recent defeats at by-elections he wanted to make sure that he did not lose a third time. After some hesitation he finally agreed to be the Conservative candidate for the Woodford constituency in Essex even though this would mean opposing a Liberal. An election was called in October and Winston began campaigning as a Conservative fighting against the dangers of a Labour party which he claimed was far too close to the Bolsheviks of Soviet Russia.

At the same time Clementine was preparing Randolph for his first term at Eton. She had been very little involved in the choice of Randolph's school. In Winston's view it was simply a matter of choosing between Eton and Harrow; any lesser establishment would have been unthinkable for his son. Remembering how disappointed her own brother had been when there was not enough money to send him to a public school, Clementine was content with Winston's decision. She hoped that the more rigorous demands of Eton would calm Randolph's wildness and that in the company of much older boys he would learn to listen to others and lose his confidence in his own infallibility. She was to be disappointed.

When the Conservatives came to power once again in November Winston had high hopes of a Cabinet position despite Clementine's view that Baldwin would see him as a threat to his leadership. But no one was more surprised than Winston when he was made Chancellor of the Exchequer, a position once held by his father. Initially Clementine was delighted: Winston would now have a salary of £5,000 a year, though this would be offset by the fact that he would have to stop work temporarily on his highly profitable book about the First World War, *World Crisis*. They had already decided that it was not financially possible to maintain both Chartwell and the house in Sussex Square. Winston had no doubt which he would choose but Clementine loved her London house and was reluctant to bury herself completely in the country. Now, suddenly, the official residence of the Chancellor, 11 Downing Street, was theirs. Sussex Square could be sold and they would still have a London house and the older girls could continue at their school. Clementine prepared for the move into Downing Street with considerably more enthusiasm than she had shown about Admiralty House. This time she could take furniture of their own and not have to rely on the Ministry of Works.

11 Downing Street was to be the Churchills' home for the next five years. Now that Winston was in office again Clementine hoped that her life, too, would improve. There was no doubt that in many ways Winston was a happier man. His old ability to delight, amuse and hold the attention of the House returned in full measure. So in her new home, with Winston's political career looking more hopeful than ever before, Clementine fully expected to cast off the depression of the previous year. She who delighted in organizing had plenty of scope for her abilities as hostess at 11 Downing Street. However, she still felt dissatisfied and tense, for in some ways Winston's new office had made them further apart, not closer. Neither Clementine nor Winston was educated in financial affairs, so when Winston needed advice it was not to his wife that he turned but to senior civil servants and the men of his acquaintance. He was drawn ever further into a male world where Clementine could not go. Because the work was new he threw himself into it with gusto; his time was fully occupied and even when he was at home he was surrounded by advisers and admirers. Clementine liked order and routine, both of which were impossible to achieve given Winston's working habits. And when he was not at work preparing for the April budget he was at Chartwell delighting in supervising the never-ending changes and improvements. The only role Clementine played in her husband's life was as a provider of an elegant setting and a good table. She did not share his pleasure in

Chartwell because she feared it represented financial ruin and she resented any interest which took him away from her.

By March she was thoroughly tired of the situation she found herself in and, as she was to do every year during Winston's Chancellorship, she escaped both Downing Street and Chartwell by going to stay with Consuelo Balsan.

At the Balsans' house just outside Eze-sur-Mer she found everything that was lacking in her life in England. The house itself was a delight to the senses. The Balsans had planned it themselves starting from scratch with an architect they knew and trusted. It was built of local stone high on a cliff overlooking a ravine and the fortressed village of Eze and surrounded by mountain peaks. Inside the house, in the panelled rooms, was carefully chosen period furniture, deep sofas with bright cushions, and Persian rugs from Isfahan on the floor. Every consideration had been made for the comfort of guests and in every room there were writing tables and lamps. Everywhere there were flowers filling the air with perfume. Outside the terraced gardens were well tended and planned so that a succession of bright flowers and blossoms grew sheltered by olive trees and cypresses. Clementine saw in Lou Sueil the antithesis of Chartwell. Here was a house which husband and wife had worked harmoniously together to achieve. Everything was planned from the start with none of the haphazardness of Chartwell where many changes were dictated by the poor condition of the existing fabric. Here was no overgrown wilderness of a garden overwhelming her with the amount of work required to tame it, but an area of calm and bright repose. Of course, Lou Sueil had been made possible by more than the loving cooperation of man and wife, though Clementine was painfully aware of the lack of this at Chartwell; Consuelo had the money to do everything properly and Clementine had not.

The routines of the household also pleased her. Mealtimes were regular and observed. Picnics and outings were carefully planned. She could play tennis, she could swim, she could visit Eze with its narrow cobbled streets and tiers of stone houses with old tiled roofs and oak doors. Here Clementine flourished, free from the irregularities of Winston's working days and his unpredictable demands. But was she free? Already by the middle of March Winston was growing restless at her absence. His letter of 15 March is a masterly piece of emotional blackmail disguised as concern for his wife. He begins by telling her not to cut short her stay at Eze, if it is doing her good, but by the end of the letter he is telling her that she is the rock on which he depends and that she should, therefore, return to him as soon as possible. No doubt Clementine would have responded to this appeal had not a more serious and genuine demand been made on her. From Dieppe came an urgent message that Blanche was very ill. Clementine immediately cancelled her return to London and joined Nellie in Dieppe. Blanche was indeed seriously ill and on 29 March, aged seventy-three, she died.

Nellie had always been closer to Blanche than had Clementine. She had lived alone with her for many years and shared her tastes and appetites. And, although Blanche owned very little, on her death she left what she had – her houses in Dieppe – to Nellie and to Nellie's younger son, Esmond. Clementine's feelings about her mother's death were complicated. For many years she had felt responsible for Blanche rather than drawn support from her. She was pleased with Winston's letters praising her mother and describing her as a great woman who had led a noble life and who had always shown great tenacity and self-denial. She did not herself, however, see her in the same light. Even so, now that she had no mother, she had to adjust her sense of herself and she was inevitably forced to consider whether she was faring any better as a mother than Blanche had done. Had Blanche failed Bill to the extent that he had killed himself? How did her relationship to Randolph compare? She had to admit that despite his remarkable good looks and obvious intelligence she found her son disappointing. She disliked his lack of discipline and his refusal to work at anything in a sustained way and she could see that these faults would be a severe disadvantage to him throughout his life. But what could she do about them? All her demands for higher standards were undercut by Winston's laughing tolerance. He saw in Randolph a great deal of himself as a boy and he confidently expected that Randolph would, as he had done, reform himself. In his desire not to treat his own son as he had been treated by his father he went to an opposite and, it seemed to Clementine, an equally dangerous extreme.

In Diana Clementine saw something of herself as a girl. Diana was becoming pretty but Clementine could see that she would never have quite the beauty that had been her own great asset. She had tried to make sure that Diana received as good an education as she had by sending her to Notting Hill High School and Diana appeared to enjoy her studies. But where Clementine had been reserved, Diana was timid and painfully lacking in self-confidence. To her dismay Clementine saw in Diana a paler, less effective version of herself. She felt more pleasure in Sarah whose health caused her concern but whose high spirits and determination she enjoyed. She did not, apparently, see how closely she was following the pattern of her own mother who had favoured Kitty and Nellie over herself for much the same reasons that she was happier with Sarah than with Diana. Of Mary she knew comparatively little. She had determined when this child was born that she would make sure that this daughter would not suffer the same fate as Marigold. The result was that Mary was being lovingly, carefully and consistently cared for, not by herself but by her cousin Maryott Whyte, a trained Norland nanny.

A distraction from these concerns was Winston's first Budget which he presented in April. Accompanied by Diana and Randolph, Clementine was in the Stranger's Gallery to hear him deliver a speech which, unlike most Budget speeches, kept the House enthralled and entertained. Winston thrived on his success, but the moment he could tear himself away from work he went to Chartwell. Despite the financial advantages he turned down offers to rent the house for the summer months. He even refused invitations to houses such as Wilton, so eager was he to be at work on his own house and grounds. He was determined to keep livestock to make the house more self-sufficient. Clementine did not like the animals nor, given the extra staff needed to look after them, did she believe that they would make a profit from them. Despite her unhappiness she worked to make a beautiful garden, carrying in her head all the time the image of the gardens at Lou Sueil. It was not in her nature to live in a house which she had not made beautiful and she was gradually recreating the inside of Chartwell to suit her own excellent taste. Had there been more money available she would have set about this work with a better grace, but to be always considering what was affordable spoilt her pleasure.

All the children loved Chartwell and they were frequently joined by cousins who also enjoyed its wildness and all the physical activity and upheaval which Winston's presence brought with it. Jack and Goonie's children spent most of their summers at Chartwell; Tom and Diana Mitford were regular visitors also. Tom was at Eton with Randolph and had a calming effect on his cousin. Diana, whom Winston nicknamed Dynamite, was a good companion for Diana Churchill, though, Clementine soon observed, she tended to overshadow her. Nellie brought Giles and Esmond, though at ages nine and seven they were often neglected by the older children. Clementine tried to organize this unruly band of children, arranging games and picnics and even amateur dramatics, but all too often they preferred their own less structured activities.

All through the summer there was a steady stream of adult visitors. By now Winston was beginning to attract younger admirers. Some of these Clementine disliked and distrusted. Brendan Bracken continued to be one of them and he was now joined on her list of those she did not readily welcome to Chartwell by Robert Boothby. The young MP for East Aberdeenshire was a frequent guest since he had been invited by Winston to be his PPS. On the other hand she did like the 'liberal' Conservative MP for Chippenham, Victor Cazalet, who always treated her with deference, had charming manners, and shared her enthusiasm for tennis. The other less likely favourite was Frederick Lindemann, Professor of Experimental Philosophy at Oxford. This man with his deep-set eyes, roman nose, flat, neat moustache and tidy hair was regarded by some of the children at Chartwell as a sinister figure. There was every reason why Clementine should have disliked him for his reactionary and anti-semitic views and his obvious influence on her husband. But on the other hand he did not smoke or drink and he was a vegetarian. He was, therefore, a less expensive guest to entertain than some of Winston's friends. He also shared with her a love of tennis and was always ready for a game. He took a great interest in Randolph and relieved some of the pressure on Clementine by taking Randolph off for visits to Oxford and for long car rides.

It may have been the death of her mother that made Clementine suddenly more conscious of the traditional family with its customs and rituals which had been lacking in her own childhood. For this year saw the first of the Chartwell Christmases when, not always successfully, Clementine attempted to gather together as many of the family as possible with Christmas tree, party games and the singing of carols. Winston loved it; it was their version of the Blenheim Christmases of so many other years.

By February, however, Clementine had had her fill of the family and Chartwell. While Winston set up an all male weekend party she escaped to the ordered luxury of Consuelo's home. She found Conseulo a congenial companion. She was well educated and well read. Unlike many of her contemporaries in the aristocracy she had courageously walked away from an unsatisfactory marriage and had been strong enough to live her own life as a busy single woman. She had been politically active and had even had a seat on the North Southwark council. Like Clementine she had a social conscience, and she had worked with the wives of prisoners and was on the Board of the Medical School for Women. Herself the daughter of a strong believer in women's suffrage she shared with Clementine a belief that women's rights should be more fully acknowledged. So the conversations in which Clementine participated at Eze contrasted strongly with the male-dominated, mostly political, arguments she was accustomed to in her own home.

From Eze Clementine went to Rome where she stayed at the British Embassy and it was from here that she wrote to Winston an extraordinary letter about her first meeting with Benito Mussolini, the Italian Fascist leader. No other letter in their correspondence describes a person or a place in such loving detail. A star-struck girl introduced to her favourite film or pop idol could not have exceeded the enthusiasm Clementine showed for Mussolini. She was undoubtedly bowled over by his smile, his penetrating eyes of deep brown. His charisma aroused in her overwhelming devotion.[1] Like any young groupie she was filled with a desire to do something, anything, for the great man. When he spoke to her she felt singled out, honoured and suddenly sympathetic to the fanatical devotion Mussolini inspired in his followers. Despite her lack of Italian she decided to go with Goonie to an open-air meeting held to celebrate five years of Fascism at which Mussolini was to speak. Her pleasure and excitement when she received a signed photo from Mussolini with 'A La Signora Winston Churchill. Devotamente B. Mussolini. Roma 25 Marzo' is unmistakable. The photograph accompanied her home and was a proudly displayed possession, at least until the political climate changed.

On her return to England the contrast between the state of affairs there and the well-ordered Italian society she had just left seemed to justify her admiration for Mussolini who had apparently achieved the impossible in making Italy function so well. In England there was trouble in the mining industry and a strike had only been averted by a government subsidy to prevent miners' wages being reduced pending the preparation of a report. On 1 March the Samuel Report had found fault with the mine owners but had acknowledged that without a continuing subsidy it would be necessary to reduce the miners' wages temporarily. When the owners did so on 1 May the TUC called for a general strike. Any hope of preventing this by negotiation was abandoned when the printers went on strike. The strike began at midnight. Six million people refused to work, so that all forms of transport and heavy industry were brought to a standstill. But not for long. The army and the police were mobilized and there was a flood of volunteer workers. In London there was almost a holiday atmosphere as the most unlikely people did the most unlikely jobs. The middle classes and the aristocracy were happy playing at being bus drivers and train drivers, not appreciating the difference between doing these jobs for a few days, dealing with a tolerant public, and grinding away day after day. Winston himself enjoyed the strike once he was made editor of the government newspaper *The British Gazette* and saw the circulation figures climbing steeply each day of printing.

Clementine simply did the same job as usual but on a larger scale, feeding and seeing to the needs of those working on the press and the constant stream of people going in and out of 11 Downing Street at all hours of the day and night. She was relieved when on 12 May the strike was called off and gradually life returned to normal. She had admired the part Winston had played but had found his exuberant energy and high spirits plus his domineering attitude exhausting.

In July 1926 Diana was seventeen years old and both parents began to think about her future. Clementine recalled that at that age she had spent time in Paris attending classes at the Sorbonne and she decided that Diana should have a similar opportunity to learn to speak French fluently. There was no question of the whole family moving to Paris as the Hoziers had done. Instead Clementine arranged for Diana to stay as a paying guest with the Bellaigue family after a short holiday in France to help her adjust to a different language and way of life. As all her children in turn were to discover, Clementine away from Winston and away from Chartwell was a much less intimidating and a much more agreeable companion than they had suspected. She now took Diana to Dinard and then to Paris where she introduced her daughter to all her own old haunts. The climax of the visit was a meal at Voisins. Clementine was again repeating the pattern established by her own mother.

By now it had come to Winston's attention that Chartwell was costing more than they could easily afford. So many of his schemes, especially his ideas for farming, had failed to prosper. Clementine urged selling the house, Winston countered by suggesting ways in which they could economize. He reasoned that if the house were let, even if only for one summer, then it would pay for itself. In the end some economies were made but the house was never let. The discussions, however, created bad feeling and tension to the extent that Clementine spent Christmas at Chartwell while Winston went to Blenheim. Then in early January he was off on a trip to Malta taking Randolph with him while Clementine went again to Eze. Winston joined her there briefly and they were reconciled, but that did not prevent Winston from rushing off to join Bendor for boar hunting.

When the four months which Diana was to spend with her French family had come to an end, Winston wanted Clementine to go to Paris and fix her up with another family. But Clementine was much too content where she was and left Winston to collect their daughter and take her home with him. Clementine did nothing to prevent the strange pattern of her own girlhood repeating itself. For Diana now found herself back at school during the day but going out socially in the evening with her father. Having apparently forgotten her own resentment at having her education brought to an abrupt conclusion and being discouraged from thinking of a career, Clementine now assumed that the next step for Diana was to prepare herself for the marriage market. Did she not take enough interest in this daughter to consider alternatives for her? Did she find it easier to fall in with Winston's ideas, his love of tradition, his sense of his family being special and his ongoing belief that women essentially belonged in the home? His attitude to women had changed very little over the years. Whatever his public position on woman suffrage he was still privately against it. In a secret memorandum written in March 1927 he expressed his worry about the extension of female suffrage as having the likely effect of transferring too much power into the hands of women.[2] So it was decided that Diana along with her cousin Diana Mitford should come out that year. She was taken for fittings for clothes suitable for a debutante and then she was taken to a succession of balls either in Oxford, close to where the Mitfords were living in Swinbrook, the ugly and uncomfortable house designed by David Mitford, or in London. Throughout the season Diana Churchill was miserable while Diana Mitford was ecstatic. Diana Churchill felt a complete failure whereas everyone agreed that Diana Mitford had been a great success. The tangible proof of that success was that by 1928, aged eighteen, she was engaged to the wealthy and very attractive Bryan Guinness.

At the end of the season Clementine took Diana off to Ireland to stay with Winston's Aunt Leonie at Castle Leslie. Anita Leslie was there at the time and it was to her that Diana confided her desperate unhappiness over the failure of her first season. She felt most bitterly that she had not lived up to her mother's high standards. Rather than commiserating with her or making light of the importance of the season Clementine had been critical of her daughter and impatient with her timidity.

Clementine's irritation which seemed to the two young girls totally unfair and unkind was the result of more than Diana's failure to shine. In June Clementine had been knocked down by a bus in Brompton Road. Although not seriously hurt, she had been shocked and her nerves set on edge with the result that she was less tolerant than she might otherwise have been of the 'busy idleness' of the season. The expense of bringing a girl out in however modest a way troubled her and she dreaded the further expense and the boredom of another season chaperoning Diana. She was in fact pulled in two directions. On the one hand she thought the whole debutante business a waste of time and money; on the other hand if she did not give her daughter this start she feared she would greatly diminish her opportunities for making a good marriage. For Clementine's pessimistic view of her daughter was that she was unlikely to succeed in any other direction.

The accident had produced one pleasant surprise. Out of the blue, having read about the incident in the newspapers, Walter Sickert had again appeared in her life. She found him as charismatic as ever and, as George Moore remarks in his autobiography, 'No one is angry when Sickert is by.'[3] In the highly charged atmosphere of Chartwell Sickert was, therefore, a most welcome guest. He took an interest in Winston's painting and he brought with him views and perspectives from a world not otherwise well represented in the Churchills' circle.

In September Clementine fell ill and her doctor advised complete rest. This was, of course, impossible at 11 Downing Street or Chartwell and so she set off for Venice and the Lido. Winston promised to join her for a few days when he could free himself from work. Venice was where the Churchills had spent some of their honeymoon. Clementine may have been hoping that in that place with its associations they could recapture some of the romantic, even passionate feeling that had been lost in the business of political life in London and practical affairs at Chartwell.

Her feeling that she never came first with Winston any more seemed to be justified when he wrote saying that, although he was attracted by the idea of joining her in Venice and having the chance to paint, he was even more enchanted by life at Chartwell. This was hurtful enough, but then in the next letter Winston announced that he did have time to go and visit the Duke of Westminster. The charms of Venice began to fade for Clementine and she was thinking of moving on, when she was urged by Winston to stay just a few days longer so that he could join her. But she now saw everything with a jaundiced eye. Mussolini, to whom she had earlier responded so enthusiastically, had become to her a 'sinister sten-cilled face' which confronted her on walls everywhere. She was not pleased to hear from Winston that Coco Chanel, for whom he had already expressed great admiration, was staying with Bendor and himself. When her husband did at last arrive in Venice it was for a brief and unsatisfac-tory stay. He brought Professor Lindemann with him as well as his paint-ing equipment so that the moments of intimacy Clementine had hoped for never materialized.

For the next few months Clementine travelled in Italy with Diana. They were perhaps not the best company for each other both being in their different ways unhappy and confronting failure. In Florence they were invited to stay with Alice Keppel whose worldliness Clementine now better appreciated.

Winston was in no doubt that Clementine was dissatisfied with him. Although she sent postcards regularly to Mary she did not write to him. Was it in an attempt to regain her favour that he wrote and promised her that he would vote for the extension of the franchise for women, the 'Flapper Vote' as he called it?

Illness rather than political compromise was what did make Clementine closer to her husband again. In February of 1928 she was racked by intense pain in her ear. Her doctors diagnosed mastoiditis and advised immediate treatment. Although this condition can now be treated with antibiotics, in 1928 the only cure was surgery in the form of an incision behind the ear to drain off the fluid collected in the air cells of the mastoid bone. Clementine was warned that if immediate action was not taken she could develop critical meningitis or even brain damage. Confronted with the possibility that he might lose his wife Winston real-ized just how important Clementine was to him. He had often asserted his love for her in letters but his actions had seemed to belie his words. Now he showed her the tenderness, devotion and concern which Clementine had longed for. Despite the pain and the anxiety of the three operations that she underwent at this time, she was able to write to her husband when she was safely in Eze to recuperate that she did not regret her illness since it had resulted in a new closeness between them: she told her husband that his tenderness while she had been ill had made her aware of her own deep love for him.[4]

Winston almost immediately put the new tenderness to the test by abstaining when the 'Flapper Vote' came before the House. Clementine's tone of reproach was softer than it might otherwise have been but she was clearly disappointed and felt that Winston had acted unwisely. She feared that the women in his constituency would not appreciate his abstention.

No sooner had Clementine returned home than Winston fell ill with influenza. Illness on top of the very heavy workload he had undertaken left him depleted for some months. So once again they spent much of the summer apart. Winston went north to stay with Bendor and Coco Chanel while Clementine did the round of balls and visits with Diana. In August a stay at Mountstewart in County Down with Lord and Lady Londonderry tried her patience sorely. She who was so fastidious and expected to have everything perfect for her own guests now found herself eating off dirty silver in a house where she could not get her shoes cleaned and where she found the conversation trite and dull. She wrote to Winston saying that however much she wanted to help Diana to make a good marriage, she dreaded more such visits. And she confessed that she preferred his own more robust if sometimes 'odious' company to that in which she found herself.

At a distance and by comparison to the Londonderrys' home, Chartwell had seemed very attractive. Faced with the reality of all the work to be done there to achieve the standards she had set herself and harassed by ongoing problems with servants, Clementine found that she could not cope. Her doctor suspected that she was feeling ill because her tonsils needed to be removed. The alternative she was given was to spend some time in a nursing home undergoing a toxic elimination programme. Clementine opted for the latter but ten days of nothing but orange juice made her feel worse and she began to have fainting fits. But by the end of November she was confidently declared to be well and able to return home.

Christmas was not, however, a happy occasion. Diana was upset and moody because her cousin was engaged and would be married in January. She envied her this escape from home to an establishment of her own and she dreaded the next season without anyone to accompany her and to confide in. Randolph was also jealous. He fancied himself in love with Diana Mitford and was annoyed that she was to be married before he was old enough to propose to her himself. Her entry into the adult world made him resent his status as a schoolboy and he now decided that he was wasting his time at Eton and should be allowed to go to university.

Winston and Clementine were far from pleased with Randolph's latest school report; though Clementine at least appreciated the accuracy of the description of Randolph as being unreachable because in his anger he would talk faster and faster, interrupt frequently and be more concerned with thinking up a crushing reply than with listening. She was quite convinced that Randolph was not ready to leave school. Winston agreed with her initially, but when Professor Lindemann took Randolph's side and undertook to get a place for him in his own college, Christ Church in Oxford, Winston allowed himself to be persuaded. Clementine's judgement that this move would simply bring out the worst in Randolph was overruled. Nevertheless Randolph resented his mother's view and continued to do so after he got his way and was admitted to the university in January.

In 1929 Winston had been Chancellor of the Exchequer for almost five years and was no longer as happy in the job as he had once been. He saw now that much of the advice he had been given in the early days had been unsound and had caused him to lose the sympathy of most working people. As the time approached when an election had to be called he began to think about what other office would suit him. But he also began to talk of the likelihood of the Conservatives being defeated. As he talked with interest about what it would be like to be on the opposition benches, Clementine thought anxiously about what it would be like to be without a Minister's salary. Winston brushed aside her fears; he was confident that he could support the family by his writing and he had anyway made a number of American investments of which he had high hopes.

As soon as the election was called Clementine rushed off to Epping to rent a house so that she and the children could be on the spot to campaign for Winston. Her husband meanwhile was on the larger campaign trail on behalf of the Conservatives as a whole rather than for just his own seat. Randolph spoke at one public meeting in Epping and was well received much to his father's joy. But it was largely due to the efforts of Clementine that, despite the Labour Party's overall victory, Winston retained his seat, though with a reduced majority.

However, with the Conservatives out of power Winston was no longer a Minister and when he gave up the residence of the Chancellor of the Exchequer the Churchills were once again without a London home.

19

Depressions

BECAUSE HE HAD anticipated a change of government Winston was not nearly as upset when the Conservatives lost the election as Clementine had feared he would be. He had, in fact, already made financial provision for the moment when his salary as Chancellor would cease by signing a contract to write the biography of the first Duke of Marlborough. Even the lack of a London house was not an urgent problem since Winston intended to make what he hoped would be a profitable lecture tour of Canada and the United States. Planning the tour and preparing lectures left him no time to miss the business of the Exchequer.

The original idea had been for Clementine and Goonie to accompany Winston, but in June Clementine had a recurrence of the throat problem which had troubled her in the previous year. To her dismay and annoyance all the time spent in the nursing home on a miserable starvation diet had only served to delay the operation for tonsillitis which was performed in July.

Worse still, Winston decided that she was not fit enough to undertake what might turn out to be a gruelling trip across North America and he decided to take Randolph and Johnny Churchill with him instead of Clementine and Goonie. Weak after her operation, Clementine initially felt lonely and abandoned. She did not even go to see Winston off when he left on 3 August but instead sent Diana and Sarah.

While Clementine drifted from one country house to another doing her duty by Diana, getting Sarah ready for school and planning a birthday party for Mary, Winston made his exuberant way across Canada, delighting in his reception and in the money he was earning and saving.

Clementine was reassured to know that Randolph was behaving well, though concerned that the way of life in California into which he flung himself with glee might have a corrupting effect. She thought he was a little young for the kind of flirtation with movie stars that Winston reported to her. She did not know, because Winston did not tell her, that he had been angry with Randolph on several occasions during the tour for rudeness and lack of discretion. As the weeks went by Clementine grew anxious that Randolph would not be back in time for the new term at Oxford. A conversation with Professor Lindemann convinced her that her son's university career would definitely be harmed if he failed to present himself on time. As always, therefore, Clementine was in the position of being the parent to urge something which Randolph felt curtailed his pleasure.

She had, meanwhile, found a temporary and inexpensive London base. Her cousin Venetia had a house at 62 Onslow Gardens in Kensington. After the death of her husband Edwin Montagu the previous year she no longer needed or wanted to be in London during the parliamentary session and she was pleased to let Clementine have the house for a modest weekly sum. As soon as he heard this news from Clementine, Winston began to plan a social calendar for the session; he wanted Clementine to organize lunches for eight or ten colleagues on a regular basis and similar dinners at least twice a week. Clementine saw that Winston's being out of office would neither lighten her burden of entertaining nor enable her to see much more of him. He clearly intended to spend his time either with other MPs or at Chartwell working on the life of Marlborough or on the grounds of the house.

To prepare herself for the months ahead she treated herself and Diana to another Italian tour, again spending time with Alice Keppel at the Villa Ombrellina in Florence before going on to Perugia, Assisi and Rome. She was confident that they could afford this holiday since Winston had reported that the American investments he had made were doing well and that he had made 'a small fortune' from his writing and lecturing, most of which money he had invested.

Such confidence in their financial stability was short-lived. In November Wall Street crashed and with it many of Winston's recent investments. The Churchills lost £40,000 overnight and all Winston's work over the summer went for nothing. Clementine's nightmare of poverty seemed close to being a reality and even Winston was shaken. They had earlier toyed with various ideas about economizing but these had rarely amounted to much. Now they were forced to act. Chartwell was all but shut down, only Mary and Maryott remaining in the cottage built specially for them. Randolph returned to Oxford, Sarah to her boarding school in Broadstairs while Winston, Clementine and Diana moved into Venetia's house in Onslow Gardens.

In 1930 Clementine would be forty-five and Winston fifty-six. They were at an age when most of their contemporaries were well established both professionally and financially and with secure homes. But they had none of these things. Winston's future in parliament looked less promising than for many years. Their income was barely enough to meet their needs and depended almost entirely on Winston's ability to write and to sell what he wrote. Their only home was Chartwell which Clementine still regarded as a burden and which they could not afford to live in. They had insufficient money to buy a place in London and would have to move to another house in Eaton Square rented on a short-term lease when Venetia needed her house at Christmas. Even the family was as much a source of concern as of comfort and pleasure. Diana was still at home with too little to do and no clear idea of a future. Randolph, apparently unmoved by their financial difficulties, continued to get into needless debt at Oxford keeping up with a group of wealthier older students. He seemed to have little interest in his work and no notion of preparing himself for a career and financial independence. In the past Clementine had always been the parent to express dismay at Randolph's extravagance and inability to apply himself to work. Now Winston began to feel let down by his son. In April, writing to the father of his hard-working research assistant, Maurice Ashley, he commented bitterly on his son's idleness and indifference to the University.[1]

Rarely had a year gone by of late when Clementine had not fallen ill in some way or another and been obliged to leave her family and husband in order to recuperate. In this most difficult year, however, she flourished. The temporary closure of Chartwell which was such a sadness to Winston was to her a relief. She was not unhappy to live frugally and she responded lovingly to Winston's need of her in his depression and sense of failure. She agreed to go to Sarah's school to present the prizes and astonished everyone with the wittiness of her speech and the elegance of her appearance. Sarah was a little overwhelmed and even embarrassed by her beautiful mother who was definitely not 'mum-shaped'.[2]

When in September one of Winston's closest friends, F. E. Smith, died of cirrhosis of the liver brought about by excessive drinking Clementine sympathized with his unhappiness. Even when she learnt that Smith had died leaving such debts that his wife Margaret would have to sell their house and its contents and move into very modest premises she did not remind Winston that she had predicted such an end. Instead she tried to bring a new interest into his life by encouraging him to play golf on the links close to Chartwell. In October Clementine was able to report to Randolph that his father had begun to like the game.[3] She clearly enjoyed sharing an activity with him rather than seeing him spend all his time either writing or working on the Chartwell estate.

The hours Winston spent in his study were now proving worthwhile. In September *My Early Life* was published, and the book Winston claimed to have written merely to pay the tax-man had an immediate success. Clementine was pleased not only by the financial implications of good sales but also by the effect on Winston of all the praise he was receiving. At a moment when he was gloomy about his political prospects his career as a writer was blossoming.[4]

At this time, against all the odds, the Churchills' marriage was close and happy. The conclusion of *My Early Life* did not seem in the context of September 1930 to be entirely inappropriate. Winston had written, 'September 1908, when I married and lived happily ever after.'[5] During the course of this year they had even found themselves in agreement about Randolph. In February Randolph had spoken at the Oxford Union against the Labour government's policy on Egypt. He had used the arguments he had heard used by his father, and it was largely because of this and his famous name that his speech had been widely reported in the English press and from there had been picked up by *The New York Times*. As a result an American lecturing agency had approached him and invited him to lecture in the States. Already in debt again and in no doubt about his parents' response to a request for more money, Randolph determined to accept. Just as they had opposed his leaving Eton early so now both Winston and Clementine were against his taking time out of his university term before finishing his degree. Clementine was confident that if he lectured in the States he would never return to university. She was right, but Randolph did not listen to her. Even his father's homilies on the importance of a university education failed to move or interest Randolph. On 1 October he sailed for New York having made no preparations whatsoever for the lectures he had engaged to deliver.

This was less of a worry to Clementine than the rumours that soon reached England that Randolph was about to become engaged to an

American girl. Knowing that Randolph would be sure to give his parents an edited version of what he was about and well aware that any advice she might write to him was likely to be ignored, Clementine resolved on a more drastic approach. From the unexpectedly good sales of *My Early Life* Winston had promised her enough money with which to buy herself a small car. Clementine decided that she would prefer to spend the money on a trip to New York to see for herself whether Randolph was contemplating marriage and, if so, to whom. She approached Randolph with her idea with great tact but was surprised by the enthusiasm of his response. Suddenly what had been planned as a journey to rescue Randolph became an adventure for her. She bought new clothes and her excitement enhanced her beauty. She was, perhaps, not simply joking when she told Randolph that she preferred to travel as herself and not as the wife of Winston Churchill.[6]

In February 1931 Clementine sailed from England on the German ship *Europa*. The crossing was rough with fogs and gales and she caught a chill. But her interest in her adventure was undiminished. The ship was delayed twenty-four hours, giving her plenty of time to observe her fellow passengers. These were mostly German Americans whom she imagined quite capable of justifying rudeness with riches.[7] She found the cold efficiency of the crew almost alarming and she imagined how readily this efficiency could be harnessed in a war situation.

The weeks Clementine spent in New York were the happiest times she had experienced with her son since he was a baby. Randolph was flattered that for the moment Clementine's concern for him outweighed that for Winston and his comforts. He saw her through the eyes of his American friends and realized fully just how beautiful she was and how readily she could charm everyone she met. Usually her qualities served to enhance Winston's position: now they reflected well on him. He was also pleased that she did not seem embarrassed or distressed by him but proud of the success he was making of the lecture tour. His unfamiliarly gallant and courteous behaviour towards her pleased and touched Clementine. The absence of Winston made Clementine view her son in a different light. Here in the States he did not have to compete with his father and so he was less loud and boastful. In England everyone was interested in the relationship between father and son; in the States they were intrigued by his relationship to his mother and how much he had inherited her good looks. It was as if Clementine had suddenly discovered that Randolph was her son as well as Winston's. Her letters home were ecstatic.

Her original intention in going to the States had been to prevent Randolph entering into a relationship which at his age and with no prospects he could not possibly sustain. But she listened sympathetically to Randolph's account of his feelings for the girl he had fallen in love with. When she met Kay Halle, the daughter of a businessman from Cleveland, Ohio, her apprehensions were dispelled. Kay, who was older than Randolph, seemed to care for him but had no intention of marrying him. Her influence on him had been a good one: she had made him prepare his lectures properly and arrive on time for his engagements. Kay could see, however, that being Randolph's wife, just like being the wife of Winston Churchill, would be more than a full-time job. She did not wish to dedicate her life to being Randolph's Clementine.

When Clementine at last left New York she was on the best of terms with her son and with Kay Halle. She was confident that Randolph would not return to England either engaged or married and she liked to think that from now on she would have a different and better relationship with him and would, perhaps, have a greater influence over him than previously.

Writing to Winston, Clementine had described her time with Randolph as a 'honeymoon'. And like all honeymoons it was soon over. For Randolph had been careful to show his mother only what he hoped she would admire. She was not aware of his rudeness, his insensitivity to American pride and his drunkenness. She did not know that his extravagance and taste for luxurious living were such that the large sums he was earning were more than balanced by those he was spending. When he returned home he was not only penniless he was also deeply in debt and completely spoilt for the life of a student.

Clementine had the doubtful pleasure of seeing her words come true again. Randolph now declared that Oxford had nothing more to offer him. Clementine insisted that he was by no means educated and entirely without qualifications. At first Winston supported her but then said that Randolph could leave Oxford on condition that he find a job. This Randolph did, and at twenty now appeared to be completely independent.

His way of life, however, angered and disquieted his mother. While she saw Winston working tirelessly at his writing to support his family she saw Randolph living the life of a young lord, even hiring for himself a car and chauffeur. What money he did earn was to a great extent earned on the back of his father. He was invited to lecture and to meet people because he was Winston's son. His willingness to cash in on his family name appalled Clementine. She had always tried to maintain family privacy and now she saw intimate details of Randolph's relationship with Winston used in an article in the *Sunday Graphic*. Then came the request from Randolph that he might write his father's biography. His motive was clearly money not filial piety. By the end of the year Winston was dealing with his son as sternly as Clementine could wish, describing him as selfishly exploiting his parents.[8] She was sadly aware that Winston's change of attitude had come too late.

For many years Clementine had been cold towards Brendan Bracken and had been angry about the rumours that Bracken was Winston's son. Now, as she compared Randolph with Bracken and saw how her son wasted what his father had worked for while Bracken was constantly on the look-out for commissions to enable Winston to earn more, she decided that she had perhaps been wrong in her judgement of the strange young man. She now made him more welcome in her home.

In June, nine months after her voyage on the *Europa*, Clementine was again on board heading for New York. This time she did have as her travelling companions her husband and also Diana, who was still living at home and feeling very much in her mother's shadow. Like Randolph, Winston had been engaged to give a series of lectures. He also planned to consult his friend Bernard Baruch about the best way to invest his earnings.

In the Waldorf Astoria where they were staying Clementine made the acquaintance of Cecil Beaton. While Winston prepared his lectures she agreed to sit for her portrait by the now fashionable photographer. She found his company soothing and his flattering attentiveness gratified her. The resulting portrait is quite unlike any other of her. Clementine is in profile and the classical line of her features is emphasized. The strength of her personality thus suggested is balanced by the soft, lacy femininity of the shawl which is draped over her arms and shoulders and from which her wrists and long, elegant fingers emerge. Clementine was very fond of dressing fashionably and in most photographs her clothes are as important as the woman. In its simplicity Beaton's uncluttered profile portrait reveals to the full Clementine's mature and characterful beauty in her forty-sixth year.

The tentative serenity of Clementine at this moment did not last. The Churchills had been in New York just a few days when on 13 December Winston left the hotel by taxi to seek out Bernard Baruch. Within a couple of hours Clementine was summoned to Lennox Hill Hospital where her husband had been taken after being knocked down by a taxi. She found Winston badly shaken and bruised. Most worrying was a severe head wound and two cracked ribs. Clearly his lecture tour could not go on. As soon as Winston was able to leave the hospital she took him to Nassau to recuperate and it was here that they saw in the New Year.

Clementine loved Nassau with its pleasant climate and relaxed way of life. She half wished that they could afford a house and a garden there. Her pleasure, however, was overshadowed by the deep depression that engulfed Winston now. He told her that he wondered if he would ever recover after three major blows in one year. First there had been the loss of money from his investments, then he had once more become politically isolated, belonging truly to neither the Conservative nor the Liberal party. Now there was this physical blow which left him feeling defeated and without that energy and capacity for work on which their future depended.

Curiously enough Clementine's letters of this time to Randolph are very affectionate. She makes none of the harsh judgements that Winston had recently made. On the contrary she confides to Randolph that she is feeling very anxious and that she often wishes that he was there to help and advise her. Had her few days in New York reminded her of how close she had been to Randolph just a few months earlier, and did she hope to revive that relationship?

By February Winston was feeling well enough to begin the postponed lecture tour, so the Churchills returned to New York. And now, as if to underline Clementine's earlier misjudgement, it was not Randolph who made an extravagant gesture of sympathy and affection for Winston after all his trials, but Brendan Bracken. Aided and abetted by Archie Sinclair he had raised enough money among their friends to buy and present to Winston on his arrival back in England an expensive motor car, a Daimler.

It was Sarah who now demanded Clementine's attention. Of her two elder daughters Clementine instinctively had more sympathy for Sarah. She admired her seeming reserve and independent spirit. She liked to think that Sarah was far more like her own younger self than Diana. So when Sarah begged to be allowed to leave school she listened sympathetically. Sarah was definitely not academic, but Clementine decided that at least Sarah should become more proficient in French and so arranged for her to continue her studies in Paris for a while before coming out.

Neither Sarah nor Clementine had much heart for this ritual but nevertheless Clementine did her best to see that Sarah would be beautifully dressed for her season. After one session with the dressmaker she happened to comment to Diana how very easy it was to dress Sarah well. Her remark solicited a family crisis the reverberations of which continued well into the future.

In Clementine's remark Diana read all the criticisms of herself she believed her mother harboured. She was jealous of Sarah as her mother's favourite and she was afraid that Sarah would have a greater success than she had done as a debutante thus making her mother favour her still more. She accused her mother of cruelty in allowing Sarah to come out before she, the older sister, was married. Diana's view of herself as the least loved member of the family was confirmed by another event in May. When Diana had reached twenty-one there had been a birthday party for her but it had not been a grand occasion. Randolph's twenty-first birthday party was, however, made by Winston into a public celebration not only of his son but of fathers and sons in general and the notion of dynasty. The family birthday party for Randolph was completely overshadowed by the all-male, fathers-and-sons dinner which Winston hosted at Claridge's. The occasion emphasized for all the Churchill women that Winston, as always, regarded men as the real force in society.

The event was widely reported in the press and, reading one account in the *Evening Standard*, Clementine was confronted with how others saw Randolph. She must have wondered if Winston's emphatic preference for his son and heir had done irreparable harm. 'What an amazing thing privilege and position still are in England. Here is a boy who, born in a less privileged circle, would have had to work hard and make his own way. As it is, he is lazy, lascivious, impudent and, beyond a certain rollicking bumptiousness, untalented, and everything is open to him.'[9]

The summer of 1932 was not a happy one for Clementine. She endured Sarah's presentation and the balls with ill-concealed boredom. It was not her style to sit on the chaperone's bench listening to the backbiting and the gossip of the other mothers and chaperones. She would have preferred to have been spending her time more usefully. Sarah, too, hated the season and being on show as a marriageable daughter. Just as Diana had come out at the same time as her cousin Diana Mitford so now Sarah's companion at this time was Diana's younger sister, Unity. Whereas Clementine had been delighted by Diana Mitford and could have wished her own daughter more like her, she was distinctly uneasy about the influence of Unity Valkyrie Mitford on Sarah. Unity was already regarded as an oddity, and many people, including her parents, were not a little afraid of her glowering stare. As a child she had been disruptive and uncontrollable and now she refused to play the role of the demure debutante. Clementine was horrified to find that Sarah was spending a good portion of those evenings when she was supposed to be on display, in the ladies' room gossiping and playing cards with her rebellious cousin.

At Chartwell Diana alternately wept and sulked while Sarah mooned around or played the same records repeatedly on her newly acquired gramophone. In doing so she brought down on herself her mother's wrath. She had broken the cardinal rule of the house that Winston must not be disturbed. Playing the gramophone during Winston's working hours – that is most of the day – was forbidden. In her desperate need to have an excuse to spend time away from her family Diana enrolled at RADA. Sarah, too, looked for an escape and begged to be allowed to take dancing lessons. She was fortunate that the painter, William Nicholson, was then in the house working on the portrait of her parents at breakfast. They admired and respected him and so when he supported Sarah and told them that his own grandchild, Jenny Nicholson, was taking lessons, they overcame their doubts and gave in to Sarah's request.

The book on which Winston was working at this time was his *Life of Marlborough*. So business and pleasure were combined in August when Clementine and Sarah accompanied him to Belgium to make a tour of the battlefields where Marlborough had made his name. But disaster struck once more when Winston contracted paratyphoid and had to be taken to hospital in Salzburg and then to a London hospital when he suffered a relapse in October.

But then there was some good news: Diana had a suitor. John Bailey, the son of their old friend Abe Bailey had proposed and Diana had accepted. It seemed like a good match; John was handsome and personable and the son of a millionaire. Diana herself was ecstatic to think that she, too, would soon have her own home and need no longer be under her mother's control and feel her disapproval. The couple did not want a long engagement and were married at St Margaret's, Westminster, on 12 December 1932.

Clementine and Winston's London home was far too small for the number of guests they wanted to invite to this, the first wedding in the family, so Sunny offered his house in Carlton Square for the reception. Sunny himself felt so ill and depressed and generally cynical about marriage that he did not attend the ceremony. His wife, the former Gladys Deacon, was there at the reception in the house from which she would shortly be evicted by force. As neither Winston nor Clementine felt kindly towards the Duchess since she had turned the Great Hall of Blenheim Palace into a glorified kennel for dozens of dogs, the occasion that Diana had so longed for was marred by tensions.

But the wedding photos show a smiling and confident Winston. By his side Diana looks small and hopeful and a little afraid. As it turned out her hopes were misplaced and her fears realized almost immediately. Had Diana been so eager to marry at any price that she had ignored any signs of future problems with her bridegroom or did she really not suspect that John Bailey was a hopeless alcoholic and impossible to live with? Had her own father's unusually large consumption of alcohol made her regard John's heavy drinking as normal? Before the honeymoon was over Diana knew that her marriage was a mistake.

Politically 1933 was a year in which far-reaching events, important for the whole world, began to unfold. The question of India and its future relationship to Britain was one on which Winston, an arch-Imperialist, felt strongly, and one on which he was prepared to diverge from Conservative leadership and even to split the party. His gloom about the future of Britain was compounded by the country's pacifism at the very moment when he believed Germany to be gaining in strength and determination and to be once again a potential enemy.

The personal lives of the Churchills, on the other hand, were quieter than for many years. Most of their time was spent at Chartwell where Winston worked long hours on his books and articles. His *Life of Marlborough* was his main preoccupation in the first half of the year. As we have already seen Winston felt a strong affinity with this ancestor and as he worked that feeling intensified. There is a great deal of Winston himself in his depiction of the Duke. When he had joined the army during the war his early letters to Clementine had been modelled on those of John Churchill to his wife Sarah. So it is worth looking at his portrait of Sarah as being likely to give some impression of Winston's view of Clementine at this time when they were more constantly together than at any other time since they were married.

Between John and Sarah as between Winston and Clementine 'It was a case of love, not at first sight, but at first recognition.' Winston had recently finished his memoirs with the words 'And lived happily ever after'; now he describes John Churchill's love for Sarah in similar terms.[10]

Sarah, like Clementine, had a devilish temper when aroused.[11] And there is perhaps a plea for understanding from Clementine for his acknowledged absorption in politics and writing in his account of John Churchill's predicament that despite his great love for Sarah he had to spend time making money,[12] and in his statement that he had not attempted to cover up Marlborough's unsavoury financial affairs.[13] Certainly Winston attributes to Marlborough and Sarah the very different attitudes towards Blenheim that were those of himself and Clementine towards Chartwell. He describes how Sarah had regarded Marlborough's obsession with Blenheim as a great weakness.[14] The Duchess is depicted as fighting with her architect Vanbrugh with the same 'zest and zeal' with which Clementine confronted Philip Tilden, the architect employed to work on Chartwell. Did Winston feel that, like Sarah, Clementine was not at her best in adverse circumstances,[15] and did he see her as a forthright, powerful and beautiful woman who could be sharp-tongued and witty and who possessed a great common-sense?[16] Certainly many of Clementine's contemporaries saw her in that light. And the 'candour' to which Winston refers again in reference to Sarah saying that it was both her strongest and weakest attribute,[17] is the side of Clementine most frequently commented on and the one from which Winston himself frequently suffered. Sarah and Clementine alike lost a child and were devastated by the loss but did Clementine feel as Winston undoubtedly did the necessity to build his name, acquire money and found a dynasty?[18]

Winston was well aware that on many occasions Clementine's warnings about the untrustworthiness of men such as Lloyd George and Herbert Asquith had been justified. He depicts Sarah as behaving in much the same manner towards her husband. She too had written many letters to her husband warning him of her instinct that his friends were untrustworthy and would eventually betray him.[19]

When Winston had written his novel *Savrola* he had not known any woman of his own age intimately. The heroine in that novel is modelled on his idealized notion of his mother, and she never really comes to life. Many of the first readers of *The Life of Marlborough* commented particularly on the vivid characterization of Sarah. It was surely his relationship with Clementine that had given Winston the experience, the insights and the knowledge that enabled him to create Sarah. What his biography also does is something of which Winston was probably not fully aware. Responding to his request for critical comment Violet Bonham Carter wrote to him on 11 June 1933 saying that Winston had captured in a moving and delicate way Marlborough's inability to completely control his attitude to his wife.[20] Like Marlborough with Sarah, Winston too was never completely master of his attitude to Clementine, a state of affairs which both husband and wife came increasingly to recognize over the years.

If their lives at Chartwell had an effect on *The Life of Marlborough* so too did *The Life* affect Chartwell itself. In January of 1933 Clementine and Winston invited their nephew John Churchill to visit Chartwell and decorate the loggia with scenes from Marlborough's victories. John had been studying art for some time and he had made a speciality of fresco painting. Unlike most visitors to Chartwell John did not dress conventionally. His arrival wearing a black Spanish cloak and orange riding breeches which had once belonged to his father caused something of a stir in the village. He had, of course, visited Chartwell frequently as a child but this was his first opportunity as an adult to witness the life his uncle and aunt led in the country, and he recorded his findings in his autobiography. He is full of admiration for Clementine's powers of organizing and describes her as an 'Extraordinary and Super Quartermaster'.[21] But despite her efforts he did not find his stay in her house a comfortable one. It was the mealtimes he found most difficult. His uncle's mood determined the tone of every meal and as Winston at this time was generally gloomy about the state of the country and the world, these twice-daily, protracted sessions were depressing. There was always a certain formality, and after dinner Clementine and any female guests who happened to be staying would leave the men to their port, brandy and cigars. If the men lingered too long Clementine would simply go to bed and suggest her female companions do likewise. When the men finally arrived in the drawing room they would find it empty and be uncomfortably aware of their hostess's disapproval.

The three older children had escaped from this stultifying atmosphere and Mary was little affected by it. But for Clementine there was no escape from the tedium of the long days except when she visited the homes of friends where time was passed in much the same way. So when in August of 1934 she was invited, along with Winston, to join Walter Guinness, Lord Moyne, for a cruise in the eastern Mediterranean on his yacht the

Rosaura, she was keen to accept and she urged Winston to organize his plans in such a way as to make the cruise possible. Winston was ready to fall in with her wishes. He had worked hard and was beginning to see results. He could even foresee a situation in which not only could they pay off their debts but also have something left over to invest.

The September and October cruise on the *Rosaura* gave Clementine infinitely more pleasure than any cruise on the *Enchantress* had done. She much preferred being a guest to being the hostess with responsibilities towards the oddly assorted guests invited by Winston. When Lord Moyne invited her to join him on a second, far longer and more adventurous cruise she very much wanted to accept. There was no question of Winston being of the party this time as he simply could not afford to be away for such a long time. If Clementine accepted she would have to join the *Rosaura* in late December and so miss the family Christmas at Chartwell. This did not weigh heavily with her since the previous Christmas had not been a very happy family occasion. Winston and Randolph had been at odds, Diana had been miserable about her unfortunate marriage and Esmond Romilly had been conspicuously in rebellion against convention by wearing at all times a large, black homburg hat and refusing to dress for dinner. Then the candles on the Christmas tree had caught fire and there had been panic until Maryott thought to get the fire extinguisher. With the memory of this occasion Clementine was not at all sorry at the prospect of being away for Christmas. Her absence would also mean that she would be away when Diana was due to appear in the divorce court.

On 18 December she put on one side all her responsibilities to her family and her husband and left by train from Victoria Station to make her way to Messina and the *Rosaura*.

20

A Romantic Adventure

WINSTON HAD ONLY reluctantly agreed to Clementine's going on this second cruise. His early letters left his wife in no doubt that he was feeling neglected and lonely. Indeed the whole series of letters written during the time Clementine was away give the impression of sadness and of a man left to cope single-handedly with the day-to-day problems of family life. It is hard to resist the idea that the tone of these letters is quite calculated, and that Winston not only had in mind his future image but was also again exercising a subtle form of emotional blackmail. The regular Chartwell bulletins which followed her round the world were perhaps intended to keep Clementine firmly attached to her home and her family. However, Clementine appeared to have had no second thoughts about her decision. The motor yacht *Rosaura* offered all the luxury and easy living she could hope for. There was a swimming pool on board, there was sunshine, good food and congenial company. Lord Moyne was a generous host and the knowledge that with his vast fortune made in the Guinness brewery in Dublin he could afford to entertain his guests well put everyone at ease, especially Clementine, who was heartily sick of money worries. She liked Lord Moyne because he was intelligent, interesting to talk to, adventurous and, unlike many of the rich people she knew, he had a highly developed social conscience. In his case Clementine was prepared to overlook the fact that he was travelling with his mistress, Vera, Lady Broughton and not his wife Evelyn. His son Lee Guinness and his wife were on board and there was a sixth member of the group to whom Clementine took an immediate liking which rapidly developed into a more intense feeling.

Lord Moyne had chosen his sixth guest carefully, knowing that he and Clementine would be in each other's company constantly over the following weeks, but he was surprised at just how well he had chosen. A man less like Winston Churchill than Terence Philip would have been hard to find and it was this very difference which so attracted Clementine. Winston was now portly, bald and showing his age. Terence Philip was forty-two and handsome. He had been born in Russia, which would certainly not have been in his favour as far as Winston was concerned, and he was now a director of the London branch of the New York firm of art dealers, Knoedlers. Charming and witty, he offered Clementine the attentive concern that had been absent from her life for some years. He was interested in her clothes, her hairstyle and her opinions. With him she could have conversations; at Chartwell Winston frequently monologized rather than conversed. Clementine had felt neglected for some years and her never very robust confidence had been undermined. Now in the company of her new friend she blossomed.

If she had stayed in England instead of joining the cruise she would at this time have been drawn into the troubles of her sister Nellie, for Giles and Esmond were proving to be just as problematical as Randolph. Esmond had carried his minor rebellion of the previous Christmas several stages further. Along with Giles, in February 1934 he had published a magazine entitled *Out of Bounds* which opposed the whole ethos of public schools, praised Soviet Russia and advocated pacificism. In other words the magazine represented everything that Winston deplored. There had been embarrassing newspaper articles about Winston Churchill's 'Red Nephew'. Esmond had been in the headlines again when he had run away from his public school, Wellington, and then, wearing a knuckleduster, had disrupted Sir Oswald Mosley's rally of the British Union of Fascists at Olympia.

But the real crisis came after Clementine left for her cruise. Along with his friend, Philip Toynbee, he had got roaring drunk and turned up at the door of Nellie's Pimlico house and caused a terrific disturbance ringing on the bell and banging on the door trying to make her let him in. Nellie had sent for the police. She had smothered him as a child with maternal solicitude but now declared that he was beyond her control. When he appeared in court on Christmas Eve she refused to speak for him. The judge was horrified to discover that this fifteen-year-old had been living alone and beyond the control of any adults for some months. So while Toynbee, who was eighteen, escaped with a fine the judge sent Esmond to a remand home. Nellie refused to visit him there. Diana, sympathetic to anyone rejected by their family, was the only relative to go to the home and to take him Christmas presents. As Clementine sailed towards Rangoon and Madras such family troubles seemed far distant and did not disturb her new serenity and happiness.

She was not entirely neglectful of family matters, however; in Singapore she not only enquired about the sales of Winston's books, she also had him in mind when she took a careful look at the docks. At Chartwell there had been so much talk of impending war that she was greatly dismayed to see how that important harbour had been neglected and allowed to become vulnerable to attack. She wrote home to Winston about her fears which in the course of time were dramatically realized.

Then she was on the *Rosaura* again sailing to Borneo, the Celebes and the Moluccas, all places which until then had been to Clementine only exotic names on maps. Lord Moyne and his guests were now in little travelled waters in New Guinea as they made their way up the Eilanden River. The sight of the inhabitants, black and stark naked, brought home to Clementine just how far she was from home and familiar things. After sailing along the Great Barrier Reef the travellers landed in Sydney in early February. Here Clementine met Margery Street, her former secretary with whom she had corresponded during the two years Margery had been living in Australia.

There were only two occasions which Clementine did not enjoy on this extended voyage. In late February they were in Deep Water Cove. Just the place for some deep-water fishing, decided Clementine's host. So he and Vera Broughton set out in one fishing boat while Clementine and Terence set out in another. Before they had even caught enough bait to lure the big fish, Clementine felt so sick that she and Terence were obliged to go ashore for a respite from the motion. Clementine hoped that some lunch would settle her stomach. After a few glasses of claret and some strong peppermints she was ready to try again. Walter Guinness and Vera Broughton managed to catch some swordfish and sharks but Clementine and Terence, who sat out in the cove in pouring rain, caught nothing at all. Clementine decided that deep-sea fishing was not for her.

But her most frightening experience was on land. The main objective of the cruise was for Walter Guinness to catch some lizards called 'tuataras' for the London Zoo. One day they left the boat to climb up the steep sides of an uninhabited island in search of the lizards. The climb to the plateau on top of the island was steep and proved too much for

Clementine. She turned back while the rest of the party continued to the top. Her intention was to scramble down to the beach and wait there, but it was not as easy to go back the way she had come as she had imagined and in a very short time she realized that she was lost. She shouted and shouted but no one called back. She felt very much alone on that island hundreds of miles from anywhere. Ironically one of the very lizards for which they had been looking now appeared and examined Clementine with a curiosity to match her own. By the time the second officer found her an hour later she was soaked from the rain and thoroughly frightened at the thought that she might never see home again.

As they sailed on from New Caledonia to the New Hebrides, the Solomon Islands and New Britain, Clementine was struck by the thought that their vessel was so very small in those vast seas and that she was an enormous distance from all that she knew and understood. There is even a slight note of fear in her description of her realization of how completely dependent they all were on the skills of the *Rosaura*'s captain. They were now heading for the island of Komodo where Lord Moyne intended to capture a giant monitor lizard – a creature which looked very much like a dragon. It took a week of patient waiting, near progressively more rotten and smelly goat meat put out as bait, before they captured five of the smaller monitor lizards. The fully grown ones were too wily for their hunters. The island itself delighted Clementine: she loved the pink coral beaches and the coral gardens and the greenness of the vegetation. She thought she had found paradise there until the *Rosaura* docked in Bali. Here again she was enchanted by what she saw: the temples, the people and, most of all, the way of life on the island. How completely different from her life was that of the islanders who worked for only two hours every day and for the rest played music, danced, made offerings to the gods, watched cock fights and made love. An 'Elysian life', a perfect life, Clementine commented enviously in her letters home.

Clementine celebrated her fiftieth birthday in Java. So far away from England, enjoying new and exciting experiences, the object of Terence Philip's attentions, she had no temptation to brood on what it meant to reach fifty as she might have done in England.

Throughout the voyage, from letters and the newspapers she read every time *Rosaura* docked, she had received plenty of information about what was going on at home. She knew all about Randolph's attempts to begin his political career at a by-election in Wavertree, Liverpool. At first Winston had been opposed to his standing but gradually he had come round and even endorsed his son's candidacy. It is doubtful whether Clementine would have approved and she would certainly have objected to investing £200 in Randolph's campaign as Winston had done. Had she been at home she would almost certainly have advised Winston to avoid damaging his own career by overt support for his son. But she was not there to advise nor to be hurt by the newspapers' contempt for the 'Fat Boy of Wavertree' as they described Randolph. Quite independently Winston expressed his strong disapproval when Randolph, assisted by Diana and Sarah, decided to back a former fascist against the Conservative candidate, Duncan Sandys, in a by-election at Norwood. He wrote to Clementine of his anger with his son and how he had quarrelled with him, alarmed as he now was himself that Randolph's antics would harm his own credibility.

He reported on Sarah's late nights and her intensity about her dancing classes, a combination he feared likely to undermine her health. Mary's whooping cough was a cause for concern as was Randolph's hospitalization with a rare form of jaundice. He grumbled a little about Horatia Seymour's exacting demands as Clementine's friend prepared to rent a Chartwell cottage from the Churchills. Clementine surely saw through his motives in his regular commendations of Diana: he writes of her beauty, her demureness, her increased maturity, her concern for her father and the sweetness of her disposition. He was obviously determined to make Clementine better appreciate her eldest daughter. Similarly, his Chartwell bulletins were an attempt to involve Clementine in the details of the place in the hope that he could make her love it as much as he did.

Clementine, however, was little perturbed or affected by the news from home. What would normally have distressed or irritated her was, by the time she heard of it, so far in the past that there was nothing she could do to affect the outcome.

At home she would have been obliged to hear the blow-by-blow progress of the India Bill. Since she was not entirely in sympathy with Winston in his desire to keep India as a part of the British Empire, she was not at all sorry to be able to view events from a great distance. As the *Rosaura* moved closer to England, however, Clementine's letters to Winston suggest that she was looking forward to being home again. A letter from Winston can have left her in no doubt that she was returning to much the same role as she had left: he tells her that he has at times been depressed by politics and he has missed the comfort that she would have given him. However glad Clementine was to be back at Chartwell she was soon writing to Margery Street in Australia that she would be quite happy to set out soon on another cruise, but that Winston had firmly vetoed this idea.

21

Disturbing Times

DURING CLEMENTINE'S ABSENCE Winston had been working on his books and attending debates in the Commons. But he had not been attentive to what was going on in his own constituency, as Clementine discovered when Sir James Hawkey, the chairman of the Conservative party in Winston's constituency, asked if he might come to lunch. His objective was to warn Winston that the constituency party was sufficiently uneasy with his stance on the India Bill and his seeming hostility to the party leader, Baldwin, that the members were seriously considering running an official Conservative candidate against him. Sir James expressed the view that Winston needed to spend much more time and effort on his constituency if he wanted its support. This was also Clementine's often-expressed view.

A way of trying to make amends for Winston's apparent lack of interest in his constituency was dreamt up by Clementine. She arranged for a series of coaches to transport constituency workers to Chartwell where she threw for them an elaborate garden party with carefully chosen food, and amusements such as fortune-tellers. She herself spent time talking and listening to each worker. The mutterings of dissatisfaction subsided for the moment.

This summer, 1935, Mary was the only one of the children still living at home. Diana had stayed in London after her divorce and Sarah, who was still taking dancing lessons, was sharing a flat with Jenny Nicholson while Randolph was living in style in Mayfair. At weekends, however, Sarah and Diana frequently visited Chartwell, and with the idea of helping Sarah to find a husband Clementine invited suitable young men to stay. She had hopes of Harry Llewellyn who was handsome, well educated and well connected. She thought that a relationship was beginning to develop when Sarah received invitations to stay at his home. But the two young people had insufficient in common for them to consider marriage: Llewellyn was chiefly interested in show-jumping – he was later to compete in the Olympics – while Sarah was keener than ever on her dancing and could not envisage living outside London. Diana, on the other hand, seemed to have found a suitor for herself. She had met Duncan Sandys when he had beaten the candidate supported by Randolph at Norwood. She had fallen in love with the tall, red-headed ex-diplomat that March, and during this summer the couple announced their engagement. Diana expected her parents to be pleased and she hoped that this engagement would erase the failure of her first marriage. Winston was in fact delighted as he saw Sandys as a rising star in the Conservative party. Clementine, however, was not impressed by Diana's fiancé and she certainly did not expect him to make Diana a good husband. She acknowledged that he had great charm but she felt that behind his rather quizzical smile there was a cold, calculating intelligence. She believed that Diana needed warmth and cherishing and she doubted that Sandys was capable of either. Being Clementine, she voiced her opinion candidly. Diana was upset and angry and ever more determined to marry the man she had chosen, believing that Clementine's comments were intended to wreck her chance of happiness.

Diana married Duncan Sandys on 16 September 1935. In the photo of her second wedding she looks triumphantly happy; her groom wears his usual impenetrable smile.

Then it was Sarah's turn to assert her independence, not in the choice of a husband as yet, but in that of a career. Without consulting either parent she had in October approached the impresario C. B. Cochran to ask for an audition as one of his 'Young Ladies'. Although Sarah used a pseudonym when she attended an interview, Cochran was never in any doubt about her identity. He had known the Churchill family since the time he had worked with Lady Randolph on a Shakespeare pageant and he had frequently seen Sarah's photograph in the newspapers. He had no desire to deceive her parents so he wrote pleasantly to Winston explaining the situation and asking permission to audition Sarah. Surprisingly enough Winston raised no objections. He may well have believed that Sarah would not succeed at her audition and if she did then the hard life of a girl in the chorus of a review would quickly disillusion her. Cochran's earlier association with his mother weighed heavily in his favour as far as Winston was concerned.

Clementine was more doubtful. She knew that C. B. Cochran's 'Young Ladies' were not all ladies as she understood the term. Indeed a follow-up letter from Cochran explaining what Sarah's working conditions would be underlined that fact. Whatever her doubts, however, Clementine did not intervene. Sarah was allowed to have her audition and then to accept the small part she was offered in the review Cochran was currently rehearsing. She was to make her debut in December.

Before that there was an election to fight. Winston was standing in his old constituency of Epping; Randolph was putting himself up for election as the independent Conservative candidate in West Toxteth. It was a difficult seat to fight as a Conservative of whatever shade: the area was largely working class and at the last election had sent a Labour MP to parliament. So in addition to speaking in Epping on Winston's behalf, Clementine agreed to speak at one of Randolph's meetings. She did not look forward to the occasion: already there had been fights and violence in which Diana had been attacked and her hat torn from her head. Clementine never lacked courage, however, and on 5 November stood up before a hostile crowd in Wellington Street School. Her fellow speaker was Lord Melchett and the two of them managed to contain a potentially hostile audience. Then Randolph arrived and Clementine saw for herself what she had only known from Winston's letters of the previous winter; that is just how much her son excited anger and resentment by his very presence. The comparatively orderly meeting suddenly erupted: there were fights, chairs were broken and used as weapons, women and children ran screaming from the hall, hecklers were forcibly ejected by stewards, some of whom had their clothes ripped and some of whom were injured in the struggles. Randolph was not elected; Winston was. The overall result favoured the National Government under the leadership of Stanley Baldwin.

Early in September Clementine had persuaded Winston to take a December holiday with her in Majorca. After the upsets of the election campaign she was eager to leave London for a while. Winston, who was hoping that Baldwin would include him in his new Cabinet, was more reluctant to leave the scene of action. Clementine had no compunctions, however, about persuading Winston that he should join her on a holiday. The newly elected National Government contained a majority of Conservatives and she was, therefore, confident that Baldwin would not feel it necessary to appoint Winston to the kind of position he aspired to. In her view he would feel only frustration in being in Baldwin's government without real power. She had her way and the couple spent their week together on Majorca and then Clementine returned to London while Winston travelled on to Tangier where he would be joined by Diana and Duncan.

Clementine's reason for returning at that particular moment was to enable her to travel to Manchester to attend the first night of *Follow the Sun*. Vic Oliver was the star of the show for which the costumes had been designed by Clementine's New York acquaintance, Cecil Beaton. Sarah's role was a small one; she danced the part of a wounded pheasant. Nevertheless she performed well and Clementine was more pleased than she would have cared to admit at her favourite daughter's small success. Sarah had after all achieved a measure of independence such as had not been available to herself at a similar age. She was in good humour, therefore, when she joined Mary, her niece Clarissa, her cousin Venetia and Venetia's daughter Judy, for a skiing holiday at Zürs in Austria. Like the voyage on the *Rosaura* this was another new adventure for Clementine. She was now fifty and had never skied before. But she was very fit as a result of swimming and playing so much tennis, and before long she began to develop a positive appetite for this new sport. She loved the place itself, 5,500 feet up in a little valley. She did not even mind the climb up the slopes – there was no ski lift at that time. She, who loved the sun so much, was not tempted now to join Winston in Morocco; she found she preferred the bright, clean light of snowy Zürs. Skiing was not the only new pleasure she discovered in January 1936. Until now she had rarely been alone with Mary, as Cousin Maryott was with her constantly. So Clementine had not fully realized what kind of person her youngest daughter, now fourteen, was becoming. Before the holiday Sarah had been her favourite child: by the end of it Mary had taken that position. Some years later Judy Montagu, who had an excellent opportunity to observe their blossoming relationship, said that it was almost as if Clementine had suddenly fallen in love with Mary. Away from the family and especially Winston she had seen her son Randolph in a new light. In a situation similarly removed from the rest of the family Clementine discovered how much she liked Mary. The rosy light in which she had seen Randolph in New York had soon faded; her relationship with Mary, however, was changed permanently by those three weeks in the mountains. She and Winston had left the bringing up of Mary almost entirely to Maryott with the result that Mary's childhood had been very different from that of her siblings. Unlike them she had not been left with a succession of unreliable nannies and governesses. Cousin Maryott had been in sole charge of her almost from the day she was born. A French governess had been employed in the holidays but for the rest she had gone to school. Her brother and sisters had not lived for long in any one place whereas Mary had been spared the moves by living always at Chartwell which she adored. The frequent comings and goings of her parents had not troubled her as there was always the reliable presence of Maryott.

Clementine now realized that Mary had none of the problems of her sisters and was less likely to present her with the worry and heartache that her other three children did. She was of a sunny disposition, friendly and affectionate, ready to do what Maryott and her parents thought best for her. Clementine could not imagine Mary making a poor marriage, going on the stage or being the object of public hostility. Here at last, Clementine thought, was a child with whom she could sustain a relationship. This was to be one of her few pleasures during the difficult year ahead.

Even while Clementine was still in Austria she was receiving disquieting news from her husband about Randolph, who was eager to snatch at an opportunity to stand for election once more. The Conservatives of Ross and Cromarty had invited him to be their candidate and oppose Malcolm MacDonald, the son of former Prime Minister Ramsay MacDonald. Had the election come at another time Winston might have supported his son, but at this moment Randolph's candidacy could only spoil his own prospects. For Winston was still hoping that Baldwin would give him a Cabinet position, and Malcolm MacDonald was Baldwin's favoured candidate. Clementine was angered by what she regarded as Randolph's selfishness, seeing that whether he won or lost he was likely to be an embarrassment to his father.

She was more shocked than angry when Winston then wrote to say that Sarah had declared that she was in love and intended to marry the star of *Follow the Sun*, the comedian Vic Oliver.

Both Clementine and Winston regarded such a marriage as completely unacceptable. Sarah was not yet twenty-two and the man she regarded as her fiancé was forty-seven. That was not all they had against him: he had already been married and divorced twice and his current marital status was unclear. Although he lived in America he was still an Austrian.

Should there be war against the Germans, which Winston firmly believed would happen, then Vic Oliver would be on the wrong side.

Like a true Victorian father Winston summoned Vic Oliver to be interviewed. His letter to Clementine after this uncomfortable occasion indicates just how hostile he was to the thought of Vic Oliver as a son-in-law. He did not think that Oliver was essentially a wicked man but – and this was almost as bad in Winston's eyes – that he was common.[1] As a gesture of how he felt, Winston had refused even to shake hands, and he had winced at the man's dreadful accent with its mixture of Austrian and American.[2] Before they parted company Winston had extracted from Vic Oliver a promise not to have any dealings with Sarah for a year. Then, because this was clearly impossible as long as Sarah was in *Follow the Sun*, he had interfered in her career and managed to have her transferred to the Liverpool Repertory Theatre. He was pleased to think that he had scotched the relationship.

Clementine was less confident. Although she was just as much against the match as her husband, she saw it as a bid for freedom on Sarah's part, just as Diana's disastrous marriage to John Bailey had been. So she tried to tackle the matter a different way. She had more opportunity of talking to Sarah than Winston did because the two of them, who both liked to get up early, often had breakfast together. Over one of these meals Clementine made a proposition to Sarah. She offered her a flat of her own in which she could lead a totally independent life, the only condition being that she gave up all idea of marrying Vic Oliver. Sarah was deeply shocked because she knew how much it went against her mother's nature to condone and promote such independence in an unmarried daughter. When Sarah did not immediately accept this offer, Clementine knew that the affair was not over. It had cost her a great deal to approach her daughter in this way. There was not only principle involved but also money. The flat would have been paid for out of what she called her 'pin money', that is the yearly allowance she received from Winston for her own use. At that particular moment she could ill afford it. She now knew that Winston was not going to be a member of Baldwin's Cabinet. Although she had earlier expressed doubts about the wisdom of Winston serving under Baldwin, she would have welcomed a Cabinet salary. Once more money was a problem. Clementine could not and did not fault Winston for failing to work hard. The trouble was that his earnings from writing did not arrive with the regularity and certainty of a salary. And, although he was capable of earning comparatively large sums, he was capable of

spending more. Already they needed an overdraft to see them through
the year, and Clementine could see that the next year was likely to be
worse rather than better. As always she blamed life at Chartwell. The
large staff the house needed for smooth running, the constant improvements Winston embarked upon, and the never-ending stream of guests
all cost more than she considered they could afford. It was all the more
worrying because the situation was one over which she had little control.

During the course of the summer Winston invited Clementine's niece,
Diana, now divorced from Bryan Guinness, to lunch at Morpeth
Mansions, the flat they currently leased for the times they spent in
London. He had always enjoyed the lively young woman's company, but
now he hoped for information from her. It was common knowledge that
Diana was very close to Oswald Mosley, usually referred to as Tom, and
Winston was interested in the young man's political potential as an ally,
leading as he did a right-wing group which included many young people.
He had some sympathy for Mosley's view that democracy was proving a
failure and that some more 'virile' form of government was needed. Even
more interesting to Winston was that Diana had met and become friendly
with the Führer and senior members of his government. She had come to
know them through her sister Unity, Sarah's fellow debutante, who now
spent as much time as possible in Germany and who was devoted to
Hitler. Winston had little doubt that Hitler represented a danger to
Europe, especially after his invasion of the Rhinelands which had been a
demilitarized zone since 1919, but he was nevertheless fascinated by this
man who had restored German self-respect and pride.

To Clementine, who of late had heard about little over her luncheon
table but the dangers of Hitler and the threat posed by the growing
strength of the Germany military, Diana's frank admiration for the
German leader was startling. Even more inexplicable was Diana's gay
assertion that her parents, David Mitford, Lord Redesdale –
Clementine's cousin – and his wife Sydney, had also been persuaded by
Unity to be vehemently pro-German. Disquieting news from Nellie
could only have added to her awareness of the irreconcilable differences
developing within the family. For a time Esmond had kept out of trouble
selling first silk stockings, and then advertising space in *World Film News*.
Then he had suddenly made up his mind to leave England and go to
Spain to fight against the fascists so much admired by one part of the
Mitford family. Since then she had received no word of him and was
fearful for his safety.

Closer to home Clementine saw another kind of danger looming when with Winston she attended a party at Blenheim. The principal guest was Edward VIII but just as much to the fore was the American, Wallis Simpson. The King's infatuation with Mrs Simpson was unmistakable. Winston found their relationship touching but Clementine thought it both dangerous and foolish. She wondered what kind of double standard allowed Winston to sentimentalize the King's love for a married woman while condemning his own daughter for wanting to marry a divorced man.

These disturbing thoughts were put aside temporarily during the pleasant days in August spent with Consuelo Balsan at her home, St-Georges-Motel, a château on the border of Normandy near Dreux. Clementine found this elegant house of pink bricks with a high, blue-slate roof, towers and a moat, soothing in its combination of luxury, elegance and seclusion. She much preferred the atmosphere in Consuelo's home to that in Maxine Elliott's equally luxurious Château de l'Horizon. So when Winston set off to pay his annual visit to his old friend, Clementine returned to Chartwell.

Mindful of the need to keep up a good relationship with Winston's constituency Clementine allowed herself to be persuaded to take part in a cricket match. As a member of the 'Lyons Girls' team she bowled against the Woodford Police Athletic Club.

She was, therefore, in good spirits until a few days later she opened the newspaper to see photos of Sarah about to embark on the *Bremen* ready to sail to New York, where, so the papers claimed, she would announce her engagement to Vic Oliver. Worse still, there was an account of Sarah's love for the comedian and her decision to join him based on an interview with Jenny Nicholson, the very young woman who was supposed to have lent respectability to Sarah's dancing career.

Clementine was shocked beyond measure. The previous morning Sarah had been with her at Chartwell. They had breakfasted together before Sarah had set off for London saying that she needed to have her hair done and that she would spend the night in the Morpeth Mansions flat. She had not actually lied to her mother but she had certainly deliberately misled her.

Then in the post came a letter from Sarah which Jenny had forwarded rather than presenting in person as she had promised. The newspapers were accurate, Clementine learned: her daughter had indeed followed Vic Oliver to New York where he was starring in a Broadway version of

Follow the Sun. She clearly had every intention of defying her parents and marrying him.

Clementine relayed this devastating news to Winston who was enraged at Sarah's flight. His immediate response was to fight back: Sarah had succeeded in joining Vic Oliver in New York, but he determined that he would prevent her marrying him. Randolph had already planned to visit the States to report on Franklin D. Roosevelt's election campaign. Winston drew him into the family drama and urged him to sail a few days early to try to dissuade Sarah from taking the next step. Randolph, eager to please his father, left for New York on the *Queen Mary* just two days after Sarah. Churchill's son in pursuit of Churchill's daughter was a story no newspaper either side of the Atlantic could resist. Reporters soon learned that the brother and sister were exchanging urgent telegrams between ships as they both made for New York. Even the weather added to the drama with rough seas and a hurricane warning.

Clementine had no difficulty in following the activities of her son and daughter over the next weeks. The newspapers reported everything they did. She read how Sarah had been greeted on arrival by swarms of journalists and that the same had happened when she had met Randolph off the *Queen Mary*. She learned that Vic Oliver had denied that he had any intention of becoming Miss Churchill's husband. Clementine did not know whether this was good news or bad. Was Sarah already so compromised that a marriage was now desirable? Winston was in no doubt, and Clementine watched with dismay as he contacted lawyers in New York and instructed them to use any means at their disposal to prevent a marriage between the comedian and his daughter. He even tried to prevent the final stages of Oliver's divorce by making it worthwhile to his estranged wife to withdraw from the proceedings.

The story took an ironical twist when in November at Chartwell Duff Cooper let it be known that the King had set his heart upon marrying Mrs Simpson and that if he persisted it was Prime Minister Baldwin's intention to advise his abdication. In Clementine's view the King should be prepared to sacrifice the woman for the sake of the country. But Winston, who was at that very moment doing his best to prevent his daughter from marrying a divorced man, took the opposite position. He became the King's confidant and was deeply sympathetic to his desire to marry the woman he loved. To Clementine's alarm and even disgust he was prepared to risk his own growing influence in the Commons by publicly opposing Baldwin's demand that the King had a duty to make up his mind either to accept that marriage to Mrs Simpson was impossible or to abdicate. Winston was deeply shocked at the hostile reaction he received when he spoke on the King's behalf.

In the matter of Sarah's marriage Winston fared no better. Neither Randolph's persuasions nor the interference of lawyers produced the results Winston wanted. Sarah first of all joined the review for its opening in Boston. By late December, despite Winston's attempts to create legal trouble and confusion, Vic Oliver was divorced. Sarah was now twenty-two and so legally able to make her own decisions. On Christmas Eve 1936 in a New York registry office she married Vic Oliver. Just a few days earlier the King had given up his throne for love of Mrs Simpson and gone into exile as the Duke of Windsor.

In no way had Clementine approved of Winston's tactics with regard to their daughter. She regarded them as grossly arrogant and unkind. Although she was deeply hurt by Sarah's behaviour she did not think it was a good idea to bully her so much that she inevitably turned more and more to Oliver as her protector and cherisher. The publicity of the affair which had so offended her had been fed to a great extent by Winston and Randolph's responses and actions. Worse still, the result of such an expenditure of money and emotions was exactly the opposite of what they had set out to achieve. Less than a year since she had announced her intentions, Sarah had succeeded in becoming Vic Oliver's wife. Looking back, Sarah herself acknowledged that the marriage had been a mistake and that she had acted from motives very similar to those which had propelled her sister Diana into an ill-judged marriage. In her autobiography, *Keep On Dancing*, she wrote: 'I had needed to get away from my happy home for it wasn't a question of having one strong parent but, as the world now knows, two great, strong parents.'[3]

'Happy' was hardly the word to describe her home that Christmas. Clementine and Winston were dismayed by Sarah's telegram announcing her marriage and each held the other in some degree responsible for all that had gone wrong. Usually Nellie brought good spirits to Chartwell but this year she was frantic with worry about both her sons. Giles who had been at Oxford but not well pleased with it had left before the end of the term and he too had gone to Spain: she now had two sons fighting against the fascists and no news of either of them.

Money worries exacerbated their misery. Winston was faced with an income tax and super tax bill for £6,000 which they did not have. A plan for him to undertake another lecture tour in the States to earn this money fell through. Although he could anticipate earning over £12,000 during the next year, this money would not be available until near the end of 1937. In the meantime they had to live and pay their bills, many of which, to Clementine's embarrassment, were from local stores in Westerham and were long outstanding. The only solution was one which Clementine hated and that was to increase their overdraft at the bank. In these circumstances it seems surprising that she planned to go once more with Mary to Austria for a skiing holiday. But she felt that whatever the financial cost of the holiday, the physical and emotional cost of staying at Chartwell with her husband was immeasurably greater. She could hardly wait for the beginning of January when she could make her escape. She was, therefore, uncertain how to respond to Sarah's urgent and heartfelt request that her parents receive her and her new husband at Chartwell. Clementine wanted to see her daughter, but to do so meant postponing her trip. For once her maternal feelings won out. She did not want to reject Sarah and she did not want to risk Winston's disgust and anger with the couple surfacing in her absence thus causing a greater rift than ever.

So Clementine presided over lunch at Chartwell on the last day of December. The occasion was inevitably strained but there were no displays of anger and resentment. If Clementine and Winston were cold to Vic at this meeting, at least the ground was established for building a better relationship. Clementine was relieved to find that the upset of the last months and her new status as a married woman had changed Sarah very little.

While Clementine was away in Austria Winston grew ever more reconciled to Sarah and her marriage, even helping her to furnish the flat she had leased in the building in Westminster Gardens where Randolph now lived.

Between Clementine and Winston, however, the tensions increased. Money and Chartwell were to a large extent responsible. Even the new croquet lawn which took the place of the tennis courts did not make Clementine look any more kindly on Winston's house. When in February an informal offer to buy Chartwell was made and Winston said that he would not sell it for less than £25,000, the extent of the folly that the house represented was fully revealed. It was true that the house had cost only £5,000 but since then money had been poured into it yearly. And now, it seemed, the house was worth less than what had been spent on it. This realization was extremely distressing to Clementine. More than ever she absented herself from home and from Winston. In July she tried to restore her undermined health by taking the cure at Badgastein in Austria but nothing seemed to help more than temporarily. She now faced the unpleasant possibility that the root cause of her problems both physical and mental was her marriage. For despite all her protestations of love, and of how much she missed Winston in her letters to him, she could observe a clear pattern over the last years. When she was at home and with her husband she was frequently ill and depressed. When she absented herself from him she felt better. Two events in 1937 brought back poignant memories of her four-month cruise on the *Rosaura* when she had felt better than at any time in her life. In May the Bali dove she had brought back from her cruise and of which she was very fond died and then, in June, she had found that Terence Philip was a fellow guest at Blenheim. For two years after the cruise she had met him occasionally, but she had not seen him at all during the previous year. Meeting him again did not so much make her wish to renew this relationship as make her aware of the deficiencies in her relationship with Winston and the nature of her life with him. For years she had made Winston and her marriage the centre of her life. What did she now have to show for this? Winston had not achieved that role in politics which they had both believed he was destined for. Now he was sixty-three, and she began to think that his best years as a politician were behind him. If he had failed, then so too had she in giving up so much for an ill-judged union. For her there was no consolation in thinking that away from the centre of political life Winston would have more time for her and more energy to devote to a full and satisfying relationship. The last few years had proved this to be another mistaken illusion. Her children were, for the most part, a disappointment. Diana and Sarah had both made unsatisfactory marriages and she was tired of Randolph and the frequent embarrassments he brought upon the family. Only Mary pleased her and she knew that she could take little credit for the way this daughter had turned out. Clementine felt strongly that her life was empty and without promise. How painfully ironic now was the picture of a fairy-tale marriage given by Winston's 'happily ever after' in *My Early Life*.

At this period in 1937 Clementine could think of only one change that might bring about an improvement and give her a life of her own and that was to end her marriage with Winston. Whether she ever discussed divorce with Winston we do not know. They would both have been careful in later years to see that no evidence of this moment of failure in their relationship survived. But Clementine did confide in her sister-in-law Goonie. For a long time Goonie's marriage had been one of companionship rather than passion. By mutual agreement she and Jack had led separate lives for years. As a Catholic Goonie could not consider divorce for herself and she did not see it as a solution for Clementine. She was not at all surprised to hear how Clementine felt, for her son Johnny had reported an occasion when he had driven Clementine back to London from Chartwell. It had been a typical weekend, with his uncle dominating the conversation at every meal and keeping the men in the dining room talking and drinking until long after Clementine had gone to bed. Once she was in the car travelling to London the rigidity and calm Clementine had maintained throughout the weekend had snapped and Clementine had cried with distress and frustration saying that she did not know how much longer she could bear Chartwell weekends.

Goonie's advice to Clementine was sensible. She suggested that Clementine should go to Austria and enjoy her skiing and then, with a different perspective, think again about her future.

Did actually saying out loud to another person that she wanted a divorce help Clementine over this crisis and help her to reach the realization that this was not really what she wanted? There are certainly signs that both Clementine and Winston were prepared to make some compromises in the interests of shoring up their marriage. For years Winston had visited Maxine Elliott on the Riviera alone. This year Clementine joined him there for a few days in February. It was in February also that Winston made clear to Randolph that certain kinds of disrespectful talk and behaviour were not acceptable at his table. Letters from Randolph which were simultaneously apologies and accusations failed to change his stance. It was a little too late in the day, but Winston was at this time adopting an attitude towards his son that Clementine had long urged.

The new understanding that was developing between Winston and Clementine was severely tested in the second week in March. A slump in the American stock market had an adverse effect on the Churchills' financial position. Not only did they lose the value of their investments, they found themselves suddenly in debt for £18,000. And there was still the bill for income tax and super tax to meet. Winston confessed to his wife that he had worked out that, with the best will in the world and writing more than ever before, he would still not be able to pay off their debts before the end of 1939.

The only solution they could think of was to sell Chartwell. It was put into the hands of agents and advertised as being available for £20,000, a sum less than Winston had been prepared to hold out for the previous year. Clementine had mixed feelings about the sale of their home. For years she had wanted rid of the burden of its upkeep. Now, seeing the catalogue prepared by the estate agents, she realized that she had made the interior of the house beautiful, that the garden was showing the results of her care and that Winston had created interesting and unusual grounds. She was aware of what a wrench it would be to him to leave the house and that he would feel its loss as another mark of failure. She also wondered, apprehensively, what would happen when he could no longer work on his projects there. She feared that Black Dog would reappear in a more devastating form than ever before.

Clementine had believed that their affairs had reached rock-bottom when another blow fell. Beaverbrook was increasingly alarmed by Winston's war-like stance, since he was himself firmly persuaded that Britain should stay out of continental wars. So he suddenly cancelled a well-paying contract for a series of articles he had commissioned from his friend. Clementine saw this action as typical of his unreliablity. She had once bracketed Brendan Bracken along with Beaverbrook as unsuitable friends for Winston. But now Bracken proved that his friendship was worth having. He had found a way of rescuing the Churchills from their financial tangles by calling on the assistance of the extremely wealthy South African financier, Sir Henry Strakosch. Bracken had for some time been attempting to build bridges between Churchill and the head of the Union Corporation, a South African mining concern. He had asked Winston to sponsor Strakosch for the Other Club; he had arranged for Strakosch to supply Winston with figures related to German war expenditure, and when Winston was in the South of France in January 1937 he had advised him to call on the South African who was also there. Now he pulled all these threads together with the result that Strakosch offered to assume all Winston's losses for three years, by which time Winston hoped that assistance would no longer be necessary.

The immediate result was that Winston felt able to take Chartwell off the market. The rosy glow with which Clementine had begun to invest Chartwell quickly faded when possession of it was restored to her. There was, however, an aspect of the relationship between the South African editor of *The Economist* and her husband which gave her a different kind of hope. At the very moment when she was prepared to see Winston as a spent force in British politics, this man clearly saw him differently. As a

Jew, his motive in backing Winston at this time had to be his faith in Winston as a potentially successful leader of the resistance to the growing threat of Germany.

There were many people who argued that Winston's position on Germany and Austria was misguided; among them was Clementine's 26-year-old cousin Unity Mitford. Not only had she actually written to Winston early in the year accusing him of being misinformed about Austria she had failed to deny reports that her adoration of Hitler embraced his rabid anti-semitism. While Clementine and Winston were being rescued financially by a Jew, Unity was reported as saying that she wanted Jews to be made to eat grass. What is more the rumour continued to circulate that it was Hitler's intention to marry Clementine's cousin.

In May 1937 George VI became King and Baldwin retired to be replaced by Neville Chamberlain. Clementine wondered whether this would be the opportunity for Winston to regain a Cabinet position. If a ministry were to be offered, could they afford Winston's acceptance, given their financial need for him to complete his writing commitments? Her anxiety was misplaced. Chamberlain took the advice of his Chief Whip David Margesson that to include Churchill in the Cabinet was to send the signal to Hitler that the government was adopting a more war-like stance.

However, an invitation to the Churchills to visit Paris in July in the entourage of the new King and Queen as guests of the French government suggested to Clementine that Winston's reputation abroad now stood much higher than at home.

22

A Fragile Peace

WHEN IN 1935 Mussolini had invaded Abyssinia there had been public outcry in Britain at the government's refusal to take any action. There was further anger when Foreign Minister Samuel Hoare had signed a treaty with Pierre Laval in Paris which put in writing the intention of both governments to allow Mussolini to keep his spoils. But after the resignation of Hoare the British public had not shown much in the way of war-like sentiments. On the contrary there was little response to the call for volunteers for the Air Raid Precautions and their training exercises were regarded as something of a joke by the press.

But in the Churchills' apartment in Morpeth Mansions there were many meetings of an oddly assorted group of men and women who did take seriously the threat posed to Britain by German expansionist policies. Hitler's annexation of Austria in March only confirmed their fears and Churchill's ringing appeal in the House of Commons for a Grand Alliance with France met with a positive response. Even if Clementine had not herself been passionately concerned about what was happening in Europe she could not have avoided hearing the blow-by-blow account of events as they happened, living as she did with a man whose attention was sharply focused on German military strength.

Early in September 1938 the Churchills entertained the German ex-Chancellor, Dr Bruening, at Chartwell. Winston had personally guaranteed that his visit would be private and secret. What he learnt from Dr Bruening about Hitler's intentions was disquieting and the German seemed very depressed about the situation in his country. When he had left, Winston and Clementine discussed the ex-Chancellor's appeal to

Winston to influence the British government to speak plainly and force-fully to Hitler. Clementine mentioned the matter to Nellie in confidence, and was therefore horrified on the next day to read in the *Daily Express* gossip column a more or less accurate account of that secret meeting at Chartwell. There could be only one possible source of this information and that was Nellie. Clementine was mortified to think that her sister could have been so indiscreet and she felt guilty that she was herself indi-rectly the cause of this breach of security. Winston wrote a sharp and crit-ical letter to the sister-in-law with whom he was much more accustomed to sharing a joke.

Everyone in Britain woke up to the fact that war was a very real possibility when the distribution of gas masks began and it became known that detailed plans were ready for the immediate evacuation of London schools. On 10 September Winston received a letter from an admirer, Eleanor Rathbone, which Clementine took to be representative of the way many people in the country were thinking at that moment. Eleanor Rathbone wrote: 'There is a great longing for leadership and even those who are far apart from you in general politics realize that you are the one man who had combined full realization of the dangers of our military position with belief in collective international action against oppression. And if we fail again now, will there ever be another chance.'[1]

But even among those who disapproved of the way Chamberlain was handling Hitler's threats to take over Czechoslovakia there was fear, and a reluctance to take action which would lead to war. Memories of the horrors of the previous war were still too vivid. Even Winston and Clementine still had some hope that the situation could perhaps be saved. Lord Moyne had invited both of them to accompany him on his next cruise. On 11 September Winston still felt that he could accept the invitation on behalf of Clementine and wanted to leave open the possibil-ity that he might join her.

A critical moment seemed to have been reached when Neville Chamberlain flew from England to Bad Godesberg to meet Hitler. That same day Morpeth Mansions was the meeting place of those opposed to appeasement-at-any-price. Although Winston announced that he thought Chamberlain's journey was unwise he agreed with all those assembled that he would not oppose Chamberlain unless the Prime Minister returned with 'peace with dishonour'. All present accepted that at least a part of Czech territory would have to be transferred to Germany. The speed with which Chamberlain returned from his meeting with Hitler suggested to everyone following events closely, which included the Churchills, that the Prime Minister's attempts at diplomacy had failed.

Hitler had indeed increased his demands and imposed new conditions, but Chamberlain, unlike most of his Cabinet, was prepared to accept the new demands in a desperate attempt to avert war. Disillusionment with Chamberlain increased at the same rate as support for Winston and his policies. But then with the mobilization of the Fleet on 27 September it seemed that after all Chamberlain was not prepared simply to hand over Czechoslovakia to the Germans.

As Winston left Morpeth Mansions for the Commons on 28 September Clementine knew he expected war to be declared that day. But on that most dramatic of occasions in the House, the arrival of a telegram from Herr Hitler at the very moment when Chamberlain was about to report the failure of his endeavours at Godesberg appeared to have pulled the country back from the very edge of war. Hitler had agreed to postpone German mobilization and summoned Chamberlain to a conference in Munich the next day.

Clementine shared Winston's scepticism about Hitler's intentions and about what Chamberlain could achieve in the Munich meeting. But it was difficult to voice doubts about any measure which might bring peace rather than war. When Winston tried to get members of his group of politicians, whose only common ground was their opposition to appeasement, to sign a telegram to Chamberlain in Munich warning him that he would be opposed in the House if he allowed further 'mean terms' to be imposed on the Czechs, he met with refusals all round. Clementine knew just how angry and frustrated he must have been when he declared that at the next election he would support every socialist candidate against every Conservative one.

Chamberlain's return from Munich declaring that he brought peace with honour was greeted with wild enthusiasm. Breaking all precedent the King invited his Prime Minister to appear with him on the balcony of Buckingham Palace and so before crowds of people signalled his complete support for the Munich agreement. The general mood was echoed in the *Illustrated London News* special two shilling Munich issue.

Yet support for the Munich agreement was not as absolute as at first appeared. The Churchills felt that, although the treaty was an improvement on the terms of the Godesberg meeting, Chamberlain was stretching the word 'honour' too far in this context. They did not agree with the

King's declaration that 'the time of anxiety is past'. Neither did Duff Cooper who, after the Munich debate, resigned from the Admiralty.

Yet for all Winston's claim that Britain had 'sustained a total and unmitigated defeat'[2] neither he nor Clementine felt that there was any danger in her accepting Lord Moyne's invitation to join him on the *Rosaura*. As Clementine was feeling the strain of all the political manoeuvring that had been going on around her over the last months she was eager for a period of relaxation.

From the outset this cruise was different from previous ones since it was not simply a holidaying and sightseeing journey that was proposed but an official investigation of social conditions in the West Indies. Along with Lord Moyne's personal guests – Clementine, Vera Broughton, Murtagh Guinness – were several members of the Commission. The atmosphere on board *Rosaura* was as a result considerably less relaxed and carefree. What struck Clementine this time was less the beauty of the places they visited than the enormous contrast between that beauty and the living conditions of the inhabitants. Writing home about Barbados she laments the way the island has been 'desecrated and fouled' by man and she describes the long-unpainted, tumbledown houses roofed with nasty corrugated iron.[3] The condition of the people was little better than that of their houses, with syphilis and yaws rampant, no sanitation, and no easy access to water. Clementine, wife of a convinced imperialist, found herself disgusted at this particular sample of imperial rule. She was also in the odd position as the wife of a Conservative MP in finding herself disagreeing with the measures proposed by the Conservatives on the Commission. They felt that birth control and sterilization would solve the problems. She was more in sympathy with the Labour members who wanted more radical measures to be taken.

Although she was enjoying the sunshine Clementine was not finding this cruise as relaxing and helpful as she had hoped. She missed home more than she had expected and this time she had no congenial companion to divert her thoughts from Winston. On the contrary events seemed to conspire to turn her thoughts ever more towards him. On New Year's Day, for example, she was in Antigua where she visited a 'sad and eerie spot', the dockyard where Nelson, one of Winston's great heroes, had served as a young man. Then there was an odd incident in Jamaica. Clementine attended the ceremony of the laying of the foundation stone for a school in a remote village. Here she was introduced as the wife of the future Prime Minister of England and was greeted with loud cheers. The

Jamaicans, it seemed, had been following European events closely in the press. Clementine too, who on previous voyages had been almost glad to be cut off from political affairs, read all the newspapers avidly whenever *Rosaura* docked. In this way she came across the announcement of the death of Sidney Peel to whom she had been engaged as a young woman. Only months before she had been talking about divorcing Winston. Now she thought about what her life would have been if she had married Sidney Peel. She would have had more security, especially financial; she would have had a husband who adored her. But her life would have been far less interesting and she would have been on the fringe of political events rather than at the centre. She was confident that, even with her backing, Sidney Peel would never have been a great or exceptional man. Clementine concluded that her marriage to Winston, despite its many real problems, had rarely been dull and had not been a mistake.

She was, therefore, feeling particularly close to her husband and beginning to think that the cruise had been a bad idea at such a difficult time. Lack of any real communication with Winston frustrated her. He had sent only telegrams which she deplored since they told her no more than the state of the weather in England. The book she was reading at this time, Prescott's *Conquest of Mexico*, suggested to her, in the treatment of Cortez by the Spanish government, a parallel to Winston's situation. She was more and more afraid that her husband had been right about Hitler and that, despite the Munich agreement, England was drifting towards war, neither thinking how to avert it nor how to prepare for it.[4] In the circumstances it took only a small incident to make Clementine decide that she should return home.

On board the *Rosaura*, docked in Barbados, everyone assembled nightly to hear on the radio the news from England. On this particular night Winston and his views were attacked by a pro-government appeaser. Somewhat tactlessly Vera Broughton expressed her approval of this point of view out loud. As she had once responded to Sunny Marlborough's criticism of Lloyd George, so now she decided that she could not possibly remain in the company of such an overt critic of her husband. Decisively she wrote a note to Lord Moyne explaining her position and the next day booked a passage on the *Cuba* which was leaving immediately for England. Neither apologies nor explanations could deter her. She left Barbados for England the next day.

Chartwell in the spring had never seemed so attractive to Clementine before and even family life, when the family consisted of Mary, Winston and herself, pleased her. Since Mary had been given a horse as a reward for doing well in her School Certificate examinations, Clementine decided to take up again the sport she had so enjoyed as a young woman and she happily joined her daughter following the hounds.

War seemed far enough away for Samuel Hoare to feel able to declare the dawn of a new golden age and for Chamberlain to meet with Mussolini. In his constituency Winston was attacked for not supporting Chamberlain's peace initiatives more whole-heartedly and he was threatened with being replaced as the Conservative candidate once more. But on 14 March he spoke about the implications of the breaking up of Czechoslovakia and when the next day Hitler's troops entered Prague his words appeared like a prophesy. But to Clementine's intense anger Chamberlain still kept her husband out of the Cabinet. Even a vigorous press campaign supporting Winston and posters in the Strand with the words 'What Price Churchill?' did not change Chamberlain's mind. Clementine was fully aware that Samuel Hoare's opinion that the vast majority of backbenchers were against Winston's inclusion in the Cabinet influenced Chamberlain. She would neither forgive nor forget his campaign against her husband.

Putting aside for a moment her concern with London politics Clementine enjoyed a weekend in Paris with Mary and in August they both joined Winston for a few days with the Balsans at St-Georges-Motel. But the pleasures of that beautiful place and the swimming and the tennis in the sunshine came to an abrupt end on 23 August. The news of a mutual non-aggression pact between Russia and Germany made Winston return to London immediately and as fast as possible. Mary and Clementine followed the next day.

23

In and Out of the Admiralty

BY THE TIME Clementine and Mary were back in London all the signs were that war was inevitable. When on 1 September Germany attacked Poland all Winston's pessimistic predictions were seen to have been right. On the very night of the invasion of Poland, during a dinner at the Savoy, Clementine was pleased to observe that her husband's confidence in the rightness of his vision was such that he would accept no defence of German policy, even from an old friend such as the Duke of Westminster. Even more important to her was tangible evidence of his political colleagues' change of attitude towards Winston when he was appointed to the War Cabinet on 2 September.

On 3 September, a beautiful sunny day with a blue sky and a few fluffy white clouds, Clementine was with Winston at Morpeth Mansions to hear Neville Chamberlain announce to the country that Britain was at war with Germany. Their response to this announcement was shared by many people all over England. As one woman later put it, 'There had been so many moves backwards and forwards that it wasn't a relief exactly when we heard there was going to be a war. But there was some satisfaction perhaps that at least now we knew.'[1]

The reality of this stark announcement was immediately brought home to all Londoners as the air-raid siren sounded. After climbing up on the roof of their building to see if there was any sign of German aircraft, and seeing only the silver shapes of the barrage balloons, Clementine along with Winston and a bottle of brandy made her way into the air-raid shelter allocated to their area. Clementine noticed that a German resident of Morpeth Mansions had stayed away from the

shelter; she soon learnt that their neighbour suddenly felt himself an
unwelcome alien. There was, in fact, no danger on that occasion; the all-
clear sounded not long after they had gone into the shelter, the brandy
bottle remained unopened and Winston was able to go to Westminster as
usual. In the debate he spoke stirringly of the need to save the world from
the 'pestilence of Nazi tyranny'. The whole family gathered in
Westminster Gardens in Sarah and Vic's flat for lunch. Here Winston
announced that he had been asked by Chamberlain to take over the
Admiralty; the toast he now proposed was 'To Victory'. For both
Clementine and Winston a new phase of their life was about to begin.

While Winston settled into the work of the Admiralty Clementine had
practical tasks of her own. She had to end the tenancy of Morpeth
Mansions and supervise the move into the Admiralty. She remembered
vividly the last time she had moved into that grand house and her uneasiness about the costs of running it. Diana and Randolph had been small
children then and Sarah had been born there. Now Diana and Sarah were
married and even her youngest child had left school and was becoming a
young woman. This time her worries were different; there was no question of the family occupying the whole house. Only the top two floors
were available; the attics and what had recently been the nursery for
Diana and Duff Cooper's baby, John. By 13 November Clementine had
her new home in sufficiently good order to be able to entertain to dinner
Mr and Mrs Chamberlain. It was not a lively or an easy meeting of two
such different couples. Perhaps only a war could have brought them
together.

The problem of Chartwell seemed to have been solved for her when
the house was commandeered for families evacuated from London. Like
many other evacuees those at Chartwell did not stay long, however, but
drifted back to London where, despite the threat of danger, they felt
more comfortable than in the country. Winston raised no objection when
Clementine proposed that the whole of the big house should be closed up
for the duration of the war. The family still maintained a presence on the
estate; Orchard Cottage was made ready for Clementine and Winston to
use at weekends while cousin Maryott together with Diana's children,
Julian and Edwina, and their nanny moved into the chauffeur's cottage.

The rest of the family was in London. Sarah and Vic were in
Westminster Gardens wondering what effect the black-out would have
on the theatre. Diana became a recruiting officer for Women's Navy
looking in her uniform smarter and more confident than she had done for

years. Her husband was a Territorial Officer with an anti-aircraft regiment while Randolph was in the uniform of the Oxfordshire Hussars.
Mary now lived with her parents at the Admiralty and divided her time
between working for a canteen and for the Red Cross and helping
Clementine with entertaining. Clementine was an excellent and experienced hostess but the entertaining at the Admiralty in wartime was a
stressful job. Many of the occasions were an extension of Winston's work
rather than simply social gatherings. Apart from seeing that her guests
were comfortable and well fed Clementine had to ensure that they were
carefully chosen. No one could be invited to a meal at which the business
of the war might be discussed who was not already inward with the government's strategies and who had not already proved themselves to be
trustworthy. All the servants had to be carefully chosen and screened for
security and even then Clementine did her best to see that no business
was discussed in front of those who waited at table. Clementine had never
forgiven herself for that leak to the press about the presence of Dr
Bruening at Chartwell as a result of her conversation with her sister.
Then only one life had been potentially endangered; now a security leak
from her luncheon or dinner table could put many lives at risk. Her position was, therefore, a lonely one. She felt the need to keep her friends at a
distance and so the company of Mary was especially important to her.
The bond that had already developed between mother and daughter was
strengthened greatly at this time.

With her son she was less pleased. Rumours had reached her that in
the short time since war had been declared Randolph had proposed to no
fewer than eight girls. By late September he had found one who would
accept him and he proudly announced to his parents that he was engaged
to Pamela Digby.

Pamela's background was impeccable. She was the elder daughter of
Lord and Lady Digby of Minterne Magna in Dorset. That September
she was working as a French translator at the Foreign Office and living in
a rented flat in London. She was prettily plump with red hair, blue eyes
and an open and vivacious manner. Although she was only nineteen and
inexperienced she had already discovered that she was attractive to men.
Unlike most of the women with whom Randolph had so far been in love
she neither looked nor behaved anything like Clementine. Randolph had
met this well brought-up young woman on a blind date and had known
her only two weeks before they became engaged.

Winston was delighted with the engagement and encouraged an early marriage; he cited his own whirlwind courtship of Clementine as an example to follow. It was not just the idea of Randolph being married that he liked. He was visibly pleased with his prospective daughter-in-law and from the outset his manner towards her was very warm.

By contrast Clementine received Pamela politely but with some reserve. She had nothing personal against the young woman but she urged Randolph not to rush into marriage. Unlike many mothers she was not influenced by the belief that her son's fiancée was not good enough for him. On the contrary, her worry was that Randolph was not good enough for Pamela. She had severe doubts about Randolph's ability to support a wife and about how this high-spirited and hopeful girl, who had clearly led a sheltered life until this time, would cope with her son's drunkenness, his rudeness, his aggression, his propensity to gamble and the likelihood that he would be unfaithful to her. She could hardly tell Pamela Digby these truths about her son; she could only hope that if the marriage were delayed Pamela would find out for herself and reconsider. Clementine had also heard of Randolph's remark that he wanted to marry quickly, before he was sent into action and possibly killed, in order to sire an heir who would carry on the Churchill name. His father's recent promotion and future prospects made him as eager as Winston himself to establish a dynasty.

Pamela's parents sided with Clementine. They were unhappy at the idea of their daughter marrying a man so much older than herself, who had a poor reputation and whom she hardly knew. Pamela had second thoughts as a result of their doubts and for five days the engagement was off. But Randolph was determined to marry and he did not want to trouble looking further for a wife. He brought to bear all his charm to change Pamela's mind and, to Clementine's dismay, succeeded.

Once the marriage was an inevitability Clementine gave in with a good grace since she had no desire to spoil Pamela's wedding day. She was kind to the young woman, noting with approval her obvious respect and affection for Winston. Since the couple intended to marry in a London registry office and not in Dorset, Clementine offered to arrange to have the Admiralty State Rooms opened especially for the reception.

The wedding was described in the press as a real war wedding. There were as many cheers from the waiting crowd for the First Lord of the Admiralty and his wife as for the newly-wed couple. But the groom in his army uniform looked plump and well pleased as the couple left the church to be greeted by a guard of honour from Randolph's regiment.

Pamela positively beamed and seemed happy and confident, even if she did look a little matronly in her suit of deep blue with a matching dyed fur and a velvet beret. Clementine hoped against hope that this happiness would last when the newly married couple settled in to everyday life in army quarters in Beverley.

Winter in London that year was a strange time. There were reminders of the war everywhere. Scarcely a window in the capital was without strips of paper pasted on to prevent the danger of flying glass in an air raid. Londoners moved about their business hampered by their bulky and frightening-looking gas masks. They stumbled over protective sand-bags and struggled with the inconveniences of the nightly black-out in bitterly cold weather. For a while the theatres and cinemas were closed. But as the months went by without any direct attacks people began to forget that there was a war on and to resent the restrictions imposed upon them.

Living in the Admiralty Clementine was always aware of the war and knew that it was not going well. There was little consolation in hearing Winston claim that he had been right about the relative strength of British and German sea power when this was no longer a question of theory but when British lives were at risk.

With Winston so necessarily occupied with his work Clementine felt the need to do more than simply run the domestic side of the Admiralty. In November 1939 she began to assist in the organization of the Fulmer Chase Maternity Home for the wives of officers away fighting. The idea was that men serving in the forces would be more single-minded if they knew that their pregnant wives were being well cared for. Ideally, as Clementine was well aware, this kind of maternity care should have been made available to everyone and not just officers' wives, but at least it was a step in the right direction. Later in the war arrangements were made for other pregnant women in areas where there was considerable risk from bombing. In Liverpool, for example, expectant mothers near their time were gathered in one place so that ambulances could take them to hospital even during the black-out.

As wife of the First Lord Clementine wanted to do something specifically for those serving at sea. She learnt that the crews of minesweepers and coastal craft who were not regular naval personnel received few of the benefits of those who were. Here was a gap that needed filling and she set about doing so by launching a fund to provide necessary comforts for those who did some of the most dangerous work in the war. She involved herself with their well-being even more directly by encouraging as many women as possible to knit thick woollen jerseys for these men. Even the totally undomesticated Diana Cooper was persuaded to take up her knitting needles as part of the war effort.

Although it was wartime, the launching of a new ship was still a glamorous event, and in March Clementine was asked to launch the *Indomitable*. The photograph taken of her as she saw the ship slide down its ramp shows her at her most carefree and happy. But this was an isolated moment in otherwise grim times, especially for those connected with the Admiralty. When Denmark and Norway were invaded in April 1940 and British forces were defeated, the lack of preparedness on the part of the navy was blamed. It was Clementine's fear that once more Winston would be the scapegoat for what she believed were the deficiencies of others. She was also very worried about her once carefree sister Nellie whose son Giles had been at Narvik and had been captured by the Germans. His relationship to Churchill was discovered and he was sent to Colditz prison camp as a potential hostage in any negotiations. Nellie's misery was compounded by the serious illness of her husband, Bertram, who was growing weaker daily. On 6 May he died at Huntington Park in Herefordshire. Clementine now found herself torn by conflicting loyalties. She wanted to be with her sister and support her through Bertram's funeral but she also knew that the affairs of the government had reached a critical point. On 7 May Winston was due to speak in the debate on Norway and Clementine knew that he faced a difficult task: to defend the navy, be loyal to the Prime Minister and keep his own reputation intact. Chamberlain was now being attacked on all sides and most politicians, including Winston, believed that he would not be able to retain the office of Prime Minister for much longer. Once she was assured that Winston's speech had silenced his opponents, on 8 May Clementine left the Admiralty for Huntington Park. On 9 May the German invasion of Belgium and Holland began and with this Chamberlain's position became impossible. Winston told her that along with Lord Halifax he had been summoned to a meeting with Chamberlain and that he believed the issue of the next Prime Minister would be discussed. When she learnt on 10 May that Chamberlain had indeed resigned, Clementine knew that Winston would ask her to return to London and he did. Just as she arrived at the Admiralty, Winston was leaving for Buckingham Palace in response to a summons from the King; husband and wife were equally aware of what this meant. As she awaited

Winston's return Clementine thought about what it would mean to both their lives if Winston was at that very moment being asked to form a government and become Prime Minister. She had little doubt that Winston was equal to the task. The Premiership was what he had been working towards his whole life; he saw this as simply a working out of his destiny. He felt confident that he was the right man to lead Britain to victory in war if only he were given a chance. Clementine was less sure that she was fitted for the difficult task which was ahead of her if Winston became Prime Minister. Although she looked much younger than her years with her slender figure and unlined skin, she had only recently celebrated her fifty-fifth birthday and for the last few years her health had been uncertain. She was by no means sure that she could stand up to all the strains that being the Prime Minister's wife in a time of war would certainly bring into her life. But when Winston returned from his interview with the King quietly jubilant that his frustration was at long last at an end, that he could now engage in winning the war his own way, she said nothing of her own self-doubt.

24

The Lady at Number 10

As WINSTON BEGAN to shape his new Cabinet Clementine watched anxiously to see that he did not ruin himself from the start by putting his trust in unreliable men. She argued fiercely against Winston making his old friend Max Beaverbrook responsible for boosting the production of aircraft. She reminded her husband of the many occasions when the tricky Canadian had let him down. But Winston was resolute in his decision. In the event both proved to be right in their assessment of Beaverbrook. He worked wonders in improving aircraft production and he caused trouble with his seemingly capricious threats of resignation. Another appointment which Clementine contested was that of Chief Whip. Winston wanted to retain David Margesson; Clementine regarded him as an old parliamentary enemy who had prevented Winston joining the Cabinet earlier. When Winston invited him to lunch to discuss his appointment, Clementine, making her disapproval clear, absented herself and went for a walk in nearby St James's Park. Only gradually did Clementine come to accept that her new position, especially in time of war, brought with it the need to be involved with men she would not have chosen for herself as friends.

Larger events overshadowed these disputes. On 13 May Germany attacked France and Paul Reynaud contacted Winston to say that France's defeat was inevitable. To stiffen French resolve and see for himself the exact situation Winston made several flights to and from France. Now began what would be for Clementine a disturbing feature of the next years: the many times when she would have to remain at home in a state of acute anxiety as Winston made frequent, and often long and dangerous, journeys to all parts of the world in the interests of winning the war. She was not alone in fearing the effects of all this travel on the health of the 67-year-old Prime Minister. Both Beaverbrook and Bracken urged her to persuade Winston to accept as his official doctor Charles Wilson who would accompany him on journeys abroad. With much grumbling Winston acquiesced and, although Clementine probably never really liked the doctor, she trusted him and had cause in the future to be grateful for his presence at Winston's side.

As a distraction from her fears Clementine made her first inspection of Chequers, the house given to the nation as a country retreat for Prime Ministers. She had visited the red-brick Tudor house when Lloyd George had been Prime Minister. But being a guest was very different from being the hostess in that attractive but inconvenient house. She was immediately aware of the inadequacy of the bedrooms and bathrooms and of how difficult it would be to find satisfactory staff. She did not on her first visit, on a sunny day in June, appreciate the two biggest problems that Chequers presented. The first was that when there was a full moon the house was totally exposed to the danger of German bombers. The second was that there was no effective central heating and that in the winter Chequers would become almost unbearably cold – especially the draughty Great Hall which was simply the central courtyard roofed over.

Italy declared war on 10 June and on 14 June the Germans took over Paris. In the context of these shattering events Clementine still had to organize the move of her family from the Admiralty to 10 Downing Street. Winston had already, with what some considered unseemly haste, taken over the offices there and installed his own staff. Clementine's arrival as Prime Minister's wife was not greeted with unreserved delight. Her predecessor had been a less forceful presence than Clementine; she had left the running of the country and the government to her husband. There were many working at 10 Downing Street who considered this to be only proper and they were not prepared for a wife so keenly alert to her husband's interests. Because she was not altogether sure of herself, Clementine managed to give the impression that she was a cold, demanding and difficult person to work with. Winston had inherited from his predecessor some of those working in the Prime Minister's office. They had resented his taking over from Chamberlain and they did not like his methods or his arrogance. Their hostility extended to Clementine and they were quick to take offence when they considered that she had exceeded her authority by asking members of the Prime Minister's staff to do things for her which they regarded as work for her secretary, Grace Hamblin. John Colville, for example, recorded in his diary his view that Clementine Churchill gave herself airs, saw it as her mission in life to put other people in their place and took pride in her blunt outspokenness. He sneered at her elegant clothes which he found totally inappropriate for wartime.

But Clementine's way of dressing was as much intended to inspire confidence as Winston's emotional speeches. Clementine knew that the reality of the situation did not in fact warrant such confidence. She was fully aware that in May at the time of Dunkirk there had been a very real fear that Germany would invade England. Wardens had been advised to maintain regular patrols and to keep a look-out for German troops landing by parachute. At the fall of France in June Winston had encour-aged the attitude that had prompted the response of a skipper on a small boat who called out to all who wished to listen, 'Now we know where we are! No more bloody allies.'[1] But Clementine had seen how oppressed Winston had felt by the situation in which Britain found herself when on 22 June France had signed an Armistice with Germany. She knew that Winston's hold on the office of Prime Minister was by no means as secure as the public believed and that some of his former allies were dissatisfied with the way he was conducting the war and plotting against him.

It was now that Clementine became especially concerned about public perception of the whole Churchill family. This was a time when few fam-ilies remained intact and untouched by the war. The men were away fighting, the young women were drafted away from home to war work either in the forces or in factories and young children were being separ-ated from their families and evacuated to safer places in the country. Other families were suddenly enlarged either by having evacuees billeted on them or by the influx of relatives and friends escaping from areas con-sidered vulnerable to bombing. Paradoxically the family as an image became more important than it had ever been. The Royal family was looked to as an example and so too was the family of the Prime Minister, since Winston had in effect set up something like a court at Downing Street.

Presenting the Churchills as a model family was no easy task. A major embarrassment to Clementine was her relationship to her cousins the Mitfords. Just before the war Unity Mitford had been in the headlines when she had unwisely attended and then spoken out at a 'Save Peace. Save Spain' rally in Hyde Park organized by the Labour Party. The crowd had turned on her, thrown stones at her and she had been only narrowly rescued by the police. Next day the papers had read 'Cries of Kill, Stones Hurled at Girl who Admires Hitler'. When other British residents of Germany had left, anticipating the outbreak of war, Unity had stayed. She had shown her solidarity with the Germans when she had taken over a flat which had belonged to dispossessed Jews and had accepted gifts of furniture from high-ranking Nazis including Hitler. At the very last moment she had realized that there would indeed be a war between England and Germany but it had then been too late for her to leave. Using a pearl-handled revolver given to her earlier by Hitler she had attempted to shoot herself in the head. Her suicide attempt had failed and for two months, unbeknown to her family, she had been unconscious in a Munich hospital. When Hitler had visited her in hospital he had decided that she should be transported to Switzerland by special train from where she could be claimed by her parents and taken home. Once Unity was back in England she was not put on trial or sent to prison because it was claimed that she had severe brain damage. But to the casual observer she seemed perfectly healthy and there was much resentment expressed that this relative of Churchill and friend of Hitler was allowed to remain free.

Clementine was anxious about the impression that Unity had been given special treatment simply because of her Churchill relatives and so she felt completely unable to intervene in any way when her other Mitford cousin, Unity's older sister Diana, was arrested in June and imprisoned in Holloway under regulation 18b. This regulation gave the government the right to detain without trial those considered a threat to the country's safety in wartime. She felt much more concern for Diana who had frequently stayed at Chartwell, who had shared her coming out with Clementine's daughter and who had only recently been to lunch and courteously answered all Winston's questions about Hitler. There were even objective grounds for giving Diana special treatment since her son Alexander was only months old when her arrest deprived him of his mother. Diana's husband 'Tom' (Oswald Mosley), who was known to be in poor health was one of the 150 prominent people arrested in May because of their known connections with Germany and Hitler. It was Winston's fear that, should Hitler succeed in invading Britain, Mosley would be a likely person for him to choose to head a puppet government. After Diana's arrest Lady Redesdale appealed personally to Clementine to do something to help the release of her daughter and son-in-law.

Sydney Mitford was not the best ambassadress for this situation. In 1938 she had attended the Nuremberg rally and accepted an invitation to a party given by Hitler for foreign guests. She was still very pro-German. Her oldest daughter Nancy wrote of her: 'she is impossible. Hopes we shall lose the war & makes no bones about it.'[2] Clementine's cousin David, who before the war had praised the Nazis, had now changed his mind and could no longer tolerate living with his fanatical wife. However, some of the Mitford family saw Clementine's response to their mother's appeal as cold and unfeeling. Clementine told Sydney that in view of the antagonism in England towards possible collaborators, Diana and Tom were probably safer in jail. She had in mind Unity's rough handling by the crowds before the war had started and she was probably right. But she was also motivated by her determination not to be responsible for tarnishing Winston's image by making him appear to treat his own family better than other people. After Clementine had spoken to him about Sydney's appeal, Winston tried to do something to improve the lot of the young woman of whom he was so fond by ordering that Lady Mosley should be allowed daily baths. He had no conception of the emptiness of this privilege in view of the conditions in Holloway at the time.

Randolph was an ongoing problem. Clementine dreaded his visits to Chequers when he would become drunk and make an exhibition of himself and Winston in front of whoever happened to be there for the weekend, no matter how important they were. She was more and more sympathetic to her daughter-in-law, Pamela, who was now pregnant and who had decided to move in with her parents-in-law. Clementine appreciated her willingness to listen to Winston's stories, to play cards with him and even to be hostess at dinners when Clementine herself felt too tired. Pamela confided in her more than her older daughters had ever done and in her turn Clementine found she could talk more openly than she was accustomed to. It was to Clementine that Pamela confessed that, try as she would, she could not prevent Randolph's extravagances, and that he had run up debts she could not meet. This was not a new situation for Clementine; she consulted Winston who agreed to put Pamela's mind at rest by paying outstanding bills. When Pamela expressed her unhappiness at Randolph's lack of attention to her Clementine advised her to leave him for a few days and perhaps go to a hotel; this was a tactic she had used herself and on her return all had been well once more.

There were, however, aspects of her own experience as a wife which she knew were unlikely to be relevant to Pamela's situation. She told the younger woman that she had early in her marriage faced the choice of devoting herself to Winston or of asserting her independence. She had chosen the former route because she believed in Winston. She could not recommend Pamela to do the same because she did not have the same faith in Randolph. Even though in September Randolph had achieved at last his ambition of becoming an MP, he had not won an election and he had been chosen as a compliment to Winston rather than as an expression of confidence in his own abilities. Clementine had no great hopes for his future as a politician and indeed she was right: he would never gain a seat through election.

Randolph's drinking had now become more than simply an annoyance. He had come home on a forty-eight-hour leave, borrowed Pamela's car, got blind drunk and left classified military maps in the car for anyone to find. When he had returned home to Downing Street he had been in such a state that Pamela had to put him to bed. Clementine was enraged that the son of the Prime Minister could behave in this way setting such a poor example. The next morning early she summoned Pamela to her room and asked about Randolph's movements the night before. She told her daughter-in-law about the maps which the police had reported finding in Pamela's car and then she summoned Randolph in order to tell him to leave the house and to stay away for the rest of his leave.

Having no illusions about Randolph, Clementine found it hard to understand why Winston set such store by him, why he tried to shelter him from danger and why he declared that he could not go on fighting to win the war if anything should happen to his son. Clementine hoped that Pamela's certainty that she would have a son was justified and that with the 'succession' assured Winston would become a little less dependent on the unreliable Randolph.

Despite all her problems, in the early months of the war Clementine found consolation in the company of her youngest daughter and her daughter-in-law. In August, however, Clementine and Winston decided that Pamela would be safer during the last months of her pregnancy if she stayed in the country at Chequers. At the same time Mary went to Norfolk to stay with Venetia and Judy Montagu.

Then there had been that dreadful day in September just over a year since war had been declared and the first air-raid warning sounded. Just as on that previous occasion it was a beautiful day when the air-raid siren went, at 4.45 p.m. By the time the All Clear sounded at 6.15 p.m. there was a huge white cloud over the East End of London. Soon the sky in the east had been a blazing red and even the barrage balloons had been tinged pink as they reflected the fire. Then there had been a second siren. All night long the bombs had fallen with their distinctive tearing and whistling sound and all night long there had been the drone of planes circling monotonously overhead. Not until dawn had the All Clear sounded the end of the first dose of what proved to be almost two months of nightly bombing. Now it seemed to both Clementine and Winston that Mary would be better off staying on in Norfolk rather than returning to London and the bombing.

So once again Clementine found herself very much on her own. She now rarely saw Winston except in company, and many nights she chose to dine alone from a tray in her room rather than be part of an otherwise all-male gathering.

In October Sarah had confessed to her mother that her marriage to Vic was under severe strain and that she needed an occupation that would justify her living apart from him. When the run of Ivor Novello's *Murder in Mayfair* in which she was playing came to an end she joined the WAAF and was sent to Medmenham to work on photographic Intelligence. Clementine was distressed that her second daughter's marriage, like that of her first, had ended in failure.

Fortunately at this time of loneliness and isolation she began to see ways in which she could use her position to help others. When she had first moved into Downing Street she had often been hurt and annoyed by her husband's peremptory and brusque way of speaking to her. It was as if being war leader had placed him above ordinary courtesies. Before long she realized that she was not alone in feeling this way and that a tension was building in the Prime Minister's office which was not likely to produce good results. How could people in a state of resentment and irritation give of their best and work the punishing hours that Winston expected of them? Occasions when she might talk privately with Winston were few and far between. In desperation she had one morning decided to catch Winston while he was shaving and talk to him then. To her dismay, when she entered Winston's bedroom she discovered she was too late: he was already conducting a Cabinet meeting in the manner of a French king's levee. And so, rather than confronting Winston in person with his insensitivity, arrogance and bullying, she adopted the technique which she was to use throughout the war: she wrote her husband a note in which she combined flattery with criticism and appealed to Winston's sense of duty to the office he held to modify his treatment of colleagues and employees alike. She asked him to combine with his unprecedented power thoughtfulness, kindness and a god-like calm.[3]

Before long many people realized that one of the most successful ways of getting the Prime Minister to take notice of things which would not normally command his attention was to filter the information through Clementine. Even John Colville, who had initially objected to being in any way regarded as part of Clementine's personal staff, now arranged for her to meet people who saw the need for government action but who had not been able to get past civil-service red tape. The first person to meet her in this way was Miriam Pease who had been inspecting armament factories. Clementine remembered what these places were like from her work establishing factory canteens in the previous war. She was dismayed to learn that the resentment against women in the factories was as bad as it had ever been. Just as in the First World War the men were reluctant to train women to take their places while they went to the Front. They were again afraid of coming back to find there were no jobs for them. Consequently many women were receiving inadequate training for their dangerous work and, because they were being taught only their own small part of a job, if one woman went sick no one could take her place and the production line was slowed down. The physical conditions for these workers were appalling, Clementine learned. Ventilation, so crucial in places where toxic substances were in constant use, was usually inadequate, and the women were being asked to work shifts which were too long. The combination of foul air and tiredness represented a real danger. Miriam Pease's argument was that armament production could not be improved until the factories were made safer and the workers' health given consideration. Clementine made notes of all she had heard and passed on the information to her husband.

Encouraged by her response, Colville then told her that not enough was being done to bolster up the morale of those living in areas subjected to heavy bombing. Clementine knew about devastated areas since she made a point of accompanying Winston whenever he visited a place which had been badly bombed. Colville pointed out that such visits were insufficient, that there were real practical problems which were not being addressed. He pointed out that in some air-raid shelters as many as eight thousand people had to spend the night in a place where the toilet facilities consisted of three feet square of floor screened off to the height of six feet with canvas tacked to a wooden frame. Inside this area was a bucket containing chemicals. There would be at best six such screened areas each for men and for women. Inevitably the smell was appalling.

It was no wonder that when the All Clear sounded and people emerged from their shelters they were usually cold, hungry and depressed. Many of them had to go straight to work having had little sleep, no opportunity to wash and no food. Because public transport stopped as soon as an air-raid warning sounded there was no way for people who had been caught far from home to get back. Clementine saw as clearly as did Colville that canteens would at least alleviate the situation, so he introduced her to Violet Markham who had been lobbying the Ministry of Food for help in organizing canteens. She had received no response and so had begun a canteen on her own initiative in Southwark. In order to present a reasoned and documented argument for more of these canteens Clementine, accompanied by Colville, visited Southwark. Colville was dismayed to see that Clementine planned to make this visit wearing a leopard-skin coat. He thought her vastly overdressed for the occasion. But Clementine's judgement was proved right; her appearance inspired confidence rather than envy. Moreover, Colville was greatly surprised to see that Clementine had no difficulty in conversing with all the people she met and in listening carefully to their accounts of the nights spent in the shelters. Once again her experience in the First World War and canvassing in Dundee had made her more prepared for such situations than Colville could have guessed from seeing Clementine at Downing Street or Chequers.

The shelter at Southwark was, like many others in London, a part of London's underground transport system. After the first night of the Blitz crowds of people had gathered outside Liverpool Street Station demanding to be allowed to shelter underground. There had been clashes with soldiers trying to prevent this mass influx of people, but eventually those who wished to do so were allowed sleep on the underground platforms. Thousands of people spent night after night there from 9 p.m. to 5 a.m. during the Blitz in extremely poor conditions with insufficient provision of blankets and inadequate sanitation. Clementine could see that such shelters were a health hazard and very bad for morale. Her visit to Southwark confirmed what she had already learnt from the many people who had written to her, as the Prime Minister's wife, asking her to do something about the shelters. She set to work by sending a memorandum to Winston which detailed measures which could and should be taken. This she followed up by regular surprise visits to shelters to see that what she had suggested was in fact being done.

Having seen how effective Clementine could be Violet Markham now brought up another problem which was not being handled well by the government. Civil Defence workers were as crucial to the country's survival as the armed forces. But like the crews of mine sweepers and coastal craft they were not entitled to the benefits of service personnel. Along with Colville, Clementine spent many hours during Chequers weekends studying the matter and deciding what might be done. Their memorandum persuaded Winston that the situation must at least be investigated.

During the heavy bombing in September the basement of Downing Street had been reinforced for the Prime Minister's protection but this did not prevent considerable damage being done to the kitchen, which was also in the basement, when a bomb fell close to the house in October. The invaluable cook, Mrs Landemare, and the housemaid, Nellie, only narrowly escaped injury because Winston had refused to let them stay in the kitchen during the raid. Now it seemed that Downing Street was no longer a safe place, and plans were made for the Churchills to move into Storey's Gate, a modern and solid block of government offices. The series of rooms – called the Annexe – allocated to them was on the first floor above the secure underground War Rooms. Undeterred by wartime conditions Clementine made her imprint on the former offices. She had them painted in pale colours and hung some of their own paintings on the walls. She had a Romney over the chimney-piece, various landscapes, and the portrait of her mother as a girl painted by Watts. Some of their furniture was brought over from Downing Street. When her Aunt Mabell, the dowager Countess of Airlie, visited her she was surprised to find such an elegant and tranquil atmosphere in such an unpromising setting. These rooms were Clementine's home for the remainder of the war.

In September Clementine had been invited to attend the christening of a son born to Mary, Duchess of Marlborough, at a time when she had believed her child-bearing days were over. When Clementine reported that the boy was to be christened Winston, in part as a compliment to her husband, Pamela unexpectedly burst into tears. She protested that this could not be allowed; the name had to be reserved for her child which was due in a few weeks. She was inconsolable and would not even consider the possibility that the child might be a girl. Her father-in-law had a good deal of sympathy with her as he had looked forward to having Winston Jr in the family. So he telephoned the Duchess and asked her as a favour to him to reconsider her child's name. Mary explained that the name was already registered. No matter, said Winston, this must be changed and the boy christened with one of the other names they had chosen for him. To please him Mary agreed. So it was a great relief to everyone when on 10 October Pamela did produce a son who could be called Winston. It should have been a proud moment for Randolph, one which might have gained him his mother's favour. But he was nowhere to be found to be told that he was now a father: he was still celebrating his introduction into the House two days earlier.

Through these difficult months, although she retained her habitual outward calm, Clementine was far from confident that she was performing her role as Prime Minister's wife adequately. There was a good deal of interest both at home and abroad in the new regime at Number 10 and *Picture Post* decided to do a feature article 'The Lady at No. 10'. Cecil Beaton was commissioned to take photographs of Clementine, and of Winston working in his office. The publication of the article brought to a head Clementine's doubts about herself, and Cecil Beaton, who had called at Downing Street for approval of the photos he had taken of Winston, found himself the unlikely confidant of a distraught Clementine. She was especially upset that the article in the *Picture Post* claimed that her marriage to Winston had been arranged by his mother. That was simply not true, she protested repeatedly to the embarrassed photographer. Winston had married her because he loved her, she asserted. The extreme distress witnessed by Cecil Beaton raises some questions about the relationship between Clementine and Winston at this time. Was the notion that Winston had married her for love so important to her because over the last years she had begun to doubt his love? Did she see the article as confirmation that other people saw her marriage as loveless? This was not the image that she had hoped to project. Perhaps even more upsetting to her were the negative reactions of her friends and acquaintances to the photo which had accompanied the article. Cecil Beaton himself may have had some doubts about this particular photograph. He had remarked in his diary after the photographic session at Downing Street that Clementine with her newly set hair looked like Pallas Athene. Was he responsible for encouraging her to dress in a manner that accentuated this Greek goddess appearance. Certainly it is a very strange photo and does nothing to suggest that the sitter is the wife of a wartime Prime Minister. In floods of tears Clementine told Beaton that one of her friends had commented that the photograph made her look like a hardbitten virago who took drugs. She raged that the article had made her a laughing stock and that those who felt that she was not fitted to be the wife of one of the three most important men in the world could point to the article and photos as evidence. She demanded that all photos of her currently in editors' offices should be returned immediately and destroyed. What concerned her most of all was that she had failed Winston by not being seen to be a fitting consort. Beaton did what he could to help. He saw the terrible loneliness that was in part responsible for this outburst. He held Clementine's hand and when she had recovered herself he kissed her on the forehead. As a further gesture to show that he saw, appreciated and admired Clementine's femininity and beauty, on the next day he sent her an enormous bunch of red and white roses, violets and yellow orchids. As he had intended Clementine was touched by his gift.

This crisis of confidence about her own public image erupted in November after months of strain resulting not only from the bombing but also anxiety about the family as a whole. Therefore more consoling to Clementine than Cecil Beaton's gift of flowers were the photos he had taken of her grandson, the five-week-old Winston, which were published internationally. With these photos the image of the Churchills as a united and happy family celebrating the birth of a boy to carry on the famous name was most satisfactorily established.

25

Fighting Against the Odds

AT THE BEGINNING of 1941 hopes that the war would soon be over and Germany defeated faded. By now Hitler's armies occupied continental Europe and Norway and under the leadership of Rommel were about to advance in North Africa. In Britain itself the effective tactics of German U-boats were being felt since the heavy loss of shipping in the Atlantic convoys was beginning to cause food shortages. Rationing had to be introduced and everyone was encouraged to eat carrots, potatoes and oatmeal in greater quantities since these food items could be grown in Britain. Lord Woolton dreamed up the idea of the British Restaurant where all meals were a fixed price. His objective was to allow the working man the same opportunity of supplementing his rations by eating out. In reality the poor were unable to afford even the moderate prices of these restaurants. Clothing the army was a major concern so that later in the year the rationing of clothes for the civilian population was introduced. Every major city had its share of derelict houses as a result of the bombing. There were neither the materials nor the labour to repair such houses and, because there was still a fear of invasion or infiltration by spies, all bomb-damaged houses were simply boarded up to prevent them being used by any Germans who had managed to make their way into England. In London the smell of burning pervaded everything as did the dust rising from bomb sites.

Like many other women during this time of little hope Clementine felt that she must extend the scope of her work to help Britain win the war. The skills she now brought into play were those organizing abilities which she had developed in the First World War and which for the past few years she had used to run her complicated household. As before her concern was first of all directed towards what was happening to women in wartime conditions. More and more of them were volunteering for or being drafted into war work. They were rarely able to live at home, but the existing numbers of hostels suitable to accommodate them was inadequate. In February 1941 Clementine became the President of the YWCA Wartime Fund. In this capacity she made speeches appealing for money, attended endless committee meetings and in 1943 even went to the Stock Exchange asking for help. If the organizers of the appeal had chosen Clementine to be their president simply as a figurehead with great charm they soon learned that she was not content to confine herself to fund-raising. She wanted to see that the money raised was put to good use and that young women away from home were given not just shelter but also some comfort. She quickly realized that any hostel was only as good as its warden and she made life hard for wardens who did not share her own exacting standards. She made it her business to enquire into such details as the number of baths in each hostel, the amount of hot water available, the quality of the mattresses and the bed-linen, the provision of adequate bedside lighting. Whenever she was offered gifts, as in September 1944 when a rich Canadian wanted to give both Clementine and Mary expensive fur coats, she delicately pointed out that as wife of the Prime Minister she was not able to accept personal gifts but that money towards the hostel fund was always welcome.

Apart from raising funds what she did for the hostels could be seen as expert housekeeping on a large scale. When she turned her attention to bomb shelters her attitude was similar. She made a thorough investigation of prevailing conditions and measured them against what could be minimally expected. Once her suggestions were officially accepted she worked relentlessly to ensure that standards were maintained. She took an interest in air-raid precaution canteens and decontamination centres. Her very presence at such places helped to focus attention on them, to make workers feel that someone took an interest in them and made government officials take notice.

Although America was still resisting government appeals to enter the war some unofficial help was reaching Britain through such organizations as the Bundles for Britain scheme. Janet Murrow, the wife of the intrepid American war reporter Ed Murrow, was one of the principle organizers at the London end. Clementine offered her services in helping to distribute the clothes and food sent by American well-wishers.

There were other Americans who came into Clementine's life now, some of whom were to have a major effect on her family. As President Roosevelt tried to help prevent the defeat of Britain without actually declaring war on Germany, he sent over representatives to negotiate the Lend-lease scheme by which help could be given to Britain in the form of much-needed equipment. Harry Hopkins was the first negotiator to suffer the bitter cold of Chequers that winter. Then came Averell Harriman and the American Ambassador, John Gilbert Winant. Averell Harriman remembered vividly his first visit to Chequers and what he suddenly realized about conditions in Britain. 'I was surprised to see how grateful Mrs Churchill was for a small bag of tangerines I had brought her from Lisbon. Her unfeigned delight brought home to me the restrictions of the dreary wartime diet, imposed by the sharp reduction of imports, even in the Prime Minister's home.'[1]

Sarah, now working at Medmenham, visited Chequers on all the weekends when she was not on duty. Clementine knew that her daughter's marriage to Vic Oliver was more or less at an end and that Vic had taken up with another young actress in a manner closely resembling the way he had begun his relationship with Sarah. So far, however, the breakup of Sarah's marriage was not common knowledge and there had been no publicity. What now worried Clementine as she struggled to maintain the image of a happy, united family was that right under her parents' noses at Chequers Sarah had begun another love affair. The man she loved was himself already married with a wife and child back in the States. The American Ambassador to London, Gil Winant, was already a great favourite of Clementine. She had begun inviting him to Chequers regularly because she felt that he was lonely and shy. This former governor of New Hampshire, with his deep-set, dark eyes and dark jutting features making him look rather like portraits of Abraham Lincoln, had refused to live in grandeur in the ambassadorial residence in Grosvenor Gardens while the people of London faced the hardships of the Blitz. He had taken a much more modest flat in Grosvenor Square where he lived alone. This was a move of which Clementine with her dislike for ostentatious luxury thoroughly approved. She had not anticipated that her daughter Sarah would find the Ambassador just as attractive as she did and that in his turn Winant would fall hopelessly in love with the vivacious red-haired actress. The two of them did their best to be discreet, knowing full well that it would not do for it to be known that the married American Ambassador was having an affair with the married daughter of the Prime Minister of England. But to Clementine it was an ongoing worry.

Meanwhile another even more potentially explosive relationship had also been begun at Chequers. Pamela Churchill no longer lived with her in-laws. After the birth of Winston Jr she had found a little house at Hitchin where she lived briefly with Randolph before he had been sent overseas to join a unit in Egypt. But before he even reached his destination Randolph had lost heavily gambling on board ship and had to appeal to his wife to send him money. Pamela was pregnant once again but the worry of the situation she found herself in brought on a miscarriage. Not caring to approach her father-in-law a second time for money, Pamela had sold most of her wedding presents and leased out the house she had been so pleased to move into. But she was still short of money. She had then decided to appeal to Randolph's former employer, Max Beaverbrook, for advice on how to raise enough money to pay her day-to-day expenses. Beaverbrook, always charmed to have a pretty young woman in his debt, had agreed to continue paying to her Randolph's journalist's wage while he was away and to enable Pamela to earn her own living he had offered to receive in his house at Cherkley baby Winston and his nanny. Pamela had found herself a job in the hostel department of the Royal Ordinance factory and had taken a room for herself at the Dorchester where Clarissa Churchill, working in the communications department of the Foreign Office, was also living. It was some time before she told her parents-in-law what she had done, and they had then insisted that she and baby Winston should visit Chequers at weekends regularly.

It was at Chequers that Pamela met Averell Harriman. Roosevelt's negotiator with Winston was quite different from the American Ambassador. Extremely rich and coldly confident he was someone Clementine enjoyed battling with at croquet but he did not appeal to her as a man at all. But Pamela, many years Harriman's junior, felt quite differently and was quickly involved in a passionate affair with him. To provide a reason for her frequent meetings with Harriman in London, Pamela had moved into a flat with his daughter.

Clementine found herself in a quandary about her daughter-in-law who in so many ways had behaved perfectly as a member of the Churchill family up to the time she met Harriman. She had produced an extremely photogenic heir to Winston. She had for a long time kept from her father-in-law the worrying news of Randolph's debt. It was a serious consideration that the good will of Averell Harriman was extremely important to the relationship between Britain and America at this time when Winston was hoping that America could be induced to enter the war. Pamela was clearly keeping Harriman happy and so, despite the fact that she was married to their son, Winston and Clementine turned a blind eye on the affair hoping that the couple would be discreet. Clementine's belief that her son had treated his wife very badly explains what was for her an unusual tolerance of marital infidelity.

Clementine began to feel that there must be something in the atmosphere at Chequers when in May 1941, when she was not yet nineteen, Mary too seemed to fall in love. Lord Duncannon was clearly enamoured of her and had succeeded in rousing her interest in him. As a concession to Mary's friendship with the young man Clementine had invited him to lunch at Chequers one weekend but she was displeased when he pretended that he had understood the invitation to be for the whole weekend. Clementine now looked with a cold eye on Mary's delighted response to being courted. Even Sarah's mocking comments did not bring her sister down to earth. On 9 May Mary told her mother that Frederick Duncannon had proposed and that she had accepted. Clementine did not forbid the marriage but she told Mary that she was far too young and inexperienced to know whether this was just a passing fancy on her part. She pointed out that she had been right about Diana's first marriage and Sarah's. Used to basking in the warmth of Clementine's affection and approval Mary was keenly aware that her engagement displeased her mother. Her attachment to her parents proved stronger than that to her fiancé and by 12 May the engagement was off. Clementine, who had been confident that Mary was more in love with the idea of being engaged than with the young man himself, was pleased.

For the most part it was left to Clementine to observe and respond to these family matters for, inevitably, Winston was concerned with larger issues. But the death of Goonie from cancer in July was a blow to the whole family. She had been the one person Clementine had looked to in times of stress, relying on her judgement far more than that of her sister Nellie. Jack Churchill, who had nursed his wife devotedly during the last months of her illness, was now drawn closer into the family circle.

Not every weekend was spent at Chequers during 1941. Because the house was highly visible from the air, especially when the moon was high, there were fears that it was not a safe place for the Prime Minister and the many people he did business with there. So Winston had asked Ronald Tree, Ethel Beatty's son by her first marriage, if he would receive the

Prime Minister and his entourage at his country house, Ditchley in Oxfordshire. The Trees really had little choice but to accept the monthly invasions of twelve or fourteen guests. Everyone enjoyed these respites from Chequers for Ditchley was a far more comfortable and very well run house with central heating and good food and drink. During these occasions Clementine began a friendship with Ronald Tree which was to last until his death.

For many years Winston had raged against communists and communism and Clementine had always resisted his violent condemnation. Winston's loathing of the Bolsheviks was one thing he had in common with Hitler, who now began to act on his hatred and to begin an invasion of the Soviet Union. Stalin now had little choice but to declare war on Germany. So in June 1941 the much reviled communists were suddenly Britain's allies and Clementine felt her attitude had been vindicated. She was further encouraged when in September she accompanied Winston on a visit to Coventry and the Whitley bomber factory which was regarded by Winston and Beaverbrook as a hotbed of communism. Everyone surrounding the Prime Minister feared that he would meet with a hostile reception. To Clementine's dismay and even anger Winston himself got the visit off to a bad start. They had travelled overnight to Coventry by special train but when the train arrived at its destination Winston was still not dressed and the official welcoming party was kept waiting. Clementine feared that the people of Coventry and Birmingham would feel insulted and she was, therefore, all the more gratified that the much-reviled communists and trade unionists at the bomber factory gave them a warmer reception than she felt they deserved.

In October 1941, as the news of the plight of millions of Russian civilians reached Britain, Clementine was asked whether she would be willing to be the chairperson of the Red Cross Aid to Russia Fund. She seized on the opportunity to counteract Russian suspicion of the Churchills as arch anti-communists by throwing herself whole-heartedly into fund-raising to send much-needed medical supplies and clothing to the beleaguered Russian people. She, who hated making speeches and especially broadcasts, made such moving appeals for money that by January of 1942 the initial target of a million pounds had been reached. All kinds of people responded to Clementine's appeal: events as different as a weekly series of piano recitals by Moiseiwitsch; an England-Wales football match; an

auction at which a beautiful enamelled clock given to the British commu-
nity at St Petersburg by the assassinated Czarina was sold; weekly collec-
tions of pennies from school children, all helped to increase the fund
which by 1945 reached the amazing amount of four million pounds. Even
having to deal with the rather difficult and critical wife of the Russian
Ambassador, Madame Agnes Maisky, did not lessen Clementine's enthusiasm for her self-imposed task. Over a period of time she became used to
Madame Maisky and a tentative friendship developed between the two
women with their mutual concern for the people of Russia. In March
1942 Clementine was invited to the Russian Embassy to be present when
four British pilots responsible for helping convoys of goods to reach the
Soviet Union were presented with awards by the Russian Ambassador
Ivan Maisky. When a new translation of Tolstoy's *War and Peace* was
published Madame Maisky presented Clementine with a copy in which
she had written '1812–1942. We destroyed our enemy then, we shall
destroy our enemy also today.'[2] In February of 1943, after she had read
War and Peace, Clementine returned the compliment presenting another
copy of the book to Madame Maisky in which she too had written. Her
message read, 'Here is a book for those who would penetrate the vastness
and mystery of Russia.'[3] The Soviet Union did indeed intrigue
Clementine more and more. Winston told the Russian Ambassador of his
wife's absorption in her task. 'All she talks about is the Soviet Red Cross,
the Red Army and the wife of the Soviet Ambassador to whom she
writes, with whom she talks on the telephone or speaks at demonstrations.'[4] There can be no doubt that the work done by Clementine in
England did much to ease the Prime Minister's way when he finally came
face to face with the Russian leader, Stalin.

A source of both pride and anxiety to Clementine was Mary's decision
in August that she should, like other young women, join the ATS. The
company of her daughter was precious to her. The kind of intimacy she
enjoyed with her is touchingly revealed in John Colville's description of
mother and daughter sitting side by side in bed enjoying breakfast
together.[5] With Mary gone her loneliness would increase. But putting a
good face on the situation, in September Clementine, along with Venetia
Montagu whose daughter Judy had made the same decision as Mary,
threw a party at the Dorchester before the two young women went to
Aldermaston to begin their basic training.

Among the guests on this occasion was Diana Sandys, no longer in
uniform and clearly feeling the odd one out in this family where she

would now be the only one not visibly involved in the war. Her husband Duncan had recently been in a car crash in which, because he was wearing no shoes at the time, his feet had been badly crushed. There had been a moment when it seemed as if his feet might have to be amputated. Although this drastic measure had not proved necessary, for some time he needed nursing and Diana had given up her work and once more dedicated herself to her husband and children. That Clementine favoured Mary far more then her eldest daughter was painfully apparent that evening. In her distress and nervousness Diana chattered obsessively about her children and whether they should be evacuated. Clementine was not pleased with her.

Throughout the war years Clementine Churchill was seen by the general public in her capacity as a fund raiser, as a woman who took a close interest in everyone she met, who answered the many letters she received with care, who was always beautifully dressed but who showed her solidarity with working women by voluntarily adopting her version of the turban that most of them were obliged to wear. She was seen frequently at Winston's side complementing his aggressive, confident posture by her smiling approachability. People responded to her as much as, if not more than, they did to the Queen. If she had done only what the public were aware of her doing, Clementine would have achieved a great deal. But the tasks she undertook and the worries she experienced were far more numerous than was generally known. As the wife of the Prime Minister Clementine was perceived as being in a privileged position. And it is true that she was far less affected by shortages of food and drink and had less difficulty in travelling than ordinary people. There was always a government car or a private train to transport her. On the other hand she was married to a man in his late sixties – and in the population at large men of that age were considered too old for military service, and stayed at home with their wives. Throughout the war Clementine suffered a special anxiety which she did not share with her contemporaries of having her husband leave her repeatedly on dangerous missions, travelling in a manner which would have taxed the strength of a much younger and fitter man.

Between August 1941 and January 1945 Winston made twelve major journeys abroad. Often he left in poor health; he was frequently ill on his return, and on one occasion Clementine was summoned to his side because his death seemed imminent.

The majority of Winston's journeys were to meet Franklin Roosevelt and Joseph Stalin, and to the other worries Clementine felt was added the need to keep Winston's movements secret. When she learned in August 1941 that her husband proposed to journey across the Atlantic on the *Prince of Wales* to meet Roosevelt at Placentia Bay she urged him to include his doctor, Charles Moran, in his entourage but Winston stubbornly refused and his return without mishap made him even more inclined to dismiss her fears as excessive.

Clementine rarely argued with Winston about such decisions. She knew, as she later told Diana Cooper in 1944, that Winston was determined to put all he had into the war and seeing the sacrifices being made by so many young men she could only sympathize with his position. The strain told on her, however, and in an effort to be in good health to support Winston to the full on his return she spent time while he was away at the health establishment of Dr Lief in Tring. He wisely advised her that she should have one rest day a week to maintain health. But in her position at such a time Clementine found such advice impossible to follow.

Clementine and Winston were at Chequers on 7 December along with Averell Harriman. Clementine had actually already retired to her room when the news came through that the Japanese had attacked Pearl Harbour and destroyed the greater part of the Americans' Pacific fleet. Then, just hours after the Americans found themselves at war with the Japanese, the Germans had declared war on the United States. Winston immediately had the news delivered to Clementine who understood what it meant to her husband that Britain now had a forceful ally.

But Winston felt that it was a matter of urgency that he consult with the President and, to Clementine's dismay, immediately made plans to set off on the *Duke of York* to Virginia for a further meeting with Roosevelt. She was concerned about the stormy weather, remembering her own winter crossing to New York at a time when there were no U-boats to add to the danger. She also had in mind the recent sinking of the *Prince of Wales* by the Japanese and she had a superstitious worry that the *Duke of York*, a sister ship, was also vulnerable. Her anxiety was increased when the President himself cautioned Winston about the dangers of the journey he proposed. However, Winston arrived safely and while he enjoyed a convivial Christmas in the White House, Clementine in London had only the company of cousin Maryott since Mary did not have leave from her unit. There seemed very little to celebrate. In November Nellie's son Esmond who had joined the Canadian air force had been reported missing presumed dead. Nellie's granddaughter, the child of Esmond and Jessica Mitford, had been born after his death in the United States and no one in the family had seen her. Giles was still a prisoner of war. Goonie was gone and the rest of the family was scattered.

26

Dangerous Journeys

AFTER THE TALKS between the new allies Roosevelt had insisted that Winston should not take unnecessary risks and repeat the dangerous crossing. Instead he offered him the use of a Boeing Clipper for his return journey. But even this comparatively luxurious form of travel meant an eighteen-hour journey, and when Clementine met Winston she found him depressed by fatigue and a heavy cold. She was even more alarmed when at a social occasion a few days later Winston had to stop dancing because of the violent beating of his heart. But nothing could prevent him from making careful preparations for the speeches he intended to make in the Commons in the debate which began on 26 January. After the heavy losses and defeats of 1941, the time had come, he felt, to call for a vote of confidence in his management of the war. Clementine was in the gallery every day of the debate. She was alarmed when Randolph got to his feet and, with his passionate defence of his father, which involved attacking all his critics, lost the Prime Minister much sympathy. It was left to Winston to make good the damage by making one of the best speeches of his life on the final day of the debate. The vote of confidence was overwhelming. Husband and wife left Westminster arm in arm and beaming. This was one of the high points in Clementine's pride in her husband and his achievements.

Such pleasure as this victory in the Commons had brought was soon dispelled by two shocking events. Firstly three major German warships – the *Scharnhorst* and the *Gneisenau* and the *Prinz Eugen* – had set off from Brest in Brittany and had managed to sail through the Straits of Dover and back to Germany. Questions were asked in the press about the effectiveness of the navy and the air force and those who gave them their orders if they could not have prevented such a thing happening. Just days later there was worse news still. As word of the surrender of Britain's important naval Pacific base, Singapore, came through, Clementine well remembered how she had written to Winston telling him how dangerously run down the port's defences had been allowed to become. In the surrender eighty thousand British and allied soldiers had been captured by the Japanese. Clementine saw how this blow had visibly aged her husband. For once his zest for war had gone. He seemed without vigour and without new ideas. She was very much aware that others, too, saw the change in him and suffered from his ill temper, and that some of the confidence in him as a leader which the vote in the House of Commons had witnessed was beginning to evaporate.

Added to her fear that Winston was dangerously undermining his health was Clementine's concern that he was putting himself into jeopardy politically when he decided on his third major journey to meet Roosevelt in June 1942. The situation of the Eighth Army fighting against Rommel in North Africa was critical. The War Cabinet and Clementine felt that Winston should be in England at such a time, not putting himself at a distance of thousands of miles. Her view appeared to be vindicated when Tobruk fell and a motion to censure the Prime Minister was tabled in the Commons. But later she wondered whether in fact her husband had made an astute move by being in the United States at Britain's moment of humiliation. The immediate offer of help from the President might not have come if Winston's presence in the States had not given the issue an immediacy for the Americans it might have otherwise lacked. Clementine waited anxiously for Winston's return on the Boeing Clipper but saw little of him after his safe arrival as he was deeply intent on preparing a speech to vindicate himself to his critics.

By now Winston was determined to meet with Stalin himself. The journey to Moscow would involve flying at greater altitudes than Winston had so far experienced. Because the planes were unpressurized Clementine, along with Moran, was concerned that such a long, high flight might bring about a coronary thrombosis. When Winston went to Farnborough at the end of July to undertake tests in the 'Chamber' to see whether he was fit for high altitude flying Clementine went along with him and watched her husband carefully through an observation porthole. She had mixed feelings when his flight to Moscow was approved. On the evening of 1 August 1942 she drove with him to the airbase at Lyneham to see him board a Liberator Commander. She stood in the dark listening as the great bomber's engines roared and then watched as the plane taxied away down the runway, its flashing blue tail-light doubly conspicuous in the surrounding darkness. There was a long pause before she saw the dim shape of the bomber slowly rising and moving out of sight. Always on such occasions Clementine wondered whether she would ever see her husband again. This time she had worries in addition to those about the dangers of flying; knowing Winston's views about communists and communism Clementine feared that her husband might well lack tact and patience in his dealings with what she described in her first message to him during this separation as being like a beast in his lair.[1] She later learned that there had indeed been moments when Winston had felt greatly provoked and angered by Stalin's attitude towards him.

In the autumn of 1942 Clementine knew that unless something happened to break the long run of Allied defeats her husband would almost certainly be obliged to resign as Prime Minister and she knew that such a failure would break his heart. So the news that General Montgomery had been successful at El Alamein was doubly welcome. Suddenly Winston was more confident and hopeful and ready to start off on yet another journey.

Each time Winston returned from his meetings with Roosevelt and Stalin Clementine hoped that he would be content to stay in England and let others do what travelling was necessary. But she knew that this was not in his nature and she was not unduly surprised when the Moscow meeting was followed quite quickly in February 1943 by plans to meet Roosevelt in Casablanca. Once again Winston flew in a Liberator. This time an attempt was made to heat the plane but this was so dangerous that this in itself could have cost him his life. Once the meeting with Roosevelt was over Clementine expected Winston to return but instead he lingered in Marrakesh and she learned that he had approached the War Cabinet with a proposal that he should fly to Turkey to meet that country's President and try to influence him personally to support the allies. It was this fruitless extra travelling that was Winston's undoing. When Clementine met his train on a freezing cold day after he had been away for four weeks she found that he was already very unwell; he looked even older and more weary than he had done at the fall of Singapore. She was not at all surprised when he was diagnosed as having pneumonia.

Yet in May 1943 he was off again to the United States, this time on the

Queen Mary. Moran had vetoed travelling again in a Liberator, the Clipper was prevented from taking off by ice and Moran felt that even the dangers of the Atlantic were preferable to those of flying. But Winston insisted on flying from Gibraltar to England by Clipper to save time. Clementine was reminded just how dangerous flying could be when on the same day that Winston was on his way home the film actor Leslie Howard's plane was shot down with no survivors. The news that the Clipper had been thrown off course by lightning reinforced her fears.

Therefore when yet another meeting between Roosevelt and Winston was proposed for August in Quebec Clementine decided that it would be easier to go with her husband than to wait anxiously at home for his safe return. On previous occasions when the two men had met, Roosevelt had always had at least one of his sons with him as official aide-de-camp. Winston decided that Mary in her uniform of the ATS should go along with them in that capacity.

On 4 August the family together with Moran and the official entourage set off from London by special train to Scotland where they were to go on board the *Queen Mary* anchored in the Clyde. The journey was uneventful and the liner arrived safely in the naval dockyard at Halifax, Nova Scotia. Then the large party of those accompanying Churchill transferred to two special Canadian National trains for the long journey through the forests of Eastern Quebec to Quebec City. The King had offered the Citadel, the summer residence of the Governor General, as a temporary home for both the Churchills and the Roosevelts. At first Clementine enjoyed being in Canada, meeting up again with the Canadian Prime Minister, Mackenzie King, whom she had already come to like during his visits to London. It was a pleasure to be in a place where there was no black-out and no shortage of food.

For some time Winston and Franklin Roosevelt had hoped that the friendship between them could be extended to include their wives. Eleanor Roosevelt had visited Chequers in October of the previous year and, on the surface at least, the two women had got along. But there was no real friendship between them as there was between the two men and there was even less between Winston and Eleanor. Indeed Clementine had spent much of Eleanor's visit trying to keep the peace between her husband and the passionately Democratic and opinionated American First Lady.

Eleanor Roosevelt was as different from Clementine as could be. She had been visiting Britain to see what life was like for women in wartime, particularly those women in the services and those working in factories. She had brought to her task a superabundance of energy which left Clementine feeling tired and inadequate. The American woman, who was almost six feet tall with short wavy brown hair going slightly grey, brilliant blue eyes and a wide mouth spoiled by buck teeth and a receding chin, knew that she was no beauty and had made a point of compensating for this by using her energy and intellect to the full. Unlike Clementine she was not content to play a subordinate role to her husband. She was a respected politician and a successful journalist in her own right. She had travelled her country tirelessly collecting information which enabled her to suggest policies to her husband who was rendered less mobile by a severe attack of polio. One one occasion Winston, with some malice, had reported to Clementine that, unlike himself, Roosevelt did not confide secrets to his wife because she was always making speeches and writing articles and might forget what was secret and what was not.

This was not the only way in which the Roosevelt marriage differed from that of the Churchills. Some years ago Eleanor had discovered that her husband was having an affair with her social secretary and the marriage had almost come to an end. It was held together now by their joint political commitment rather than physical passion. So far apart were the couple in this respect that Eleanor had her own houses on the Roosevelt estates at Shangri-La and Hyde Park, and in Washington she had her own quarters where her close woman friend, the journalist Lorena Hickock, also lived. Clementine felt somewhat threatened by Eleanor's independent life-style and this example of a marriage without physical love or intimacy. Elliott Roosevelt, the eldest son, had been with his mother on that visit to Chequers and Clementine had not taken to him either. His good looks, hooded eyes and wolfish grin and his instant, easy camaraderie with everyone he met made her suspicious of his integrity. Everything Winston had told her about the young man subsequently had not improved her sense of him. She had not yet met Franklin Roosevelt. His assumption that his intimacy with her husband would automatically include her alarmed her.

Although the Churchills were supposed to go by train to spend a few days with the Roosevelts at Hyde Park, Clementine felt too tense and upset after so many days of living constantly in public view to go through with the arrangement. She desperately needed some privacy and she was sure that at Hyde Park with the larger-than-life presidential family she would not get this. An announcement was made that on the advice of Dr Moran Clementine Churchill would stay in Quebec and rest before the conference while Winston and Mary visited Hyde Park.

They returned for the conference which began on 14 August. Clementine now met Roosevelt and was immediately offended by his addressing her familiarly as Clemmie, a privilege accorded to very few and certainly not on first acquaintance. However, for the days of the conference she saw little of either her husband or the President so taken up were they with discussions. Then when the conference was over Winston had plans to go to Washington to stay with the Roosevelts once more. This time Clementine felt obliged to accompany her husband, but first of all she enjoyed a few days of respite in the Laurentian Mountains. Colonel Clarke, a wealthy Canadian who owned forests and papermills had hospitably put at the disposal of the Churchills his house, La Cabane Montmorency, at Lac des Neiges in a clearing in virgin forest on the bank of a river. The two-storey house built of roughly hewn logs looked entirely appropriate for that isolated place. But its primitive appearance was deceptive. To Clementine's relief the house did in fact have electric lights, a proper bathroom and was well stocked with food and drink. The party was welcomed by the sight of a blazing log fire in front of which lay a huge black bearskin rug, a reminder of the kind of place they were staying in.

While Winston fished, Clementine rested and enjoyed the peace and quiet. Thoroughly recovered from her earlier nervous tension she was ready to take on the White House. This famous official residence of Presidents of the United States failed to impress her as much as she had expected. Evidently Eleanor Roosevelt had not taken the same personal interest in making the place elegant as Clementine had even with her temporary quarters at Storey's Gate. Everything seemed old fashioned and of another generation. The heavy Victorian furniture was neither comfortable nor appropriate to the setting. A further disappointment was the food. There was no shortage of good ingredients available in Washington. But unlike the Churchills' invaluable and inspired cook, Mrs Landemare, Mrs Henrietta Nesbitt, the cook employed by Eleanor Roosevelt, believed in very plain food, simply prepared. To Clementine it suggested a lack of care and she found her meals in the White House boring and unappetizing. To add to her general discomfort she cracked her elbow and was forced to wear her arm in a sling for most of the visit.

Mary had rejoined them in the White House after paying a courtesy visit to a Women's Army Corp base in Georgia so that the family was reunited ready for the train journey to Hyde Park where they were to spend a few days before returning to Halifax. During this visit Clementine and Winston celebrated their thirty-fifth wedding anniversary. During their marriage they had spent many anniversaries apart and it was not inappropriate that on this occasion the context was a semi-official visit. Nevertheless Winston was at pains to reassure Clementine that he loved her more than ever. Was it a measure of Clementine's previous uncertainty about whether this really was so that she hastened to repeat her husband's words to her daughter?

The return journey to Scotland was made not on the *Queen Mary* but on the battle cruiser *Renown*. During the voyage there were two notable events: the first was that Mary celebrated her twenty-first birthday. The second event was a less happy one. Mary had insisted on going on deck during heavy seas. She was taken by surprise when a heavy swell swept over the deck and without the intervention of a quick-witted sailor would have been dragged overboard.

Despite being able to keep an eye on Winston's health for herself Clementine had not greatly enjoyed the Quebec Conference. She decided that, however painful the uncertainty of staying at home whilst Winston travelled might be, she was herself too old and too nervous for any more long official journeys. In future, she decided, another member of the family must take on the responsibility of looking after Winston. So when a meeting with Chiang Kai-shek and Roosevelt in Cairo to be followed by a meeting of the two leaders with Stalin in Teheran was arranged, Sarah was asked to accompany her father as his aide-de-camp.

Once again Churchill arrived for the conference suffering from a heavy cold. Sarah, however, kept her mother well informed both about Winston's health and about what was going on. Clementine was glad that she had not gone to Cairo when she learned that the only other woman present was the powerful wife of Chiang Kai-shek and that at an evening's entertainment Sarah had been obliged to dance with all the men in turn. She was confident that Sarah performed her duties with more pleasure and a better grace than Clementine could have mustered. But even Sarah had not been able to prevent her father from staying up too late and drinking too much. The news that Moran had made Winston go to bed to nurse a fever even though it meant missing an evening meeting was disquieting to Clementine but she was hardly prepared to learn that on the first stage of the journey home after the conference Winston had once again developed pneumonia and that, worse still, he had suffered another heart attack.

Sarah and Moran grew increasingly alarmed at Winston's condition and eventually, fearing that he was near death, decided that Clementine must be sent for. So with this terrible anxiety about her husband weighing on her mind Clementine faced making the long journey to be with him by the form of transport which she had always feared. A Liberator similar to the one she had seen carry Winston off to Moscow was assigned to take her to Carthage. Her troubles began before she ever reached Lyneham airport, for the drive on which Mary and Grace Hamblin accompanied her was made dangerous and difficult by dense fog and the black-out. She was relieved to discover John Colville, smart and confident in his RAF uniform, had been summoned to go with her on the flight. But first they all had a meal in the RAF Mess. Colville describes the tense occasion as 'a rather sticky dinner'[2] but says that throughout the meal Clementine appeared to be calm, even cheerful. She was in fact terrified as she put on her padded flying suit and then saw the interior of the plane with mattresses laid out on the floor. The plane was unheated so that Clementine appreciated the bulky flying suit. At eleven-thirty Clementine began her first flight. After the difficult take-off the weather was perfect and the flight was calm. Nevertheless neither Clementine nor Grace felt safe enough to settle to sleep and so all three passengers spent the night sitting up and talking and drinking coffee. Early in the morning the plane stopped at Gibraltar for refuelling while breakfast was served for the travellers at Government House. Then it was time to board the plane for the last stage of the flight to Tunis where they landed at three o'clock to find Sarah waiting to meet them. She reassured her mother that Winston was much improved but when Clementine reached the White Villa she was shocked to see how frail and ill her husband looked. For his part Winston was pathetically grateful to see her. Everyone was touched by his response, but Clementine, perhaps hiding her own emotions, commented, 'Oh yes, he's very glad I've come, but in five minutes he'll forget I'm here.'[3] This had often been Clementine's experience in the past but this time was different. Winston had himself been shocked by the seriousness of his illness and he found his wife's presence a confirmation of how ill he had been but also a great comfort. Despite his awareness of how tired she must be after her long and frightening journey Winston was reluctant to let his wife leave his side and go to her bed. At last she was able to sleep, but not for long. At one o'clock she was awakened by sounds of activity in the Villa; she went to Winston's room to find that he had suffered a setback during the night. Despite this, from the time of Clementine's arrival Winston began slowly but surely to recover. He was impatient at just how slow his progress was and at how easily he became tired. For example, the excitement of a visit from high ranking military personnel who had been captured by the Germans and escaped was almost too much for him. Then there was Randolph. His father was pleased by his presence and liked to play bezique with him. But to the annoyance of Clementine and the consternation of Moran, Randolph could not resist talking to his father in a way that upset and overexcited him.

Tunis did not greatly impress Clementine. She did not like the food and she found the place dirty. She occupied her time as best she could touring the battlefields and visiting what remained of the docks. Like Winston she longed to leave and go to Marrakesh but unlike Winston she realized that their departure on the twenty-sixth as Winston planned would deprive all his staff of a proper Christmas holiday. So that there would be no argument and upset she wrote a note to Winston asking that their departure should be postponed until 27 December. Her appeal was successful, and so Winston, Clementine, Sarah and Randolph spent Christmas of 1943 in Tunis. The Christmas service took place in very unfamiliar surroundings. All that could be arranged was a space in a corrugated-iron shed in which ammunition was stored. But there was one moment that restored some sense of the magic of Christmas. Whether it was contrived or whether it happened by chance, the flight of a white dove from the shed at the end of the service moved everyone. There was an attempt at festivity at the Christmas lunch and the evening cocktail party.

To everyone's relief Randolph left on 26 December on a mission contrived specifically to prevent him causing further upset. Then on the twenty-seventh the remainder of the party left for Marrakesh and the Villa Taylor, or the Flower Villa as it had been nicknamed, which had been put at the Churchills' disposal by Roosevelt. Clementine was reminded of how frail Winston still was when Moran decided that he needed to be given oxygen during the course of the flight.

The luxurious Flower Villa, surrounded by beautiful vegetation and close to the Atlas mountains, was much more to Clementine's taste than Tunisia. Here it was possible to have picnics most days by a river in the foothills of the mountains. Though still weak Winston could be included in these outings and the clean mountain air seemed to speed his recovery. Along with Colville, Clementine explored the foothills further, walking up the valley to the nearest village, a ramshackle Jewish settlement. At one point they had to ford a stream by taking turns to ride across on a donkey.

Guests arrived who took the burden of entertaining Winston off Clementine. Among them was Beaverbrook whom she made welcome on this occasion because he was so good for Winston's spirits. Another guest more to her taste was General Montgomery. She found him interesting and refreshingly sincere and good natured. She was amused rather than put off by his conceit, comparing him to Nelson. Unlike many people, especially women, Clementine was never overawed by Montgomery. She was even prepared to risk a tiff with him. After she had invited his aide-de-camp, Noel Chevasse, to dinner he protested that this broke protocol. Clementine answered him haughtily, saying, 'In my house, General Montgomery, I invite whom I wish and I don't require your advice.'⁴

At this time Bryce Nairn was the British Ambassador in Marrakesh. His wife Margaret was a painter and on the basis of this shared interest she was well received by Winston. She suggested that Sarah and Clementine, the advocate of women's suffrage, might be interested to visit the Pasha's palace, a bastion of male privilege and female subordination. The three women were well received and offered mint tea and sweetmeats while the Pasha conversed politely in French. The inside of the palace was strangely just as they had imagined, with a row of myrmidons on guard in the outer vestibule and black slave girls to wait on them. But they did not see what they were most curious about – the harem. When their visit ended they were given gifts which clearly indicated the Pasha's attitude to women, even western ones: a dagger in a gold scabbard was the gift for Winston the fighter, but the ladies were presented with gifts for their homes: each one was given a carpet.

The exotic mood of the palace contrasted with the diplomatic manoeuvring taking place back at the Villa Taylor. For despite the fact that Winston was convalescing there was still work he insisted on doing. For a while the war had seemed less immediate but now with the arrival of General de Gaulle it was once again to the forefront of everyone's mind.

Even before the General arrived he had upset Winston by a message abruptly refusing the latter's invitation to dine and stay the night. Clementine herself was not feeling pleased with the General. She had never quite forgiven his rude behaviour at a Downing Street luncheon shortly after the fall of France even though he had later apologized and sent her flowers. She knew of his many public anti-British declarations. But she also knew that such personal considerations must be put aside in the interest of larger issues. She was fearful that Winston's irritation would prevent any fruitful negotiating. She had hoped that the arrival of Duff and Diana Cooper would put him in a better mood but in fact their pro-French attitude irritated him further. She urged on him the necessity of calm good manners but, although Winston appeared to agree with her, she could not predict how he would behave when confronted with the General. Then there was the problem of language. Her own French was good but Winston's was less so. General de Gaulle was likely to refuse to speak or understand any English. Bryce Nairn offered his services as interpreter at what was likely to be a most difficult luncheon. In the event a touch of boyish humour from Winston and his evident delight in making his French understood broke the ice and the two leaders managed to remain civil throughout the meal.

By 14 January Winston, who was eager to return to the centre of action in London, claimed that he was well enough to return to England. Although they flew to Gibraltar, to Clementine's relief the remainder of the journey was completed on board the battleship *King George V* and not by plane.

In March 1944 Clementine visited Bevin's 'Back to Work' exhibition at Burlington House. The exhibition's aim was to show how the many men who had returned disabled from the war did not need to feel themselves useless and incapable of ever working again and showed how they could be retrained and taught new trades. Before the visit Clementine made herself familiar with the problems and the solutions proposed so that when she was at Burlington House she was able to talk to the men there with real concern and sympathy. No one present felt that this was simply the Prime Minister's wife making a courtesy appearance but a woman who really cared and who would do her best to make the ideals of the exhibition become practical realities.

Now tired and shaken by how close to death Winston had come, in April Clementine felt the need for a week's rest in Weymouth with only quiet and easy-going Jack Churchill for company. But Winston was in no way deterred by his recent illness from carrying on as usual. Although she had told Diana Cooper that she did not expect either herself or Winston to last beyond the war Clementine began to fear that Winston would drive himself to death even sooner. As preparations for the D-Day landings intensified Winston planned to be present himself and this despite the fact that he was convinced that something like twenty thousand men would be killed in the action. Clementine's pleas went unheeded; it was only when the King himself intervened and more or less ordered Winston to stay in England that he took notice. Six days after the landings Winston was in Normandy and then in August he flew to Algiers. But all the travelling was beginning to tell on him once more and when Clementine met him at Northolt on his return he was ill with pneumonia.

After her experience in Quebec Clementine had decided that it would be unwise for her to attend any more conferences with her husband. Now she faced a quandary for, despite his illness, Winston was about to set off for a second Quebec Conference on 5 September. She felt she had no choice but to put aside her own feelings and to accompany him. She faced the possibility that if she did not go with him she might anyway be summoned to Canada just as she had been to Tunis. So on the morning of 5 September three Churchills – Mary, Clementine and Winston – were on the train for Greenock where they went on board the liner *Queen Mary* which was on this occasion carrying American troops returning home for leave or because they were wounded. During the voyage Winston was depressed and irritable; anti-malaria pills that he had taken before going to Italy and Algiers were still having a bad effect on him. It was Clementine's responsibility to ensure that he did little socializing and got sufficient sleep to prepare himself for the meeting ahead.

An enthusiastic reception at Halifax raised his spirits and Clementine hoped that the worst was over. Once again they travelled by train to Quebec and on this occasion the President and his wife were there to greet them on their arrival. Clementine was less hostile to Roosevelt by now and would anyway have found it hard to dislike a man who was so clearly very ill. The strain of the war years had affected the handicapped American far more than his older English counterpart. As if to make up for the lethargy of their husbands Eleanor drew Clementine into a hectic round of public appearances. To Clementine's dismay the First Lady had arranged that they should make a joint broadcast. In itself this was an ordeal for Clementine but then she found that she was expected to repeat bits of the performance for the benefit of the News Reel. She was no sooner over this than she was a guest of honour at a luncheon given by Lady Fiset, the wife of the Lieutenant Governor of Quebec. It was altogether a strange experience, for although the meal took place during broad daylight all the curtains in the state room had been drawn and there were candles on the tables. Seven courses of rich food with suitable wines were served and with coffee came liqueurs. Fully aware of the responsibility of her role, Eleanor Roosevelt rose after the meal and made a stirring speech. With horror Clementine realized that the same was expected of her. She managed to acquit herself with her usual dignity despite feeling the effect of the food and drink. Before she had fully recovered from this experience there was an evening reception and a supper with Mackenzie King to which seven hundred guests had been invited. And so it went on for the rest of their stay with luncheon, tea and dinner parties to attend every day. Nevertheless Clementine made a determined effort to escape her hosts and hostesses to do some shopping. In Britain everything was in short supply, but in the shops of Quebec City it was possible to buy soap and nylons and lingerie trimmed with the lace forbidden at home. So Clementine bought such luxuries not only for herself but to take back to her family and friends. The conference came to an end but was followed by a visit to Hyde Park. Here Clementine had an opportunity to continue her self-appointed task of determining the way in which Winston would be seen by posterity. In the President's collection of photos were some of her husband which displeased her. With Roosevelt's permission she removed and destroyed them.

By 27 September they were back in London but already Winston was planning a flight to Moscow for 7 October. Still exhausted by the Quebec Conference Clementine had no desire to go to Russia so soon. She was greatly relieved when Moran gave his opinion that her presence was not absolutely necessary. During the first week of Winston's absence Clementine took full advantage of being free of her official duties and went to the theatre most nights with Mary, who was on leave. But she paid close attention to the news and was delighted to hear that Winston had received a warm welcome from the Russian people when he had attended the ballet. As was her custom she was there to meet him at Northolt on his return.

Just before the couple set off for Paris as the guests of the reinstated General de Gaulle news came of the assassination of Lord Moyne by Zionist terrorists, the Stern Gang, in Cairo. Deeply distressed by the violent death of her old friend Clementine was newly aware of just what dangers Winston faced every time he travelled abroad. She was deeply grateful that Winston was still alive to celebrate his seventieth birthday with a family party at the Annexe and touched by the many, many telegrams and good wishes he received. Such appreciation increased her sense of her husband's stature and the importance of her role as his sustainer.

In private, however, she still acknowledged and criticized Winston's shortcomings. She was, for example, horrified when, after there had been communist demonstrations in Athens, Winston began very publicly and vehemently to denounce communism. Clementine could not rest until she had warned him of the danger of such sweeping statements at a time when the Russians were still their allies. She drew his attention to the fact that, however sinister and dangerous he felt communists to be, they had during the war shown a courage which at other times he had been willing to praise. Hoping that her note to him had modified his rhetoric she then began to plan as elaborate a family Christmas at Chequers as conditions would permit. She was, therefore, greatly upset on more than one account when on Christmas Eve Winston arrived at Chequers to announce that he was leaving immediately for Athens. He was no sooner back from Greece than he was off again, this time to Versailles.

The War Cabinet was no happier than Clementine at the Prime Minister's frequent absences from England. There were, after all, growing problems at home in a country where people were hungry and cold, where many were homeless and where a war-weary population was now facing new and more deadly attacks in the form of flying bombs and the terrifying menace of the V2 rockets. As Winston planned another conference to be held in Yalta, Clement Attlee wrote to him protesting about his lack of attention to affairs at home, about his dismissing and ridiculing papers he had not read and for relying too much on the opinions of Brendan Bracken and Lord Beaverbrook. Fully expecting his wife to share his anger at this letter Winston immediately showed it to her. As scrupulously honest as ever, whatever the cost, Clementine who had a great respect for Attlee disagreed with her husband's response saying that she thought it was a good and fair letter.

Winston persisted with his preparations for a Yalta Summit and once again invited Sarah to be his aide-de-camp and accompany him on the long and difficult journey to the Crimea. As Clementine was now making her own plans for a good-will visit to Russia later in the year there was never any question of her being his travelling companion. There was a moment, however, when Winston felt ill and wanted the comfort of Clementine's presence. But Sarah wrote reassuringly to her mother and she was spared the need to fly to the rescue. By the time she met him on his return he was well and already talking about the need for him to go to Germany. This time Clementine had a commitment of her own on the continent. She had been invited to Brussels to inspect the YMCA and YWCA hostels and service clubs there and for her was the added bonus that she could see Mary who was now stationed in the Belgian capital. Visiting hostels and clubs was far more to Clementine's taste than making speeches to well-heeled ladies at luncheons, and as always she impressed everyone with her appearance and the trouble she had taken in advance to be able to talk intelligently and with interest to all she met.

Hope was growing steadily that the end of the war was in sight. During its course Winston Churchill had made twelve major journeys abroad as well as many shorter ones to France and Germany. For much of the time Clementine had been the one to stay at home and worry and wonder. It was, therefore, a great irony that at this very moment it should be Clementine who set off on a long journey on her own account leaving her husband safely at home in England.

27

A Journey Through the Soviet Union

CLEMENTINE WAS APPREHENSIVE about the journey to Russia and so, just as Winston had made provision for her whenever he went into danger, now she thought about what would happen to him if she did not come back safely. What she wanted was for one of the family to take over her own role of looking after Winston and making sure he would be remembered as a great man. As she considered to whom she should assign this task she looked back over the years of the war and considered how each of her children had responded to this time of stress and how the war had affected the Churchill family as a whole.

The last few years had neither brought her closer to nor made her respect any better her two oldest children. That Randolph's marriage was now at an end she blamed entirely on her son for treating his wife badly and for putting her in an impossible financial position. Both she and Winston had seen the necessity of making their daughter-in-law an allowance to protect her and young Winston from Randolph's fecklessness. Randolph had bitterly resented this move which he saw as favouring Pamela above himself and he had been angry to learn that his parents had done nothing to discourage Pamela's affair with Harriman. Although Randolph had shown courage in joining the Commandos and being parachuted into Yugoslavia, Clementine could not forgive him for wilfully going into danger when he knew how much this worried his father. What she had heard of Randolph's behaviour in Cairo further inclined Clementine to view her son as irresponsible and unfit to be entrusted with his father's welfare.

Diana had done nothing wrong during the war years but neither had she done anything to enhance the family's image. Clementine felt a coldness towards this daughter who had put her husband and children before everything else. Although Winston was fond of her and enjoyed her company Clementine did not regard Diana as a sufficiently strong personality to undertake the care of her father.

Although Sarah had been an invaluable help in accompanying her father on his journeys to meetings Clementine believed that this daughter, of whom she was very fond, lacked judgement. The failure of Sarah's marriage confirmed this view.

So that left Mary whose behaviour and progress once she had joined the ATS had been entirely a cause for parental pride. After a period at Enfield in December she had joined an Anti-Aircraft unit in Hyde Park. Her promotion to lieutenant was swift and earned. Newspaper pictures of Winston inspecting his daughter's unit created exactly the right impression. She was in uniform when she accompanied her parents in the role of aide-de-camp to her father on their two journeys to Quebec. Not only did she enhance family prestige by her charm on a good-will visit to a Women's Army Corp in Georgia, she was an invaluable support to Clementine on that first visit to the Roosevelts when she was able to send Winston off to Hyde Park without her while she recuperated, confident that Mary would look after him. Then in November 1944 when she was still only 22-years-old Mary had been promoted to junior commander in charge of 230 women in a battery scheduled to go to the Front in January. When Clementine made her visit to Brussels in March she felt very proud of her youngest daughter's accomplishments. Mary was a good example of the abilities of young women in which Clementine had always believed.

Success in the ATS had not made Mary distant from her parents. Whenever she was away from home she wrote regularly and it was to her that Clementine reported closely on the state of Winston's health and spirits in much the way that one mother might write to another about a beloved child. If her work commitments allowed, Mary joined in family occasions such as birthdays and Christmas whenever possible.

So for the most part Clementine found Mary a source of pride and contentment. But she was not perfect even in her mother's eyes. Clementine worried about her susceptibility to the sort of young men she would never have met in the ordinary course of a season and coming out. But the war had changed the way that young people related to each other. They were readier to fall in love and to marry since the war had made them aware of the vulnerability and brevity of so many lives. In this respect Mary, who until she joined the ATS had led a very sheltered life, was no exception. There had been the brief engagement to Lord Duncannon followed by another short-lived romance with an officer on board the *Renown*. Even the fact that he prevented her daughter from drowning did not make Clementine view him any more favourably as a suitor. More alarming still was the occasion when Mary fell in love with a French parachutist during their second visit to Quebec in September 1944. Perhaps because they were able to spend so little time together, since the young man was serving in the Far East, this relationship lasted longer than the others. In March 1945 Mary confided in Colville that she was wondering whether she would have to become a Catholic to marry her suitor on his return from the war. Once again, however, Mary bowed to her parents' wishes and the affair came to an end. Both Clementine and Winston were keen for their daughter to make a good match and they determined that after the war they would try to bring this about.

On the whole Clementine did not take Mary's romances seriously; they were known of only within a tight circle of family and friends and they did nothing to harm the idea the public had of a thoroughly nice and wholesome daughter.

And so, as she confronted her journey to Russia, Clementine decided that she would entrust Winston into Mary's care. She would have liked to have taken her daughter with her but felt the task of looking after Winston was a more important one. John Colville had proved a comforting travelling companion during her first flight and so she asked him if he would be willing to go to Russia with her but he did not feel able to leave England at that particular time. Clementine braced herself for the journey without familiar companions.

The Queen invited her to tea on the day before she was due to leave as a mark of how highly she regarded Clementine's work with the Aid to Russia Fund. Clementine herself held a small party to thank those who had worked with her throughout the years of the war. During the last few days before she set off Winston was away in Germany but he returned in time to have dinner alone with her on the eve of her departure and then to drive with her to Northolt from where she was to fly on 27 March.

The journey to Moscow was far too long to make in one stage and so Clementine first touched down in Cairo where she was to stay overnight with the British Minister Resident and his wife, Sir Edward and Lady Grigg. But the weather was considered too bad for her to continue and so she remained in Cairo for some days. Typically Clementine did not waste her time nor did she simply have a holiday. She investigated local YWCA hostels and hospitals. In the course of this she met Anita Leslie, the granddaughter of her godfather John Leslie who had died the previous year, and the daughter of Shane Leslie, Winston's cousin. There had been a time when Anita had resented Clementine because she believed her insensitive to the feelings of Diana. But now with shared work interests the two women got on so well that Clementine wrote to Winston suggesting that Anita should be invited to lunch as soon as possible.

On 1 April, Clementine's sixtieth birthday, the small party of Red Cross workers was able to resume the journey to Russia. Like the rest of them Clementine was wearing uniform to underline the official nature of the visits. She was a little alarmed at the prospect of meeting with Soviet officials for she was aware that the Allies and Russia were at odds over Soviet treatment of and intentions for Poland. She had herself only recently studied papers sent to her by the Duchess of Atholl describing the unacceptable treatment of Poles deported to Russia in 1939 and 1940. She knew that Stalin had recently sent an acrimonious and even insulting letter to Roosevelt. So despite her unwillingness to condemn outright communism and communists she did not approach Russia with blind idealism nor with any reluctance to look closely and critically at all that she saw in that country.

When Clementine arrived at Moscow airport she was glad to see the familiar faces of the British Ambassador, Sir Archibald Clark Kerr, and Averell Harriman. Ivan Maisky, who was no longer the Soviet Ambassador in London but who had become Deputy Foreign Secretary, and his wife, Madame Maisky, seemed like old friends in this context. Mr Molotov and his wife along with Dr Kolesnikov, the President of the Red Cross and Red Crescent Societies of the USSR, were also of the reception committee. The next few days were spent visiting some of the hospitals and projects which had been funded by the money she had helped to collect. She was greatly moved by the warmth of the reception she received everywhere she went and so felt readier to face Stalin, the Russians' war-like leader[1] at an official reception in the Kremlin on 8 April. The meeting began with a slight awkwardness. Clementine had brought for Stalin from Winston a gold pen but, when she presented it, Stalin made a point of letting her know that he wrote with a pencil only. She received with more grace and genuine appreciation The Order of the Red Banner of Labour which Stalin now presented to her.

Moscow was not the only place the Red Cross workers were scheduled to visit. For the next weeks, accompanied by Madame Kislova of the Society for Cultural Relations with Foreign Countries and Mr Zinchenko, head of the Press Department of the Foreign Office, they covered great distances by train. As the train travelled at only twenty miles an hour they had ample opportunity of seeing for themselves the vastness of the country and the extent of the task faced by the Russians as they began to rebuild the country ravaged by war. When the party arrived in Leningrad on 13 April Clementine knew immediately that something had happened. She was met by the Molotovs who told her that on the previous day Roosevelt had died. Now she felt very far from Winston who would, she knew, be very distressed by this news even though he had seen for himself at their last meeting that the President's death must be close.

Clementine was delighted with Leningrad which she described as the most beautiful city she had ever seen. She wrote to Winston saying that she would love to spend a whole summer there with him and Mary boating on the Neva and swimming in the Baltic. The exhibition showing how Leningrad had been defended impressed her greatly as did the Paediatric Institute and Children's Home she visited. She was fascinated by the children she met there, writing of them that there was something in traditional Russian upbringing of children which made them well-behaved and obedient but unafraid.[2] She was taken to the ballet where she was given an enthusiastic reception but then it was time to leave the quiet villa in the suburbs where she had been living for a few days and in bright and beautiful weather set off on the train to Stalingrad. Here Clementine confronted an 'appalling scene of destruction' for which nothing in badly bombed Britain had prepared her. She wrote that the enormity of the disaster was more than the imagination could assimilate.[3] The party of Red Cross workers travelled by car to see the prefabricated villages being put up to house the homeless. But they were also aware of the misery of large numbers of the population living in the cellars of ruined buildings and even in fox holes.

Then it was back on the train to the Caucasus spa towns of Kislovodsk, Essentuki and Pyatigorsk, and then on to Simferopol in the Crimea. In the Crimea she felt a strong connection with Winston as she stayed in the very same palace in which he had stayed during the Crimean Conference. She had the opportunity to visit Chekhov's house and even to meet his 82-year-old sister.

Her itinerary over the next weeks reads like a whistle-stop tour of the Soviet Union, but it was the contact with people wherever they stopped that gave Clementine most pleasure. In particular she enjoyed meeting the Chairman of the Council of Kursk, Madame Maslennicova, who had telegraphed to her an invitation to visit the city. Clementine described her as unlike any other woman she had ever met. Active and efficient, despite her youth, she had the full confidence of the citizens.[4] To Clementine the active role in the city played not just by Madame Maslennicova but other women who had volunteered to help in the rebuilding of the city was a confirmation of all that she had long believed about the capacities of women. And it was not just in the one city that she saw women doing work traditionally done by men. In Moscow she was vastly impressed to discover that the Assistant to the Head of Movement Control in the metro was a woman and that there were two women engineers in charge of construction.

She was full of praise for the courage and ingenuity she encountered in hospitals where some basic essentials were lacking. She could see that ideally the Aid to Russia Fund should continue to help supply these deficiencies. Those she met responded to her just as positively as she to them. The good will her visit was inspiring was responsible for Stalin sending a very friendly telegram to Winston.

As she travelled news of the winding down of the war reached her. On 29 April Mussolini was shot and then on 1 May the death of Hitler was announced. Winston sent his wife a telegram saying that their two major enemies were dead[5] while she in turn sent him telegrams saying how she longed to be with him in those 'tremendous days'. Back in Moscow on 4 May Clementine received a telegram from Winston congratulating her on her 'triumphant tour' and complaining about the difficulties of those last few steps towards making peace. Stalin himself was insisting on strict observance of protocols and there were disagreements about when peace should be officially announced. Once Winston knew that a firm date had been agreed upon, he was anxious for Clementine to return immediately to be with him in his moment of greatest triumph. For her own part Clementine would have been happy to do so, but she saw herself more as a symbol than an individual at that moment and as such she regarded her continued presence in Russia as essential. The British Chargé d'Affaires, Frank Roberts, urged her stay for the same reason and he wrote to Winston saying that Clementine's presence in Russia as peace was declared 'symbolized more than anything else could have done the friendship between the two peoples of the two countries and also the personal ties between the two leaders of the two countries.'

So Clementine was not with Winston when he made his way through boisterous, affectionate crowds to the House of Commons nor did she appear with him on the balcony of Buckingham Palace along with the King and Queen. But in the British Embassy she did hear his broadcast to the nation and telegraphed her congratulations not only on his broadcast but on all that he had achieved in leading Britain to victory. She urged on him the importance of keeping the celebrations going on the second day with a special reference to Russia, and on that day she made a broadcast to the Soviet Union on Winston's behalf using notes he had sent to her. Then, at last, she could go home.

Throughout the journey back to England Clementine thought about all that she had seen in those exciting weeks and she resolved to share her experiences with others. She now began to plan the pamphlet which she would publish in June as *My Visit to Russia*. She resolved that in this piece her emphasis would be on the women she had seen and on their courage and hard work, on the way they saw themselves as equal to men and were willing to take equal responsibilities. She thought that, perhaps, there was a lesson there for her own society.

28

Aftermath

DURING THE LAST months of the war Winston had been confident of his re-election. While Clementine was in Russia he had written to her telling her about how he was supervising the restoration of Number 10 ready for them to take up residence there once more. He seemed to have forgotten the moment a few years earlier when he had led Clementine and his family to believe that, having at last achieved his ambition to be Prime Minister, once he had brought the war to a successful conclusion he would be ready to resign office and even leave politics altogether.

There was growing evidence that Winston was not now eager to give up the power he so enjoyed but, despite this, Clementine began to try to turn his thoughts towards a life of gracious retirement. Her first step had been to take him to see a London house which she liked and which she thought they might buy. Winston's immediate enthusiasm for 28 Hyde Park Gate took her by surprise and she felt she must curb his reaction in case he decided on the spot to buy it and begin to spend on it money which they did not have. At the same time it was apparent to her that he saw this as a possible residence for a more distant future than she envisioned.

Winston's attitude was not entirely unreasonable. The overwhelmingly enthusiastic reception he had received from the crowds when the end of the war was announced coupled with the fact that he was greeted warmly and affectionately every time he appeared in public had blinded him to realities of which Clementine showed herself much more aware. As she later confided to Lord Moran she realized that the war had isolated Winston more than ever before. He had wielded a power rare for a

Prime Minister and had carried such great responsibilities that there were few of those who worked with him who felt able to stand up to him once he had made up his mind. He was curiously unaware that this acquiescence in time of war did not signify complete acceptance of himself and his policies. Clement Attlee had been a notable exception and his criticism had struck Winston like a bolt from the blue.

Clementine, who had visited the shelters and the hostels and who had an extensive correspondence with a wide range of people, had a far better idea of how the war had affected the lives of ordinary people and she was aware of a growing discontentment in the country as a whole just as there had been after the First World War. She saw, as Winston did not, that those who had sacrificed so much during the war now looked for some recompense for their hardships; they would no longer be content to return to a form of society in which the upper class had both the power and the wealth. During the war Winston had been able to make decisions on a non-party basis. It seemed to Clementine that her husband had lost sight of the fact that when the inevitable election was held party politics would again come into play and that the country as a whole would almost certainly not want a Conservative government, even one led by the hero Winston Churchill.

The first clear sign that this was so came less than a month before the peace was signed at a time when an Allied victory seemed certain. At the end of April in a by-election at Chelmsford the Conservative candidate was defeated. Then Randolph, who had held the seat at Preston as a courtesy to his father, was ousted by Julian Amery; the Churchill name no longer had quite the magic of earlier years. Even more worrying to Clementine who could see that Winston's heart was set on being a peacetime Prime Minister were indications that members of the Conservative party were not happy with this prospect. There were rumours that the party was considering debarring anyone over seventy from standing for election. Winston was obviously the target of such a measure and if the policy were to be adopted he would not only lose the leadership of the party but also his seat in the Commons.

Clementine wanted Winston to retire before the election at the moment when his image was most potent. She dreaded what would happen if what she feared came about and the Conservative party was defeated. She was also very tired; she had not exaggerated when she had told Diana Cooper that both she and Winston had given everything to the war. Winston, too, was showing signs of fatigue. He did not take enough interest in the details of government and he was enormously frustrated by the bickering and jostling of those who had been allies. He wrote to Clementine in May that underlying the victories were nasty political manoeuvres and terrible rivalries between nations.[1]

Hours after her return from Moscow Clementine accepted the fact that nothing she could say or do would make Winston voluntarily give up his position as Prime Minister. That being so she focused her energies on the election. She began by consulting party organizers about the timing of the election, which was to some extent in Winston's hands. After discussion her advice to Winston was to delay until the war with Japan was over. Perhaps she hoped that by then Winston would have had enough of politics and have become aware of the very different nature of the job that faced a Prime Minister attempting to put the country back on its feet. But she knew her husband well enough to recognize that this course of action was unlikely to appeal to him; she saw that he was eager to have his position confirmed by the electorate and to start planning the future. Her second suggestion was that if Winston decided on an early election he should make very clear to the electorate that the decision to end the coalition had been Labour's and that he would have been happy to continue to work with his former colleagues. For a few tense days Winston debated about what to do. As Clementine had feared, he resolved to have the election sooner rather than later and on 23 May he resigned as Prime Minister of the coalition. He was asked by the King to form a caretaker government until the results of the election were announced.

The campaign began, as it was to continue, with radical disagreements between Clementine and Winston. She was, for example, horrified to learn that in a broadcast speech Winston intended to compare the Labour party to the Gestapo. He ignored her advice that this would lose not win votes. While he toured the country making speeches which were provocative but lacked the impact of his wartime rhetoric, Clementine worked hard in the constituency stressing the need for cooperation and emphasizing how well Winston had worked within a coalition. Once again she was dismayed at Beaverbrook's influence on her husband and she feared their plan of fighting the campaign on the basis of Winston's personality and war achievements was unlikely to appeal to an electorate which was tired of war. What people wanted was the forward-looking plans of the Labour party not the backward-looking ones of the Conservatives. Disagreements about the campaign spilled over into their personal life. Winston was angry to receive a letter from Clementine's friend Horatia Seymour announcing that she would not vote Conservative but Liberal. Clementine had to point out that there was truth in Horatia's statement that Winston had himself once been a Liberal and that she herself was not altogether happy to vote Conservative. Then Clementine said that she was unwilling to start opening up Chartwell as a family home. Already at this point in her life she wanted to make the house into a museum and a monument to Winston's remarkable period of office. She urged more modest premises and a quieter life-style. Winston refused to hear of this.

In the middle of the month they flew to Bordeaux and then drove to Hendaye where they were the guests of the Canadian vineyard-owner Brigadier-General Brutinel. Despite the beauty of the setting on a tongue of land north of the Bidassoa River on the border of Spain, despite all the efforts of their host and despite the company of Mary and John Colville, Winston was bad tempered and difficult. He blamed Clementine because his painting gear was not as he wanted it and then he complained because he was too tired to paint anyway. Clementine could do nothing with her husband whom she considered to be behaving like a spoilt child. Only a visit from Mrs Nairn, who took a quiet but professional interest in his painting, roused him from his cross dissatisfaction. Clementine was not unhappy to leave on her own for London while Mary dutifully accompanied her father to Berlin. But the respite was brief. On 25 July the family was reunited for the election results. On 26 July Clementine, who had regularly visited the constituency throughout the war when Winston was rarely free to do so, went to Woodford to hear the count there. She returned to the Annexe for lunch with her family as well as Max Beaverbrook, David Margesson and Brendan Bracken. All followed the incoming results with increasing dismay as it became clear that the Conservatives were being defeated by Labour and that the next Prime Minister would not be Winston Churchill but Clement Attlee. At 7 p.m. Winston accepted the inevitable and resigned before broadcasting to the nation in very different circumstances from those he had become accustomed to.

Clementine felt for her husband who took the defeat of his party personally. She tried to comfort him by saying that perhaps the defeat was a blessing in disguise. Bitterly Winston retorted that it was certainly well disguised. When he musingly commented that it seemed to be women who had given him most votes, Clementine sharply reminded him that it was no thanks to him that they were in a position to vote at all. As on that other wrenchingly disappointing occasion when Winston had lost his position as First Lord of the Admiralty so now Clementine was anxious to leave as quickly as possible the premises to which they no longer had any entitlement. In vain the Attlees reassured her that there was no urgency but, with no home of their own to go to, the Churchills immediately moved into Claridge's and Jack, who had lived with them throughout the war, now moved in with his son Johnny on Campden Hill. Realizing that her parents needed privacy in which to come to terms with their position Diana offered them the use of the Sandys' London flat and this was gratefully accepted as a short-term solution. But a fretful Winston soon wanted to be even further from what he regarded as the scene of his defeat and humiliation and so Clementine accompanied him once more to Hendaye where the two tired, depressed people, both now feeling their age, began to think about the shape of their future.

As soon as they returned to the cottage at Chartwell the trouble began. Never had the carefully created image of a smiling Clementine on the arm of her jaunty confident husband been further from reality. The harmony between man and wife it suggested simply did not exist. The main problem was that they were not used to being forced so much into each other's company. Throughout the time Winston had been Prime Minister they had not even dined as a couple very frequently, and he had always been busy with his mind fully occupied. The loneliness Clementine had sometimes experienced now seemed highly preferable to the constant company of a bored and bitter husband who looked to her to relieve his misery. Every detail of their everyday life seemed to cause friction. Always interested in good food and drink Winston looked to them for solace even more during this period of inactivity. What he refused to understand was that they had been in a privileged position during the war and the food shortages which had made the lives of most people miserable had not much affected them. Winston believed that the man in charge should be well fed and he had eaten better than the King himself. Now they were dependent on rations like everyone else. Worse still Cousin Maryott was now in charge of cooking and she was not able to meet the high standards set by Mrs Landemare. To Clementine's intense irritation Winston found fault with every meal. Refusing to understand the very real difficulties of housekeeping in a time of rationing Winston accused Clementine of cheeseparing.

It was the same with Chartwell itself. Clementine saw problems in opening up the whole house immediately. Winston was eager to resume life on a large scale to compensate himself for some of the humiliation he felt. He would not face facts and instead attributed Clementine's dilatoriness to her old antagonism to the house which he loved. But as Clementine began to confront this task of opening up the house she felt vindicated. As she unpacked box after box of stored curtains and unrolled carpets and removed dust covers from furniture she discovered that many of their possessions were now useless; moths and mice, damp and dirt had wreaked havoc during the years the house had been closed. To replace everything would have been a vast expense at the best of times, but as long as there was rationing even money would not buy all that was necessary. She fretted about how she could find servants to run the house and about how the enormous job of restoring the garden and the grounds could be accomplished without the help which was no longer readily available. Winston would not listen to her tales of woe; he had ideas about how the house and gardens could be turned around and made to yield money. But Cousin Maryott, who had become rather proprietory about Chartwell during the years when she had been in sole charge of it, was always ready to point out difficulties and dismissed most of Winston's schemes as impractical. The arguments and rows seemed endless and Clementine's despair grew as she realized that Winston had every intention of having a London home as well as Chartwell and that he had made up his mind that he would continue as leader of the opposition.

Desperately at odds over almost everything Clementine and Winston could not even easily escape each other's company. Without a staff of helpers to make arrangements, without a chauffeur to drive them, restricted by petrol rationing, they suddenly found that travel was difficult. Clementine had the loan of a car but she wondered how they would manage once the car was returned to its owner.

Greatly disturbed about their financial position Clementine challenged her husband about where the money was to come from to do all that he planned. They had, after all, saved nothing during the war and they now had expenses from which holding office had sheltered them. His answer was the same as it had been at other times when they had faced seeming ruin. He would earn the money with his pen. The lucrative contracts which he set about securing brought for Clementine new worries. She was far from sure that he had the right to use some of the papers from which he now proposed to make money. And although he negotiated a most favourable contract for his war memoirs, Clementine feared that he had made a commitment that would require more time and energy than he perhaps had. The sums of money seemed huge and promised security, even wealth, but it was money which she felt might never materialize. And even these contracts did little to solve immediate problems of ready cash.

As long as Winston had been leader of a coalition party Clementine had taken a close interest and often offered sound advice. But she could not now sympathize with his political position. She was not a Conservative and she found little to approve of in their policies. This did not stop her from berating Winston for failing to do adequately the job of leader of the opposition, and from pointing out that his writing commitments would leave him little time for his political position.

In his diary for this time Anthony Eden wrote, 'fond as I am of Winston, I do not feel I have the strength to undertake life and work with him again; it is too much of a strain and a struggle'.[2] These sentiments were shared by Clementine. After failing once again to persuade Winston to retire while his stock was at its highest, she decided that the situation had got beyond her. She could no longer cope with her husband and all that she had to do. She saw the irony that she, who had been so praised for her organizational abilities during the war, now found that she could not organize her own affairs. She did not say so, but it was the demands her husband made which reduced her ability to act efficiently. She could not turn to Randolph for help; he was as bitterly at odds with Winston as she was herself. Diana was preoccupied with her family so that left Mary and Sarah. Sarah was only recently divorced and trying to establish a new life for herself; Mary was still abroad with her unit. But it was to Mary that Clementine appealed for help, asking her to try to arrange to return to England as soon as possible.

Mary responded by asking for a transfer to the War Office Holding Unit in Radnor Place and because she was a Churchill this request was quickly granted. She understood that it was of major importance to see that husband and wife were separated in order to break the pattern of bitter reproach and sharp recrimination into which they had fallen. Mary could not herself take immediate leave so she asked Sarah to accompany her father to Lake Como leaving Clementine in peace to organize not only the restoration of Chartwell but also the preparation of the newly acquired house in Hyde Park Gate. So that she could better supervise both projects Clementine rented a house in Woodford, Winston's constituency. Gradually she recovered her equanimity. She solved the problem of removing all the barbed wire and camouflage from the grounds at Chartwell by arranging to employ German prisoners of war once they had helped with the local harvest. Then she turned her attention to Hyde Park Gate. This she loved far more than Chartwell and she lavished care and attention on its redecoration. The question posed by the press at this time as to where Clementine got the means to achieve her richly decorated interiors when labour and materials were in such short supply remains unanswered. Clementine, who was usually so careful and so keen to avoid ostentation, was certainly made very uneasy by public criticism of her extravagance.

From Winston came loving letters far removed from the sharp tone he had habitually used during the weeks he had been in England. He even conceded that perhaps losing the election had been a blessing in disguise but he made no mention of retirement. What worried Clementine was his proximity to Monte Carlo and the casino. She took the step of writing to the young men who had been assigned to look after him asking them to try to keep him from gambling. Despite their real efforts to comply with Clementine's wishes they were no match for Winston's wiles. Fortunately Clementine was unaware that in one night Winston managed to lose £7,000 and he never had to confess because the casino owner never presented the cheque that Winston handed over as payment for his debt.

By the time Winston returned to England in October, 28 Hyde Park Gate was ready to live in and it was here late in the month that they entertained the Canadian Prime Minister Mackenzie King and in December gathered the family together for Christmas in London rather than Chartwell where work was still in progress. Neither Pamela nor Randolph joined in the celebrations and in the New Year they were divorced, with Pamela being given custody of her son. Clementine tried to make the best of the situation by writing to Pamela's parents suggesting that all four grandparents should now join forces to ensure young Winston's well-being.

Clementine continued to worry about the cost of running both Chartwell and Hyde Park Gate so that she was very uncertain when number 27 Hyde Park Gate came on the market and the Churchills were given the first refusal on the freehold. She admitted that their house was proving too small for the combination of living, entertaining and working. As Winston's writing contracts grew more numerous he needed more and more help in the form of researchers and secretaries and they all needed a place to work. Clementine tried to encourage the researchers to do their work at home but Winston still needed to meet with them for consultations. Buying number 27 would solve the problem of office and work space but Clementine blenched at the idea of buying a whole house when they needed the space of the ground floor only. Then it occurred to her that the top two floors of the house could be turned into a financial asset if they were converted into a maisonette suitable for letting and she withdrew her objections to the purchase.

It was while these negotiations were taking place that Lord Camrose came up with an idea which would provide the Churchills with some much-needed capital. He proposed joining with other wealthy friends to buy Chartwell with the intention of handing it over to the nation to be preserved as a kind of Churchill museum. The idea of the museum pleased and interested Clementine, who had for some time been thinking along similar lines. There were two drawbacks, however. The first did not greatly concern her: Winston had originally bought Chartwell with the idea of establishing a Churchill family home which would pass from generation to generation. He was still reluctant to give up this idea but he was far less set upon it now that Randolph was out of favour. He saw the point that his name might well be far better preserved by a museum than by his troublesome son. What gave Clementine pause was that at a very modest rent the couple would be entitled to live in the house for the rest of their lives. Any hopes she had of persuading Winston to sell Chartwell and be content with one house and perhaps a small cottage would be lost for ever. And she knew that the rent would not be all the house would cost. It would still need servants, and Winston would still spend money on the grounds and on animals. But the idea that the image of Winston as the man who won the war would be preserved indefinitely was a potent motive for accepting Lord Camrose's idea.

She was pleased, too, that the country's apparent rejection of all that her husband had done was now softened by the honours he received. First of all came the Freedom of Wanstead and Woodford. Appropriately, since she was the one who had taken most care of the constituency, this was given to Clementine also. In the New Year's Honours of 1946 Winston was awarded the Order of Merit, while in April Clementine was awarded the Grand Cross of the Order of the British Empire which gave her the right to call herself Dame, a title she never in fact used. But what gave Clementine greatest pleasure was being awarded an Honorary Degree by Glasgow University, specifically as a symbol of the part women had played in the war and as a public acknowledgement that she had done valuable work as a wife in sustaining Winston during those years.

Winston's stature as a figure of international importance was under-lined by the many invitations he now received. In 1946 alone he was invited to Cuba, the United States, to the Hague, to Brussels, Geneva and Paris. In this year Clementine usually accompanied him on his visits, thus preserving the appearance of the perfectly matched couple. But they were not happy together. During the first days of their visit to the States when they were the guests of Colonel Clarke once more, they went for two days without speaking to each other except in public. When Winston made his famous Iron Curtain speech in Fulton, Missouri, in March, Clementine was highly critical of his attitude towards Russia. So critical in fact that on the occasion of receiving her Honorary Degree from Glasgow she chose also to speak about Russia and to take a line inde-pendent of her husband's, asserting that 'we do not want to be cut off from one sixth of the human race'.[3]

After the visit to the Hague Clementine had felt it necessary to remind her husband of his manners and to write a letter of thanks to Queen Wilhemina. In Geneva she advised him to visit some departments of the International Red Cross before the official lunch so that when he spoke with the President he would know what he was talking about. Such actions suggest that increasingly Clementine's attitude towards her husband was a divided one. On the one hand she revered and respected what he had achieved and stood for during the war. But her letters to her daughters show that she also regarded the real man she had to live with as a wilful, troublesome and often misguided, if highly talented, child. Only the helpful presence of Mary, who had been demobbed on Clementine's birthday, enabled her to get through the hectic and often distressing first postwar year. For with Mary she could relax in visits to galleries and the theatre; she could confide in her and, with Mary in the house to defuse some of the tensions, the rows with Winston were fewer and less fierce.

She had recognized at the end of the war that Mary was probably ready for marriage and a home of her own. But she expressed to her daughter the hope that she would spend some time at home making the adjustment to civilian life which Clementine herself was finding difficult. She wanted Mary to make a good marriage, a better one than her siblings had managed. For a time she encouraged Mary to reciprocate the interest shown in her by Prince Charles of Belgium but, much as Mary wanted to please her parents, she could not marry someone on that basis. It was, therefore, a great blow to Clementine when Mary suddenly became engaged to Christopher Soames.

Mary had met him in September while staying with her parents at the British Embassy in Paris where he was Assistant Military Attaché. The two young people were immediately attracted to each other and Christopher had arranged to spend his leave in October in London so that they might spend more time together. But this plan was suddenly threatened when Mary was unexpectedly sent to Rome to look after Sarah who had fallen ill while filming there. Unbeknown to Winston and Clementine, Mary agreed to let her admirer accompany her to Rome. The first they knew of the relationship was when Mary told them that she wanted to marry Christopher Soames.

In November Mary's fiancé was invited to lunch at Chartwell. His background of Eton, Sandhurst and the Coldstream Guards did not put him on a par with Prince Charles of Belgium. Moreover his immediate prospects were doubtful. Clementine made her disappointment at Mary's choice clear. But this time her disapproval did not make Mary change her mind and wedding preparations began. For Clementine the prospect of losing the one member of the family whom she loved unreservedly and on whom she could rely was too much. She became ill and depressed and was ordered by her doctor to take three weeks' rest away from the demands of her family.

But after this all too short respite Clementine was back at Chartwell planning Christmas and Mary's wedding. There was little festive spirit in the house in 1946. Clementine was not only upset with Mary she was also annoyed to find that no sooner had the burden of Chartwell been eased by the National Trust Scheme than Winston had extended their responsibilities once more by buying the two farms which adjoined Chartwell. It was the old conflict: Clementine wanted to consolidate while Winston was determined to expand. At the back of his mind was a certain guilt that he had sold Randolph's inheritance, and indeed in January of 1947 he told Randolph that the farm would be part of his inheritance.

The winter of 1946 to 1947 was especially cold. Fuel was in short supply and coal was rationed. Keeping Chartwell warm was a big problem but the situation was even worse at Hyde Park Gate which relied entirely on electricity, since there were electricity cuts lasting up to five hours a day. Conditions in England generally were grim and morale was low. There was no war to make people feel they were suffering in a good cause and there was not the hope that once the war was over things would change. Resentment ran high that those who had been victorious in the war were now much worse off than those in France and Italy where conditions were gradually improving.

So the two noteworthy weddings that took place in this bleak year provided a much-needed sense of occasion and glamour. Mary's wedding to Christopher Soames took place in February in St Margaret's, Westminster, where Clementine and Winston had been married. Clementine was proud of her daughter and considered she looked just as beautiful as she herself had done all those years ago. By now she had become more reconciled to Christopher and after the wedding she wrote warmly to the young couple in an attempt to make up for her earlier coldness. The second wedding of the year in November was that of Princess Elizabeth to Prince Philip. This was a far more glittering occasion in Westminster Abbey with a grand party held afterwards at Buckingham Palace.

Between the two weddings a great deal had taken place. When Clementine had seen her daughter depart for her honeymoon in Switzerland she had believed that the close relationship she had so enjoyed with her would now be ended. But then from Mary in St Moritz came an urgent call for help: her new husband was seriously ill with a duodenal ulcer. Clementine immediately flew out to join the young couple, quite prepared for all the jokes about the mother-in-law on the honeymoon. What now became clear was that Mary's husband would have to leave the army. The couple faced a difficult future with no home and no job. Clementine saw a way of solving her own loneliness and giving her daughter and son-in-law a secure future. She suggested that Chartwell Farm, the purchase of which she had once opposed, should be turned to good account. It could be a home for the Soameses and since a manager for the estate was needed anyway it could provide Christopher with a job.

Other events during this period were less happy. Jack Churchill who had been ill for some years now was taken once more into University College Hospital where on 26 February he died. Winston had always been very close to his admiring brother and he felt the loss keenly. His brother had been younger than he and so now he worried increasingly whether he would live the necessary five years to secure from taxes the Trust Fund he had set up for his children. Both he and Clementine felt ill and weary; in Clementine's case it was nervous exhaustion which she could alleviate by a short holiday in France, but in Winston's case it was a hernia which required an operation in July. Their misery was increased in October by the news that Gil Winant, Sarah's former lover, had shot himself. Clementine mourned his loss because she had been genuinely fond of him. It fell to her to inform Sarah, knowing that Sarah would feel guilty that it was in some part because she had rejected him that Winant had been driven to suicide. Clementine was now aware that when Sarah was upset she drank.

She was, therefore, simultaneously relieved and concerned when Winston persuaded Time-Life to finance a working holiday for him in Marrakesh and since all his expenses were being paid he felt able to invite Sarah to go with him. Her relief was in being able to spend a quiet and relaxed Christmas with Mary and Christopher; her concern was that Winston was not really fit to travel and the chances were that he would fall ill and she would be summoned to his side. It was just as she had feared. With the help of Brendan Bracken, who was somehow able to charter a plane, Clementine, accompanied by Winston's doctor and his wife Dorothy, flew in late December to Marrakesh. Winston was soon recovered from the effects of his hernia operation and resumed work on his World War Two memoirs. But these were quickly the cause of disagreements. He would read extracts aloud to his wife ostensibly for her opinion but actually for her reassurance and praise. This she was not able to give since she had many reservations about the work. In particular she disliked the use of initials rather than names and undigested material from memorandums and government documents. Matters were not improved when Clementine's criticisms were echoed by Emery Reves, Churchill's literary agent. Another aspect of the memoirs troubled Clementine; she feared that the work was making Winston live almost exclusively in the past and she was alarmed when some of his old animosities began to inform his present opinions. She was particularly upset by his rages against communism. He went so far as to say that he would be prepared 'to throw a bomb amongst the most subversive people'.[4]

Clare Sheridan who spent a day with Winston at Chartwell in May 1948 described him at that time. She was very fond of Churchill and he would have been on his best behaviour with her. Clementine would have had to put up with much worse. 'Dear Winston in his dreadful boiler suit was looking pale. He rants, of course, about the inefficient crowd now in power . . . He is almost heartbroken. He tried so hard, bless him, to be interested in my concerns, but he can't sustain interest outside himself for more than a few minutes.'[5]

Yet somehow Clementine managed to preserve the image so important to her of a devoted couple. In July they were together to receive visitors to the first public opening of Chartwell, the proceeds of which were to go to the YWCA. Clementine had resigned the presidency of the organization in March of 1947, but she continued to take a close interest in its work. In the same month they made two joint appearances when they were the centre of attention. The first was when they had to walk through Claridge's to a private party and those who were dining in the restaurant stood up and clapped them. The second was a rather embarrassing occasion when at the royal garden party they were cheered as they left the royal pavilion and followed by the crowds so that the royal family was upstaged and neglected. When Time-Life once again financed a working holiday for Winston in August Clementine accompanied him so that they could celebrate their fortieth wedding anniversary in public together as guests of the Duke and Duchess of Windsor. But while Winston remained in the South of France staying at Max Beaverbrook's villa La Capponcina on the Côte d'Azur Clementine returned alone to Hyde Park Gate.

Accustomed as she was to acting as a go-between for Winston's petitioners, she was nevertheless surprised when in October Randolph asked her to raise a matter with his father on his behalf. He now told her that he was about to marry again and he wanted to know if the terms of the Trust would make it possible for it to buy him a house. He wanted the house, he said, not only as a home for his new wife but also as a proper place where he could entertain Winston Jr. This latter point was calculated to engage Clementine's sympathy since she was not altogether happy about the way her grandson was handed round like a parcel. Along with Brendan Bracken and Lord Cherwell, Clementine was one of the trustees who administered the Literary Fund set up by Winston for his children. But in fact none of the Trust's money was spent without Winston's consent. So she agreed to write to Winston and the money towards a house in Westminster was forthcoming. But when Clementine met Randolph's fiancée she realized that he was repeating his earlier pattern and entering a marriage which had little chance of success. She did not dislike June Osborne any more than she had Pamela Digby; in fact she saw in her some of her own characteristics. June was a colonel's daughter who dressed well and created an impression of quiet confidence. But as

Clementine quickly discovered this was a façade to hide an essentially neurotic, vulnerable and conventional young woman. She was entirely unsuited to be the wife of Randolph Churchill. However, despite violent rows, many of them public, between the betrothed couple, they were married at Caxton Hall on 2 November 1948. Clementine could only sit back and wait for the inevitable to happen.

At the same time she saw Sarah, too, beginning to repeat the mistakes of her first marriage. Sarah had already confided to her mother that she had begun a new relationship, so when both couples were in Monte Carlo at the same time Clementine invited Sarah to bring her friend along to dinner with herself and Winston at the Hôtel de Paris. Antony Beauchamp, a photographer, did not appeal greatly to Clementine. She was, for example, struck by the fact that, just like Vic Oliver, he too had taken an assumed name. She was, however, prepared to be cordial, not knowing how serious the relationship was and very well aware that Sarah was not nicknamed the Mule for nothing. She understood the need to tread carefully for fear of driving Sarah into a premature commitment. But Winston had no such tact. He treated Beauchamp with a rudeness similar to that he had meted out to Oliver. Unlike Vic Oliver, however, this suitor was not prepared to stay and be insulted publicly and so along with Sarah he left the hotel. In great anger Sarah wrote to her father saying that she would never again risk her friends being subjected to such a scene; that she was glad that she had built a life for herself and that Churchill family life was more than she could endure. Clementine did her best to effect a reconciliation but both parties were now on their dignity.

In October 1949 came the news that Sarah had married Antony Beauchamp in the States. As on that previous occasion Sarah claimed that she had intended to tell her parents before the story appeared in the press. But once again it was from the newspapers that they learnt of the marriage. Even now Clementine tried to restore harmony but Winston was adamant. Not until a letter came from Beauchamp to Clementine telling her how ill the estrangement was making Sarah did Winston relent. The Churchills lunched with Antony's parents and for the time being the breach was healed. Clementine, however, had little hope that the marriage would last.

Throughout the almost five years that Winston had been leader of the opposition he had been working with great intensity on the books which provided the family with a good living. With the help of his financial advisers he had been able to create a situation in which he minimized taxes by having all his literary earnings paid into the Trust from which he was able to draw a salary of £20,000 a year while leaving money to accumulate for the benefit of the children. To achieve this he had spent more time on writing than on politics and a good deal of responsibility for maintaining his credibility as the opposition leader had fallen on Clementine. She it was who regularly visited the constituency, took an interest in its problems and communicated any concerns to her husband. She had more than once had to coerce him into attending events he was inclined to miss because she thought his absence would be rude and damaging to his image. The memorial service held in London after the death of Winant was one such occasion. She had tried to keep him in contact with his fellow Conservatives by arranging a series of lunches to which backbenchers were invited. By March of 1949 she had already held twenty-six such lunches.

She was, therefore, very angry when in that month Winston accepted an invitation to have a holiday in Jamaica as the guest of Max Beaverbrook prior to fulfilling a speaking engagement in the States. Her objection was that she was very much aware that there were murmurings of dissatisfaction with her husband's lack of interest in the party at a time when, after almost five years of Labour government, there was low morale among Conservative politicians. An election in the near future was inevitable and Clementine, like others, felt that Winston should earn his position as leader by working for the party rather than leaving all the work to others while he holidayed in luxury in Jamaica. She appealed to his sense of his image; she reproached him for doing only just as much as would keep him in power. Finally, in her letter explaining her position, she told him that her conscience would not allow her to accompany him to Jamaica. Churchill gave in and cancelled the proposed visit. Was he perhaps influenced by a telling indirect comment on what kind of a husband he had been all these years? Clementine had begged Winston to take Mary as well as Christopher with him to the States because she thought it most important for the two newlyweds to be together and share every possible experience whilst they were still young and passionate. She was thinking of the many, many times as a young wife when politics had deprived her of her husband and she wanted things to be different for Mary.

Winston's strange insensitivity to the feelings of others continued even in the States. His visit to MIT had been planned to last two days and

President Truman was supposed to join him there. But after the first day, when it became clear that the President would not after all be able to come, Winston lost interest in the whole enterprise and was prepared to cancel the second day of his visit. It took a great deal of persuasion on the part of Clementine to convince him that many people had made a great effort on his behalf for the second day of his visit and that to simply walk away would be insulting and damaging to his reputation. Then on the voyage back to England on the *Queen Mary* Winston refused to sign a letter of appeal for funds for a memorial to the Polish leader General Sikorski. Clementine had to remind him that his refusal would cause great offence, especially since he had already agreed to give his signature.

All Clementine's careful plans to maintain Winston's image as a strong political leader were, however, threatened in August of 1949 as the country prepared for the announcement of the general election. For while he was staying with Max Beaverbrook at La Capponcina he suffered a slight stroke. Every effort was made to keep the illness secret but there was nevertheless speculation in the press about the physical fitness of the leader of the opposition who in November of that year had his seventy-fifth birthday.

As if to show the world that all was well in the Churchill family Clementine entertained on something like a prewar scale that Christmas at Chartwell before she and Winston set off with Diana and Duncan for a holiday in Madeira. They had been there just two weeks when the long-expected election date was announced. Winston immediately set off for London making it quite clear to Clementine that he fully intended to stay on as leader of the Conservative party whether they won the election or not. For a few more days Clementine lingered in the warm climate preparing herself for the struggles of the coming year.

29

Reluctantly to Downing Street

AT THE END of January Clementine returned to England to await the election results. Her lack of enthusiasm for a Conservative victory showed in the more limited part she took in this election campaign. When Labour was restored to power, though with a greatly reduced majority, she was by no means sorry and hoped that time would take care of Winston's ambition to be Prime Minister once more. She now felt free to continue with the job she had accepted in January of 1949 as Chair of the National Hostels Committee of the YWCA and she threw all her energies into improving the conditions in the hostels. Now that the war could no longer be given as an excuse for poor standards she was sharp in her criticisms of wardens whom she saw as failing in their duties and her surprise visits to individual hostels to see the state of affairs for herself struck terror into wardens whose standards were laxer than those of the formidable Mrs Churchill. In order to ensure that certain minimum standards were met even when she was no longer in a position to oversee them, she worked hard on producing a handbook which set them out clearly and in detail. In time for the Wardens' Conference in March of 1950 her handbook was published and Clementine then turned her attention to another activity at which she excelled, the raising of money for a special fund which would help provide much needed new equipment for the hostels.

But, having as usual given rather more energy to her work than was wise, in April Clementine was exhausted and took a short holiday travelling in Italy with her secretary Penelope Hampden-Wall. Even on holiday, however, her critical faculties were still at work and when she visited the Annual Milan Fair she found the British exhibition inadequate and uninspiring; this at a time when the need to earn money from exports was critical. On her return to England she quickly drew this sad state of affairs to the attention of Clement Attlee with whom she continued on good terms.

Mary's husband, Christopher, had infected Winston with his own enthusiasm for racing and was responsible for Winston buying race-horses of his own. As this interest became a passion and took up ever more time Clementine had even more reason to be glad that Winston was not Prime Minister. As matters stood, racing and writing came well before the duties he should have performed as Leader of the Opposition. Clementine had some sympathy with Attlee's comment in response to harsh criticism from Winston that the former Prime Minister seldom attended the House except to make speeches. Clementine had to be always on the alert to make sure that his neglect of official business did no harm. For example, when Queen Juliana of the Netherlands was visiting England Winston would have thought nothing of declining two invita-tions to meet her using pressure of work as an excuse had not his wife intervened. Clementine's own health was still poor and she escaped to Spain in June 1950 and again in March 1951. Her problems, however, were more serious than could be cured by holidays and changes of scene. In May 1951 she was admitted to hospital for three weeks and she under-went a gynaecological operation. To recover from this she travelled in the company of Mary to Hendaye and then went on to Annecy where she was joined by Winston before they set off together to the Hotel Excelsior on Venice Lido.

Was there any relationship between Clementine's ill health and her growing realization that Winston, who for years had taken a minimal interest in the day-to-day affairs of the country, had since the last election been calculatedly wearing down the government with repeated attacks in the Commons with a view to making Attlee call another election? She must have found her loyalty to her husband strained when he made speeches in the Commons designed to ensure his own election without thought for the ill effect his words were having on England's image abroad. She who had supported Lloyd George's People's Budget cannot have been happy when Winston called the Labour government's mea-sures for social welfare 'Reckless expenditure'. And, whatever her per-sonal feelings for her husband, she would have been the first to admit the truth of Attlee's words when he said, 'I am afraid that nowadays the strength of Mr Churchill's language is in inverse proportion to his knowledge of the subject. It is unfortunate that his words are taken at their face value in other countries. They don't realize that it is just Winnie's Way.'[1] But to her dismay Winston's tactics worked, aided by some unpopular government measures such as the devaluation of the pound, reduction of housing targets and the imposition of a charge for National Health prescriptions, along with the high cost of living and growing unemployment. In September, only eighteen months after taking office for a second time, Attlee called an election.

The Korean War which had begun in June 1950 had raised fears of a third world war. Labour politicians played on the fear that if Winston became Prime Minister he would almost certainly lead the country into war. The *Daily Mirror* went so far as to depict Winston as a war-monger with his hand on the trigger of a gun. Winston successfully sued the paper and, despite the fears it had inspired, the Conservatives were victorious, largely because they were not associated with the wearing austerity of the previous few years. Churchill was once again Prime Minister. He was just a month away from his seventy-seventh birthday as he prepared to take up office once more. Clementine was herself sixty-six and by no means certain that either of them had the energy or the health to do the task that lay ahead of them. She immediately resigned her position on the National Hostels Committee in order to devote herself full-time to being Winston's consort once again. The immediate problem was the recurrent one of moving house. This time Clementine was determined not to lose her London home since there was no telling how long Winston could manage to do the job he had undertaken. So 28 Hyde Park Gate was let to the Cuban Ambassador and 27 was maintained as very necessary office space for Winston's literary enterprises. When the Attlees had first moved into 10 Downing Street Mrs Attlee had consulted with Clementine about how best to cope with the house. Clementine had encouraged her idea of converting the top floor of the house into a self-contained flat and using the other large rooms for state occasions only. Clementine was confident that what had been big enough for the Attlees who still had children living at home would be quite adequate for herself and Winston. But Winston wanted no corners cutting during what even he acknowledged would be his last term of office and he was in favour of opening up the whole house. From the moment they moved into the house in November until February of 1953 Clementine managed to get her way. But with the death of the King and the prospect of the coronation things changed. She had to acknowledge that the coronation would put England on show to the rest of the world and that the Prime Minister's residence must create a good impression. Reluctantly she began to supervise the opening up of all the state rooms which during her previous residence had been closed for the duration of the war. She saw that her husband's insistence on this grand setting was of a piece with his general sense of himself. As a wartime leader he had been an international figure and this was how he continued to view himself. He was not much concerned with nor temperamentally suited to deal with the urgent domestic problems of Britain – the housing shortage, labour unrest, lack of industrial productivity, the need to export more and import less and the continuing weakness of sterling – which the election of a Conservative government had done nothing to solve. He began as he meant to go on by setting off just months after the election to the United States which he visited again less than a year later.

Clementine saw her hope that the mere achievement of office would encourage and enable Winston to retire gracefully fade away. The need to ease the new Queen into office was his first reason for refusing to consider retirement. Then he took an almost childlike pleasure in the preparations for the ceremony of the coronation and his own important part in it. But others, like Clementine, could see that the Prime Minister was often not up to the task of governing the country. His cousin Clare Sheridan recorded that at a lunch with him in January he seemed an old man: 'Winston just gave grunts, he was dead tired and his chin sunk down in his chest. No brandy, no champagne, only a little white wine which obviously fails to cheer him.'[2] Then one morning in late February 1952 Winston appeared in Clementine's room accompanied by Charles Moran. He had woken up to find he had some difficulty speaking and moving. Moran's verdict was that small vessels in Winston's head had suffered a spasm. But even when Moran advised him to give up office because his heart would not take the strain Winston continued to insist that he must at least see the coronation through. Clementine kept a careful watch on him for further signs of illness; she did her best to prevent others seeing him at his worst moments. But those who worked with him could not fail to see that their leader was deteriorating. John Colville commented on Winston's lack of concentration and his apparent tiredness and that, despite some moments when his old self shone through, old age was beginning to show.

Such constant vigilance was tiring and from time to time Clementine needed desperately to get away from both Winston and Number 10 where she was so much in the public eye. In July 1952 she went with Mary, Duchess of Marlborough, to Montecatini where the two women tried to refresh themselves by taking the mudbath cure. And then, responding to an urgent invitation from Sarah, Clementine went on to Capri to visit her daughter and son-in-law. She loved Capri though she had some worries about the relationship between Sarah and Antony and the life they were leading: she saw that Sarah was drinking more than was good for her.

Her stay was cut short, however, by Winston's appeal to her to come home to deal with another family matter. Much to everyone's surprise, and the dismay of some, Clarissa Churchill, Goonie's daughter, had announced her engagement to Anthony Eden, Winston's Foreign Secretary. Clarissa was considerably younger than her fiancé and had previously led a life very different from the one she would have to lead as a politician's wife. Her friends and associates had all been involved with the arts and she had herself worked for the film producer and director Alexander Korda and then for the publisher George Weidenfeld. She had always kept her family at a distance and had professed herself bored with politics. Many people found her difficult to deal with and were intimidated by her beauty, her intelligence and her sharp wit. Clementine wondered how a marriage between two such different people could possibly work. Nevertheless she wanted to do her best by this daughter of the sister-in-law and brother-in-law of whom she had been so fond and to whom she had been so close. So on 14 August Winston was principal witness at the registry office wedding and Clementine arranged a reception for the newly-weds at Number 10. She had little time to dwell on how this marriage would fare before her attention was once more engaged in trouble within her own family.

It was apparent to everyone that Christopher Soames was very close to Winston. Winston had made him his Principal Private Secretary as soon as he had become Prime Minister and so whenever he travelled Christopher, and very often Mary too, went with him. At Chartwell the two families lived at close quarters while Christopher's involvement with Chartwell Farm and his interest in racing meant that he had an intimate involvement with his father-in-law on a personal as well as a political level. So close was Soames to Churchill that John Colville had seen fit to warn the former against making the fact that he had the ear of the Prime Minister too apparent. Randolph, who had not even managed to get himself elected to parliament looked on enviously as the young man appeared to fill the place that he should rightly have had. To make matters worse Clementine herself seemed more loving to her son-in-law than to her son. Randolph was not happy that the promise that he would inherit Chartwell Farm seemed to have been forgotten now that it was the Soameses' family home. He still resented the way Winston had initially refused to tell him the details of how he stood in relation to the Trust. The Conservative party conference brought his jealousy to the surface and was the occasion of yet another quarrel with his father. It was Randolph's contention that Winston had deliberately and hurtfully made sure that his son did not travel to the conference on the same train as himself, despite the fact that he was willing to have Clementine and Christopher with him.

To smooth over family quarrels and to present the Churchills to the world as a united family Clementine organized a Christmas party at Chequers which was large even by her standards. Randolph was invited, along with Winston Jr, but June was absent. For, despite the birth of their daughter, Arabella, in November 1949, the couple had become irrevocably estranged. Randolph was deeply resentful that Clementine had been prepared to listen to June's grievances and to offer sympathy to her rather than to him. He could not understand why his mother blamed him for his broken marriages while apparently giving support to Sarah when her marriages looked equally disastrous. While he had needed to ask for money from the Trust to buy a house when he married June, Sarah had been presented with a house in Ebury Street which Clementine had chosen, decorated and furnished herself so that Sarah would have a place of her own if she left Antony.

Until now Clementine had done her best to pretend that Randolph could be contained within the image of the Churchill family. But at this stage she appeared to have decided upon a different tactic. If Randolph could not be assimilated then he must be rejected. The first sign of her changed attitude was noted by Noël Coward shortly after the family Christmas. Winston had travelled to the United States to meet President Eisenhower accompanied by Clementine and the Soameses and they had met Sarah in Washington. Once official business was concluded the family went to Jamaica where they had been loaned a villa by Sir Harold Mitchell, Vice Chairman of the Conservative party. Here they met Noël Coward at social occasions. Like Cecil Beaton, Coward inspired Clementine to speak frankly of family matters. In a long talk she told him her view of Randolph's severe failings. Coward was somewhat surprised that as Randolph's mother she should take such a trenchant tone. She was clearly making sure that Winston's image was not tarnished by the suggestion that Randolph's parents in any way condoned his behaviour.

The pleasures of holidaying in Jamaica were soon followed by a return to public life. In February Clementine was reminded of the time when Winston had been First Lord when she was asked to launch the *Hermes* at Barrow in Furness. Then memories of wartime visits to devastated cities were revived as she accompanied Winston on a tour of East Anglia. This time the devastation was not the result of bombing but of severe floods which had left many people homeless. Other memories were evoked in March when the death of Stalin was announced. There had been a time when Clementine had defended Stalin and the Soviet Union. Now she was no longer confident that she had been right. She could easily discount Winston's extravagant and hostile rhetoric against communists and communism but she found it much harder not to take seriously Clement Attlee's condemnation of Soviet expansion of power and his concern to dissociate socialism from communism.

Yet at this time of looking back there was also a keen sense of the future inspired by the coronation and the beginning of a new era. For Clementine, however, the months preceding the coronation were less a time of anticipation than one of great stress. Acute neuritis racked her with pain and then she was greatly concerned that when Anthony Eden became ill in April 1953 Winston refused to appoint someone else as interim Foreign Secretary but instead combined this position with that of Prime Minister. There were family troubles too. One day Sally Churchill, the teenage daughter of Johnny from his first marriage, turned up at Number 10 and asked if she might stay. She claimed that she found living with her father and his third wife intolerable. Clementine, who found Johnny's marriages and divorces difficult to understand, had some sympathy with the girl who had been repeatedly farmed out with other people. But at sixty-eight she did not feel able to take on a teenager. She did her best to resolve the matter but was aware that Johnny Churchill resented her for interfering.

By the time the long-awaited coronation arrived both Clementine and Winston were feeling distinctly jaded. But there were pre-coronation parties to attend before the ordeal of the big occasion itself. On 2 June Clementine had some difficulty in rousing Winston to dress up in the uniform of the Warden of the Cinque Ports and to at least look pleasant.

She herself gave no outward sign of tiredness but looked quite radiant in her coronation attire. There were many members of foreign royal families and political leaders from all over the world in London for the occasion so there were more parties and more dinners including a banquet at Lancaster House where Winston and Clementine were the hosts in place of Anthony Eden and Clarissa. This was followed by a dinner at Number 10 for the Commonwealth Prime Ministers. Immediately after this the weary couple retreated to Chartwell only to be followed by a request from the Queen to advise her in the matter of Princess Margaret's expressed desire to marry the divorced Peter Townsend. After only a few days respite it was back to London to host a dinner at Downing Street for the Italian Prime Minister, Signor de Gasperi. Despite his fatigue Winston made a good speech and Clementine relaxed, thinking that the evening had been successful. In fact what Clementine had long feared and dreaded had happened. Winston had suffered a stroke in public. Fortunately most of the guests had not noticed. Everyone had attributed Winston's immobility and silence to tiredness. Only Jane Clark, wife of the art historian Kenneth Clark, noticed anything amiss and quietly let her hostess know. Clementine was able to organize the departure of the guests, leaving only family and intimates to cope with the situation. Somehow Winston was put to bed and Charles Moran sent for. In the morning Winston was worse rather than better but he managed a Cabinet meeting where his unusual silence was put down to the effect of the previous night's party. By now his left side was affected and his speech was slurred. With some careful planning Churchill was more or less smuggled out of Downing Street and taken to Chartwell where greater privacy gave everyone time to consider the situation. There were fears that Winston would die that weekend at Chartwell but the public was only told that he had gone to the country for a month's rest.

Against all the odds Winston slowly began to recover. The news of the death of long-time friend Bendor, Duke of Westminster, from a coronary thrombosis seemed to increase rather than diminish his will to get better. Not only did Clementine have to worry about whether her husband would recover and, if he did, whether he would be a helpless invalid, she had also to fall in with the wishes of Winston's political staff and help to maintain secrecy about his condition. Eden was still ill and there was no clear leader to take Churchill's place. The fear amongst those in the know was that the news of Winston's illness would split the party, a fight for the leadership would begin and in the process confidence in sterling would evaporate. Owners of the main newspapers were summoned to Chartwell where they, too, in the interests of the country as a whole, agreed to refrain from any suggestion about the seriousness of the Prime Minister's state. Even the new Queen was kept in ignorance and assumed that Winston was simply suffering from overwork.

As the weeks went by Winston became less helpless and with increased strength came boredom and irritation at his weakness and a desire to have everyone pay attention to his needs. Clementine hoped that this shocking experience would make her husband realize that it was definitely time for him to retire. In August he gave the impression that he accepted the idea of resignation in October. But first he set himself the objective of getting successfully through the Conservative party conference.

Feeling that Winston was no longer in danger and could safely be left to the care of his attentive nurses, Clementine left Chartwell to spend a few days in London to see that all was well at Downing Street. Her difficulties were compounded when she fell and cracked some ribs. For some time she had been urging Winston to find some excuse for not attending the Doncaster races even though he had been invited by the Queen to attend and afterwards to travel in the royal train to Balmoral. But Winston had made up his mind that this outing would be a test of whether he had recovered sufficiently to pass in public as a healthy man. Clementine was quite unable to change his mind. He survived the self-imposed ordeal but at a cost. He returned tired and grumpy and behaving like an overexcited child. Clementine had to rebuke him for bad table manners and for insisting on talking about 'blackamoors' and 'niggers'. She was greatly relieved when Mary and Christopher took him off to the South of France to Beaverbrook's villa for his final recuperation before the big ordeal of the party conference in October. Her doubts about whether he really could pull off this appearance were increased by the letters she received from him. He clearly had great difficulty in writing and was pathetically pleased when he could put a few words on paper. He was also very anxious that these letters should be burnt so that in the future no one would know how reduced he had been by his illness. Clementine wondered how he could possibly be sufficiently recovered to present himself before a highly critical audience.

When Winston returned to Chartwell he began immediately to prepare himself for the conference. Clementine was in a quandary. She did not want Winston to make a speech; she did not want him to continue as Prime Minister; she did not even want him to be an MP. If he was to put on a credible performance before his peers then he would need her to help him by listening to his speech and coaching him. She could have achieved her objective of making him retire by simply refusing to help him. But she did not seriously consider this option. It was as important to her as to Winston that he should retire with his dignity unimpaired. She was prepared to sacrifice her own peace of mind for a little longer to make this possible.

The conference in Margate on 10 October was nerve-racking for all those who knew the secret of Winston's illness. But he amazed everyone with a flawless performance. Clementine was proud of the sheer willpower he had shown to make this possible. But there was a drawback: with newly restored confidence Winston retreated from his earlier commitment to retire once the conference was successfully over. Now he expressed his determination to stay in office until the Queen returned from her Australian tour in May.

Clementine escaped from the irritation experienced by all those who worked with Winston, especially Anthony Eden, by accepting an invitation to stay with Lord and Lady Ismay in Paris. It was there that she learnt that Winston had been awarded the Nobel Prize for Literature which would be presented in December in Stockholm. She wondered whether Winston would be well enough to be present. But when she returned to London her husband informed her that he would be absent from the Nobel ceremonies, not because he thought the occasion would make too great a demand on him, but because he still saw himself as an international politician and he was planning to meet President Eisenhower for a top-level conference in Bermuda. Clementine would have to be his representative in Sweden.

So it was Mary and Clementine who set off for Stockholm rather than Winston and Clementine. There is no doubt that she graced the occasion better than her husband would have done. Everyone was delighted with her and at the ball after the ceremonies the orchestra paid her a special compliment by playing 'My Darling Clementine'. They could not have known that she hated this song; certainly the words are at odds with her carefully maintained dignity.

Winston's deafness was now a real problem and he refused to use a hearing aid. Eden who was with him at the Bermuda conference was fully aware that the Prime Minister had missed most of what was happening. President Eisenhower himself expressed concern at the way Winston looked to the past and still tried to relive the days of World War Two. For it was now Winston's declared ambition to achieve a meeting between the heads of the three countries who had been the principle allies in that war, despite the fact that neither the United States nor the Soviet Union was at all interested in such a meeting and Britain was no longer a power to influence the two superpowers.

Clementine learnt just how serious Winston was about this ambition early in 1954. The Queen returned from Australia on 14 May and Winston was there to meet her as he had earlier determined. But when Clementine reminded him of his promise to retire once the Queen was safely home Winston announced that he still had work to do and that he was planning to visit President Eisenhower in June. Clementine was in despair and it is probably no coincidence that the neuritis, which had never really left her, now flared up again. She set off to try yet one more cure in Aix-les-Bains. But more trouble awaited her on her return. Having forced a meeting with the American President, Winston had begun to try to arrange a meeting with the Soviet leaders. Every member of the Cabinet was opposed to this but Winston ignored them. Harold Macmillan was deputed to approach Clementine and secure her support in opposing such a journey. She listened to what he had to say and, though she basically agreed with him, she decided to enlist the help of John Colville. He was invited to be present at the lunch when Clementine broached the subject with Winston. This she did, but her comments were received angrily by Winston who later complained to Colville that Clementine always put the worst complexion on his actions. It was a situation in which Clementine simply could not win. At every turn she was met by Winston's stubborn refusal to accept that he was simply not doing his job. Her sense of what was ethically proper was offended by his remaining in a position for which he was no longer fitted. Winston, on the other hand, saw her acting as a go-between for Macmillan and Eden as disloyalty to him. There was at this time little harmony between them and even small incidents could cause upset. Clementine felt unappreciated and resented Winston's failure to send his secretary out of the room when she wanted to speak privately to him. She was also upset when he brought colleagues who were there to do with business with him into her private sitting room. More than ever she wanted a division between her public position and her private life.

Then in July came a blow of another kind. Clementine's sister Nellie, who had been unwell for some time, discovered that she had cancer and that her only hope was to have radiotherapy. Clementine feared that her

66-year-old sister would not survive this difficult treatment that was still in a comparatively crude state of development. Clementine's circle of intimates had never been large and it was shrinking rapidly. She had felt the loss of Duff Cooper earlier that year. Now she might well lose Nellie and she feared that Winston who was complaining of dizzy spells could easily succumb to another illness.

Having been thwarted in his desire to go to Russia and feeling that there was really little left for him to accomplish, Winston talked of retiring in September. He irritated Clementine beyond measure as throughout August he debated whether this was the right decision and then changed his mind yet again and put off the day until Easter. Clementine was glad to be diverted from this frustrating process by the arrival at Chartwell of Graham Sutherland and his wife Kathy. The House of Commons had commissioned Sutherland to paint a portrait of Winston to mark his eightieth birthday in November 1954, just three months away. Clementine was familiar with Sutherland's work and was pleasantly surprised at the difference between the man and his paintings. She characterized these as savage and cruel but Sutherland himself she declared to be a most attractive man. While he was at Chartwell Sutherland had three sessions with Winston in which he made preparatory drawings. Only Winston was allowed to see these and he told Clementine that he was impressed by the power of the drawing. No one saw the portrait until it was finished.

Kenneth Clark was one of the first to see Sutherland's portrait. Did he perhaps feel a little anxiety about how Winston would react? Why otherwise did he carefully arrange an occasion at Saltwood Castle when Clementine and Mary would be invited to see the painting in his company and with another art critic, Maurice Bowra, present? At Saltwood Castle Clementine expressed herself pleased with the portrait. Her reputation for outspokenness is such that it seems unlikely that she would have hidden her feelings and merely responded politely.

On Winston's birthday the Churchills were inundated with letters, gifts and messages of good will and congratulation. Winston revelled in thus being the centre of attention. Then came the ceremonial presentation of the portrait. Winston accepted this token of appreciation from his peers graciously. His immediate dislike of the portrait showed, however, in his ironic comments on its being a fine example of modern art. When he was safely back at home his anger was loud and bitter. He left Clementine and anyone else who would listen in no doubt that he was horrified by the portrait. Whereas Sutherland had intended to 'paint him with a kind of four-square look . . . as a rock' what Winston saw was a man who looked 'like a down-and-out drunk who has been picked out of the gutter in the Strand'.[3] He described the portrait as filthy and malignant. Clementine could see how very much he saw it as a criticism, and that he did not want to be remembered as the man suggested by it. She had the offending painting sent to Chartwell where for the time being it was stored in the cellars.

Now at last, having reached eighty and still in office, Winston agreed to retire shortly after Clementine's seventieth birthday. They spent their last Christmas at Chequers with a family party. There was one sad absence from the occasion. As Clementine had feared, Nellie had reacted badly to the radiation treatment, experiencing sickness and weakness. For months she had tried to put a cheerful face on the situation and had spent most weekends at Chartwell or Chequers. She had struggled to be present at Winston's eightieth birthday. But by Christmas it was apparent that Nellie was not going to recover and she lacked the stamina to face a family Christmas. Clementine arranged for nurses to look after Nellie in her own home and it was there on 1 February 1955 that Nellie died. Now Clementine was the last survivor of the Hozier family.

Grief at the loss of her lively sister had to be suppressed for the moment as Clementine began to plan the removal from both Downing Street and Chequers. There were parties to organize and farewell presents to select. Her own birthday party was not such an occasion as Winston's had been. As an assertion that she was shortly to be a private person and not a public one and thus able to choose her guests regardless of their political persuasion, she insisted that the Attlees should be invited. Then just three days later the Queen was to mark the occasion of Winston's retirement by taking the unusual step of dining at Downing Street.

Clementine did everything possible to make the evening a superlative one and in terms of food and organization she was successful. But this time the guests were not necessarily of her choosing and their behaviour gave the evening an element of farce. Anthony Eden who had waited a long time for this moment was so eager to shake hands with the Queen that some people suggested he jumped the queue. In retaliation the Duchess of Westminster attempted to put her foot through Clarissa's train. Randolph, predictably, got drunk and spent the evening in pursuit of his cousin Clarissa trying to read to her a derogatory article he had written for *Punch* about her husband. Mrs Herbert Morrison, who had been overcome with shyness at the beginning of the evening, became so elated by the occasion that she could hardly be persuaded to leave the Queen's side. It was not the kind of dinner party that Clementine had hoped for at all. But at last it was over and she could look forward to a life of greater privacy. But Winston was not glad. He was tired and depressed and resentful that his cherished position would pass to a man he considered less worthy and capable than himself. His last words before he went to bed were, 'I don't believe Anthony can do it.'⁴ Clementine had won a victory in getting her husband to retire but she was about to pay the price.

30

Friendships and Family

WHAT CLEMENTINE HAD been working to achieve for many years had now come about; Winston had retired from office, though he still clung to his seat in the Commons. At last they had leisure, they had plenty of money, they owned a London house and they had the permanent use of Chartwell. What remained of their lives should have been happy, but in fact the next ten years were troubled and difficult.

Immediately after his resignation Winston set off for Chartwell and immersed himself in his writing, taking up where he had left off on *The History of the English-Speaking Peoples*. But he was resentful that he was no longer the centre of things and everyone in his immediate circle felt the force of this. On 12 April the couple set off for a holiday in Sicily where they were to stay in the Villa Politi. But both Clementine and Winston were nervous about being alone together and so with them went Lord Cherwell and the indispensable Colvilles.

It was on this holiday that Clementine faced up to the fact that her husband really was an old man. Until now his position and his necessary dealings with a large number of people had to some extent masked this reality. Now she realized how little interest he had in anything outside politics and that even this interest was only as great as his personal involvement in affairs of state. The silences that had of late overcome him from time to time now became the rule rather than the exception and he said quite frankly to those who attempted to rouse him from his stupor that he simply had nothing left to say. And yet he did not want to be left alone. The situation required patience and tact both of which Clementine felt she lacked especially when the tormenting pain from neuritis was made worse when she broke her wrist. She could see that a long hard haul lay ahead of her and she was desperate to find a cure for her illness so that she had the strength to do what was necessary. So, despite Winston's needs and her fear that he could at any moment suffer another stroke, she determined to spend a month in Switzerland where she hoped she would become well. Over the years she had learnt that a certain amount of self-defensive selfishness was necessary to survive living with Winston.

At Suvretta House at St Moritz she began to feel better and it was here that she met Lewis Einstein, a man whose cultured conversation and sympathetic attention enlivened her cure. While she was away Winston began a painting of her from an old photograph taken as she launched the *Indomitable*. On the one hand she was touched at this clear sign that he was missing her but on the other hand she was troubled that it was an old and untypical image of her he had chosen. She had rarely felt as carefree as that photograph suggested and she certainly did not feel like that in her seventieth year.

As soon as she returned to England Winston wanted to be off. He craved the warm climate of the South of France and the comforts of the Villa Capponcina that Max Beaverbrook had put at their disposal in his absence. Clementine who did not much enjoy life among the kind of people who spent the winter on the Riviera was willing to accompany her husband on this occasion partly because she felt it her duty to do so. She enjoyed herself far more than usual because this time in addition to swimming they had the pleasure of using a motor yacht, the *Aronia*, which Jack Billmeir, a millionaire ship owner, had put at their disposal for some weeks.

As he grew older Winston yearned more and more for the warmth of the South of France. He began to think that it was not enough to rely on the hospitality of others but that he should have a villa of his own. And so for the next three years, whenever he was in France and Clementine was not, he began the search for a villa to meet his needs. In October 1956 he got as far as going into detailed negotiations with the company who controlled Monaco casino for a villa which needed restoring but which he otherwise considered perfect. He wrote to Clementine telling her that the villa would be put in order by the company and then he could have it for the rent of £1,500 a year. The only drawback as far as he was concerned was that the work would take a year, and at eighty-one he was in a hurry. Despite reassuring letters from Sarah saying that she was confident that her father would not do anything rash, Clementine was terrified that the Chartwell experience would be repeated and that one day she would find herself responsible for another house which she did not want. She saw, as Winston apparently did not, that buying or renting a villa was simply the first step. Then there would be furniture to find and servants to employ. He failed to see that the luxury which was part of his enjoyment of Max's villa had to be paid for by someone. Clementine did not believe that they had that kind of wealth. This was one more worry which exacerbated her nervous ill health.

Her good intentions of spending more time with Winston did not last for more than a few months and for the next five years she saw comparatively little of him except in company. On the one hand this was actually something of a relief to her, because for much of the time Winston was in England he was depressed and unhappy and said to many of his visitors that he was simply waiting for death but that it would not come. His silent company could be oppressive and his increasing deafness made conversation difficult since he still refused a hearing aid. What little interest he had ever had in art galleries was gone and Clementine could no longer share with him the pleasures of the theatre. So the freedom of Winston's absences was not entirely unwelcome but was tinged with a growing anxiety about the influence on him of the new friendships which dominated these five years.

Although the hospitality of Max's villa was always lavish Max himself was frequently absent when Winston was in residence so that an invitation of a more personal kind was very attractive. In January of 1956 Winston received such an invitation to Roquebrune from his rich and successful literary agent Emery Reves. Reves was a Hungarian-American Jewish millionaire. In 1953 he had bought from Coco Chanel, at one time the mistress of Winston's great friend the Duke of Westminster, her villa La Pausa. It was marked by her style, being light and elegant and casually luxurious. Its setting was perfect, on a hillside above the sea and surrounded by olive groves. Here Reves had hung his collection of Renoirs, Cézannes and Degases and had stocked the cellars with fine wines. To complete the picture he had installed his beautiful young mistress, a New York model, Wendy Russell.

When Winston arrived at the airport Reves met him in his Rolls Royce and from the outset treated his guest like royalty. He took care that the other guests were to Winston's taste. He made sure the food was to his liking. He talked to him about his paintings and when he thought the old man was showing signs of boredom played Mozart to him and taught him a little about the music. Wendy Russell was equally attentive and before long was on sufficiently close terms with Winston to be addressing him as 'Darling Sir' or 'Pumpkin Pie'. Winston was in his element and wrote home ecstatically about his treatment. It was what he had always wanted. Clementine, who had gone into University College Hospital for a few days to have injections to ease her neuritis and who had there caught an infection which kept her in the hospital for three weeks, received these paeans with suspicion and irritation. She felt somehow criticized for having failed to give Winston this happiness herself. She was also disapproving of the unmarried status of Miss Russell and wondered what the American couple hoped to gain from their slavish attention to her husband. While Winston was in England she made a great effort to ensure that press photographers did not take him off his guard and she tried to keep any rumours of his illness or depression reaching the papers. She was, therefore, alarmed by the amount of publicity her husband was getting during his stay at La Pausa. She had received a letter from Winston after he had been introduced to Aristotle Onassis at a dinner party at La Pausa saying how much he disliked the man's 'Levantine servility'.[1] The next thing Clementine knew was that the papers were full of photos of Winston with Onassis, apparently the greatest of friends as Winston arrived to have lunch on Onassis's yacht *Christina*. She was by no means sure that it was good for Winston's image to be seen in the company of this man whose integrity had often been questioned.

It was with this matter of her husband's image in mind that Clementine now took a step which later shocked everyone. She was becoming concerned about the number of books about Winston that were appearing and the light in which they showed him. Some years ago she had managed to prevent Inspector Thompson, who had attended Winston as his guard, from publishing his memoirs on the grounds that when he had entered Winston's service he had guaranteed not to take advantage of his position by publishing details of Winston's life. But she could not prevent private individuals from writing about him. What she could do was to make sure that Graham Sutherland's image of Winston, which caused him such distress and which was certainly not how he cared to be remembered, never again saw the light of day. During these weeks in January she cut up the canvas and then burnt it.

Winston was now urgent that she should join him at La Pausa for her convalescence. But Clementine had no intention of going to a place which she feared would irritate and upset her rather than relax her. Already much keener on cruises than holidays in one place she arranged to go with her cousin Sylvia Henley on a voyage to Cyprus. She wrote to Wendy Russell explaining that her condition required her to find a hot climate and so she must decline the invitation to La Pausa. That this was not her only reason for refusing was made clear when on her return journey she stopped in Marseilles. She could have easily driven over to La Pausa, and this time her excuses were rather flimsier: her clothes were crumpled, she said, and she had nothing fit to wear and she wanted to finish the cruise without interruption.

It was mid-April before Clementine was back in London; Winston had arrived a few days before her. By now Winston was infatuated not only with the villa at Roquebrune and the way of life there but also with his beautiful and attentive hostess. When he decided to return there in May Clementine did not go with him, preferring to spend her time in Paris with Lewis Einstein. With him she visited the Louvre, Carnavalet, Malmaison, Versailles and St Germain-en-Laye as well as going to plays and concerts. These activities and this company was far more to her taste than Roquebrune. But having insisted on this time in Paris she felt obliged to follow it with an appearance at La Pausa. The situation she found there appalled her.

Noël Coward recorded how he and his companion, Edward Molyneux, had dined with Pamela Churchill in Avignon on 3 June. The subject of discussion was Churchill's apparent infatuation with Wendy Russell, which Pamela said was causing dismay to Clementine. On 9 June Coward and Molyneux were invited to lunch at La Pausa and so were able to judge the situation for themselves. Clementine had already departed, having spent only a few days at the villa but Sarah had stayed to keep her father company and perhaps to keep an eye on him. Coward wrote in his diary after the visit how upset he was to see the great man, 'historically one of the greatest our country has produced . . . absolutely obsessed with a senile passion for Wendy Russell. He followed her about the room with his brimming eyes and wobbled after her across the terrace, staggering like a vast baby of two who is just learning to walk.'[2]

If Noël Coward found the situation distressing how much greater must Clementine's upset have been, especially that such behaviour would be seen by anyone Reves invited to his home. In July Winston returned home but by the end of the month Clementine was off again to

Switzerland. It was no coincidence that Lewis Einstein was already there at St Moritz ready to entertain her by taking her for rides in his car. In her absence Winston began to plan his next stay at La Pausa in September. Clementine thought about accompanying him mainly to keep him out of mischief. But in the end she could not face going and Sarah went in her place. Clementine took the opportunity to see as many plays as possible. By now Winston acknowledged that his refusal to use a hearing aid put a great strain on anyone in his company and while he was at La Pausa he tried hard to come to terms with an instrument given to him by his New York friend Bernard Baruch. But Clementine had reason to regret that she had not gone to La Pausa for while he was there Winston suffered another stroke and had to be flown home at the end of October.

In 1957 there was a similar pattern. In the middle of January Winston was once again on his way to La Pausa where he would in all spend five months of the year. His brief visit to London for a few days in February was as much to attend meetings as to spend time with Clementine. However, shortly before he arrived, the Alanbrooke diaries were published. Lord Alanbrooke, who had been General Alan Brooke during the war, had published his wartime diaries to give his perspective on events. The Ulsterman with a sharp tongue had a reputation for outspoken bluntness and had not always agreed with Winston in the past, so Winston had every reason for expecting to find himself criticized in the diaries. He was anxious before they appeared and upset afterwards at the picture they gave of him. Charles Moran records a conversation with Clementine at this time in which he reports her as saying 'You know Winston has become a legend . . . I am not really angry with Alanbrooke. We must get used to criticism of Winston. I realise the poor darling cannot be a demi-god for ever.'[3] Nevertheless Clementine's protective instincts were aroused and she determined that she would accompany Winston when he returned to Roquebrune. Despite her good intentions, she was not happy at La Pausa and her general disapproval was felt by all the company. After a short stay she returned to London leaving Winston behind. When he returned it was with complaints that she had upset Wendy by her attitude and by the fact that she was said to have listened to unkind rumours about the young woman from Daisy Fellowes. Winston wrote to his host and hostess denying that Clementine had felt anything other than friendly during her stay. But was he really being candid? Subsequent events suggest that Wendy Russell's perception of Clementine's feeling were entirely accurate. The letter which Winston wrote to Clementine on his return to La Pausa in May suggests that his departure had caused a rift between them which he was anxious to mend. In the same letter he comments that Wendy is unhappy that the Churchills are planning to visit La Capponcina in September rather than La Pausa. This was exactly the kind of comment calculated to anger Clementine since it suggested an intimacy and a possessiveness that she could not condone. Whereas she had not before shown much enthusiasm for La Capponcina she was now willing to go if this would hinder Winston's contact with Wendy. There was now enough bad feeling between the two women for a visit planned by Wendy to Chartwell in June to be cancelled. When Winston returned to La Pausa in October after the visit to La Capponcina Clementine returned to London.

None of this affected Winston's determination to enjoy Reves's hospitality once more in January of 1958. He was even willing to spend a few days at the Hôtel de Paris waiting for the central heating at La Pausa to be repaired. Asserting her superior knowledge of what was good for Winston Clementine wrote to Wendy suggesting a modified timetable for his visit and once again requesting that great care be taken to keep Winston out of the limelight. At this point she had no intention of going to La Pausa herself. Then came word that Winston was ill and that he needed her. The very reasons for this illness angered her. Reves had taken Winston to have lunch with Onassis on the yacht. Lunch had been extended into a gambling session during the course of which Winston had eaten and drunk too much. It was exactly the kind of situation which Clementine was always trying to avoid.

Although Emery Reves and Wendy Russell were by now married, Clementine was still determined that the close tie Winston had formed with them must be loosened. Ironically the means of achieving this were put into her hands by the Reveses themselves. It was they after all who had introduced Winston to Onassis who was now anxious to ingratiate himself with Winston. In September 1958 Onassis invited the Churchills to be his guests for a cruise on *Christina*. As an enticement he gave them the last word on the guest list. Clementine made quite sure that the Reveses were not invited.

Cruises with Onassis now began to take the place of visits to La Pausa, so that in 1959 Winston spent only two months there. The Reveses were, not unnaturally, offended and felt that they had been dropped in favour of Onassis, with the result that when in 1960 Winston confidently proposed himself for a visit to Roquebrune he was for the first time turned down. Reves wrote to say that they could not receive him because Wendy had been made ill by all the scheming and gossip that she felt had attended his switch of loyalty to Onassis.

The contentious visit to La Capponcina in September was the occasion of Clementine and Winston's golden wedding anniversary. They had already been guests in July at a dinner given by the Marlboroughs to celebrate the fiftieth anniversary of their engagement at Blenheim. On 12 September Randolph, with his daughter Arabella, arrived at the villa bearing the Golden Rose Book. In this volume were paintings of roses commissioned by Randolph from many artists. Some of the artists, such as Augustus John, Paul Maze, Matthew Smith and Cecil Beaton, were professionals. But there were also paintings from less well-known artists, among whom were Randolph's daughter, Arabella, and Margaret Birkenhead, the widow of Lord Birkenhead. Randolph presented this heavy volume on the twelfth as a token of the real anniversary present from the four Churchill children – an avenue of golden roses to be planted at Chartwell.

A perfect image had been achieved: the smiling old hero with his still beautiful wife receiving a token of love and esteem from a united family after many years of happiness together.

The photo of the occasion masked a situation so bad that at times Clementine had felt her sanity threatened. Over the last three years she had rarely been free of illness which had its root cause in worry and distress and indeed most recently during her August visit to Tangiers to stay with her most calm and reassuring friends the Nairns she had been afflicted with a severe case of shingles. Winston's infatuation with Wendy Russell, his unrealistic search for a villa in France, his silences and his brooding on death had been perhaps the least of her worries. Of her four children only Mary had continued on a stable course and even she had brought an unwelcome change in Clementine's life when in October 1957 she had moved from Chartwell Farm to Mansell Manor near Tunbridge Wells. The old tight intimacy had seemed less possible after the move. Chartwell Farm had been sold at that point.

There was nothing new in the problems presented by Randolph. He continued to quarrel with his father, especially after the sale of the farm which he had been led to believe he would inherit. He had caused great embarrassment by his drunken behaviour at Winston's last public appearance as Prime Minister, his dinner for the Queen; his repeated derogatory and scornful remarks about Anthony Eden were doubly embarrassing now that Eden, as Clarissa's husband, was a member of the family. In October 1956 Clementine had expressed herself as being ashamed and mortified when Randolph had taken the newspaper the *People* to court in a libel action for calling him a 'paid hack'. His divorce from June had long been expected but was, nevertheless a blow when it was made absolute in April 1958. But Clementine by now expected little but trouble from the son of whom she had been so proud when he was born. She was to some extent hardened against him and his antics.

She had not, however, expected her two older daughters to be responsible for completely shattering the notion of the Churchills as a happy family.

By the time Winston became Prime Minister in 1950 there was only minimal contact between Clementine and Diana. By that time, too, everyone in the family was aware that Diana's husband was having affairs, although he tried to be discreet, and they thought no better of him for it. Clementine, who had never really trusted him, was increasingly distant in her manner towards him. But she was not able to comfort her unhappy daughter as she had never thought much of the marriage and she felt that Diana's docility and weakness had done nothing to save the situation. When Diana suffered a complete mental break-down it was not surprising that it was against Clementine she turned, going so far as to take a knife and threaten to kill her mother with it. She did not pose a real danger to Clementine's life and she was pathetically easily disarmed. But the shock to Clementine and the realization of how completely she had failed her daughter was a terrible blow to her sense of herself. Diana clearly needed help that her family and her husband could not give her and she was put in a private nursing home for treatment. It was, however, the effectual end of her marriage though she was not formally divorced until 1960. Clementine's fear that it was her own weakness which she had passed on to her daughter only increased her own tendency to nervous depression and illness. She worried also about the effect on Diana's children of their mother's break-down and, remembering how her own mother had not been able to do anything for her coming out, she arranged that she and Winston would give Edwina Sandys her coming out dance at Claridge's in May of 1957.

Clementine had always had a special affection for Sarah. Even when she had felt that Sarah had let her down it had never been long before she was willing to be reconciled. She appreciated Sarah's help in keeping an eye on Winston at times when she herself did not want to be in France with him. For a long time she had known that Sarah's second marriage was not working and had even helped Sarah to be independent. In 1955 the couple had gone their separate ways: Antony Beauchamp to pursue his career in London while Sarah pursued hers in the States. But it was a situation more of Sarah's choosing than her husband's, and now the pattern of her relationship with Gil Winant began to be repeated to the extent that in August 1957 Beauchamp committed suicide by taking an overdose of drugs. Again Clementine had to phone Sarah with the news. When Winant had died few people had known of his connection with Sarah, but the suicide of Sarah Churchill's husband was headline news and some reports suggested that Sarah and her family were to blame for Beauchamp's unhappiness. Altogether the Churchill family received a great deal of exactly the kind of publicity that Clementine was always trying to avoid. When a guilty and distraught Sarah tried to restore her place in the family by spending Christmas at Chartwell with her parents, Winston wrote to her saying that Clementine was in a state of nervous exhaustion and could not face the strain that a visit from Sarah would involve. It was an unfortunate decision. Left with her unhappy thoughts in her Malibu home Sarah got well and truly drunk. She caused such a disturbance that the police were called and because of her violent behaviour she was arrested for being drunk and disorderly. Her appearance in court where she pleaded guilty was highly publicized. It was an added humiliation to Clementine that she was paying one of her rare visits to La Pausa when the news broke. And when Sarah was brought to La Pausa it was clear to her that both Winston and Wendy Reves were more able to be helpful to Sarah than she was herself. Just as Diana had been admitted to hospital for treatment for mental disorder so now Sarah was sent to a clinic in Zürich in an attempt to cure her of what everyone now accepted as chronic alcoholism. Remembering her own mother's propensity to drink and the rumours she had heard of her grandfather's failings in that direction, Clementine wondered if she was to blame for this failing too in Sarah and Randolph. Had she passed on to them a 'drinking gene'?

When Sarah tried to pick up her acting career in England Clementine supported her loyally, attending performances whenever possible and even organizing a big family party to see Sarah star in *Peter Pan*. At the back of her mind always was the fear, that proved to be well founded, that before long Sarah's drinking would cause more trouble and unhappiness.

Against this background the prospect of a cruise on the *Christina* was especially attractive. On 22 September Winston and Clementine joined

Onassis's other guests in Monte Carlo ready for a cruise through the Mediterranean to the Straits of Gibraltar stopping off at Tangier and then going up the river Guadalquivir to Seville. There was much about this cruise to please Clementine. The company was congenial, including Lowell Guinness and his wife, Margot Fonteyn's lawyer husband, the familiar Montague Brownes, Onassis's sister Artemis as well as his wife Tina and his two children. She looked forward to meeting Margaret and Bryce Nairn again in Tangier where they had been invited to come on board. She had loved cruising and seeing new places ever since the days when she had sailed with Lowell Guinness's father, Lord Moyne. It was an ideal way for her to spend time with Winston without having the whole burden of entertaining him. Onassis went out of his way to see that his honoured guest had everything that he wanted. He was willing to listen to him with respectful attention and had even learned to play Winston's favourite card game, bezique, so that he could play with him. Clementine did not need to worry about going ashore and leaving her husband since there was always someone at hand if he wanted company. And the yacht itself was amazing and luxurious beyond belief. Three hundred and twenty-two feet in length, the *Christina* had originally been a Canadian frigate. Her conversion into a luxury yacht had cost Onassis more than four million dollars. In the dining room were frescoes by Marc Vertes which depicted the seasons with family members engaged in suitable activities: Tina skating was the focus of the winter panel while the children picnicking on a lawn represented summer. There were nine luxury suites on board each one named after a Greek island. Onassis himself had a four-room suite on the bridge deck in which he had installed a sunken bath of blue Siena marble, a replica of one built for a Minoan king. The walls were lined with Venetian mirrors. In the bar were bar stools covered with white leather. Onassis was enough of a judge of character not to explain to Clementine, as he usually did to other female guests, that the white leather was in fact white whale foreskin. And he did not treat her to his usual line, 'Madame you are now sitting on the largest penis in the world.'[4] On this cruise Clementine was more relaxed and happier than she had been for some time. Other guests who were accustomed to hearing about Winston and his great speaking abilities were surprised to see Clementine engaged in animated discussion of English literature while Winston sat silently in the background. When the cruise ended in Gibraltar Clementine was inclined to look favourably on the idea that there should soon be other such voyages.

The advantage of being a friend of Aristotle Onassis was apparent again in January of 1959 when Winston expressed a desire to return to Marrakesh. The party, which included the Colvilles and the Montague Brownes as well as the Churchills, was flown out in a private aircraft of Olympic Airways of which Onassis was the owner. Marrakesh seemed more run down than on previous visits but before long they left, driving to the coast at Safi where they boarded the *Christina*. This time they sailed to the Canary Islands calling at Lanzarote, Santa Cruz and Las Palmas before returning to the Moroccan coast at Agadir and then sailing north to Tangier where Clementine had the opportunity of spending time with the Nairns before returning to London.

There were to be three more cruises on the *Christina* for Clementine. None of them gave her quite the same pleasure as that first one. She grew progressively disillusioned with Onassis himself and thoroughly disapproved of some of the things that happened on board the yacht. She continued to accept invitations only because they solved for some weeks at a time the problem of what to do with Winston. On the yacht he was happy; in England he was bored and depressed and none of the efforts made by Clementine or the friends she invited to entertain him distracted him from his own misery at his physical and mental condition and his desire to die. Seeing his condition Clementine recalled sadly that Winston had written on the death of Jennie that his mother had not had to suffer the miseries of old age.[5]

In July 1959 Onassis proposed a tour of the Greek Islands. It was the most ambitious cruise to date taking in places as far apart as Portofino, Istanbul, Smyrna and Athens. The places they visited interested Clementine greatly but the company on board was less pleasing. On this occasion Winston had asked that Diana and her daughter Celia be invited too. Although Clementine and her daughter were on better terms Diana's presence made her uneasy. She was not at all pleased by the occasion on which Onassis boasted that his wine glasses were special and unique and could be squeezed into shape. Diana took him at his word and squeezed her wine glass, breaking it and splashing red wine all over the spotless white dinner jacket of another guest, the British Ambassador to Greece, Sir Roger Allen. Clementine was as distressed as her daughter at the awkwardness of the situation.

The tension created by Diana, however, was as nothing compared to that brought by Maria Callas and her manager husband. Everyone on board was uneasily aware that these two were not on the best of terms since their quarrels could be heard all over the yacht. Then just before the *Christina* returned to Monte Carlo there was trouble between Onassis and his wife Tina after she discovered her husband making love to the opera singer. Clementine was by now fond of Tina, who was young and beautiful with the excellent manners of a girl raised in an expensive English boarding school. In contrast Clementine had no time for the extravagances of the flamboyant and temperamental Callas and she resented the breach of decorum her presence had brought about.

So when the Greek millionaire invited the Churchills to join him on the *Christina* in February 1960, tempted as she was by the prospect of visiting Barbados, Trinidad, Tobago and Santa Lucia, Clementine made it a condition of her accompanying Winston that Callas was not of the party. Even so this cruise did not get off to a good start. Bad weather forced their plane to land unexpectedly in Tangier where no provision had been made for their stop-over. Winston was in a bad mood and his irritation grew as his food failed to arrive promptly; he became abusive to the waiters. Clementine was ashamed of his behaviour and told him so in no uncertain terms, threatening to leave the table and retire to bed without a meal if he did not behave better. The bad weather continued and the passengers on board the *Christina* were greatly discomforted by a storm at sea as they approached the Canary Islands.

Nevertheless Clementine joined Winston one more time when the *Christina* sailed first to Venice and then to Split, Dubrovnik, Corfu, Athens, Crete and Rhodes. But the pleasures of travel were no longer adequate compensation for Clementine's growing distaste for the company of Onassis. Although he was always extremely polite to her she was left in no doubt that the real focus of his attention was Winston. She saw more clearly now that his attitude to women in general was one that she did not like. There was now a whiff of scandal about whatever he did. His tempestuous affair with Callas was receiving enormous publicity, and Clementine was no longer pleased to be associated with him. Winston made three more cruises with Onassis, the last one being in June 1963, but Clementine was no longer willing to accompany him. As far as she was concerned the friendship was at an end.

31

Uphill all the Way

ONE OF THE difficulties Clementine faced in the years between Winston's leaving office and his death in 1965 was the fact that, although in his eighties and often in poor health, Winston continued to be a public figure. The man who would sit slumped in his chair silent and apparently unseeing, who could behave like a petulant child and who could be pathetically dependent on his wife still fulfilled official engagements. Time after time Clementine experienced the fear and dread she had felt before and during the Margate conference in October 1953. There was always the question in her mind as to whether Winston would pull off an occasion or whether he would make a dreadful exhibition of himself.

For some years he enjoyed his occasional public appearances for the precious confirmation they gave him that in his life he had achieved something. He was pleased to be consulted by the Queen in January 1957 when, as he had predicted, Anthony Eden found the Prime Ministership too much for him and resigned. The occasion of the funeral of his old friend Lindemann, Lord Cherwell, in July of that year was a sad one but Winston was moved when the entire congregation rose as a mark of respect when he entered the church for the service.

He felt he still had a part to play internationally and persisted in the idea that he should go to the United States. Clementine resisted this notion and when Montgomery heard of the plan in March 1958 he supported her position. Nevertheless Winston was only temporarily deterred and in May 1959 aged eighty-five he journeyed to Washington to stay in the White House. In the meantime Clementine had accompanied him to Paris where he had received from General de Gaulle the

Croix de la Libération. His role as an international statesman was further underlined by a visit to Hyde Park Gate from the German Chancellor Dr Adenauer. But on this visit, as was to happen increasingly, communication between the two men was hampered by Winston's deafness. The burden of making the occasion a success fell on Clementine who summoned up the German she had learnt so long ago.

There was one public involvement which Clementine actively encouraged and this was the planning of the opening of Churchill College, Cambridge, to which Winston intended to leave his papers. A meeting of the Trustees was held over lunch at Chartwell in May 1958. Clementine took a prominent part in this meeting making sure that Winston understood what was going on. She was as concerned as ever about the education of women and at this meeting she urged that Churchill College should be open to women as well as men. When in May 1959 there was a ceremony at which an oak tree was planted in the grounds where the college was to be built Winston was still strong enough to attend. But this was not the case when the college was formally opened in June 1964, and Clementine went instead as his representative.

What did make her unhappy and put an unnecessary burden on her was Winston's selfish refusal to give up his seat as an MP. He had never taken as much interest in or care for his constituency as Clementine had done and now he did not even appear as its representative in the Commons any more. Constituency matters were filtered through Clementine as was the growing dissatisfaction of the local party with their invisible MP. In April 1959 Winston did make one of his rare appearances in the constituency. Clementine was torn by conflicting emotions: on the one hand she was pleased that Winston was doing the right thing; on the other she was afraid that he would not do it well. She even hoped that this would be his resignation speech and she was upset when it was not. Winston stood again for election in the October election and was returned although with a greatly reduced majority. And so Clementine struggled on until April 1963 when she became seventy-eight years of age. Now she enlisted the help of Christopher Soames in trying to persuade the stubborn old man that he had no business clinging to his position and so depriving his electorate of someone young enough to truly represent it. In May 1963 he finally gave in and it was with pleasure and relief that Clementine held a garden party in July at Chartwell for the new Conservative candidate.

Just how long overdue that resignation was and the strain endured by

Clementine every time her husband spoke in public is made clear in an account by Diana Cooper of an occasion in the very month that Winston stood down. A literary prize had been established in memory of Diana's husband, Duff Cooper, and Winston had offered to make the first presentation. Clementine invited Diana to lunch before the occasion. Diana, who had known Winston since she was a girl and he had come courting Pamela Plowden, was pleasantly surprised by Winston's healthy appearance but found his mental state less easy to deal with: 'his mind is like love; when you think you are sure of it, it's flown, and giving up pursuit, it's back with you'.[1] Diana witnessed with some alarm how Clementine tried over and over again to explain to her husband exactly what was expected of him. He clearly found her explanation hard to grasp. There was a moment when the three of them wondered if he should withdraw from the occasion. But he determined to go through with it. He made his speech without a hitch and the two women sat back in relief. But then he stood up again and to the surprise of everyone present made a second impromptu speech. 'He was for a flash the real Winston and ended with a joke about Gallipoli,' Diana recorded.[2]

It is not surprising that from this point on Clementine discouraged public appearances. When Winston Jr married Minnie D'Erlanger in June 1964 she attended the ceremony without her husband. Then the wedding party returned to Hyde Park Gate for the new bride to be presented to Winston. There were photographs taken and one of these offers an interesting perspective on the family at this time.

The central figures in the group are not, as you might expect, bride and groom, but grandfather and grandson. What is important in this portrait is the notion of the Churchill line being continued from one Winston to another. But the old man looks bewildered as if he is not quite sure why he is there. The bride is on the extreme edge of the picture looking resigned as if waiting patiently for the occasion to come to an end. Behind the two Winstons stands Randolph with a startled expression on his face as though the camera has interrupted his flow of speech. Next to him, but clearly not with him, looking challengingly at the camera is the most expensively and smartly dressed member of the wedding party, Randolph's former wife and young Winston's mother, Pamela. Mary stands next to her looking slightly anxious as if not sure what might happen next. Clementine is on the extreme right of the group. She holds her spectacles in her hand as if she has taken them off in order to look her best on this family occasion. But she does not look at the camera at all: her attention is entirely focused on Winston as she leans forward as if to reassure him and to tell him what to do. It is a gesture which tellingly characterizes her care for her husband during these most difficult years.

There are two notable absences from this family group. Neither Sarah nor Diana is visible. At the time Sarah was in the States in retreat from the scandalous reputation she had established for herself in England and which had been a contributing factor in pushing her mother to such an extreme of anxiety that in March of 1961 she had been forced to spend a month in St Mary's Hospital in Paddington. Evidently the time Sarah had spent in the Zürich clinic had completely failed to cure her of alcoholism. During the course of 1960 she had been arrested three times for drunkenness; she had been put on probation which she had broken and as a result had been confined in Holloway Prison. Clementine had been distraught at her daughter's imprisonment. She could not help remembering Sydney Mitford's distress when her daughter Diana had been imprisoned there during the war and the anguish of the Lyttons when Lady Constance was incarcerated.

On her release from jail Sarah had left England and gone to Spain where she had met, and in April 1962 married, Henry, Baron Audley. The Churchills knew little about him except that he came from a good family. Clementine did not attend the wedding but sent Diana in her place, remarking tartly that Sarah's third husband was the first to go by his real name. For just over a year Sarah kept out of the headlines and seemed to be happy. But in July 1963, without warning, her world once more crashed around her when Henry suffered a cerebral haemorrhage and died. Although Diana was given money by Clementine to go to Spain and look after her sister she feared that this blow would drive Sarah further into alcoholism. She was relieved that Sarah was not at young Winston's wedding. Noël Coward who visited Sarah in July describes a woman who would certainly not have graced the family portrait. In his diary he writes that Sarah looked 'beaten up', a 'pretty woman now aged fifty and quite obviously done for'. He describes the apartment where Sarah was living with her lover, an abstract painter, 'three quarters Negro and one quarter Arab' as 'ghastly, squalid, incense burning, tatty'.[3] And, as Clementine herself had spent many painful hours doing, he wondered what could have gone wrong in Sarah's upbringing to lead her to such a state.

At least, though absent, Sarah was alive. Diana was dead. On 20 October 1963 she had been found dead in her flat having taken an overdose of drugs. Had she done this some years earlier after her mental breakdown and the failure of her marriage her family would not have been surprised. But she had appeared to have overcome her difficulties. She had taken up work with the Samaritans and she had proved herself strong and caring in her dealings with Sarah. She was on good terms with her father and even with Clementine. Indeed on the day before she died she had told her daughter Edwina, now married, that she planned to spend the following day visiting her mother in hospital and then going on to have dinner at Hyde Park Gate with her father. The only possible clue to her decision to kill herself was the fact that her death followed immediately on the news that Duncan's new wife, Marie-Claire, had just given birth to their first child.

Clementine was in Westminster Hospital when Diana died. She had been admitted for electrotherapy treatment having broken down under the strain of being in constant attendance on Winston who had suffered another stroke in August. Montgomery who had visited the Churchills at Hyde Park Gate had foreseen Clementine's collapse. He was entirely sympathetic to the difficulties that Clementine, now seventy-eight, was facing and he had written to Mary saying that in his view Clementine was worn out and urgently in need of a rest. So neither of Diana's parents was able to attend her funeral. She would, perhaps, have seen this as typical of her relationship with them when she was alive. Both of them, however, attended the Memorial Service held in the crypt of the church where Diana had worked for the Samaritans.

After young Winston's wedding Clementine and Winston spent what would prove to be their last summer at Chartwell. The time was enlivened for Clementine by the presence of Mary's children who stayed with her while Mary nursed her husband who had injured his pelvis. But Chartwell had many disadvantages now. Because of its isolation it was harder for Clementine to have much life of her own there. In London there were friends who were willing to take turns playing cards with Winston or even just sitting with him to enable her to get out. Hyde Park Gate was a more convenient house in which to look after Winston as a result of the changes Clementine had made there in August 1962. While Winston had been in hospital after breaking his hip she had created a bedroom and bathroom for him on the ground floor of 27 and had installed a lift in 28 to enable him to move from the dining room to the ground floor. In October Winston left Chartwell for the last time; he no longer cared where he lived, being weary of life itself.

Later in the month Clementine had a few days in Paris where she stayed with Edwina's parents-in-law. The purpose of her visit was to unveil in the Embassy a bust of Winston by Oscar Nemon. She had the strange feeling that to the rest of the world Winston was already a figure of the past. While she was in Paris she dined with another survivor of World War Two, General de Gaulle. Both of them were now mellower and sharp exchanges between them were a thing of the past.

In November Winston reached his ninetieth birthday. The occasion meant more to his family than to him. Clementine did not know what to give to her husband who had outlived his need for any more possessions. She settled on a token, a small gold heart. Throughout December Winston lingered on, cut off from his family by deafness and indifference. His only desire seemed to be to have Clementine close at hand. When the massive stroke came on 10 January Clementine knew that this time he would not recover. But for fourteen days he remained alive though unmoving. Clementine was calm as the family came and went and crowds gathered outside. To one observer Clementine, drifting through her house, her face expressionless as though she was in a trance, seemed as remote from life as Winston himself. But she was not so distant from the present that she did not realize that the crowds of people in Hyde Park Gate were beginning to interfere with the lives of other residents and so she issued a request that they move and promised regular bulletins on Winston's condition.

Lord Randolph Churchill, Winston's father, had died on 24 January. And, as if his iron will had exerted itself even in unconsciousness, Winston reached that date and then quietly died without regaining consciousness.

Unlike most widows Clementine was spared the need to turn her thoughts to the funeral. That was in the hands of others and the arrangements had been in place for some years since the Queen had expressed the wish that Churchill should be given a state funeral. Now an efficient, organized operation swung into movement and after a couple of days for the family's private grieving Winston became once more a public figure. The coffin was taken from Hyde Park Gate to Westminster Hall for a lying in state. Hundreds of thousands of people, undeterred by bitterly cold weather and snow, queued to file past the coffin to pay their last respects, and every day Clementine too visited the Hall. It was some recompense to her for the misery of the last years to see the man she had cared for respected as a hero by ordinary people.

The funeral took place on 30 January. After Big Ben struck 9.45 a.m., the last time that it sounded out on that day of public mourning, the coffin was taken to New Palace Yard and there loaded onto a gun carriage to process down Whitehall past silent crowds. Clementine with Mary and Sarah drove in the procession to St Paul's in a carriage loaned by the Queen. In the cathedral the Queen herself was there for the funeral of the man she had known for as long as she could remember.

Throughout the proceedings Clementine maintained a calm dignity, just as she had done on so many other public occasions, whatever her private emotions. This could not be said of Sarah who was overcome by grief and drink. As the family left St Paul's at the end of the service Clementine quietly arranged for Sarah to be taken home.

The coffin made its ceremonial journey across the Thames and then onto a special train pulled by the engine named 'Sir Winston Churchill'. At Clementine's request this marked the end of the State's involvement. Only family and those who had known Winston personally accompanied the coffin to Bladon where Clementine saw her husband buried, as he had wished, alongside his mother and father in the graveyard of the little church of Bladon close to the Palace of Blenheim where he had been born and where he had made the proposal that had bound his life to Clementine's.

There were only two wreaths on the coffin; one was from Clementine with the message 'To my Darling Winston. Clemmie.' The other was from the Queen and the message read, 'From the Nation and Commonwealth. In grateful remembrance. Elizabeth R.'

Even at his burial Clementine had shared her husband with the nation.

32

Endings and Beginnings

THE VASTLY IMPRESSIVE and emotionally charged funeral brought to an end a long phase of Clementine's life. She had lived with Winston for more than fifty-six years and, although they had often been apart during that time, he had always been at the centre of her life and she had seen her primary role as being his wife. His death left a great gap in her life but her grief was undoubtedly tinged with relief that a great responsibility had come to an end. She was now approaching her eightieth birthday. Was it too late for her to have those things in life which she had given up for Winston and to express that side of herself which she had consciously repressed? Could she now at last enjoy the pleasure of being a private person?

After two weeks, staying with Mary and her family at Hamsell, Clementine began to take some decisive steps to change her life. Despite the inevitable infirmities of age, her basic health was from this time until close to her death as good as could be expected. All signs of nervous illness and neuritis disappeared as she began to lead a life chosen by her and not by Winston. Her first and highly significant act was to hand over Chartwell together with most of its furnishings immediately to the National Trust. She had no desire to exercise her option to remain there until her own death.

She had once confided to Mrs Graebner, the wife of one of Winston's agents, that she would like to have a small flat with three or four rooms and one maid. She had even apologized for needing a maid but explained that she was getting too old to do everything for herself.[1] The big houses and the staff to run them which had been so important to Winston had never been to her taste. She had disposed of Chartwell and now considered putting the two houses in Hyde Park Gate up for sale so that she could achieve her ambition of a smaller, easily managed home.

But it was too soon to make such a drastic change and so to give herself time to clear her mind and recover from the tiredness which had been accumulating for years she accepted two invitations. In February, along with Mary and her husband, she left Southampton on the *Queen Mary* for New York. Clementine remembered the days when it had been denuded of all its luxury and used as a troop ship. From New York she flew to Barbados to stay with the Trees at Heron Bay. Ever since the weekends of the full moon during the war when she had gone to Ditchley rather than to Chequers she had remained close to Ronald Tree and had written to him regularly. The Duke of Marlborough, the grandson of the cousin to whom Winston had been close all his life, had invited her to stay with his family in Montego Bay, Jamaica, and so she made this her next stopping place. To her family she seemed remote as she thought about the past and tried to plan her future.

In the past she had always been the one to organize family occasions so it was a pleasure to her on her return to England to have her eightieth birthday party arranged for her by Randolph. After the death of Winston his relationship with his mother became less fraught. He was no longer in competition with his father and he was a much happier man than he had been before, as he lived in his country house and worked hard on the biography of Winston which had finally been entrusted to him. There were times when Clementine could help him by dating photos and identifying people he did not know. It was too late for them to become close and Randolph had only three years to live. But there were no more debilitating quarrels.

There were various tasks which Clementine had to complete once back in London. The insignia of the Order of the Garter which Winston had been awarded in 1953 had to be returned. It was Randolph who accompanied his mother to a lunch with the Queen at which the Order was handed over. Then there was the matter of the Sutherland portrait. Since 1956 Clementine had put off everyone who wanted to see the painting. However, there was now talk of its being handed over to the Commons to be hung at Westminster. With no sign of remorse Clementine broke her long silence on the matter and told her horrified daughter that the portrait would never again be seen in public as she had destroyed it. Fearful of a hostile response from the art world and from the general public Mary made the decision to keep the secret until after Clementine's death.

The most important matter as far as Clementine was concerned was to find a suitable place to live. She had not changed her mind about wanting a flat but she did not want to move too far away from the area where she had lived for so long. By September she was installed in a pleasant apartment in Princes Mansion close to Hyde Park. Her cook moved with her as did her secretary-companion Nonie Chapman. The Hyde Park Gate houses were auctioned in October and at last Clementine was free of those many responsibilities which had irked her.

In her new home she began a life of orderly routine such as she had never been able to achieve with Winston. She continued her life-long habit of keeping herself up to date by reading the newspapers daily and she continued to protect her hands as she read with white cotton gloves. Every evening she changed for dinner. Now she began the habit of visiting Sarah once a week and taking her out for lunch and a drive. By so doing she ensured that there was one day in Sarah's week on which she made an effort to remain sober.

Into this routine she introduced a new activity. As a young girl she had been religiously inclined and a regular church-goer. Winston, however, attended church only for formal occasions, and during her life with him Clementine had fallen into this way also. Now she began to attend services at Holy Trinity, Brompton. When she became unable to go on her own her children and grandchildren would take her occasionally. In her last years the Vicar would go to her apartment at Christmas and Easter and take Holy Communion to her.

This was the first assertion of her difference from her husband, and there were others. In 1965 the Queen made her a life peer and she took the title of Baroness Spencer-Churchill. When she was introduced into the House on 15 June by Lords Ismay and Normanbrook she did not, as many expected, take her seat with the peers of the party of which her husband had been the leader. Instead she sat on the crossbenches asserting that belief in Liberalism and government by coalition to which she had held all her life. When it came to the vote on the abolition of the death penalty she did what Winston would not have done and voted for abolition. Even in the matter of making gifts of Winston's books she made sure that while the Napoleonic collection which Winston assembled went to Churchill College, the de Gaulle speeches went to the library named after the Labour politician Ernest Bevin. Her opportunity to express her admiration for the Labour Prime Minister came when she not only became a trustee of the Lord Attlee Memorial Fund she also took part in a film in April 1968 made with the aim of raising money for the fund.

In the matter of holidays, too, she eschewed Winston's habits. Whereas he had always flown whenever possible, Clementine had never enjoyed that form of transport. Now when she visited the Soameses in Paris where Christopher had been made ambassador she chose to travel by ferry and train rather than plane. Staying in luxurious villas and cruising on the yachts of the wealthy had always given Winston pleasure, but bothered Clementine. When she made two cruises in the Mediterranean in September 1970 and 1971 she paid her own way and chose her own company.

Her fierce financial independence led her into a somewhat embarrassing position. In 1972 she became President of the National Benevolent Fund for the Aged. In the same year, realizing that as she got older and weaker she would need more nursing and help and wanting to pay for these herself rather than be a burden on her children she decided to sell some of Winston's paintings. This decision, which was much publicized, coupled with her involvement with the Benevolent Fund led people to believe that she had fallen on hard times financially. To her great embarrassment there were moves to raise money to help her which she had to explain were quite unnecessary.

She had not, despite these assertions of independence, lost her keen desire to ensure that her husband's image remained untarnished. It had been put in her power to get rid of Sutherland's warts-and-all portrait but she had less control over books which were being published. In 1965 Violet Bonham Carter's book on Winston appeared. Clementine disliked it because of the undue prominence in Winston's life Violet gave herself, but it was clearly a book written by an admirer. More devastating was the knowledge that Lord Moran who had been Winston's doctor for so many years and who had, therefore, seen him at his most vulnerable, was writing a book about his former patient. She first learnt of this in July 1964 and immediately wrote to Moran expressing her view that such a book would be improper. Moran, however, went ahead and in January 1966 wrote to Clementine asking for the use of an Orpen portrait of Winston. Clementine simply replied that the permission was not hers to give. When the book was published later in the year she was greatly upset. Moran had shown a side of Winston she had been at pains to disguise because it threatened the notion of Winston as a hero. He had also, she felt, robbed her husband of dignity by describing such occasions as the one when he clambered about in a plane wearing only his pink silk vest. She was, therefore, delighted and supportive when a counterbalancing book of essays was proposed and eventually published under the title *Action This Day*.

Randolph was trying to do his part to perpetuate his father's memory but Clementine understood in the summer of 1967 that it was unlikely that he would live to finish his task. Although he now lived more quietly at his country house under the watchful eye of the woman he loved, Natalie Bevan, who lived close by and was herself married, he still gambled and kept strange hours. More distressing to Clementine was the fact that he continued to drink heavily and had developed cirrhosis of the liver. So it was not a shock or surprise to her when she received the news on 7 June that during the night Randolph had died in his sleep. When she attended his funeral she gave the impression to onlookers of being far less emotional about Randolph's death than a mother might be expected to be. But she had long been able to hide her feelings under a mask of impenetrable calm. She knew that her own relationship with her son had not been a success. Although she had loved him dearly when he was a baby, she had not been able to maintain a strong maternal attitude towards him. Randolph had been quite explicit about her failure expressing his preference for the company of the Duchess of Buccleuch because 'she's maternal and you're not'.[2] Her memories of Randolph were likely to bring her pain rather than pleasure.

In contrast, it seemed as if the nation as a whole positively wanted to remember Randolph's father, Winston, as the man who had led England to victory in the war. In December 1969 Clementine was asked to unveil a bronze statute of Winston by Oscar Nemon in the House of Commons. Then in 1970 the Lord Mayor of London made a public appeal for funds to commission a statue of Winston which should stand in Parliament Square. This too Clementine unveiled in November 1973. In the year which saw the hundredth anniversary of Winston's birth the appeal for the Churchill Centenary Trust was launched on Clementine's own birthday with a party in the Banqueting House. The objective of this Trust met with Clementine's approval because its aim was to enable people who were not necessarily academics to carry out research in a wide variety of fields. This same year the Queen Mother opened a Churchill exhibition in Somerset House to which Clementine made many visits.

The biography begun by Randolph was being continued by Martin Gilbert who would visit her from time to time and read extracts to her. She had every confidence that Winston's papers and Winston's image were in good hands. She was also aware that Mary had begun a biograhy of her and she trusted this daughter to present the family in a good light. Chartwell was proving a great success as year by year the number of visitors grew, far exceeding the Trust's expectations.

On 1 April 1975 Clementine reached the age of ninety and celebrated her birthday with a party given in her honour by her granddaughter Celia. This was the age at which Winston had died. She thought more and more about her own death which she knew could not be far off. Already she had been pre-deceased by three of her children. De Gaulle, Clement Attlee and his wife, and Horatia Seymour were now dead. The next year she would spend her birthday attending the funeral of Field Marshal Montgomery in St George's Chapel, Windsor. In the same year her cook Mrs Douglas and her old friend Ronald Tree would die followed in 1977 by Anthony Eden.

However, unlike Winston, she did not retreat into silence nor express longings for death. She took an interest in the exploits of her grand-children and the growing number of great-grandchildren. She began a new friendship with Edward Heath who invited her to lunch at Chequers where she inspected with great interest all the changes he had made. With him she joined the thousands of other Londoners who went to see the Tutankhamen exhibition at the British Museum. She no longer read or had read to her the kind of books which had occupied her when she was younger. Now she read Barbara Cartland as if seeking in her novels the romance she had always wanted but rarely had in her own life. In 1976 she was still receiving representatives of foreign governments. This was the year President and Madame Giscard d'Estaing sought her out.

She now met Margaret Thatcher who was already making her presence felt in the Conservative party. The two women discussed the gaining of the vote for women. What did Clementine make of this woman so different from herself but who expressed the greatest admiration for Winston? She was a woman who had reached office in government through the earlier courage of women such as Constance Lytton, but who did not care for the rights of women in general as the suffragettes had done and who would use her power to destroy those very social measures which Clementine had once urged Lloyd George to fight for whatever the political costs. Admirer of Winston Margaret Thatcher might be, but would she have put his career and interests before her own in the way that Clementine had done?

In 1977 after her ninety-second birthday Clementine became ill and had to be admitted to King Edward VII hospital for an abdominal operation. She did not recover her strength afterwards and she knew with some certainty that her end was close. But with the careful habits of a lifetime she set about ordering Christmas presents for a festive season in which she did not expect to participate.

Her departure from life when it came was very different from that of Winston. There was no agonized waiting around her deathbed. The twelfth of December 1977 began like an ordinary day. She had lunch and was ready for her drive in the park. Suddenly those with her realized that she was dying but barely had time to put her to bed before she was gone.

There was no elaborate state funeral this time. But, as if to bring to completion that entwining of Clementine's life with Winston's which had begun on that day in September of 1908, the day chosen for her memorial service in Westminster Abbey was 24 January, the anniversary of Winston's death.

Notes

Prologue: Two Wilful Women
1 Lord Redesdale, *Memoirs*, p. 29
2 Quoted by Nancy Mitford in *The Stanleys of Alderley*, p. 5
3 *Idem.*
4 Virginia Surtees, *The Artist and the Autocrat: George and Rosalind Howard, Earl and Countess of Carlisle*, p. 50
5 Quoted by Nancy Mitford in *The Stanleys of Alderley*, p. 150
6 *Ibid.*, p. 151
7 Virginia Surtees, *The Artist and the Autocrat*, p. 134

1. An Unexpected Family
1 Mabell, Countess of Airlie, *Thatched with Gold*, p. 89
2 Virginia Surtees, *The Artist and the Autocrat*, p. 134
3 Quoted by Nicola Beauman, *Cynthia Asquith*, p. 5
4 See Joan Hardwick, *Addicted to Romance*, p. 275
5 Anita Leslie, *Edwardians in Love*, p. 15
6 Elizabeth Longford, *A Pilgrimage of Passion*, p. 271
7 *Ibid.*, p. 272
8 For a full account of Caroline Norton see Margaret Forster, *Significant Sisters*, pp. 15–52

2. An Unconventional Childhood
1 Nancy Mitford, p. xiii

3. A Little Knowledge
1 Clare Sheridan, *Naked Truth*, p. 65
2 Mabell, Countess of Airlie, p. 67
3 Quoted by the Earl of Birkenhead, *Churchill 1874–1922*, p. 176
4 Quoted by Ted Morgan, *Churchill 1874–1915*, p. 167
5 Anita Leslie, *Cousin Clare*, p. 43

4. Love at Last
1 Ted Morgan, p. 206
2 Anita Leslie, *Jennie: The Life of Lady Randolph Churchill*, p. 100
3 Randolph S. Churchill, *Winston S. Churchill*, Vol. II, Companion 2, p. 697

5. Marriage
1 John Grigg, *Nancy Astor: Portrait of a Pioneer*, p. 55

6. Adjustments
1 Nicola Beauman, p. 72
2 *Ibid.*, p. 100
3 The Duke had been christened Hugh Richard Arthur but when his grandfather's horse Ben d'or won the Derby in 1880 the name was used as a nickname for the grandson and subsequently he was rarely called by any other name.
4 Ted Morgan, p. 100

7. Maternity
1 James Lees-Milne, *Ancestral Voices*, p. 19
2 Violet Bonham Carter, *Winston Churchill As I Knew Him*, p. 25
3 Mary Soames, *Clementine Churchill*, p. 56
4 *Winston S. Churchill*, Vol. II, Companion 2, p. 207
5 Mary Soames, p. 57
6 *Winston S. Churchill*, Vol. II, Companion 2, p. 914
7 For a discussion of this nickname see Marvin Rintala, *Lloyd George and Churchill*

8. Women's Rights
1 *Winston S. Churchill*, Vol. I, p. 337
2 David Morgan, *Suffragists and Liberals*, p. 48
3 *Ibid.*, p. 18
4 *Winston S. Churchill*, Vol. II, Companion 2, p. 918
5 *Ibid.*, p. 915
6 Betty Balfour, ed., *The Letters of Constance Lytton*, p. 185
7 David Morgan, p. 52
8 John Grigg, *Lloyd George: The People's Champion 1902–1911*, p. 223
9 *Winston S. Churchill*, Vol. II, Companion 2, p. 917
10 Violet Bonham Carter, p. 146

9. Conflicting Loyalties
1 *Winston S. Churchill*, Vol. II, p. 320
2 *Ibid.*, p. 379
3 *Ibid.*, p. 381
4 Lucy Masterman, *C.F.G. Masterman: A Biography*, p. 149
5 Violet Bonham Carter, p. 217

10. Seduced by the Enchantress
1 Violet Bonham Carter, p. 244
2 Betty Balfour, ed., *The Letters of Constance Lytton*, p. 222
3 *Idem.*
4 David Morgan, p. 87

11. Fears and Anxieties
1 Violet Bonham Carter, p. 284
2 *The Times*, 28 March 1912
3 *The Times*, 30 March 1912
4 Violet Bonham Carter, p. 271
5 Anna Gerstein (Nellie Romilly), *Misdeal*, p. 107
6 *Winston S. Churchill*, Vol. II, Companion 3, p. 1790
7 Michael and Eleanor Brock (eds), *H.H. Asquith to Venetia Stanley*, p. 62
8 Mary Soames, p. 100
9 Simona Pakenham, *Sixty Miles from England*, p. 209

12. 'This is your war station'

1 Joan Hardwick, *An Immodest Violet*, p. 128
2 Violet Bonham Carter, p. 331
3 Richard Hough, *Winston and Clementine*, p. 258
4 Martin Gilbert, *Churchill A Life*, p. 252
5 Violet Bonham Carter, p. 335
6 Clayre Percy and Janet Richley (eds.), *The Letters of Edwin Lutyens to his Wife, Lady Emily*, p. 301
7 Violet Bonham Carter, p. 384
8 Ralph Martin, *Jennie: The Life of Lady Randolph Churchill*, p. 335

13. Disgrace

1 Michael and Eleanor Brock, pp. 385, 465
2 *Winston S. Churchill*, Vol. III, Companion 2, p. 921
3 *Ibid.*, pp. 926–7
4 Ralph Martin, pp. 371–2
5 *Winston S. Churchill*, Vol. III, p. 722

14. A Soldier's Wife

1 Gail Braybon, *Women Workers in the First World War*, p. 134
2 *Ibid.*, p. 128
3 Anna Gerstein (Nellie Romilly), p. 21
4 *Ibid.*, p. 35
5 *Ibid.*, p. 3
6 *Winston S. Churchill*, Vol. III, p. 623
7 Mary Soames, p. 155
8 *Idem.*
9 *Ibid.*, p. 178
10 *Ibid.*, p. 164
11 Violet Bonham Carter, p. 449
12 Mary Soames, p. 178
13 Richard Hough, p. 351
14 Violet Bonham Carter, p. 453
15 Mary Soames, p. 179
16 *Ibid.*, p. 150
17 *Winston S. Churchill*, Vol. III, Companion 2, p. 1530
18 Mary Soames, p. 180

15. False Friends

1 Quoted by Richard Hough, p. 306
2 Lady Cynthia Asquith, *Diaries 1915–1918*, p. 269

16. Life and Death

1 Richard Hough, p. 306
2 Lady Cynthia Asquith, p. 269
3 Cynthia Asquith's 7 October diary entry quoted in Nicola Beauman, *Cynthia Asquith*, p. vii
4 *Winston S. Churchill*, Vol. IV, Companion 1, p. 479
5 Quoted by Richard Hough, p. 384

17. A Country Estate

1 *Winston S. Churchill*, Vol. IV, Companion 3, p. 1895
2 *Ibid.*, p. 1899

18. 11 Downing Street
1 *Winston S. Churchill*, Vol. V, Companion 1, p. 675
2 *Ibid.*, p. 852
3 George Moore, *Hail and Farewell*, p. 219
4 *Winston S. Churchill*, Vol. V, Companion 1, p. 1238

19. Depressions
1 *Winston S. Churchill*, Vol. V, Companion 2, p. 145
2 Sarah Churchill, *Keep on Dancing*, p. 8
3 *Winston S. Churchill*, Vol. V, Companion 2, p. 190
4 For full details see Keith Alldritt, *Churchill the Writer*
5 Winston S. Churchill, *My Early Life*, p. 387
6 *Winston S. Churchill*, Vol. V, Companion 2, p. 236
7 *Ibid.*, p. 248
8 *Ibid.*, p. 369
9 Brian Roberts, *Randolph: A Study of Churchill's Son*, p. 95
10 Winston Churchill, *Marlborough: His Life and Times*, Vol. I, p. 117
11 *Idem.*
12 *Ibid.*, p. 128
13 *Ibid.*, Vol. II, p. 172
14 *Ibid.*, Vol. IV, p. 319
15 *Ibid.*, Vol. IV, p. 642
16 *Ibid.*, Vol. IV, p. 640
17 *Ibid.*, Vol. II, p. 478
18 *Ibid.*, Vol. II, p. 187
19 *Ibid.*, Vol. II, p. 313
20 *Winston S. Churchill*, Vol. V, Companion 2, p. 616
21 John S. Churchill, *A Churchill Canvas*, p. 149

21. Disturbing Times
1 *Winston S. Churchill*, Vol. V, Companion 3, p. 53
2 *Idem.*
3 Sarah Churchill, *Keep on Dancing*, p. 56

22. A Fragile Peace
1 *Winston S. Churchill*, Vol. V, Companion 3, p. 1154
2 Quoted by John Charmley, *Churchill: the End of Glory*, p. 353
3 Mary Soames, p. 277
4 *Ibid.*, p. 280

23. In and Out of the Admiralty
1 May Lawton, 'What the Teacher Learned', *What Did You Do in the War, Mummy?*, p. 161

24. The Lady at Number 10
1 Norman Longmate, *The Home Front*, p. 53
2 Charlotte Mosley, *The Letters of Nancy Mitford*, p. 89
3 Mary Soames, p. 291

25. Fighting Against the Odds
1 Averell Harriman and Elie Abel, *Special Envoy*, p. 21
2 Ivan Maisky, *Memoirs of a Soviet Ambassador*, p. 320
3 *Idem.*
4 *Ibid.*, p. 323
5 John Colville, *The Fringes of Power*, p. 247

26. Dangerous Journeys

1 *Winston S. Churchill*, Vol. VII, p. 161
2 John Colville, *The Fringes of Power*, p. 454
3 Lord Moran, *The Struggle for Survival*, p. 164
4 John Colville, *The Fringes of Power*, p. 459

27. A Journey Through the Soviet Union

1 Clementine Churchill, *My Visit to Russia*, p. 14
2 *Ibid.*, p. 24
3 *Ibid.*, p. 30
4 *Ibid.*, pp. 47–8
5 *Winston S. Churchill*, Vol. VII, p. 1332

28. Aftermath

1 *Winston S. Churchill*, Vol. VII, pp. 1332–3
2 Robert Rhodes James, *Anthony Eden*, p. 313
3 Mary Soames, p. 403
4 Lord Moran, p. 352
5 Anita Leslie, *Cousin Clare*, p. 258

29. Reluctantly to Downing Street

1 Kenneth Harris, *Attlee*, p. 434
2 Anita Leslie, *Cousin Clare*, p. 261
3 Anthony Montague Browne, *Long Sunset*, p. 171
4 John Colville, *The Fringes of Power*, p. 709

30. Friendships and Family

1 Peter Evans, *Ari: The Life and Times of Aristotle Onassis*, p. 157
2 Graham Payn and Sheridan Morley (eds.), *The Noël Coward Diaries*, p. 323
3 Lord Moran, p. 768
4 Peter Evans, p. 147
5 *Winston S. Churchill*, Vol. IV, Companion 3, p. 1530

31. Uphill all the Way

1 Philip Ziegler, *Diana Cooper*, p. 309
2 *Ibid.*, p. 310
3 Graham Payn and Sheridan Morley (eds.) *The Noël Coward Diaries*, p. 603

32. Endings and Beginnings

1 Walter Graebner, *My Dear Mister Churchill*, p. 113
2 Anita Leslie, *Cousin Randolph*, p. 161.

Select Bibliography

Airlie, Mabell Countess of, *Thatched with Gold*, London, Hutchinson, 1962
Alldritt, Keith, *Churchill the Writer: His Life as a Man of Letters*, London Hutchinson, 1992
    The Greatest of Friends, Franklin Roosevelt and Winston Churchill 1941–45, New York, St Martin's Press, 1995
Asquith, Lady Cynthia, *Diaries 1915–1918*, London, Hutchinson, 1968
Balfour Betty, ed., *Letters of Constance Lytton*, London, Heinemann, 1925
Balsan, Consuelo Vanderbilt, *The Glitter and the Gold*, New York, Harper & Bros., 1952
Barker, Dudley, *Prominent Edwardians*, London, Atheneum, 1969
Beauman, Nicola, *Cynthia Asquith*, London, Hamish Hamilton, 1987
Birkenhead, Earl of, *Churchill 1874–1922*, New York, Harrap, 1989
Bonham Carter, Mark, ed. *Margot Asquith: The Autobiography*, London, Eyre & Spottiswoode, 1962
Bonham Carter, Violet, *Winston Churchill as I Knew Him*, London, Eyre & Spottiswoode, 1965
Braybon, Gail, *Women Workers in the First World War*, London, Routledge, 1989
Brock, Michael and Eleanor, *H.H. Asquith Letters to Venetia Stanley*, Oxford, Oxford University Press, 1982
Browne, Anthony Montague, *Long Sunset: Memoirs of Winston Churchill's Last Private Secretary*, London, Cassell, 1995
Campbell, John, *F.E. Smith First Earl of Birkenhead*, London, Pimlico, 1983
Cartland, Barbara, *The Private Life of Elizabeth Empress of Austria*, London, Frederick Muller, 1960
Charmley, John, *Churchill: The End of Glory*, London, Hodder & Stoughton, 1993
Churchill, Clementine, *My Visit to Russia*, London, Hutchinson, 1945
Churchill, John Spencer, *A Churchill Canvas*, Boston, Little Brown & Co., 1961
Churchill, Randolph and Gilbert, Martin, *Winston S. Churchill*, Vols I–VIII, London, Heinemann
Churchill, Randolph S., *Twenty-One Years*, Boston, Houghton Mifflin, 1965
Churchill, Sarah, *A Thread in the Tapestry*, London, André Deutsch, 1967
Churchill, Sarah, *Keep On Dancing*, London, Weidenfeld & Nicolson, 1981
Churchill, Winston, *His Father's Son: The Life of Randolph Churchill*, London, Weidenfeld & Nicolson, 1996
Churchill, Winston S., *Memories and Adventures*, London, Weidenfeld & Nicolson, 1989
    Marlborough: His Life and Times, London, George Harrap, 1933
    My Early Life, London, Macmillan, 1944

Collier, Peter and Horowitz, David, *The Roosevelts: An American Saga*, New York, Simon & Schuster, 1994

Colville, John, *The Churchillians*, London, Weidenfeld & Nicolson, 1981
    The Fringes of Power: Downing Street Diaries 1939–1955, London, Hodder & Stoughton, 1985

Cooper, Artemis, ed., *A Durable Fire: The Letters of Duff and Diana Cooper 1913–1950*, London, Collins, 1983

Cooper, Diana, *The Rainbow Comes and Goes*, London, Rupert Hart-Davis, 1958

Cooper, Duff, *Old Men Forget*, London, Rupert Hart-Davis, 1953

Cowles, Virginia, *Winston Churchill. The Era and the Man*, New York, Grosset & Dunlap, 1953

Eade, Charles, ed. *Churchill by His Contemporaries*, London, Hutchinson, 1953

Edel, Leon, *Henry James: The Middle Years*, New York, J.B. Lippincott, 1962

Edel, Leon, ed. *Henry James Letters Vol. 1*, Cambridge, Harvard University Press, 1974

Erskine, Angela St Clair, *Fore and Aft*, London, Jarrolds, 1932

Evans, Peter, *Ari: The Life and Times of Aristotle Onassis*, New York, Summit Books, 1986

Fedden, Robin, *Churchill and Chartwell*, Over Wallop, Hampshire, The National Trust, 1968

Field, Leslie, *Bendor The Golden Duke of Westminster*, London, Weidenfeld & Nicolson, 1983

Flower, Raymond and Wynn Jones, Michael, *Lloyds of London*, Newton Abbot, David and Charles, 1974

Gerstein, Anna (Nellie Romilly), *Misdeal*, London, Cassell & Co., 1932

Gibb, D.E.W., *Lloyds of London: A Study in Individualism*, London, Macmillan, 1957

Gilbert, Martin, *In Search of Churchill*, London, Harper Collins, 1994

Goodwin, Doris Kears, 'Chronicle of Washington: The Home Front', *The New Yorker*, 15 August, 1994, pp. 38–61

Graebner, Walter, *My Dear Mister Churchill*, London, Michael Joseph, 1965

Grigg, John, *Nancy Astor: Portrait of a Pioneer*, London, Sidgwick & Jackson, 1980

Guinness, Jonathon & Catherine, *The Mitford Family*, London, Hutchinson, 1984

Halle, Kay, ed., *Randolph Churchill The Young Pretender: Essays by His Friends*, London, Heinemann, 1971

Hardwick, Joan, *Addicted to Romance: The Life and Adventures of Elinor Glyn*, London, André Deutsch, 1994

Harriman, W. Averell and Abel, Elie, *Special Envoy to Churchill and Stalin 1941–1946*, New York, Random House, 1975

Harris, Kenneth, *Attlee*, London, Weidenfeld & Nicolson, 1982

Haslip, Joan, *The Lonely Empress*, London, Weidenfeld and Nicolson, 1965

Hassall, Christopher, *Edward Marsh Patron of the Arts: A Biography*, London, Longmans, 1959

Hastings, Selina, *Nancy Mitford a Biography*, London, Hamish Hamilton, 1985

Hough, Richard, *Winston & Clementine: The Triumph of the Churchills*, London Bantam Press, 1990

Ingram, Kevin, *Rebel: The Short Life of Esmond Romilly*, London, Weidenfeld & Nicolson, 1985

Jolly, W.P., *Marconi*, London, Constable, 1972

Jones, Mervyn, *A Radical Life: The Biography of Megan Lloyd George 1902–66*, London, Hutchinson, 1991

Judd, Dennis, *Edward VII: A Pictorial Biography*, London, MacDonal and Jane's, 1975

Lascelles, Sir Alan, *End of an Era: Letters and Journals 1887–1920*, ed. Duff Hart-Davis, London, Hamish Hamilton, 1986

Lavery, John, *The Life of a Painter*, London, Cassell & Co., 1940

Lees-Milne, James, *Ancestral Voices*, London, Chatto & Windus, 1975

Leslie, Anita, *Jennie: The Life of Lady Randolph Churchill*, London, Hutchinson, 1969
    Cousin Clare: The Tempestuous Career of Clare Sheridan, London, Hutchinson, 1976

The Gilt and the Gingerbread, London, Hutchinson, 1981

    Cousin Randolph: The Life of Randolph Churchill, London, Hutchinson, 1985

Longford, Elizabeth, *A Pilgrimage of Passion: The Life of Wilfrid Scawen Blunt*, London, Weidenfeld & Nicolson, 1979

Longmate, Norman, *The Home Front: An Anthology of Personal Experience 1938–1945*, London, Chatto & Windus, 1981

Lutyens, Emily, *A Blessed Girl: Memoirs of a Victorian Girlhood*, London, Heinemann, 1919

Lysaght, Charles Edward, *Brendan Bracken*, London, Allen Lane, 1979

Lytton, Constance, *Prisons and Prisoners: Some Personal Experiences*, London, Heinemann, 1914

Maisky, Ivan, *Memoirs of a Soviet Ambassador: The War 1939–43*, trans. Andrew Rothstein, New York, Charles Scribner's & Sons, 1968

Manchester, William, *The Last Lion: Winston Spencer Churchill Visions of Glory 1874–1932*, New York, Little Brown & Co., 1983

Mantle, Jonathan, *For Whom the Bell Tolls: The Lesson of Lloyds of London*, London, Sinclair-Stevenson, 1992

McCormick, Donald, *The Mask of Merlin. A Critical Study of David Lloyd George*, London, Macdonald, 1963

McGowan, Norman, *My Years with Churchill*, London, Souvenir Press, 1958

Marsh, Edward, *A Number of People: A Book of Reminiscences*, Harper & Bros., 1939

Masterman, Lucy, *C.F.G. Masterman. A Biography*, London, Frank Cass, 1968

Mendelssohn, Peter de, *The Age of Churchill. Heritage and Adventure 1874–1911*, London, Thames and Hudson, 1961

Mitford, Jessica, *Hons and Rebels*, London, Gollancz, 1960

Mitford, Nancy, *The Stanleys of Alderley*, London, Hamish Hamilton, 1939

Moore, George, *Hail and Farewell*, ed. Richard Cave, Gerrards Cross, Colin Smythe, 1976

Moran, Lord, *Churchill Taken From the Diaries of Lord Moran. The Struggle for Survival 1940–1965*, Boston, Houghton Mifflin, 1966

Morgan, David, *Suffragists and Liberals. The Politics of Woman Suffrage in England*, Oxford, Basil Blackwell, 1975

Morgan, Janet, *Edwina Mountbatten*, London, Harper Collins, 1991

Morgan, Ted, *Churchill 1874–1915*, London, Jonathan Cape, 1983

Mosley, Charlotte, *The Letters of Nancy Mitford: Love from Nancy*, London, Hodder & Stoughton, 1993

Mosley, Diana, *A Life of Contrasts*, London, Hamish Hamilton, 1977

Murphy, Sophie, *The Mitford Family Album*, London, Sidgwick & Jackson, 1985

Nicholson, Mavis, *What Did You Do in the War, Mummy?*, London, Chatto & Windus, 1995

Nicolson, Nigel, ed., *Harold Nicolson: Diaries and Letters 1930–1939*, London, Collins, 1966

Ogden, Christopher, *Life of the Party: The Biography of Pamela Digby Churchill Hayward Harriman*, London, Little Brown and Co., 1994

Pakenham, Simona, *Pigtails & Pernod*, London, Macmillan, 1961

    Sixty Miles from England: The English at Dieppe 1814–1914, London, Macmillan, 1967

Pawle, Gerald, *The War and Colonel Warden*, London, Harrap & Co. Ltd., 1963

Payn, Graham and Morley, Sheridan, eds., *The Noël Coward Diaries*, London, Weidenfeld & Nicolson, 1982

Pearson, John, *Citadel of the Heart: Winston and the Churchill Dynasty*, London, Macmillan, 1991

Percy, Clayre and Ridley, Jane, eds., *The Letters of Edwin Lutyens to his Wife, Lady Emily*, London, Collins, 1985

Ponting, Clive, *Churchill*, London, Sinclair-Stevenson, 1994

Priestley, J.B., *The Edwardians*, London, Heinemann, 1970

Pryce-Jones, David, *Unity Mitford: A Quest*, London, Weidenfeld & Nicolson, 1976

Pugh, Martin, *Women's Suffrage in Britain 1867–1928*, London, The Historical Association, 1980

Quennell, Peter, *Customs and Characters: Contemporary Portraits*, London, Weidenfeld & Nicolson, 1982

Redesdale, Lord, *Memoirs*, 2 vols, London, Hutchinson, 1915

Rhodes James, Robert, ed., *Chips: The Diaries of Sir Henry Channon*, London, Weidenfeld & Nicolson, 1967

Rhodes James, Robert, *Anthony Eden*, London, Weidenfeld & Nicolson, 1986

Rintala, Marvin, *Lloyd George and Churchill: How Friendship Changed Politics*, Maryland, Madison Books, 1995

Roberts, Andrew, *Eminent Churchillians*, London, Weidenfeld & Nicolson, 1994

Roberts, Brian, *Randolph: A Study of Churchill's Son*, London, Hamish Hamilton, 1984

Rose, Norman, *Churchill. An Unruly Life*, New York, Simon and Schuster, 1994

Roskill, Stephen, *Admiral of the Fleet Earl Beatty. The Last Naval Hero: An Intimate Biography*, London, Collins, 1980

Rowland, Peter, *Lloyd George*, London, Barrie & Jenkins, 1975

Seymour-Jones, Carole, *Beatrice Webb. Woman of Conflict*, London, Allison and Busby, 1992

Shaugnessy, Alfred (ed.), *Sarah: The Letters and Diaries of a Courtier's Wife 1906–1936*, London, Peter Owen, 1989

Sheridan, Clare, *Naked Truth*, New York, Blue Ribbon Books, 1928

Shone, Richard, *Walter Sickert*, Oxford, Phaidon, 1988

Soames, Mary, *Clementine Churchill*, London, Cassell, 1979

Storr, Anthony, *Churchill's Black Dog, Kafka's Mice, and other Phenomena of the Human Mind*, New York, Grove Press, 1965, 1988

Surtees, Virginia, *The Artist and the Autocrat*, Wilton, Michael Russell, 1988
    Jane Welsh Carlyle, London, Michael Russell, 1986

Townsend, Colin and Eileen, *War Wives: A Second World War Anthology*, London, Grafton Books, 1989

Toynbee, Philip, *Friends Apart*, London, MacGibbon & Kee, 1954

Tree, Ronald, *When the Moon was High, Memoirs of Peace and War 1897–1942*, London, Macmillan, 1975

Tuchman, Barbara, *The Proud Tower. A Portrait of the World Before the War 1890–1914*, London, Macmillan, 1962
    The Guns of August, New York, Macmillan, 1962

Vickers, Hugo, *Cecil Beaton: The Authorized Biography*, London, Weidenfeld & Nicolson, 1985
    Gladys, Duchess of Marlborough, London, Weidenfeld & Nicolson, 1979

Wheeler-Bennett, Sir John, ed., *Action This Day. Working with Churchill*, London, Macmillan, 1968

Winstone, H.V.F. *Gertrude Bell*, London, Jonathan Cape, 1978

Young, Kenneth, ed., *The Diaries of Sir Robert Bruce Lockhart, Vol. 2 1939–1965*, London, Macmillan, 1980

Ziegler, Philip, *Diana Cooper*, London, Hamish Hamilton, 1981
    London at War: 1939–1945, London, Sinclair Stevenson, 1995

Index

Index